D0987030

THE COMMUNIST PARTY
OF BULGARIA

AMS PRESS
NEW YORK

JOSEPH ROTHSCHILD

THE
COMMUNIST PARTY
OF BULGARIA

ORIGINS AND DEVELOPMENT

1883-1936

NEW YORK 1959

COLUMBIA UNIVERSITY PRESS

Library of Congress Cataloging in Publication Data

Rothschild, Joseph.
    The Communist party of Bulgaria.

    A revision of the author's thesis, University of
Oxford.
    Bibliography: p.
    1. Bŭlgarska Komunisticheska partiîa--History.
I. Title.
JN9609.A8K6847 1972   329.9'4977   72-174967
ISBN 0-404-07164-3

ERINDALE
COLLEGE
LIBRARY

Copyright ⓒ 1959 by Columbia University Press, New York

Reprinted from the edition of 1959, New York
First AMS edition published   in 1972
Manufactured in the United States of America

International Standard Book Number: 0-404-07164-3

AMS PRESS INC.
NEW YORK, N.Y. 10003

PREFACE

It is a pleasant tradition in the academic community for the author of a book to record his gratitude to those who have given him support and rendered help.

The first version of this study was written as a doctoral dissertation in the University of Oxford which I attended from 1952 to 1955 as Euretta J. Kellett Fellow from Columbia College to Oriel College. The richest sources of research material were the libraries of the British Museum, the School of Slavonic and East European Studies of the University of London, the Royal Institute of International Affairs in London, the Bibliothèque de Documentation Internationale Contemporaine of the University of Paris, and the Internationaal Instituut voor Sociale Geschiedenis in Amsterdam.

Mr. F. W. D. Deakin, Warden of St. Antony's College, Oxford, under whose supervision the work was undertaken, gave me unfailing support and wise direction. I should like to thank my examiners, Professor Edward Hallett Carr, then of Balliol College, Oxford, and today Fellow of Trinity College, Cambridge, and Mr. David Footman, Fellow of St. Antony's College, Oxford, for the careful readings which they gave the manuscript. Mrs. Jane Degras of the Royal Institute of International Affairs made valuable suggestions in matters of both style and substance. My editor, Mrs. Kathryn W. Sewny, was an invaluable assistant in the preparation of the final version of the manuscript. Mr. Edward M. Siegel helped me read the proofs.

Publication of this book has been made possible thanks to generous subsidies from the Subcommittee on Grants of the Joint Committee on Slavic Studies of the Social Science Research Council and the American Council of Learned Societies and from the Columbia University Council for Research in the Social Sciences.

In conclusion, I wish to pay tribute to the memory of the man whose teaching first elicited my interest in the study of politics and has influenced my general approach to it, the late Professor Franz Neumann of Columbia University.

JOSEPH ROTHSCHILD

New York City

February 27, 1959

CONTENTS

Note on Dates

The difference between the Gregorian (Western) and the Julian (Eastern) calendars was twelve days in the nineteenth century and thirteen days in the twentieth. Bulgaria adopted the Gregorian calendar on April 1, 1916, which thereby became April 14, 1916. Events occurring in Bulgaria before this day are dated in both styles.

INTRODUCTION

The Communist Party of Bulgaria was shaped by the Socialist movement from which it evolved. The distinctive factor in the history and development of the Bulgarian Socialist tradition was that it was the offspring of the Russian, not the German or French one. Dimitar Blagoev, one of the half-dozen important leaders of Bulgarian Socialism, had, as a student at St. Petersburg University, founded in the winter of 1883-84 the first known Marxist circle in Russia.[1] Georgi Kirkov and Yanko Sakazov, who were to become leaders of the Bulgarian Communist and Socialist Parties respectively, received their political education in the Populist and Socialist student circles at the gymnasia of Nikolaev and Odessa in the early 1880s.[2] Nikola Gabrovski and Nikola Kharlakov, who both repeatedly transferred their allegiance from one to the other wing of Bulgarian Marxism before being finally reconciled to Communism, had likewise studied in Russia, the latter at Kiev University.[3] The Communist leaders Vasil Kolarov and Khristo Kabakchiev were initiated into the Marxist movement by Plekhanov while studying in Geneva in the 1890s, as was Georgi Bakalov, who in 1900 organized the smuggling of Lenin's *Iskra* (Spark) into Russia via the Varna to Odessa shipping route.[4] Georgi Dimitrov, indeed, is exceptional in having achieved a prominent position in the Bulgarian Communist movement without a period of apprentice-

[1] Nevski, *Materiali dlya biograficheskogo slovar' Sotsial-Demokratov*, p. 84.
[2] Trotsky, "In den Balkanländern," p. 74, and *Yanko Sakazov yubileyen sbornik*, p. 3.
[3] For Gabrovski's career, see Blagoev, *Prinos kam istoriata na sotsializma v Bulgaria*, p. 577; For Kharlakov's, see the obituary in *La Fédération Balkanique*, III, No. 70-71 (July 1, 1927), 1370-71.
[4] *Vasil Kolarov: Important Dates of His Life and Work*, p. 8; Karakolov, "Revolyutsionniat i tvorcheski pat na Kh. Kabakchiev," p. 195. For Bakalov's smuggling of *Iskra* into Russia, see Bakalov, "Staraya 'Iskra' sredi Bolgar," pp. 73-81. While Bakalov organized these clandestine shipments of *Iskra*, the agent who actually traveled with the contraband-filled suitcases was another Bulgarian named Ivan Zagubanski. Apprehended by the Odessa police in December, 1901, released and expelled from Russia in September, 1903, Zagubanski died in his native Bulgarian town of Sopot in 1904 of tuberculosis contracted in prison.

ship in a Russian Socialist organization, but he rose out of the ranks of the trade unions and not the political Socialist movement.

It is not surprising that these men, on returning to Bulgaria, should organize the Socialist movement of their native country along lines similar to those of the Russian model. Indeed, on a visit to Bulgaria in 1910, Trotsky noted that the Bulgarian Socialist leaders aped even the peculiar rhetoric and phraseology of their Russian tutors.[5] This copying of outward forms reflected the fact that these Bulgarians had been stamped with the narrow intensity so characteristic of the Russian intelligentsia. This was deepened yet further when, on returning to Bulgaria, they were faced by the fact that social conditions and the development of social classes there did not correspond to their historical generalizations and political convictions. Whereas in Western Europe liberalism, socialism, and even conservatism developed as ideologies roughly corresponding to class structures, in Bulgaria as well as in Russia the conflict of ideologies was fought out within a small, closed circle of revolutionary students and teachers bound together only by a common psychological alienation from the existing social and political structure of their country and by faith in the almighty power of ideas and cells of ideologists as motors of social change. Ignored or treated with suspicion by the backward peasant mass, their entire existence was internalized in the agonizing and vituperative thrashing out of ideas, ideas, and yet again ideas, which became their daily bread. This atmosphere bred doctrinairism and fanaticism and a spirit of schism.[6] It comes as no surprise to learn that by 1904, at a time when the industrial proletariat of Bulgaria was still insignificant, the Socialist Party had already split twice. It was to split yet twice again in the next four years. The fanaticism and intolerance of the Bulgarian Socialists, their complete absorption in the world of political ideology—a result of their Russian schooling

---

[5] Trotsky, "In den Balkanländern," p. 74.

[6] The Russian intelligentsia is well described by Berdyaev: "It acquired the power of living by ideas alone. . . . The thoroughly true to type intolerance of the Russian intelligentsia was self protective; only so could it preserve itself in a hostile world, only thanks to its fanaticism could it weather persecution and retain its characteristic features. . . . What was scientific theory in the West, a hypothesis, or in any case a relative truth, partial, making no claim to be universal, became among the Russian intelligentsia a dogma, a sort of religious revelation." Berdyaev, *The Origin of Russian Communism*, pp. 17-18. Blagoev and his disciples were products of this tradition and of the conditions which shaped it.

and of Bulgarian social conditions—is well illustrated by the example of Blagoev, the founder of the Party, who forbade his disciples, on pain of expulsion, to maintain personal friendships with "bourgeois" elements and even with adherents of Socialist groups other than his own. He was proud of the fact that only once in his life had he allowed himself to go to the theater (a bourgeois obscurantist institution); he spent his days between his library and the Party headquarters.[7]

Just as the intensity and fanaticism of the early Bulgarian Socialists is largely attributable to the fact that only shadows of future social classes existed in Bulgaria at the turn of the century, so too, and for the same reasons, this condition explains why at one time or another most of the political and intellectual leaders of Bulgaria had been Socialists. Indeed, socialism was really the major intellectual tradition of the Bulgarian intelligentsia; bourgeois, monarchist, and even reactionary politicians and journalists had almost invariably spent a period of apprenticeship in it and had left the Socialist movement when they saw that it was still, at the turn of the century, a general staff without an army and without immediate prospects of coming to power. In 1910, for example, with but two exceptions, every minister in King Ferdinand's cabinet had only a few years before been a zealous Socialist.[8] This inconstancy was rooted in that disparity of educational levels which tends to arise in all backward countries where social classes are as yet only emerging. More foreign-trained university graduates accumulate than social development or primary educational standards warrant. The relatively few who enjoy the opportunity of higher education prefer for reasons of prestige to study law or history or politics or any of the other "superstructural" subjects instead of acquiring a training in engineering or agronomy or medicine or such other professions objectively most needed by their backward peoples. And precisely because the social development of their countries does not correspond to the presuppositions of their advanced level of edu-

---

[7] Kolarov, "Dimitry Blagojew—der Gründer und Führer der Bulgarischen K.P.," p. 204.

[8] Trotsky, "In den Balkanländern," p. 71. Another indication of this political orientation of the Bulgarian intelligentsia is that most of the schoolteachers of the country were organized into professional unions affiliated to one of the Socialist Parties.

cation, they tend either to gravitate toward radical political theories or to drift into political opportunism. Thus it was with the Bulgarian intellectuals who returned to their native towns and villages from St. Petersburg or Geneva or Heidelberg or Paris, psychologically and educationally prepared only for politics, that is, only for becoming either sectarian Socialists or, subsequently, "renegades" from Socialism. These are the general characteristics of a relatively backward nation in flux and slowly emerging into the more advanced economic and political arena centered on Western Europe. Bulgaria had been experiencing this phase of development since the mid-nineteenth century.

With the revival of trade along the Danube River at the end of the eighteenth century following the Treaty of Kuchuk Kainarji of 1774 and the Austro-Ottoman trade treaty of 1780, the backward economy of Bulgaria was exposed to contact with the economy of the West, initially chiefly that of Austria, though English merchants also soon established themselves in the Black Sea ports of Varna and Burgas.[9] The process of opening Bulgaria to the influx of Western goods was accelerated by the Treaty of Paris of 1856, by which the Danube was declared a free international waterway, followed in 1866 by the construction of the Russe-Varna railway line on the initiative of the energetic reform governor Midhat Pasha.[10] The artisans of central and northern Bulgaria were hard hit by this process and requested protection through tariff walls.[11] As the international obligations of the Porte prevented its acceding to these demands, the artisans of the Bulgarian towns concluded that their economic interests as well as their political and cultural aspirations required the establishment of independence for their country in order

---

[9] The first cargo ship to sail from Vienna down the Danube and through the Black Sea to Constantinople after the treaty of 1780 was despatched by Joseph II in 1782. Balugdgitsch, "Die Oekonomischen Ursachen der Gährung in Makedonien," p. 294. In 1783 a Russo-Ottoman trade treaty opened the Straits to trade and thereby stimulated greater traffic on the Danube. Ivan Sakazov, *Bulgarische Wirtschaftsgeschichte*, p. 253.

[10] Rainoff, *Die Arbeiterbewegung in Bulgarien*, p. 21.

[11] The once highly prosperous spinning industry of Russe (Rustchuk), for example, had disappeared by 1878. See Staneff, *Das Gewerbewesen und die Gewerbepolitik in Bulgarien*, p. 21. In the days of their greatest prosperity, the second half of the eighteenth century, the Bulgarian guilds had produced for markets as distant as Mesopotamia and Abyssinia. See Sakarov, *Die Industrielle Entwicklung Bulgariens*, p. 12.

that they might protect themselves against the influx of Western goods.[12] But even after the establishment of the Bulgarian principality it proved impossible to insulate the country against Western economic penetration, for Article Eight of the Treaty of Berlin of 1878 initially bound Bulgaria to the same conditions of trade and tariff (8 percent ad valorem) which had been imposed upon the Porte by the European Powers in 1861 and were not due to expire until 1890. Only toward the Ottoman Empire, Serbia, Rumania, and those industrially weak states with which the Porte had no trade treaties could Bulgaria conduct a tariff policy free from these limitations of the Treaty of Berlin.[13] Their products, however, hardly represented the same threat to the native *esnafi*, or artisan guilds, as did those of the West. Due to the steady influx of Western goods, the decay of the *esnafi*, far from being halted with the Liberation, even accelerated after 1879. By the time new agreements were concluded with the Western states in 1895, permitting a rise in import tariffs, the artisan industry was in ruins.[14]

The modernization of the Bulgarian economy was an extremely slow and painful process. The first modern textile mill had been built in Sliven in 1834, followed by others in 1840-43. Stara Zagora saw its first factory erected in 1860 and Karlovo in 1873.[15] By the time of the Liberation in 1878, there were about twenty industrial establishments, chiefly spinning mills, in the country.[16] Though the revolutionary leader Khristo Botev did organize a few workers' communes among the Bulgarian colonies of Reni, Oltenița, Galați, Brăila, Bolgrad, and Ismail in 1870 and 1871, one cannot speak of a proper and organized Bulgarian labor movement until the end of the century, in part because the declining artisan guilds fought a rear-guard action against this native and therefore vulnerable manifestation of the capitalist offensive which was destroying them.[17]

An examination of the economic and social condition of the

---

[12] Blagoev, *Prinos kam istoriata na sotsializma v Balgaria.* On page 85 of this book, which was first published in 1906, Blagoev recalls that, after the occupation of northern Bulgaria by the Russian armies in 1877, the local artisans and merchants petitioned the Russian authorities through appropriate decrees to stem the inflow of Western goods.

[13] Kaltscheff, *Die Bulgarische Zollpolitik seit 1878*, pp. 17-19.

[14] Sakarov, *Die Industrielle Entwicklung Bulgariens*, p. 79.

[15] Ivan Sakazov, *Bulgarische Wirtschaftsgeschichte*, p. 275.

[16] Pandov, *Grazhdanskata Voina*, p. 67.

[17] Black, *The Establishment of Constitutional Government in Bulgaria*, p. 16.

peasantry at this time provides no relief from the picture of decay and hardship. Indeed, while the town population was stirred and aroused by its fate, the peasantry remained inert. But though they remained passive until well into the nineteenth century, the peasants' system of feudal obligation was also profoundly altered by the opening up of Bulgaria to Western contacts. These brought about the abandonment of the military-feudal *sipahi-timar* system of land tenure under which the peasant had been obliged to deliver to the local *sipahi*, or resident knight, a fixed proportion of the produce of his holding, from which he could not normally be evicted and which on his death passed to his sons, in favor of the *bey-chiflik* system of obligations by which the local owner could lease his land to any peasant under conditions renegotiated with each new tenant. As the peasant was usually indebted and in arrears on his tax payment, this development, completed, except in Macedonia, by the time of the *tanzimat*, or Ottoman reform movement of the middle decades of the nineteenth century, far from ameliorating his lot, in fact worsened it from an admittedly servile but not materially unbearable one to a condition of well-nigh total depression.[18] Thus precisely at the time when the towns began to stir owing to a social revolution among the artisan classes, the peasantry, also subjected to a revolution by the same causes, sank yet deeper into degradation. Yet the peasants were the chief immediate beneficiaries of the revolutionary movement, for the Liberation of 1878 resulted in the flight of the Turkish landlords and the possession of the land by the Bulgarian peasants, who were legally confirmed as owners in 1885.[19] Even this was not an unmixed blessing for their new state insisted on taxing them in money whereas the Ottoman tithe had been paid in kind.[20] In 1885 the government granted the peasants a loan for the payment of compensation claimed by the previous Turkish owners of their holdings. Though this debt of the peasants to the government was ultimately canceled, the usurers had in the meantime gained a tight grip, for despite a law of 1880 intended to

[18] Balugdgitsch, "Die Oekonomischen Ursachen der Gährung in Makedonien," p. 294. The agricultural system of Rumelia and Anatolia is discussed by Gibb and Bowen, *Islamic Society and the West*, I, 235-58.
[19] Cf. Petkoff, *Die Sozialen und wirtschaftlichen Verhältnisse in Bulgarien vor der Befreiung*, p. 44.
[20] Ivan Sakazov, *Bulgarische Wirtschaftsgeschichte*, pp. 265-66.

defend the peasant against the usurer, it was a number of years before the state banking system was sufficiently developed to give him a reasonable measure of protection.[21] The backward Bulgarian peasant had enjoyed some security within the market of the Ottoman system but now, outside that system and burdened with antiquated tools and techniques, he found himself well-nigh defenseless. The drastic consequences of these developments are illustrated by the following statistics: [22]

Number of peasants owning their land: *1888*, 529,771; *1893*, 416,199; *Decline*, 113,572 or 21 percent

Number of hired agricultural workers: *1888*, 715,308; *1893*, 955,281; *Rise*, 239,973 or 33.5 percent

The total population of Bulgaria at the time of the census of 1881 had been 2,008,000. The union with Eastern Rumelia in 1885 added 816,000 people.[23]

Many of those who hired themselves out as agricultural workers during the ploughing and harvesting seasons would drift into the towns in the winter to seek employment in the young industrial system. The already low wage scales were thereby depressed even further.

This drifting potential proletariat from the countryside was joined in the towns by the ruined artisans. The Liberation and the severing of Bulgaria from the Ottoman system had combined with the

[21] Petkoff, *Die Sozialen und wirtschaftlichen Verhältnisse in Bulgarien vor der Befreiung*, p. 45.

[22] Rainoff, *Die Arbeiterbewegung in Bulgarien*, p. 35. In the last years of the century there began, despite a general agrarian depression in Bulgaria, a slow reversal of this trend. By 1900 the number of peasants owning their own land increased over the 1893 figure by 20,893, or 5 percent, to 437,092 and the rate of increase of peasants hiring themselves out as agricultural laborers had slowed down from 33.5 percent for the years 1888-93 to 15 percent for the span 1893-1900. By the latter year their number stood at 1,099,241. The two groups are not of course mutually exclusive. Peasants whose own plots were too small to provide a livelihood would also seek work as laborers. It should further be noted that the statistics for peasants owning their own land enumerate only the male head of the family while those for agricultural laborers include all individuals falling into this category. The children of even a prosperous peasant might work on a neighbor's holding and would be classified as hired laborers. In the first two decades of the twentieth century the position of the small peasant was stabilized and with the legislation of Stamboliski's premiership (1919-23), which limited the size of holdings and enabled landless peasants to acquire plots, the small-holder nature of the Bulgarian rural economy was confirmed. These later developments do not, however, alter the fact that during the immediate post-Liberation years Bulgarian agriculture was shaken by a severe crisis, aggravated by falling wheat prices.

[23] Gopčević, *Bulgarien und Ostrumelien*, p. 18.

pressure from the West to deal the death blow to the Bulgarian artisan industry.[24] The result was the economic extinction of many towns. The union of Bulgaria and Eastern Rumelia in 1885 deepened yet further the economic crisis, and a quarter of a century after the Liberation, a Bulgarian economic historian not particularly friendly toward the Turks had to admit that economically the Liberation had been anything but a blessing and that the Bulgarian economy had not even by 1900 recovered to the level at which it had stood in 1876.[25] The ruined artisans joined the ruined peasants to form the labor reserve. Thus did Bulgaria enter the phase of the primitive accumulation of capital which Western Europe had experienced a century and more earlier. In consequence, however, of many pressures, political and economic, foreign and internal, Bulgaria did not follow the path of Western capitalist development very far. The problems of underemployment and underconsumption, of agricultural rationalization and capital investment were never solved, and notwithstanding the confident prediction to the contrary of Bulgaria's early socialists,[26] she, like her neighbors, remained a backward, at best semicapitalist, country.

Already at this early stage Bulgarian social development deviated from the Western pattern. Precisely because the Bulgarian government sought to emulate in outward appearances the higher cultural level of the West, the sons of the declining artisans, instead of being proletarianized in accordance with the Marxist analysis, were sent to acquire a higher education in the West and in Russia from where they would return home to join the swollen ranks of that "bureaucratic proletariat" which was to become an endemic sore in Eastern Europe. Those who found no place in the state administration would often append themselves to one of the too numerous political parties whose main *raison d'être* was the desire for spoils. Politics, in effect, came to be one of the chief national industries of Bulgaria.

---

[24] Rainoff, *Die Arbeiterbewegung in Bulgarien,* pp. 23-24 presents a statistical analysis of the post-Liberation collapse of the artisan industry. Whereas in 1876 there had been 50-60 shoemakers in Sofia, their number had declined by 1896 to 4-5. Of 700-800 spindle makers in Pirdop in 1876, only 20-30 survived twenty years later. The story is the same for the other towns and crafts.

[25] Staneff, *Das Gewerbewesen und die Gewerbepolitik in Bulgarien,* pp. 21-29.

[26] See, for example, Blagoev's pioneer work, published under the pseudonym D. Bratanov, *Shto e sotsializam i ima li toi pochva u nas?* Tirnovo, 1891. Blagoev argued that Bulgaria, like all countries, must inevitably develop along the same lines and to the same levels as had industrial Western Europe.

The original controversies of her political leaders in the 1880s over the issues of dependence upon Russia and of constitutional arrangements had at least been rational in the sense that they involved real and fundamental issues. The subsequent proliferation of National, Liberal, Democratic, National-Liberal, Young-Liberal, Radical, and several Socialist Parties—significantly, no group any longer called itself "conservative"—was, however, largely artificial and in no way corresponded to social development or class differentiation. The elaborate and top-heavy political superstructure of Bulgaria was the most striking aspect and consequence of the unevenness of her cultural and educational development. The political consciousness ot the intelligentsia was as modern as the foreign universities at which it was bred, while the peasantry, which formed 80 percent of the population until the Second World War, continued to be the user and victim of obsolete production methods. The intellectual awakening of Bulgaria occurred in the first half of the nineteenth century, and the formation of her intelligentsia began in its middle decades. Both were concomitants of Western economic and ideological penetration and of Russian political and cultural expansion.

Though Bulgarian political and ecclesiastical national aspirations —two aspects of the same phenomenon—were originally directed against Phanariot domination, the cultural and spiritual awakening of the Bulgarians had in fact been stimulated in the Greek schools of Salonika, Ioánnina, Athens, and Andros which the more fortunate among them attended.[27] Bulgarian modern popular education began in 1835 with a Western-type school in Gabrovo, and in 1856 reading rooms for adults were opened in Shumen, Lom, and Svishtov. By the time of the Liberation there were 131 of these.[28] Progress was slow. In 1843, for example, only fifteen books were published in the Bulgarian language.[29] Culturally most advanced were the 30,000 Bulgarians living in Constantinople. In the 1850s American Protes-

[27] Arnaudov, "Bulgariens nationale Wiedergeburt," p. 617.

[28] Black, *The Establishment of Constitutional Government in Bulgaria*, p. 26.

[29] Handelsman, "La Guerre de Crimée, la question polonaise, et les origines du problème bulgare," p. 281. In 1844 the number of books published was 18; in 1845, 11; and in the following year, 12. Many were published at Salonika where the first Bulgarian printing press was established in 1838. Prince Miloš Obrenović had permitted others to be produced by the Serbian State Press. Wendel, *Der Kampf der Südslawen um Freiheit und Einheit*, p. 226.

tant missionaries began to establish schools in Bulgaria, and the American-founded Robert College in Constantinople graduated 45 Bulgarians before the Liberation.[30] Others studied in the West and in Russia. The development of political aspirations accompanied the spread of education. The establishment of Greek and Serbian independence early in the century served as a spur to Bulgarian nationalism. In the aftermath of the Galician revolt of 1846, two thousand Polish refugees arrived in 1849 at Shumen and brought the ideas of 1848 to the Bulgarians, whose nationalist hopes they encouraged.[31] Wealthy Bulgarian merchants traveled to Vienna, Leipzig, or Paris, where they were exposed to the intellectual currents of the West.[32] All these influences were, however, secondary to that exerted by Russia.

In 1840 a program of scholarships for Bulgarian students was instituted at the Odessa seminary and after the Crimean War the Slavonic Benevolent Committee of Moscow was given state aid to provide for the education of young Bulgarians in Russia. Between 1856 and 1876 about 500 Bulgarian students studied in Russia with the aid of such scholarships.[33] The purpose of the program was to imbue the Bulgarians with Slavophilism. They were, accordingly, usually sent to theological academies in Moscow, Kiev, and Odessa, though some were enabled to study also at the Universities of Moscow and Odessa and at the Richelieu High School of Odessa. Far from absorbing there the principles of orthodoxy and conservative Slavophilism, the young Bulgarians were usually initiated into revolutionary student circles, particularly in Odessa which was swarming with these groups in the 1860s and 1870s.[34] Thus Botev and Stambolov, for example, were expelled from Odessa for nihilist connections, while Lyuben Karavelov returned to Bulgaria from his Moscow studies a revolutionary socialist and a violent opponent of Pan-Slavism. It was in these Russian academies and universities that Bulgarian Socialism was born, and it was on the Russian model that the Bulgarian leaders shaped their young Socialist Party.

[30] Black, *The Establishment of Constitutional Government in Bulgaria*, p. 28.
[31] Chilingirov, *Balgarski chitalishta predi osvobozhdenieto*, p. 37.
[32] Black, "The Influence of Western Political Thought in Bulgaria," p. 508.
[33] Stavrianos, *Balkan Federation*, p. 119.
[34] Summer, *Russia and the Balkans: 1870-1880*, p. 112.

I

THE EARLY SOCIALIST MOVEMENT

Just as the development of a modern political and administrative superstructure in Bulgaria preceded the economic and social growth which would have warranted it, so too did the birth of the Socialist movement anticipate the formation of that proletariat for which it claimed to speak. Not in the ranks of a vigorous working class but in the revolutionary circles of the Russian universities was Bulgarian Socialism bred. The most formidable figure of its first three decades was Dimitar Blagoev.

A Macedonian, born in either 1855 or 1856 in Zagorichane, a village in the Kastoria District of what is today Greek Macedonia, Blagoev was sent to Constantinople as a boy to become a cobbler's apprentice but while there won a scholarship to a Bulgarian school in the Ottoman capital. After further study at the gymnasia of Gabrovo and Stara Zagora, he was awarded, partly through the influence of the poet and publicist Petko Slaveikov, a scholarship to the seminary of Odessa whither he went in 1878.[1] Here he made the acquaintance of another Bulgarian student who was destined to be the second great figure of the early Bulgarian Socialist movement and his most formidable antagonist in it: Yanko Sakazov (1860-1941), son of a prosperous merchant.[2] Blagoev was to develop into a sectarian Marxist, while Sakazov became the leader of the moderates. The trend of their future ideological development was foreshadowed by the paths they took after leaving Odessa. Whereas Sakazov went to the West to pursue his studies in Germany in 1881,

[1] "Nachruf: Dimiter Blagoeff," *Inprekorr*, IV, No. 54 (May 13, 1924), 653-54; Kolarov, "Dimitry Blagojew—der Gründer und Führer der Bulgarischen K.P.," pp. 197-204.

[2] Blagoev, *Kratki belezhki iz moya zhivot*, p. 34.

to attend Huxley's lectures in London in 1883 and Taine's in Paris the following year,[3] Blagoev remained in an exclusively Russian environment, first transferring from the theological seminary to the Odessa gymnasium, at that time a hive of revolutionary student circles, then in 1880 going to St. Petersburg, there becoming first a visitor to lectures and in 1881 a matriculated student at the University. He participated in the activities of the capital's Black Partition group and associated briefly with the People's Will movement before its destruction after the assassination of Tsar Alexander II on March 1/13, 1881.[4]

In 1883 Blagoev discovered the writings of Lassalle and of Marx, the first volume of whose *Kapital* had appeared in a Russian translation in 1872. Toward the end of the year, he began expounding this new revelation to his friends at the University whom he organized about the turn of the year 1883-84 into the first known Social Democratic group in Russia. It consisted of fifteen or sixteen students, an architect, a journalist, and two members of the Black Partition movement living illegally in St. Petersburg.[5] Calling itself The Party of Russian Social-Democrats, the group in 1884 established contact with the metal workers of St. Petersburg and in January, 1885, began publishing a clandestine paper, *Rabochii* (Worker), in issues of a thousand copies for distribution among the workers of St. Petersburg and other cities. The second, and final, number of the paper contained articles by Plekhanov and Aksel'rod, who had founded their Liberation of Labor group in Geneva in the summer of 1883 and with whom Blagoev was in correspondence over the projected program of his group.[6] Though Blagoev took

[3] *Yanko Sakazov yubileyen sbornik*, p. 3.

[4] Nevski, *Materiali dlya biograficheskogo slovar' Sotsial-Demokratov*, p. 84. Blagoev, first an "auditor," matriculated in the spring of 1881 in the Physical-Mathematical Faculty of the University. In November, 1883, having become interested in the social sciences, he applied for transfer to the Faculty of Law. His request was approved.

[5] *Ibid.*, p. 84.

[6] In his posthumous memoirs, *Kratki belezhki*, p. 64, Blagoev apologizes for the fact that his views and the propaganda in *Rabochii* at that time were not yet thoroughly Marxist but "a concoction of scientific socialism with Lassalleianism or, if you will, with Lavrovism." He was of course tempted in his later years as a Communist to disparage in retrospect his own views at a time when they had been so largely shaped by Plekhanov. The latter's article for *Rabochii* is reprinted in his *Sochinenia*, II (1923), 263-72. For further details on Blagoev's correspondence with Plekhanov in 1884-85 see Kabakchiev, "Dmitri Blagoev i Bolgarskie Tesnyaki," p. 32. For Plekhanov's own brief reference to it, see his "Introduction" of 1903 to the Russian translation of Alphonse Thun's book, *Geschichte der revolutionären Bewegungen*

measures to conceal his identity, adopting the pseudonym "Peter Egorov," the police arrested him in February, 1885, before he could bring out a third number of the paper, and expelled him from Russia in mid-March. After his return to Bulgaria he managed to maintain contact with the rest of the St. Petersburg group until it was uncovered by the police in August and its members banished to Siberia.[7] By this time it had established seventeen cells among the workers of St. Petersburg.[8]

Thus Blagoev returned to his native country in 1885, not yet a complete Marxist but a revolutionary thoroughly of the Russian pattern. A year before, Yanko Sakazov had returned from the West and taken a position as teacher of natural science and history in Shumen.[9] After a brief stay in 1885 in Sofia, where, using the pseudonym "Zhelyazov," Blagoev had published three issues of a rather eclectic socialist journal named *Savremenni Pokazatel* (Contemporary Index),[10] he too accepted a teaching position in Shumen in 1886.

At this time Bulgarian socialism existed exclusively among the intelligentsia. In the 1880s teacher-student discussion circles, or *krazhotsi*, were organized in the larger towns and soon came to own libraries and reading rooms. Though most of the students and teachers who went abroad to study on their return entered the government service and, after a short spell of socialist conviction, the bourgeois parties, a number of the *krazhotsi*, those of Gabrovo, Shumen, Tirnovo, Sliven, and Kazanlak, came under the control of Socialists and were used by them as indoctrination centers for the propagation of their ideology among the students.[11]

---

in Russland (Leipzig, 1883), in his *Sochinenia*, XXIV, 120. By 1909, when he wrote "The First Steps of the Social Democratic Movement in Russia" (*Sochinenia*, XXIV, 174-82), Plekhanov had apparently forgotten Blagoev's group and does not mention it. The entire episode is discussed in exhaustive detail in Sergievski, "Plekhanov i Gruppa Blagoeva."

[7] Nevski, *Materiali dlya biograficheskogo slovar' Sotsial-Demokratov*, p. 84. From Bulgaria Blagoev sent to the St. Petersburg group the program of Plekhanov's Liberation of Labor group in Geneva and recommended its adoption with minor alterations. See Blagoev, *Kratki belezhki*, p. 81.

[8] Kolarov, "Dimitry Blagojew—der Gründer und Führer der BKP," p. 198.

[9] *Yanko Sakazov yubileyen sbornik*, p. 4.

[10] Blagoev, *Prinos kam istoriata na sotsializma v Balgaria*, p. 115. See also Khristov, "Dimitar Blagoev—Osnovatel na Balgarskata nauchna istoriografia," p. 8. The coeditor of *Savremenni Pokazatel* was Blagoev's wife, V. Zhivkova.

[11] Assen Tsankov, "Der Sozialismus in Bulgarien," p. 626.

In 1881 Georgi Karjiev, influenced by the Serbian Socialists Svetozar Marković and Vasa Pelagić and by the Bulgarian revolutionary hero Khristo Botev, had published a utopian-socialist, semianarchist paper, *Rabotnik* (Worker), in Russe. Closed down before the year was out, it was replaced by *Bratstvo* (Brotherhood). In 1885 Karjiev launched *Napred* (Forward) along the same ideological lines.[12] It is typical of the Bulgarian intelligentsia that Karjiev soon tired of the unrewarding role of a socialist pioneer and jumped on the Liberal bandwagon. Blagoev had issued *Savremenni Pokazatel* also in the summer of 1885, and in June of the following year Evtim Dabev (1864-1946) began publishing the weekly *Rositsa* (Dew), in which translations of the early writings of Karl Marx appeared for the first time in Bulgarian, though the journal was by no means consistently Marxist.[13] After eighteen issues it was closed down during the political crisis created by the abduction of Prince Alexander of Battenberg in August, 1886.[14] The subsequent rule of the controversial Stambolov imposed a temporary halt upon socialist propaganda.

In the spring of 1888 Yanko Sakazov undertook a sixteen-day trip to all the socialist *krazhotsi* and cells of Shumen, Dzhumaya, Kotel, Sliven, Kazanlak, Yambol, Gabrovo, and Tirnovo in order to repair the now secret organizational contacts,[15] and a year later a cautious revival of socialist propaganda, though not of legal organization, began with the appearance of a challenging brochure by Nikola Gabrovski, who had been educated in Russia and in Geneva, entitled *Nravstvenata Zadacha na Inteligentsiata* (The Moral Obligation of the Intelligentsia). In somewhat Aesopian language Gabrovski called upon the intellectuals to organize themselves into a federation devoted to "developing an intellectual interest in society." [16] His specific views on the regeneration of society were at this time influenced more by the Russian Populists than the Western Marxists.

---

[12] *Yanko Sakazov ijubileyen sbornik.* p. 10; Blagoev, *Prinos kam istoriata na sotsializma v Balgaria,* pp. 112-13.
[13] *Yanko Sakazov yubileyen sbornik,* p. 27; Blagoev, *Prinos kam istoriata na sotsializma v Balgaria,* p. 121.
[14] Assen Tsankov, "Der Sozialismus in Bulgarien," p. 627; *Yanko Sakazov yubileyen sbornik,* p. 10.
[15] *Yanko Sakazov yubileyen sbornik,* p. 10.
[16] Gabrovski, quoted in Blagoev, *Prinos kam istoriata na sotsializma v Balgaria,* p. 128.

Just as Gabrovski had to use seemingly innocuous language because of the Stambolov dictatorship, so Evtim Dabev, another gymnasium teacher, was careful to hide behind the pseudonym "Druzhelyubov" when in 1890 he published and prefaced a translation of Engels's *Die Entwicklung des Sozialismus von der Utopie zur Wissenschaft*,[17] while a year later Blagoev also thought it advisable to conceal his identity behind the nom de plume "Bratanov" when he wrote his ground-breaking work *Shto e sotsializam i ima li toi pochva u nas?* (What is Socialism and Do We Have a Basis for It [i.e., in Bulgaria]?), the first publication of the Bulgarian Social Democratic Library. In the history of Bulgarian Socialism this book occupies a position similar to that of Plekhanov's *Nashi Raznoglasie* (Our Differences) in the Russian, and it argued the same case: that the country must and will pass from the peasant economy into and through a capitalist phase to socialism, and that all hopes of avoiding this development through the resurrection of the largely defunct *zadruga* and of artisan industry are vain.[18] The book was provoked by articles in the government press claiming that there was no basis for socialism and hence no justification for a socialist party in Bulgaria[19] and was soon attacked by Russian Populist writers living in Bulgaria, such as Prokopiev (pseudonym of Debogori-Mokrievich) and Boris Mintses, who believed that Bulgaria would be able to avoid the capitalist phase of her social development.[20] Their argument was even more unrealistic in respect to Bulgaria than to Russia for while the *mir* and the *artel'* were still functioning relatively satisfactorily in the latter country in the last two decades of the nineteenth century, the Bulgarian *zadruga*, or communal multiple family,[21] and *esnaf*, or guild, were rapidly declining. Though the Populists were wrong in claiming viability for these institutions, Blagoev proved to be equally mistaken in his confident prediction that Bulgaria would develop in the Western industrial pattern.

[17] *Ibid.,* p. 133.
[18] D. Bratanov, *Shto e sotsializam i ima li toi pochva u nas?* Reviewed in *Lacha* (Ray), I, No. 1 (November 1, 1893), 17-18.
[19] Blagoev, *Prinos kam istoriata na sotsializma v Balgaria,* p. 140.
[20] Karakolov, "Kharakterni momenti ot borbata na Balgarskata Rabotnicheska Partia—Komunisti," p. 135. The polemic between the Populists and Blagoev was conducted in the columns of *Lacha.* Debogori-Mokrievich settled in Bulgaria in 1894.
[21] Cf. Mosely, "The Distribution of the *Zadruga* within Southeastern Europe," pp. 219-30.

In 1887, before the appearance of Blagoev's book on the inevitability of capitalist development, a group of teachers from the trade school in Svishtov had founded the journal *Promishlenost* (Industry) in which industrialization was also advocated though without Blagoev's socialist assumptions.[22] Encouraged by the fact that this journal was allowed to appear regularly without governmental interference, Sakazov in January, 1891, founded *Den* (Day), a socialist monthly to which Blagoev for a time contributed. A translation of *The Communist Manifesto* was published in the same year.[23] Stambolov's police, however, subjected *Den* to regular censorship and intermittent confiscations.[24] A year later the quarterly *Sotsial Demokrat* was founded in Sevlievo on the model of a journal of the same name which Plekhanov was then publishing in Geneva and from which it frequently reprinted articles. The chief contributors were a group of Bulgarian students gathered around Plekhanov in Geneva, the most prominent among whom were Slavi Balabanov and Christian Rakovski, the latter destined to achieve fame as a Soviet politician and diplomat. After four issues it had to be closed.[25] The editors were Sava Mutafov and Andrei Konov.

A number of ardent young intellectuals were determined to found a socialist party despite police repression. Already in 1890 twelve delegates from the socialist *krazhotsi* had discussed this issue at Buzluja without coming to a decision.[26] A year later Nikola Gabrovski, who had been dismissed from his teaching post for his radical political views and was then practicing as a lawyer in Tirnovo, summoned about ten socialists, including Blagoev, to a secret conference in his vineyard, taking advantage of the cover afforded by the crowds assembled for the Orthodox Easter celebrations. Gabrovski thought that it was essential to organize a social demo-

---

[22] Blagoev, *Prinos kam istoriata na sotsializma v Balgaria*, p. 140.

[23] Tchitchovsky, *The Socialist Movement in Bulgaria*, p. 11.

[24] *Yanko Sakazov yubileyen sbornik*, p. 4. After the fall of Stambolov in 1894, *Den* became the official organ of the Social Democratic Party. Assen Tsankov, "Der Sozialismus in Bulgarien," p. 626.

[25] Blagoev, *Prinos kam istoriata na sotsializma v Balgaria*, p. 571. Balabanov and Rakovski were medical students. A digestive illness led Balabanov to commit suicide in 1893. His funeral was a veritable parade of the East European refugee and student socialist colonies in Switzerland. Plekhanov delivered the eulogy. See Bakalov, "G. V. Plekhanov v Bolgarii," p. 46. For an interesting account of the life of the Bulgarian socialist students living in Geneva during the early 1890s, see Nokov, "Studentski spomeni ot Zheneva (1889—1894g.)." Here (p. 92) the date of Balabanov's suicide is given as March, 1892. This appears to be an error.

[26] Assen Tsankov, "Der Sozialismus in Bulgarien," p. 626.

cratic party if only to demonstrate to the people the falseness of the government's propaganda that socialists were dangerous conspirators. Sava Mutafov and Konstantin Bozveliev, representing respectively the socialists of Sevlievo and Kazanlak (all the participants were from towns in north-central and central Bulgaria), deprecated this proposal, arguing that the premature abandonment of secrecy would simply provide Stambolov with the opportunity to destroy the still embryonic socialist movement. To this objection it was replied that even if the government persecuted the new party, at least it would then be demonstrated that Stambolov's policy was to suppress socialist ideas as such and not simply conspiratorial groups.[27] After much debate, it was finally resolved to call a larger general conference in the summer at which a decision on this question would be taken.

Thus it came about that on the evening of July 19/31, 1891, and early the next morning, more than twenty men gathered around a campfire among the beeches on Mount Buzluja, near Sofia, where the national hero Haji Dimitar had fallen in 1868 in the struggle against the Turks, to decide whether the moment was opportune to found a socialist party. Once again the gathering assembled under the cover of the celebration of a national holiday, this time Ilinden, or St. Ely's day. Once again Bozveliev and Mutafov opposed the formation of an openly socialist party. This time, however, they were outvoted by the supporters of Gabrovski and Blagoev. The Buzluja conference then unanimously (with even the skeptics joining in) founded the Bulgarian Social Democratic Party.[28]

But the fears of the cautious had not been unfounded for just at this time the government, alarmed by a rebellion of the students of the Shumen gymnasium against their principal, decided to crush the socialist circles which it considered responsible.[29] In 1892 Blagoev was dismissed from the directorship of the Vidin gymnasium to which he had been appointed in 1889.[30] District police commissioners were instructed to denounce all socialist teachers—and

[27] Blagoev, *Prinos kam istoriata na sotsializma v Balgaria,* pp. 140-41.

[28] *Ibid.,* pp. 142-45. The program adopted for the Party was a modified translation of the Belgian Socialist Party's. Two years later, at the Tirnovo Congress of 1893, this program was replaced by one modeled on that of the German Social Democratic Party.

[29] *Vasil Kolarov: Important Dates of His Life and Work,* p. 4.

[30] At Vidin he had founded the first Bulgarian teachers' association and edited its journal.

these formed a large percentage of the profession—to the Ministry of Education. In Sliven and Khaskovo a curfew was imposed upon all workers suspected of socialist sympathies and in June, 1893, all the known socialists of Vidin were arbitrarily imprisoned.[31] The socialist ranks were decimated, and the movement was barely kept alive through literature and articles sent from Geneva by Rakovski.[32]

At the Socialist Party Congress in Plovdiv in August, 1892, those who had opposed the founding of the Party in the previous year were naturally more firmly convinced that they had been right. This time Bozveliev and Mutafov were joined by Sakazov and Dabev, the editors of *Den* and *Rositsa*. They argued that the organization of a political socialist party had been premature and dangerous because police persecution, by isolating the Party from the masses, would lead to its degeneration into a sectarian cabal. The need of the moment was not a political struggle for "socialism" but a campaign to obtain better working conditions, higher wages, and shorter hours for the still undeveloped proletariat, then the victim of the crude exploitation which accompanied the birth of capitalism everywhere. Not only could such a policy be undertaken without exposing the small socialist movement to the full force of persecution, but, by building bridges to the workers, it would exorcise the threat of sectarianism. As Sakazov put it at the time, "We think that the need is for quiet and systematic work, propagandistic and organizational, for the preparation of our workers." [33] This argument is deeper than the earlier objections of Mutafov and Bozveliev, which had been based on the fear of persecution. The gulf between the views of Sakazov's and Dabev's groups and those of the circle around Blagoev and Gabrovski, whose faith in the political party remained unshaken, proved unbridgeable and the former seceded and founded

[31] *Progres*, Vol. I, No. 35 (July 10, 1893). *Progres* was a nonsocialist but strongly anti-Stambolovist weekly. Because of the latter tendency, its offices were wrecked. A number of issues are available at the Internationaal Instituut voor Sociale Geschiedenis in Amsterdam.

[32] *Yanko Sakazov yubileyen sbornik,* p. 28.

[33] Quoted in *Yanko Sakazov yubileyen sbornik,* p. 28. Sakazov reviewed these ideas in his "Ziele und Wege der Bulgarischen Sozialdemokratie," pp. 649-54. For Blagoev's reminiscences of this episode, see his *Prinos kam istoriata na sotsializma v Balgaria,* pp. 149-58. Writing in 1906 he claims (p. 153): "Essentially Yanko Sakazov was in his views a liberal-democrat of the Karavelovist type, by nature a bourgeois politician." These lines, like Sakazov's article of 1907, must be read against the background of a split (1892), a reconciliation (1894), and a second split (1903), which embittered both.

the Social Democratic Union (Sayuz) for the implementation of their theories.[34] Sakazov put *Den* at the Union's disposal as did Mutafov the *Sotsial Demokrat* for its few remaining issues.[35] Blagoev's Party was thus obliged to found in November, 1892, its own mouthpiece *Rabotnik* (Worker), edited by Gabrovski. In 1893 Dabev launched *Drugar* (Comrade) for the propagation of the Union's policy.

The leaders of the Bulgarian socialist colony in Geneva, Rakovski and Balabanov, who were in Bulgaria for their 1892 summer vacation, supported the Union to which the socialist groups of Shumen, Sevlievo, Kazanlak, Gabrovo, and Sofia affiliated. The backbone of the Party remained the socialist groups of Stara Zagora and Tirnovo.[36]

The Union held its first and last conference at Shumen in the summer of 1893.[37] The Party assembled in congress at Tirnovo early in July of the same year and resolved to participate independently in the elections for the national parliament, the Sobranie, to be held later in the month.[38] It received a grand total of 571 votes.[39]

The schism was short-lived for the leaders of both groups saw that in the face of Stambolov's ever-increasing persecution, which took a particularly sharp turn in 1893 with a severe censorship law, the temporary suspension of *Rabotnik*, numerous arrests, and considerable bloodshed,[40] it was essential to avoid weakening the socialist ranks. Though the doctrinaire Blagoev at first hesitated to effect a reconciliation with "traitors," a month's imprisonment in November, 1893, on the alleged suspicion of being involved in a plot

---

[34] In subsequent Bulgarian Communist historiography, which is dominated by the frantic desire to find parallels with the Russian experience, this period is referred to as the Bulgarian equivalent of Plekhanov's and Lenin's struggle against the "Economists." The first instance of this juxtaposition of "Economists" and "Union," which is now the standard Communist interpretation, is the article of Bakalov, "Die Sozialdemokratische Bewegung in Bulgarien," p. 597. Cf. also Trotsky, "In den Balkanländern," p. 74, and Kabakchiev, "Der Weg zur Kommunistischen Internationale," p. 617.

[35] Blagoev, *Prinos kam istoriata na sotsializma v Balgaria*, p. 571.

[36] *Progres*, Vol. I, No. 30 (June 5, 1893); *Yanko Sakazov yubileyen sbornik*, p. 5.

[37] *Yanko Sakazov yubileyen sbornik*, p. 5.

[38] Blagoev, *Prinos kam istoriata na sotsializma v Balgaria*, p. 166.

[39] Karakolov, "Kharakterni momenti ot borbata na Balgarskata Rabotnicheska Partia—Komunisti," p. 130.

[40] Blagoev, *Prinos kam istoriata na sotsializma v Balgaria*, p. 233; Tchitchovsky, *The Socialist Movement in Bulgaria*, p. 12.

against the life of Prince Ferdinand,[41] gave him occasion to re-consider, and on his release at the end of the month he took up the question with Sava Mutafov. In January, 1894, Sakazov went to Plovdiv to discuss with Blagoev arrangements for reunification. An agreement was signed on February 10/22, but the arrest of Sakazov in March, from which he was released only after the overthrow of Stambolov in May, 1894,[42] delayed the unification congress until July, when it assembled in Sofia.

It had been agreed in February to unite in a new political party, to be called the Bulgarian Social Democratic Labor Party. On this issue, then, the Blagoev faction had its way. The leaders of the old Party and Union were to fuse into a united Central Committee pending the election of one by the coming congress. The revived *Rabotnik* was to be the official political organ of the new Party, *Drugar* to be a paper for the workers, and *Den* to become the Party's monthly journal.[43]

When the unification congress met early in July, however, Stam-bolov had been overthrown and the main cause of the sense of urgency which had animated the February conversations was re-moved. The debates were, accordingly, bitter, but the new unity survived. The Sakazov group had yielded in February to the demand that a political party be formed and now with the end of Stambolov's dictatorship one of the reasons for its previous opposition to such a course was removed. But the danger that the Party would degenerate into sectarianism continued to be acute. The implications of the paltry 571 votes cast for the old Party in the elections of 1893 were clear, and the congress adopted the following policy to be pursued by the new Party in regard to elections: [44] (1) No Socialist may vote for a candidate from Stambolov's Liberal Party; (2) No electoral agreements compromising the Socialist program shall be made with another party or with a non-Socialist political leader; however: (3) In electoral districts where a Socialist candidate obvi-ously has no chance at all of election, the Party may endorse "honest and progressive" candidates of parties other than the Liberal Party.

---

[41] Blagoev, *Kratki belezhki iz moya zhivot*, p. 89.

[42] *Yanko Sakazov yubileyen sbornik*, p. 5.

[43] Blagoev, *Prinos kam istoriata na sotsializma v Balgaria*, p. 220. Within a short time *Drugar* was replaced by *Sotsialist*.

[44] Blagoev, *Prinos kam istoriata na sotsializma v Balgaria*, p. 244.

The heart of this policy was the third provision, and it represented a victory for Sakazov's faction which Blagoev later reproached himself for having accepted.[45] In his "Russian" mania for heresy-hunting and for ideological purity he suspected all contact of any kind with non-Socialist parties and personalities. Whereas Sakazov believed in the desirability of cooperation with non-Socialist progressive groups in the fight against dictatorship and for the establishment of "bourgeois democracy" in Bulgaria, Blagoev declined to make distinctions among the various forces in the bourgeois camp. Whereas the Union's *Drugar* had hailed the dismissal of Stambolov as a step which, if properly followed up, could lead to the normalization and democratization of Bulgarian politics, the Party's *Rabotnik* had warned that the event simply marked the substitution of one party of the class enemy by another, a change of little significance for Socialists.[46] Apparently Gabrovski, the paper's editor, and Blagoev, its ideologue, considered the fact that the coming unity congress could for the first time be held openly and legally to be irrelevant.

The mildness of the succeeding Stoilov regime, which made it safe to be a Socialist,[47] and the unification of the Party and the Union, brought an inflow of intelligentsia into the reunited Party. The dearth of serious non-Socialist political literature in the country contributed to this movement. The peasants, who had as yet no political organization of their own, were also attracted to vote for this Socialist Party which talked so much about justice for the underdog. Consequently in 1894 Sakazov and Gabrovski were elected to the Sobranie from completely rural electoral districts in which the new Party had no organization whatsoever and which were among the most backward in the country, inhabited by the poorest peasants. In the next election these seats were lost but two others were gained in districts of a similar character in which the Party had again made no particularly strenuous efforts.[48]

---

[45] *Ibid.,* p. 244.

[46] Blagoev, *Prinos kam istoriata na sotsializma v Balgaria,* pp. 239-40. Between the February agreement and the July congress each faction continued to publish its own paper.

[47] Symptomatic of the change was the fact that Blagoev was reinstated into the state school system with an appointment as teacher of Russian at the Plovdiv gymnasium Alexander I.

[48] Rainoff, *Die Arbeiterbewegung in Bulgarien,* p. 79; *Yanko Sakazov yubileyen*

Sakazov and his friends were entranced by these electoral successes and, to Blagoev's alarm, began actively to court peasants and middle-class elements. When the second Party congress of 1895 even deprecated a series of small-scale strikes in Sofia as being useless and harmful in the absence of strong workers' organizations,[49] Blagoev became seriously alarmed. He regarded the appeal to the peasants combined with this resolution on the strike question, which he admitted to be objectively correct although psychologically defeatist, as the beginning of the degeneration of the Socialist Party into an electioneering club of petit-bourgeois progressives. Like his teacher Plekhanov, Blagoev, distrustful of the peasant, demanded that the Party cease to woo this incorrigibly conservative creature who could only corrupt it.[50] Whereas Sakazov viewed the agrarian depression of 1895-99, which brought many peasants to support the Socialist Party out of desperation, as an opportunity for winning them to it permanently, Blagoev insisted that since the peasants would inevitably become either an urban or an agricultural proletariat, it was pointless and dangerous to court them *qua* peasants.[51]

But Blagoev's warnings went unheeded, for the supporters of Sakazov were at this time in a majority among the Party leaders, Blagoev thereupon founded in January, 1897, the monthly *Novo Vreme* (New Time), which was intended to serve, like the German publication (*Die Neue Zeit*) after which it was named and patterned, as a theoretical journal expounding "scientific" Marxism.[52] As

---

sbornik, p. 5; Yanko, Sakazov, "Ziele und Wege der Bulgarischen Sozialdemokratie," p. 650. The election of Gabrovski seems to have been the consequence of a misunderstanding on the part of the mayor of the village in the district for which he was elected. Gabrovski, in order not to be obliged to explain what a Social Democrat was, distorted the truth and announced himself as a *Narodnyak*, by which he meant a former participant in the Russian *Narodnaya Volya* revolutionary movement. The local mayor, however, assumed him to refer to the Bulgarian People's (*Narodnata*) Party, which the mayor supported, and recommended Gabrovski's election. In the backward Bulgarian villages of the time, such a "recommendation" was often tantamount to election. See Blagoev, *Prinos kam istoriata na sotsializma v Balgaria*, p. 281.

[49] Blagoev, *Prinos kam istoriata na sotsializma v Balgaria*, p. 277.

[50] Dimker, "La Crise socialiste en Bulgarie," p. 67.

[51] Blagoev, "Die Sozialistische Arbeiterbewegung in Bulgarien," p. 564. This fear of and contempt for the peasant was an old Marxist tradition. Karl Marx had despised the peasantry as "a class of barbarians standing half outside human society and combining all the coarseness of primitive social forms with all the miseries of civilized countries." *Das Kapital*, Vol. III, Part II, Book III.

[52] An incomplete file of *Novo Vreme*, which was published by Blagoev uninterruptedly from January, 1897, until the Communist uprising in September, 1923 (at

Blagoev grew more and more dissatisfied with the Party's policy, his editorials in *Novo Vreme* became increasingly critical. Finally, after the fifth Party congress, held in Yambol in July, 1898, he gave vent to his resentment in a bitter article purporting to be a report on the congress.[53] He begins by complaining of the neglect shown toward "the most essential need of the Party—propaganda ... among the working class and the arousing within it of a class consciousness, a feeling of solidarity, and an appeal to organization." The Party press, Blagoev continues, appeals to "the broad masses," where it should direct itself at the workers, and rationalizes this opportunistic policy with the claim that the peasantry and the urban petite bourgeoisie are "tomorrow's proletarians." Singling out his former collaborator Gabrovski, who now subscribed to the majority view, for a particularly resentful tirade, Blagoev reproaches him with endorsing policies which will "degrade the Party from a socialist to a radical or democratic one of petit-bourgeois character." Surely Gabrovski must realize that "a social democratic party can be nothing other than ... the representative of the proletarian class ... the vanguard of the workers' movement." The Party is organizationally still too weak and ideologically too impure to indulge in questionable, nay dangerous, accommodations with "tomorrow's proletarians." [54]

Sakazov and Gabrovski were also aware of the fact that in the long run it was quite impossible for a Socialist Party to become the spokesman of the peasantry in a country in which 80 percent of the population belonged to that class. Though he had energetically championed the peasants' complaints and demands at the time of the disorders of 1899, which had been evoked by a combination of

---

which time it was the journal of the Bulgarian Communist Party), is available at the Internationaal Instituut voor Sociale Geschiedenis in Amsterdam. It was revived after the Second World War.

[53] *Novo Vreme,* II, No. 9 (September, 1898), 860-66.

[54] *Ibid.,* II, No. 9 (September, 1898), 866. Gabrovski's position was not inconsistent with his stand in 1891. At that time the issues had been whether primary emphasis should be placed on the political or the economic struggle and whether or not a political party ought to be organized. He had then stood for the political solution. Now the controversy concerned the extent to which this political struggle should be broadened to cover various strata of the population and once again Gabrovski advocated the widest range of political activity. He was to remain a supporter of Sakazov until 1919 when he joined the then newly founded Communist Party. He was killed in the White Terror which followed the dynamiting of the Sofia Cathedral in April, 1925. See the obituary in *Inprekorr,* V, No. 111 (July 21, 1925), 1543.

harvest failures and government efforts to impose a burdensome new tax, Sakazov realized that eventually the peasantry would form its own political party. This happened later in 1899. Sakazov, far from boycotting the new Peasant Union, attended its first congress at Plevna in 1900 and welcomed it into the political arena.[55] His aim had not been to forestall the formation of a peasant party but rather to draw together all the economically productive and politically liberal elements of the country in an alliance against governmental corruption and the system of palace intrigue which Prince Ferdinand was manipulating and perfecting. Sakazov wanted to see established in Bulgaria as an essential prerequisite for effective socialist activity, the rule of law, responsible cabinets, parliamentary government—in short, that "bourgeois democracy" which Blagoev contemptuously dismissed as "not being socialism." [56] To promote his policy, Sakazov founded in 1900 a semimonthly journal to which he gave the descriptive name of *Obshto Delo* (Common Action). It was intended to counter Blagoev's *Novo Vreme*. The difference in the policies of the two journals was revealed most strikingly when in 1902 Prime Minister Danev, in order to prevent the alliance between the Socialist and Peasant Parties for which Sakazov was striving, took advantage of the political ignorance of the peasant to spread the rumor that, given the opportunity, the Socialists would take away the peasant's plot, house, and animals. Sakazov took great pains to correct this impression by assuring the peasants, in *Obshto Delo*, that it was the intention of his Party to socialize only large capitalist enterprises, leaving untouched all small property, urban or agricultural, which was worked by the owner and his family. Blagoev in *Novo Vreme*, however, sneered at such assurances and thundered that the Socialist Party would "vigorously fight for the complete abolition of private

---

[55] *Yanko Sakazov yubileyen sbornik*, p. 6. The assertion that the Peasant Union would never have been formed had the Socialists resolutely pursued Sakazov's policy is made by Petkov in "Die Bulgarische Sozialdemokratie und die Bauern," p. 114. The claim is quite improbable as the general development of agrarian politics in Eastern Europe has demonstrated. A peasant ideology was developed, confused but distinct from Marxism and opposed to it. A Socialist Party could not cater to this without abandoning its own ideology. In a country with hardly a proletariat and where 80 percent of the population were peasants, that an avowedly proletarian party should have been formed before an agrarian one is another indication of the over-intellectualization and sociological artificiality of Bulgarian party politics.

[56] Blagoev, *Prinos kam istoriata na sotsializma v Balgaria*, p. 425.

property—from the biggest machine to the tailor's needle, from the large tracts of land to the last inch of land." [57] If this statement alienated the peasants and artisans, so much the better. They were in any event incorrigibly reactionary, and their objective class interests were opposed to those of the proletariat, which they would betray at the first opportunity. Sakazov decried Blagoev's attitude as narrow-minded, and the latter with alacrity appropriated the rebuke as his banner. Henceforth he and his followers proudly referred to themselves as the "Narrow-Minded" Socialists (*Tesnyatsi*) and derisively denounced Sakazov's supporters as "Broad-Minded Collaborators" with other classes (*Shiroki Obshtodeltsi*) [58]— a play upon the name of their journal.

Sakazov soon had an opportunity to implement his theory. When in May, 1903, the Stambolovist Liberals led by Petrov and Petkov replaced the Progressive Liberal government of Danev, they revoked the law for the irremovability of civil servants on political grounds which had been passed by the Sobranie under the preceding government. When the opposition deputies thereupon wrote a joint letter to Prince Ferdinand protesting against this reintroduction of the spoils system, Sakazov and Gabrovski also appended their signatures, an action which the doctrinaires around Blagoev denounced as an act of servility before the Prince, an acknowledgment of monarchism, and a lowering of the Socialist movement to the level of the bourgeois parties.[59] Another time Sakazov suggested that the opposition parties remind Prince Ferdinand, who appointed and dismissed governments at his pleasure without reference to the parliamentary strength of the parties, of his constitutional limitations. Blagoev not only felt that Sakazov had again contaminated himself by giving such advice to the bourgeois parties but, in his pedantic and barren interpretation of Marxism, insisted, quite contrary to the facts, that the Prince was "objectively powerless," was but a "tool" of the bourgeois class, and that to attack him was but to beat a straw man.[60]

---

[57] Quoted by Tchitchovsky, *The Socialist Movement in Bulgaria*, p. 15.
[58] G. B., "Shiroki Sotsialisti ili Obshtodeltsi," pp. 581-87. The author of this article was probably Georgi Bakalov. A few issues of *Rabotnichesko Delo* are preserved at the Internationaal Instituut voor Sociale Geschiedenis in Amsterdam.
[59] Dimker, "La Crise socialiste en Bulgarie," p. 73.
[60] Assen Tsankov, "Der Sozialismus in Bulgarien," p. 628.

The quarrel between the two wings of the Party extended also to the conception of the proper relationship between the Party and the fragile young trade-union movement. Sakazov believed that the trade unions should be open to all workers irrespective of political sympathies and should be organizationally independent of the Party. The conditions of the trade-union struggle would then arouse a class consciousness in the hearts of the workers who would thus be educated to socialism within their movement. Blagoev regarded this as an incorrect theory of trade-union "neutrality" in the class struggle, a theory which, by not requiring a tight organizational connection between the unions and the Party, would allow the former to degenerate into nonpolitical wage-and-hour pressure groups.[61] To this charge the Broad Socialists retorted that trade unions free from organizational control by the Party were not necessarily neutral and nonpolitical, nor was it intended that they should be. The trade-union movement, on the contrary, by developing the workers' solidarity, raising their cultural level, fighting for the improvement of their conditions, would necessarily take on a political character. Precisely because they fought for these general interests of the laboring class, it was essential that the trade unions be open to all workers irrespective of political conviction. Though the organizational independence of the trade-union movement from every political party was therefore necessary, it was clear that as the fight for the objectives of this movement had to be waged on the political as well as on the economic front, the unions would support that political party which showed itself the firmest champion of working-class interests—the Socialist Party.[62]

This controversy on the proper relationship between the Socialist Party and the trade unions must be viewed against the Party's strength and social composition. The Party was not then and never became proletarian despite the fact that industrialization, particularly mining and railroad development, was creating a small proletariat. In 1900, for example, the total Party membership was 1,761, of whom only 496 were workers, the rest being intellectuals, peasants, and artisans. By 1902 the number of members had increased to

[61] G. B., "Shiroki Sotsialisti ili Obshtodeltsi," p. 586; Blagoev, *Prinos kam istoriata na sotsializma v Balgaria*, p. 542.
[62] "Tekhniat Sindikalen Kongress," *Rabotnichesko Delo*, II, No. 10 (October, 1904), 594.

2,507; the number of workers rose to 982, but this was still a relatively low percentage of the membership.[63]

The Party suffered from a high turnover in membership as many of its numerous intellectuals passed into the bourgeois parties. The high proportion of artisans saddled the Party, which claimed to be the political arm of a "rising class," with recruits from precisely that class which capitalism was threatening to exterminate. Nevertheless, this was the strongest Socialist Party in the Balkans and boasted of being "the rampart of the social revolution in the Orient." [64]

The Party scored further electoral successes but, to the chagrin of its leaders, all of its Sobranie deputies, with one exception, continued to be elected by rural constituencies. The first Socialist deputies had been Sakazov and Gabrovski, elected in 1894. By 1899 there were six in the chamber[65] and in the following year, though their number declined to one, the member for Sliven, the only Socialist to be elected from a town in these years,[66] a total of 13,800 ballots were cast for the Party's candidates by an electorate disgusted with the corruption of the Radoslavov government.[67] In the elections of 1902, eight Socialists, among them Blagoev, were sent to the Sobranie and 20,300 ballots cast for the Party's candidates.[68] As these Socialists continued to be elected by rural constituencies, it seems probable that the victories were due less to their political ideology than to their revolutionary phraseology and promises to fight corruption and exploitation. The government was alarmed and in 1903 altered the electoral law to introduce the single-member constituency system. This law, together with the rapid growth of the Peasant Union as the class party of the peasantry, hit

[63] Compiled from Blagoev, *Prinos kam istoriata na sotsializma v Balgaria, passim.* In 1901 the Party had 2,180 members. The proportion of workers in this year is not known. A breakdown of the 1900 figure is given by Staneff, *Das Gewerbewesen und die Gewerbepolitik in Bulgarien,* p. 51. He divides the 1,761 members into 496 proletarians, 430 artisans, 420 intellectuals, 250 peasants, and 165 others.

[64] Denkoff, "Le Huitième Congrès National du Parti Ouvrier Social Démocrate Bulgare," p. 568.

[65] It was in this year that the Peasant Union entered the political arena and won twenty-five seats in the Sobranie. See X.Y.Z., "Le Peuple bulgare et l'Union Paysanne," p. 239.

[66] Rainoff, *Die Arbeiterbewegung in Bulgarien,* p. 81.

[67] Denkoff, "La Lutte de la social democratie bulgare contre l'opportunisme," p. 435.

[68] *Ibid.,* p. 435.

the Socialists hard. In the towns they were unable to compete with the bourgeois parties and it was henceforth impossible for them to ride into the Sobranie from the villages in the teeth of the new Peasant Union. As a result, no Socialist sat in the chamber from 1903 until 1912, when Sakazov broke through the single-member constituency system to be elected in Sofia.[69]

The electoral successes of 1899, 1900, and 1902 widened rather than healed the rift within the Party. Whereas Sakazov was sufficiently exhilarated to cast his net ever wider for peasant and middle-class support for his policy of common action to bring bourgeois democracy to Bulgaria, Blagoev was profoundly disquieted by what he felt was the debasement of a Marxist-proletarian party into a radical-bourgeois one. The disagreements became ever sharper, and at each annual Party congress the chasm between the two factions widened.

Early in 1900, after the appearance of the first numbers of Sakazov's *Obshto Delo*, Blagoev attacked it in his own *Novo Vreme* and demanded its suppression as an "un-Marxist and un-Socialist" journal and therefore one which it was improper for a member of the Party to publish.[70] As the Bernstein controversy was then convulsing the German Socialist Party[71] and heresy-hunting had come into fashion, Blagoev had little difficulty in rallying the majority of the Central Committee of the Bulgarian Party to his side. Sakazov retorted with the charge that Blagoev was transforming living socialism into dry formalism. He refused to close *Obshto Delo*. Blagoev, taking advantage of his control of the Central Committee, sought to have the Eighth Party Congress, meeting in Plevna in the summer of 1901, censure Sakazov. He incited his supporters to propose a resolution stating that "The Eighth National Congress of the Bulgarian Social Democratic Labor Party . . . considering that for the realization of its ultimate aim—the political and economic emancipation of the working class—the Party draws its strength principally from the development of the class consciousness of the proletariat and its organization on the basis of class struggle . . . that the urban and rural elements standing close to the proletariat

---

[69] *Yanko Sakazov yubileyen sbornik*, p. 46.

[70] Assen Tsankov, "Der Sozialismus in Bulgarien," p. 627.

[71] Eduard Bernstein, *Die Voraussetzungen des Sozialismus und die Aufgaben der Sozialdemokratie* had been published in 1899.

constitute a reliable support for the Party only insofar as they are imbued with the class interests of the proletariat ... reaffirms once again the purely proletarian character of the Bulgarian Social Democratic Labor Party." [72] Sakazov, however, did not fall into this trap and, pretending to be unaware that the proposed resolution was an attack upon himself, voted for it. Of the 60 delegates to the Congress, 46 endorsed the resolution outright, 11 did so with reservations, and only 3 opposed it.[73] Thus Blagoev's lunge, which had been intended as the final stroke in the long duel over Sakazov's theory of common action with other classes, was parried by its intended victim.

The stalemate at the Plevna Congress only spurred Blagoev to renew the attack at the next Congress held in the summer of 1902 in Tirnovo, this time directing it against Sakazov's conduct in the Sobranie—his joining with bourgeois opposition groups to protest against the cancellation of the tenure of civil servants, his speeches assuring the peasants and petite bourgeoisie that the Party had no intention of socializing small family property. After this tirade Blagoev had his young protégé Vasil Kolarov tender a motion expressing concern over the alleged tendency of the Party to concentrate excessively on gaining the support of nonproletarian elements "in the pursuit of immediate political successes" and its supposed neglect of its primary task, "the political and economic organization of the proletariat on the basis of the class struggle and in the name of the socialist ideal." [74] This time, to prevent the recurrence of Sakazov's tactical escape from the implied censure at the Plevna Congress, Kolarov's motion contained an explicit indictment of *Obshto Delo*. But the Tirnovo Congress simply deleted this clause after Sakazov had explained that he did not advocate the destruction of the Party's proletarian base but only its extension to include other exploited classes and progressive strata. The emasculated resolution was then accepted by Sakazov's faction and

---

[72] Quoted in Denkoff, "Le Huitième Congrès National du Parti Ouvrier Social Démocrate Bulgare," p. 570.

[73] Blagoev, *Prinos kam istoriata na sotsializma v Balgaria*, p. 450.

[74] For the full text of Kolarov's resolution, see Blagoev, *Prinos kam istoriata na sotsializma v Balgaria*, pp. 511-12. Cf. Denkoff, "La Lutte de la social democratie bulgare contre l'opportunisme," p. 445. The Party had at this time 2,507 members. The previous year it had 2,180.

the intention of its sponsors once again foiled.[75] As its last act, however, the Congress, which was not animated by sympathy with Sakazov's program but rather by anxiety to avoid a split in the Party, instructed him to present within six months a brochure summarizing his theories in order that they might be judged by the Party.[76]

As the Party's Central Committee, which was to examine this statement, was controlled by the partisans of Blagoev, making it a foregone conclusion that the brochure would be condemned, Blagoev, expecting Sakazov to plead "freedom of criticism," sought to anticipate this defense by making a violent attack upon the doctrine of freedom of criticism in the December, 1902, issue of *Novo Vreme*. In this article, entitled "Socialism or Opportunism?", Blagoev quoted heavily from Lenin's *What Is To Be Done?*, which had appeared in March of that year, lauding in particular the lines " 'freedom of criticism' means freedom for an opportunistic drift in social democracy, freedom to transform social democracy into a democratic party of reform, freedom to inject into socialism bourgeois ideas and bourgeois elements." [77] Early in 1903 Blagoev published in *Rabotnicheski Vestnik* (Workers' Newspaper) that part of Lenin's pamphlet which dealt with this issue.[78]

One remarkable aspect of this incident is indicative both of Lenin's position in the Socialist world at this time and of Blagoev's ideological heritage. This Bulgarian who, having emerged from the Russian Socialist movement, always sought to keep himself informed of developments within it, was in 1902 under the firm impression that the name "Lenin" which appeared on the title page of the book he was commending was, like "Beltov," but a pseudonym concealing the identity of Plekhanov.[79]

As it was, these preliminary skirmishes on Blagoev's part against

[75] Assen Tsankov, "Der Sozialismus in Bulgarien," p. 629.
[76] Dimker, "La Crise socialiste en Bulgarie," p. 72.
[77] Lenin, *Sochinenia*, 3d ed., IV (Moscow, 1927), 368.
[78] *Rabotnicheski Vestnik*, No. 41 (1903).
[79] Kabakchiev, "Lenin i bolgarskie Tesnyaki," p. 174. Whereas Plekhanov's writings were published by Blagoev in Bulgarian as soon as they appeared, those of Lenin were not published until after his coming to power in Russia. Before that Blagoev repeatedly attacked Lenin in *Novo Vreme*, emphasizing that the "social-democratic centralism" upon which he himself insisted in the Bulgarian Party had nothing in common with Lenin's "Blanquist" and "conspiratorial" centralism. Cf. Blagoev, "Po vaprosa za organizatsiata na Partia," p. 89.

what he expected would be Sakazov's response to the Tirnovo Congress were quite unnecessary, for before the required brochure could appear the Party was rent asunder. The break came within the Party organization of Sofia, where the old Union had been in control ten years before and in which the supporters of Sakazov were now in the majority.[80] In March, 1903, a group of about fifty followers of Blagoev seceded from the Sofia organization, charging it with flouting the resolution of the Party Congress on the necessity of recentering the Party's activity upon its proletarian base, and applied to the Central Committee for recognition as the official Party organization in the capital—an application which, in view of the Committee's control by Blagoev, was immediately granted. The Central Committee then declared the organization of the Sofia majority dissolved "in view of the fact that they have become unworthy of the name of Socialists."[81] The Broad minority led by Sakazov thereupon quit the Central Committee. As Evtim Dabev, now secretary-treasurer, was of this minority, the Party funds came into the possession of the Broad faction[82] while the weekly *Rabotnicheski Vestnik*, founded by Georgi Kirkov in September, 1897, was put by him at the disposal of Blagoev's Narrow group.[83]

The Narrow majority of the Central Committee immediately dispatched ultimatums to the secretaries of all the local organizations demanding that they declare their adherence. In most cases the local secretary decided this issue without consulting the membership.[84] By May, 1903, about forty local Party organizations had sent affirmative replies and half as many had declared in favor of the Broad position.[85] As to membership, however, the latter was the

[80] Yanko Sakazov, "Die Spaltung in der Bulgarischen Sozialdemokratischen Arbeiterpartei," p. 474.

[81] For the Broad interpretation of this incident, see Assen Tsankov, "Der Sozialismus in Bulgarien," p. 629. The Narrow retort is given by Blagoev *(Prinos kam istoriata na sotsiatizma v Balgaria*, p. 520). The two accounts are in agreement on the basic facts. See also Bakalov, "Die Sozialdemokratische Bewegung in Bulgarien," p. 598, for the account of one who in 1903 had sided with Blagoev but had later quarreled with him.

[82] Blagoev, *Prinos kam istoriata na sotsializma v Balgaria*, p. 521; Karakolov, "Kharakterni momenti ot borbata na Balgarskata Rabotnicheska Partia—Komunisti," p. 130.

[83] "Nachruf: Georg Kirkov," *Die Kommunistische Internationale*, No. 14 (1920), p. 331.

[84] Dimker, "La Crise socialiste en Bulgarie," p. 72.

[85] Avramov, "Der Zehnte Kongress der Sozialdemokratischen Arbeiterpartei Bulgariens," p. 208.

stronger faction,[86] for it included the majority of the large Sofia group as well as the strong Party organization of Tivorno, led by Blagoev's erstwhile ally in the struggle against the Union, Nikola Gabrovski. The backbone of the Narrow section were the Party organizations of Russe, Plovdiv, and Sliven.[87] Of the four Socialist cooperatives, only that of Plovdiv opted for Blagoev's group while those of Sofia, Yambol, and Kazanlak adhered to Sakazov's. As for the Party's leaders, Kirkov, Bakalov, and Rakovski[88] sided with Blagoev as did many of the young students just returned from abroad who, like Kolarov and Kabakchiev, were subsequently to make their names in the Bulgarian Communist movement. Gabrovski and Dabev supported Sakazov.

In the summer of 1903, when the Russian Socialist movement was splitting into the Bolshevik and Menshevik sections, Blagoev summoned a congress of his adherents at Russe at which Sakazov and his colleagues were formally expelled. These promptly formed themselves into another party of the same name, and subsequently the two identified themselves by the designations "Narrow" and "Broad." Blagoev was determined to make a clean sweep of "compromises" and "deviations." Henceforth, the Congress decided, there would be no more attempts to attract nonproletarian support and no cooperation either in or out of the Sobranie with other groups. In the elections scheduled for October the Party would put up candidates only in the cities (for it spurned peasant support), and it would henceforth be extremely cautious in founding new cells, since no doubtful Socialists were wanted and a small pure party was preferable to a large but "compromised" one.[89] A reeducation campaign was begun to correct the ideological errors taught by Sakazov. "Common action" of the Socialist with other parties for the replacement of corrupt royal rule by "formal" democracy was

---

[86] Assen Tsankov, "Der Sozialismus in Bulgarien," p. 629.

[87] Blagoev, *Prinos kam istoriata na sotsializma v Balgaria,* p. 521.

[88] Both Bakalov and Rakovski broke with Blagoev within a few years. In 1920 Bakalov rejoined him in the new Bulgarian Communist Party. Rakovski soon extended his activities to the Rumanian and international Socialist movements and devoted only a small part of his energy to the Bulgarian, though he long sought to effect a reconcilation between its Narrow and Broad wings. He became a Soviet official and diplomat after 1917.

[89] Avramov, "Der Zehnte Kongress der Sozialdemokratischen Arbeiterpartei Bulgariens," p. 208.

denounced—only class interests existed for a Socialist.[90] Blagoev's Party, purged to wage the "pure" class struggle on behalf of the proletariat, consisted now of 1,174 members of whom only 480 were of that class.[91]

Sakazov defended himself with vigor. Scoffing at the Narrow Socialists' pretensions to be the only defenders of the proletariat, he pointed out that it had been his own supporters who had first organized the workers and established schools for them. The Sofia Party organization, which overwhelmingly endorsed his policy, was the only one essentially proletarian in membership. The only constructive resolutions adopted at the Narrow Party's Russe Congress, he claimed, were repetitions of those passed in previous years by Broad majorities. Though Blagoev was trumpeting his new electoral policy of nominating candidates only in the cities as a return to proletarian purity, in fact his party had in the October, 1903, elections simply put up rival candidates in every locality where a Broad Socialist was standing, regardless of whether or not the Narrow Party had an organization in the town. This policy of spite had only confused the electorate and contributed to the elimination of all Socialist representation in the Sobranie, thus playing into the hands of the government and its new electoral law.[92]

Sakazov did not limit himself to verbal counterattacks. While Blagoev was purifying his Party at Russe, he called a congress of his own supporters in Sofia. A semiweekly, *Rabotnicheska Borba* (Labor Struggle), was founded. It soon had 2,000 subscribers as compared to 1,500 for the Narrow Party's *Rabotnicheski Vestnik*.[93]

Thus the Bulgarian Socialist Party split at the same time as did the Russian. It is interesting and instructive to compare the two cases. Outwardly they seemed to have little in common as to the immediate causes of the schism: in the Russian case it involved contrasting definitions of party membership[94] and in the Bulgarian differences over relations with peasant and other nonproletarian elements and over collaboration with other parties against palace

[90] G. B., "Shiroki Sotsialisti ili Obshtodeltsi," p. 583.

[91] Blagoev, "Die Sozialistische Arbeiterbewegung in Bulgarien," p. 569.

[92] Yanko Sakazov, "Die Spaltung in der Bulgarischen Sozialdemokratischen Arbeiterpartei," p. 474.

[93] Assen Tsankov, "Der Sozialismus in Bulgarien," p. 629. Before the split *Rabotnicheski Vestnik* had 3,000 subscribers.

[94] Wolfe, *Three Who Made a Revolution*, p. 240.

rule. Another dissension which arose in the Bulgarian camp, that over the degree of control to be exercised by the Socialist Party over the labor unions, resembled more the quarrel between the Russian Economists and the Iskra group than the Bolshevik-Menshevik struggle. There were other contrasts in the two cases. The split in the Russian Party at the London Congress in August, 1903, came suddenly and took everyone by surprise, with the possible exception of Lenin. The Bulgarians had stood on the verge of theirs for a decade. In 1903 none of the Russians thought that the split would harden into a permanent schism, efforts were made throughout the succeeding decade and a half to effect a reconciliation, and many, such as Plekhanov and Trotsky, were to cross and recross the dividing line several times. Both Mensheviki and Bolsheviki retained until 1919 the same program, the one presented by Plekhanov at the 1903 congress, and during the First World War Lenin worked with the Menshevik leaders Martov and Aksel'rod in the antiwar Zimmerwald Movement.[95] In Bulgaria, on the other hand, Blagoev not only considered the split irrevocable, not only immediately drafted a new program, but also refused ever again to cooperate in any way with Sakazov.[96]

Despite the differences between the two cases there also existed a fundamental similarity. Though he did not possess an iota of Lenin's flair for revolutionary strategy and tactics, Blagoev shared with him a temperamental "hardness" on the issue of "proletarian" dictatorship, whereas both Martov and Sakazov were "soft." In both the Russian and Bulgarian splits the real issue was the question of the nature of the Party. That Blagoev purged the Bulgarian Party in the same year as Lenin split the Russian and that these were the only two parties of the Socialist International to be thus rent asunder before the First World War have always been matters of intense pride to Bulgarian Communists, the heirs of the Narrow Socialists.[97]

[95] Fainsod, *International Socialism and the World War*, pp. 67, 86, 153.

[96] When in 1910 a conference of Balkan Socialist Parties met in Belgrade, Blagoev successfully insisted upon the exclusion of the Broad Party. The Serbian Socialists, led by Tucović and Lapčević, in general preferred the Narrow Party to its rival while Rakovski's Rumanian Socialist Party favored now the one, now the other.

[97] See, for example, Kabakchiev's chapter on the Bulgarian Communist Party in Kabakchiev, Boshkovich, and Vatis, *Kommunisticheskie Partii Balkanskikh Stran*, pp. 52 ff., and Dimitrov, *Politicheski otchet na Ts. K. na BRP (k)*, pp. 9-11.

While Blagoev hardened the rift, purging the labor unions a year after the Party, Sakazov considered it a tragedy and did his best to heal it. A split in the Socialist Party of a Western industrial state, he reasoned, would have been bad enough, but in backward Bulgaria, where the proletariat was weak, where the bourgeois parties were largely personal coteries held together by hope for office and spoils, where, therefore, it was particularly important for the Socialists to set a different example by maintaining a strong party united around principles, it was nothing short of a catastrophe.[98] Sakazov refused at first to consider it final. Wiser counsel, he was sure, would prevail as the suicidal nature of the split became manifest. Objective conditions must eventually reimpose unity.[99] While Blagoev was expelling him from the Party at Russe in August, 1903, Sakazov extended the olive branch, declaring that though his own followers were more numerous, he was yet willing to compromise; their differences were not irreconcilable. He appealed to Blagoev's sense of responsibility in the face of the recent return to power of Bulgarian Socialism's chief enemy—the Stambolovist Liberal Party.[100] Later in the year he began publishing a weekly leaflet entitled *Edinstvo* (Unity) which, as its title suggests, was devoted to agitating for reconciliation.[101] In vain—Blagoev would have none of it. Unity with "opportunists" and "traitors" was out of the question. To every overture he responded with abuse. Sakazov appealed to the International, the supreme authority of the Socialist world, to mediate. Since his Parisian student days Sakazov had maintained connections with the French Socialist movement and he hoped that Jaurès, who had often deplored Blagoev's doctrinairism in the years when the split was developing,[102] could persuade the International to compel Blagoev to reunite. The report of the Broad Party to the Copenhagen Congress of the Socialist International in 1910 was a plea that the International endorse the current attempt of Rakovski, then active in the Rumanian and international Socialist movements, to

[98] Yanko Sakazov, "Die Nächsten Aufgaben der Bulgarischen Sozialdemokratie," p. 1075.
[99] Yanko Sakazov, "Was geschieht in Bulgarien," pp. 645-52.
[100] Yanko Sakazov, "Die Spaltung in der Bulgarischen Sozialdemokratischen Arbeiterpartei," pp. 474-75. The Stambolovist Liberals had returned to power under Racho Petrov in May, 1903.
[101] *Yanko Sakazov yubileyen sbornik*, p. 6.
[102] Articles by Jaurès in *La Petite République*, 1901-3, *passim*.

mediate between the Narrow and Broad Parties, a mission to which the latter had invited him.[103] The response of Kolarov, one of the Narrow Party's delegates to the Congress, was to demand the expulsion of the rival party from the International.[104] The International Socialist Bureau authorized Rakovski and Trotsky, who also enjoyed high prestige among Balkan Socialists, to bring about a reconciliation, but both were rebuffed by Blagoev.

Trotsky approached the problem with an open mind, though with his natural inclination to favor "hard" Socialists. He considered ideological impurity particularly dangerous in a Socialist movement such as the Bulgarian, with its preponderance of intelligentsia. He considered the high turnover rate of intellectuals as evidence that Sakazov's "common action" policy was dangerous, but he was appalled by the fanaticism of Blagoev and his circle, whom he dubbed "the seminarians," and vainly sought to effect a reconciliation between the two parties.[105] In 1911 Rakovski, authorized by Huysmans, the secretary of the International Socialist Bureau, to use any appropriate means to bring about unity, and despairing of bringing the respective leaders together, founded the daily *Napred* (Forward) to further his cause by means of propaganda among the rank and file which, he hoped, would evoke a ground swell of pressure forcing the leaders to begin serious negotiations. After publishing the paper from June, 1911, to January, 1912, he abandoned the effort as futile.[106] In 1911, in an attempt to compel unity on the trade-union level, the International Federation of Trade Unions at its Budapest Congress decided not to recognize either of the Bulgarian trade-union federations affiliated with the two respective

---

[103] "Rapport du Parti Ouvrier Social Democrate Bulgare (Unifié) au Bureau Socialiste International," p. 5.

[104] Kabakchiev, Boshkovich, and Vatis, *Kommunistischeskie Partii Balkanskikh Stran*, p. 71.

[105] For Trotsky's overtures to Blagoev, see his "In den Balkanländern," pp. 68-74. Blagoev published his reasons for rejecting them in an article entitled "Sotsializm na Balkanakh" (Socialism in the Balkans) in the Russian journal *Sotsial Demokrat* (Social Democrat), No. 19-20 (January, 1911). See also Kabakchiev, "Lenin i bolgarskie Tesnyaki," p. 178; Kabakchiev, "Dmitri Blagoev i bolgarskie Tesnyaki," p. 55; Logio, *Bulgaria: Problems and Politics*, p. 77.

[106] Dimitrov, *Der Kampf um Arbeiterschutz in Bulgarien*, p. 4. Rakovski, another "hard" socialist, also came to the conclusion that Sakazov's program of cooperation with other classes and parties was dangerous. As Sakazov refused to abandon it, Rakovski berated him in the last issue of *Napred*, that of January 7, 1912, as an "opportunist" and a "scoundrel." By this time both Parties considered *Napred* simply a nuisance.

political parties. In 1914 Karl Legien, secretary of the International Federation, went to Sofia to plead that at least the unions be reunited. But Georgi Dimitrov, secretary of the labor federation affiliated to the Narrow Party, was no less adamant than Blagoev. Legien, too, had to acknowledge defeat.[107]

The two rival parties had meanwhile developed along lines suggested by the theories of their leaders, a development which drew them ever further apart. In 1906 Sakazov formalized and expanded the theory of cooperation with other classes in a book entitled *Caesarism or Democracy?*,[108] and in January, 1907, he gave it practical application when he and Gabrovski joined the leaders of the four bourgeois opposition parties in a protest against the government's ordering the closing of the Sofia University for six months and dismissal of several professors as punishment for a hostile reception accorded by the students to Prince Ferdinand.[109] The leaders of the Broad Socialists repeatedly joined other opposition leaders to condemn the censorship and other arbitrary policies pursued by the Stambolovist Liberal Party and Prince Ferdinand, and to denounce the corruption which characterized their government. This agitation helped bring about the fall of the cabinet in January, 1908, and the replacement of Liberal Premier Petar Gudev by the Democrat Alexander Malinov. The first actions of the new government were to reopen the University and to relax the censorship, but Sakazov soon learned that while it was easy to cooperate with other parties to bring about the fall of a government, it was quite another matter to exert any influence over a new cabinet of his erstwhile allies. Malinov was no sooner in power than he abandoned the six-point reform program drawn up before Gudev's fall by the opposition parties, including his own and Sakazov's. He was also as docile as his predecessors toward Ferdinand. Sakazov's policy of "common action" foundered on the rock of the bourgeois parties' opportunism

---

[107] Dimitrov, "Die Gewerkschaftsbewegung Bulgariens," *Inprekorr*, III, No. 24 (February 5, 1923), 183. The various individual Bulgarian craft unions continued, however, to be affiliated with their respective international trade secretariats.

[108] Reviewed by G. Wassileff in *Die Neue Zeit*, XXIV, No. 49 (1906), 773-74.

[109] Rainoff, *Die Arbeiterbewegung in Bulgarien*, p. 127. A few weeks after these incidents the Prime Minister, Dimitar Petkov, was assassinated. He was the father of the Peasant Union leader Nikola Petkov whose judicial murder in 1947 was one of the milestones in the process of the Communist *Gleichschaltung* of postwar Bulgaria. Dimitar Petkov was succeeded by Petar Gudev, another Liberal.

and his subsequent disillusionment makes pathetic reading.[110]
Malinov in opposition had been righteously indignant over the
corruption and terror practiced by the Liberal government. Malinov
in power applied them profitably in the elections of 1908, which he
scheduled as soon as he felt firmly in control of the state machine.
Of the 175 members of the prorogued Sobranie, 150 had been
Liberals and 6 belonged to Malinov's Democratic Party. In the
newly elected chamber of 203 members, however, the Democrats
boasted 166 members while the Liberals were unrepresented.[111]
Though the Broad Socialists received 10,260 votes to the Narrow
Party's 1,809 (both parties remaining, however, unrepresented in
the chamber) and though a year later Konstantin Bozveliev, of the
Broad Party became the first Socialist to be elected mayor of a
Bulgarian town, that of Kazanlak, these petty triumphs[112] were no
consolation to Sakazov.

Developments in the Narrow Socialist Party were proceeding in
the opposite, though no less disastrous, direction. As Blagoev had
always been more concerned with the internal soundness of the
Party than its electoral success, it is not surprising that the parallel
crisis in his party was one of strained relations among its leaders
rather than with outside politicians. Desperate to prevent the corruption of his party's Marxist purity, of which he came to consider
himself the sole guardian, he ruled it with an iron hand. Opposition
within the Central Committee was crushed and initiative from below
stifled. It was not long before resistance to Blagoev's dictatorship
developed. The first revolt occurred in 1905 and was led by Georgi
Bakalov and Nikola Kharlakov who protested that Blagoev was
isolating the Party from the proletariat by his insistence that all
wisdom resided with him and his small clique of intellectuals in the

[110] Yanko Sakazov, "Die Nächsten Aufgaben der bulgarischen Sozialdemokratie,"
p. 1078.

[111] That this startling reversal was due not to a genuine change in the opinion of
the electorate but to political corruption and public cynicism is indicated by the
results of the election of 1911, when Ferdinand appointed a coalition government of
Nationalists and Progressive Liberals (the heirs of Dragan Tsankov) with Geshov as
prime minister. This new government also scheduled elections as soon as it felt itself
in control. This time the Democrats' seats fell from 166 to 4 while the Nationalists'
rose from 3 to 80 and the Progressive Liberals' from 1 to 79. These and other
piquant accounts of Bulgarian politics are reported in the articles which Trotsky
wrote in 1912 as Balkan War correspondent for the liberal *Kievskaya Mysl'*. They
are reprinted in Trotsky and Kabakchiev, *Ocherki politicheskoi Bolgarii*.

[112] "Rapport . . . au Bureau Socialiste International," p. 5.

Central Committee, and that the workers had only to obey, not to show initiative. Such centralization may have been justified at a time when there was no proletariat and it was necessary to guard against ideological impurity in a Socialist party composed almost exclusively of the intelligentsia. By 1905, however, with the growth of a working class, and the eruption of a strike movement (albeit on a small scale),[113] this centralization had become a fetter upon the development of the movement.[114] Expelled from the Narrow Party in July, 1905,[115] Bakalov and Kharlakov received the support of many hitherto unaffiliated workers while most of the intellectuals of the Party remained faithful to Blagoev. By 1906 their new Liberal Socialist group, as Bakalov and Kharlakov called it,[116] had 425 members of whom 230 were workers. A year later it had 647 members of whom 349 were workers. In 1907 the membership of the Broad Party was 1,063 and that of the Narrow 1,795 of whom 690 and 1,189 respectively were workers. Though the Liberal Socialists thus had only 18 percent of the total membership of all three Socialist Parties, the trade unions attached to the Liberal Socialist group accounted for 25 percent of all organized workers: 1,176 belonged to their unions, 1,689 to the Narrow Party's, and 1,884 to the Broad Party's.[117]

These statistics indicate the weakness of the Bulgarian Socialist movement and the senselessness of its schisms. Compared with those of Western European Socialist Parties, they suggest an inverse

[113] In 1904 there had been thirty strikes throughout the country, of which the most important were those of the tobacco workers and bakers of Plovdiv and the textile workers of Samokov. A year later the movement had snowballed to sixty-six strikes. Rainoff, *Die Arbeiterbewegung in Bulgarien,* p. 94.

[114] Bakalov, "Die Sozialdemokratische Bewegung in Bulgarien," pp. 600-601. See also Manoff, "Ce qui se passe en Bulgarie," pp. 254-63. Years later an anonymous author, probably Blagoev, ridiculed the charge of excessive and dictatorial centralization and explained the episode in terms of "the individualism of a group of party intellectuals and the petit-bourgeois ideology of their adherents." Quoted from B., "Die Kommunistische Bewegung in Bulgarien," p. 132.

[115] It was at this congress that Vasil Kolarov was first elected to the Central Committee in place of Bakalov. See *Vasil Kolarov: Important Dates of His Life and Work,* p. 15.

[116] Present-day Communist historiography follows Blagoev in referring to this group as "the anarcho-liberals." See Blagoev, *Prinos kam istoriata na sotsializma v Balgaria,* p. 32 and Karakolov, "Kharakterni momenti ot borbata na Balgarskata Rabotnicheska Partia—Komunisti," p. 139.

[117] These and the preceding statistics are from Rainoff, *Die Arbeiterbewegung in Bulgarien,* p. 94. The journal of the Liberal Socialists was *Proletarii* (Proletarian), edited by Kharlakov.

proportion between the strength of the working class in a country and the ferocity of the quarrels within its Socialist movement. The Liberal Socialists were aware of the futility of these splits, and one of the causes of their expulsion from Blagoev's party had been their demand that unity negotiations be reopened. In June, 1908, the Liberal Socialists merged their trade-union federation with the one under the influence of the Broad Party.[118]

In that same year Blagoev excommunicated yet another band of heretics from his party. This time Nikola Sakarov, Genko Krastev, Koika Tineva, and a certain Ilyev had made the demand for a resumption of negotiations with Sakazov the core of their agitation.[119] After a few months of existence in limbo, this group of Progressive Socialists, as they called themselves, joined with the Liberal Socialists of Bakalov and Kharlakov and Sakazov's Broad Socialists to form one party calling itself the Bulgarian Social Democratic Labor Party (United).[120] Colloquially, however, it continued to be known as the Broad Party.

[118] "Rapport . . . au Bureau Socialiste International," p. 3.

[119] Tchitchovsky, *The Socialist Movement in Bulgaria*, p. 19; Kabakchiev, Boshkovich, and Vatis, *Kommunisticheskie Partii Balkanskikh Stran*, p. 61; Trotsky, "In den Balkanländern," p. 70.

[120] The subsequent careers of these Liberal and Progressive Socialists were highly erratic and extremely interesting. Kharlakov (born 1874), who had been secretary of the Central Committee in the crucial year of the split of 1903 when he had sided with Blagoev, and had been on the editorial boards of *Novo Vreme* and *Rabotnicheski Vestnik* as well as of several other papers, organized the Liberal Socialists in Varna in 1905. After the Balkan Wars he was elected to the Sobranie as Broad deputy for Vidin. In 1917, however, he left the Broad Party in protest against its support of the Bulgarian war effort and joined Lenin's antiwar Zimmerwald Movement. For some years thereafter he was one of the leaders of a splinter group which stood for a policy of trade-union independence from the control of the Communist Party— the issue which had prompted his rupture with Blagoev in 1905. In 1921, however, he was reconciled to the orthodox Communists and in 1924 played an active part in fashioning the abortive alliance between the Comintern and IMRO (see pp. 184 ff.). He died in Moscow on June 23, 1927.

Georgi Bakalov (born 1873 in Stara Zagora), the organizer of the smuggling of Lenin's *Iskra* into Russia and a "hard" socialist by nature, joined the Communist Party in the revolutionary enthusiasm after the First World War. Fleeing from the Tsankov regime to Moscow in 1925, he became a contributor to *Inprekorr* and a literary historian, being elected a member of the Academy of Sciences of the USSR. The coming to power of the milder Malinov-Mushanov government in Bulgaria enabled him to return home in 1932 to take up the editorship of the literary journal *Zvezda* (Star). Bakalov wrote studies of Khristo Botev and Vasil Levski and other monographs on Bulgarian literature and the national revolutionary movement. He died in 1939.

Koika Tineva became Kharlakov's wife and followed his checkered political career. In the 1920s she was a contributor to *Inprekorr*.

Nikola Sakarov was the most chauvinistic of Bulgarian Socialists during the First

The Socialist Parties maintained their slow growth in the years before the wars. The membership statistics of the Narrow Party in the decade between the break with Sakazov and the outbreak of the Balkan Wars are: [121]

Year	All Members	Proletarian Members
1903	1,174	480
1904	1,195	613
1905	1,475	774
1906	1,234	748
1907	1,795	1,189
1908	1,661	1,103
1909	1,870	1,230
1910	2,126	1,519
1911	2,510	—
1912	2,923	—

Party membership thus more than doubled in the decade. The two short periods of decline following 1905 and 1907 were due to the expulsion of the Liberal and Progressive Socialist groups. Though the proportion of workers rose from 41 percent in 1903 to 71 percent in 1910, the leadership continued to be confined to a Central Committee composed almost exclusively of intelligentsia. By 1909 about 1,100 readers subscribed to *Novo Vreme*, and in September of that year the appearances of *Rabotnicheski Vestnik* were increased from twice to thrice weekly. It had 2,700 subscribers, and the Party's propaganda-laden almanac, *Red People's Calendar*, was distributed in 15,000 copies. The Party's publishing firm, founded four years earlier and devoted to the issuing of translations of the socialist classics as well as the writings of the Party's own authors, prospered. [122]

World War but after its conclusion joined the Communist Party, from which he was, however, expelled in 1923 for opposing the Moscow-ordered September uprising of that year. He is the archfiend of "right-opportunism" in the orthodox Communist eschatology.

[121] Compiled from the following sources: Blagoev, "Die Sozialistische Arbeiterbewegung in Bulgarien," p. 569; Rainoff, *Die Arbeiterbewegung in Bulgarien*, p. 94; Trotsky, "In den Balkanländern," p. 72; Rakovski, "Aus Bulgarien," p. 687; Pandov, *Grazhdanskata Voina*, p. 75; Yotsov, "Upravlenieto na 'Demokraticheski Sgovor'," p. 18.

[122] Blagoev, "Die Sozialistische Arbeiterbewegung in Bulgarien," p. 570. By 1910 the circulation of *Novo Vreme* had increased to 1,275 and a year later *Rabotnicheski Vestnik* had 4,300 subscribers. The latter paper was expanded into a daily after the Party congress of July, 1911. Rakovski, "Aus Bulgarien," pp. 687-88.

Though statistics for the Broad Socialist Party during these years are confused, it also appears to have slowly expanded. Its strength may be surmised from the following estimates: [123]

Year	Number of Members
1904	1,210
1905	908
1906	1,014
1907	1,063
1908	1,221
1909	2,427
1910	2,431
1911	3,102

The decline after 1904 was probably due to disillusionment after the split. The doubling of membership between 1908 and 1910 was a consequence of the fusion with the Liberal and Progressive Socialists. On the eve of the Balkan Wars the Broad Party was somewhat stronger than its rival.

As for the number of proletarian members in the Broad Party, in 1905 there were 548; in 1906, 655; and in 1907, 690. A detailed breakdown of its membership in 1909 is revealing: apprentices in artisans' shops, 720; master artisans, 156; civil servants and state employees, 774; members of the liberal professions (chiefly lawyers), 196; merchants, 285; peasants, 157; workers, 139.[124]

Though a considerable proportion of the 774 state employees were railway men and should be listed as proletarians, yet the working-class element in the Broad Party was weaker than among the Narrow Socialists. Where the social composition of the two parties differed most was in the relative strength of the intelligentsia and artisans. Sakazov might taunt Blagoev with having hammered the Narrow Party into a club of sectarian intellectuals, but the composition of his own group seemed to have borne out his rival's warnings that solicitation of petit-bourgeois support would result in the domination of the Party by this class.

[123] Compiled from the sources listed on p. 41, footnote 121 as well as from "Rapport . . . au Bureau Socialiste International," pp. 7-8, and from "Rundschau: Sozialistische Bewegung: Bulgarien," pp. 848-49.

[124] "Rapport . . . au Bureau Socialiste International," p. 7. As regards the educational qualifications of the members, 102 had a university education, 645 had completed secondary school, 638 had only completed primary school, and 10 were illiterate.

The age structure reveals a young party: 1,114 were between the ages of 21 and 25; 1,150 between 26 and 40; only 163 were over 40 years of age.

The voting strength of the Parties also rose, though the electoral law of 1903 prevented Socialist representation in the Sobranie between that year and 1912. The figures are: [125]

Year	Votes Cast for Socialist Candidates
1900	13,815
1901	13,283
1902	20,307
1904	10,652
1908	12,466
1911	25,666

In 1908 the Socialist vote was divided among the three parties, as follows: Broad, 10,260; Narrow, 1,809; Liberal Socialist, 397. In 1911 the Narrows polled 12,923 votes, the Broads 12,743.

The decline of votes between 1902 and 1904 was due partly to the split, partly to the electoral law of 1903, partly to coercion by the Petrov-Petkov government, but chiefly to the rise of the Peasant Union which attracted many votes in the villages that had previously been cast for Socialist candidates.

The year 1911 marked the beginning of a sharp rise in Socialist electoral fortunes. The main political issue was the coming constitutional convention called to amend Article 17 of the Constitution so as to permit the government to conclude secret treaties with Serbia and Greece in preparation for the First Balkan War. Both Socialist Parties were alarmed but, characteristically, reacted in opposite ways. The Broad Party came to an electoral agreement with the Peasant Union to fight the proposed amendment, and five of its candidates were elected to the convention on 18,351 votes. The Narrows spurned alliances and, though their candidates received 12,300 votes, only one was elected and he from a completely peasant constituency near Troyan.[126]

---

[125] Compiled from Denkoff, "La Lutte de la social democratie bulgare contre l'opportunisme," p. 435; Yotsov, "Upravlenieto na 'Demokraticheski Sgovor'," p. 19; "Rapport ... au Bureau Socialiste International," p. 10; *The American Labor Year Book, 1916*, p. 169. The total vote was just below 500,000.

[126] Rakovski, "Aus Bulgarien," p. 685. The Narrow Party indulged in much soul-searching before accepting this seat presented by the "reactionary" peasants. About 50 percent of the Broad and 30-40 percent of the Narrow vote was polled in the villages. The total Broad vote was one and one half times as large as the Narrow one; in Sofia it outran the latter by a 3 to 1 margin, but in Sliven and some other towns the Narrow poll was the larger. The constitutional convention, or Grand National Sobranie, was twice as large as the ordinary Sobranie of 225 members.

The electoral policy of the leaders of both parties aroused some dissatisfaction among the rank and file. Certain elements in the Narrow Party criticized Blagoev's refusal to conclude agreements with other parties and claimed that this refusal was throwing away the Party's votes and allowing the liberal constitution to be whittled away. At the Plovdiv Party Congress in July, 1911, Blagoev's favorite disciple, Kolarov, had to exert himself to still these murmurs. The congress was persuaded to accept the criticized policy but only on the understanding that it would be abandoned if any more basic constitutional guarantees were threatened.[127] A week later, the Broad Party assembled in Sofia for its congress. Here the leaders were able to obtain endorsement of their policy of electoral alliances but only after promising that just the Narrow, Peasant, and Radical Parties would be considered eligible partners and that among these the Narrows would be given preference. Even then, the policy was approved only by a close vote of 53 to 38.[128]

In one of the first of a series of Socialist successes, 7 Broad and 2 Narrow delegates were elected in 1911 to the 30-member Sofia Municipal Council.[129] In June, 1912, Sakazov ended the decade of Socialist absence from the Sobranie by winning a by-election in Sofia.[130] He was thus the only Socialist in the chamber when the First Balkan War erupted in October, and he courageously spoke out against it in the chamber with the result that he was howled off the tribune and, upon leaving the parliament building, was assaulted by a mob of students.[131]

With the defeat of Bulgaria in the Second Balkan War in the summer of 1913, however, the antiwar stand of both Socialist Parties was rewarded. In the elections of December, 1913, 21 Broad and 16 Narrow deputies were sent to the Sobranie, and respectively 54,369 and 52,777 votes cast for the two parties, accounting for one fifth of the total number of ballots.[132] This quadrupling of the

---

Though 600,000 voters (about 55 percent of all those entitled to vote) went to the polls and cast only 245,000 ballots for the government party, through gerrymandering this latter party won 375 of the 450 seats. The Peasant Union polled 160,000 votes.

[127] Rakovski, "Aus Bulgarien," p. 688.
[128] *Ibid.,* p. 688.
[129] Stavrianos, *Balkan Federation,* p. 183.
[130] *Yanko Sakazov yubileyen sbornik,* p. 46.
[131] *Ibid.,* p. 14.
[132] Walling, *The Socialists and the War,* p. 110; Kabakchiev, "Balgaria v Pervata

1911 vote for the Socialist Parties was, however, a measure of the electorate's resentment against the lost war, not an endorsement of socialism. Prime Minister Radoslavov, unable to govern with the hostile Sobranie, quickly dissolved it. In the last pre-First World War elections of February 23/March 8, 1914, the Socialist vote, in consequence of police pressure and the partial evaporation of the hot antiwar resentment, fell by one fifth to 85,939, that for Broad candidates declining to 47,107 and that for the Narrow Party even more precipitously to 38,832. The combined Socialist representation in the Sobranie was reduced to twenty seats of which the Narrows occupied eleven.[133] Thus, to Blagoev's chagrin it was demonstrated that the Socialist Parties had won increased electoral support for policies which had nothing to do with socialism and from people who were not proletarians.

Before the Balkan and First World Wars, both parties were mainly propaganda institutions,[134] and it was only in the course of these conflicts that the Narrow in particular developed into a mass party with substantial political power. Until then the strength of socialism lay in its influence over the intelligentsia. Nevertheless, though the small proletariat did not form the center of gravity of the Socialist movement, the two parties were able to ensure that no working-class organization developed outside their control. The painful birth of the Bulgarian trade-union movement warrants a discussion at this point, not only for the information it offers in regard to the problems created by the partial and stunted industrialization of a backward agrarian state, but also for the light it throws on the early career of the best known of Bulgarian Communists, Georgi Dimitrov.

Imperialisticheska Voina," p. 43. The Peasant Union won 49 seats in a Sobranie which Prime Minister Radoslavov denounced as "poisoned with socialism." See Yanko Sakazov, "Bulgarien nach den Balkankriegen," p. 1671.

[133] Walling, *The Socialists and the War,* p. 110. See also *The American Labor Year Book, 1916,* p. 169. The decline was heaviest in the cities.

[134] This is admitted in Communist apologia for the Narrow Party. See, for example, Kolarov, "Die Taktik der K. P. Bulgariens im Lichte der Ereignisse," p. 255 and Kabakchiev, Boshkovich, and Vatis, *Kommunisticheskie Partii Balkanskikh Stran,* p. 54.

II

THE EARLY LABOR
MOVEMENT

In 1877, when the Russian armies liberated Bulgaria from five centuries of Turkish rule, the entire industry of the country consisted of 19 small factory-shops, mostly producing textiles. Railways covered 523 kilometres of track.[1] In 1894, less than two decades after the Liberation, Bulgaria could boast of 501 factories and mills, employing 5,732 workers, an average of 11 per unit.[2] By the last year of the century railroads had been extended to 1,570 kilometres.[3] Though unimpressive by Western standards, this development was considerable by Balkan ones.

Bulgarian Socialists observed these developments, noted the crises of agriculture and artisan industry,[4] and joyously prophesied that Bulgaria stood on the threshold of an era of intensive industrialization which would shape the country in the Western European mold.[5] This, however, was not to be. On the eve of the Second World War, 79.8 percent of the people of Bulgaria were still engaged in agriculture and of the remainder only 8.2 percent earned their living by work in industry.[6] Had these Socialists examined the

---

[1] Rainoff, *Die Arbeiterbewegung in Bulgarien*, pp. 20-21.

[2] Staneff, *Das Gewerbewesen und die Gewerbepolitik in Bulgarien*, p. 94.

[3] Sakarov, *Die Industrielle Entwicklung Bulgariens*, p. 27.

[4] See pp. 4-8.

[5] For example Blagoev's *Shto e sotsializam i ima li toi pochva u nas?* published in Tirnovo in 1891 under the pseudonym D. Bratanov. Also Sakarov, *Die Industrielle Entwicklung Bulgariens,* and Rainoff, *Die Arbeiterbewegung in Bulgarien.*

[6] *Bolshaya Sovetskaya Entsiklopedia,* 1949, s.v. "Bolgaria." Far from becoming an urban industrial country as the early socialists predicted, the proportion of Bulgaria's population engaged in agriculture had probably increased between the first and fourth decades of the twentieth century. According to the census of 1911 as analyzed by Ivan Sakazov *(Bulgarische Wirtschaftsgeschichte,* pp. 286 ff.), the percentage of Bulgaria's population employed in agriculture had then been 74.7, that is, less than on the eve of the Second World War.

nascent industrial development of the 1880s and 1890s more carefully, their confidence might have been shaken by the observation that with the exception of some coal mining at Pernik and two cement factories, all of this industrial development encompassed only light consumer industries. Fully half of the 5,732 proletarians of 1894 were employed in textile, ceramics, and tobacco-processing factories and the great majority of the remainder were scattered among the chalk, vodka, nut-oil, soap, perfume, and other fragrant industries. With no rich deposits of coal or iron, Bulgaria could not become an industrial power.

The origins of Bulgarian industry lie in the disintegration of her artisan guilds.[7] At first the decline of the guilds was more rapid than the growth of industry, creating pools of unemployed in the towns, but with the beginning in 1898 of governmental attempts to shore up the artisan system[8] many craftsmen who would otherwise have disappeared were enabled to survive, and the expansion of the proletariat and salaried middle class outstripped the contraction of the artisans, as the following figures show:[9]

[7] The severity of this process is indicated by the following figures (taken from Sakarov, *Die Industrielle Entwicklung Bulgariens*, p. 29) showing the reduction of guild strength within a relatively short period: The shoemakers' guild of Sofia had 50-60 artisan shops in 1876, 4-5 in 1896; the spindle makers' guild of Pirdop 700-800 in 1876, 20-30 in 1896; the cutlers' guild of Kazanlak 25 in 1876, 3 in 1896; the metal smiths' guild of Karlovo 40 in 1876, none in 1896; the rope and saddle makers' guild of Panagyurishte 100 in 1876, 5-6 in 1896; the textile printers' guild of Sopot 100 in 1876, 1 in 1896. For further details see Spassow, *Der Verfall des alten Handwerks*, pp. 18-47.

[8] In 1898 there was enacted a law to preserve the guild system, but as no provision was made for cheap credit to artisans, its purpose remained a pious hope. No party endorsed it enthusiastically while the two Socialists in the Sobranie denounced it as reactionary. In 1899 the law was suspended but reintroduced two years later and amended in 1904. This version was designed not so much to reinvigorate the defunct guilds as to load the main burden of their deterioration on the shoulders of the journeymen and apprentices. The poorer masters also did not benefit since the law, by not regulating home industry, enabled the wealthier masters with liquid capital to farm out their spinning or weaving work and thereby legally to undersell the guild price. The main effect of the law was to impose sanctions under which apprentices could be compelled to remain in the factories. In 1907 a petition to the government signed by 6,000 workers demanded the repeal of the law. It was ignored. See Staneff, *Das Gewerbewesen und die Gewerbepolitik in Bulgarien*, pp. 42-51 and Rainoff, *Die Arbeiterbewegung in Bulgarien*, pp. 50-54. Another abortive attempt to preserve the artisan industry was the founding in the 1880s and 1890s of state schools where the traditional trades were to be taught to aspiring carpenters, dyers, weavers, smiths, and potters. See Sakarov, *Die Industrielle Entwicklung Bulgariens*, p. 46 and Spassow, *Der Verfall des alten Handwerks*, pp. 48-49.

[9] Pandov, *Grazhdanskata Voina*, p. 66 and *Bolshaya Sovetskaya Entsiklopedia*, 1927, s.v. "Bulgaria."

Year	Independent Artisans	Wage and Salary Earners
1887	105,400	—
1900	91,900	50,619
1905	76,000	71,507
1910	70,400	93,964

The exploitation of labor in the young industries was as naked as it is everywhere during the period of the primitive accumulation of capital. Failure on the laborer's part to complete a work period was punished as theft. Stambolov's police smashed strikes.[10] Until 1905-6 there was no legislation regulating work conditions and hours, limiting child and woman labor, or setting minimal safety and hygienic standards in the factories. These conditions created labor unrest and provoked the formation of several trade unions in the 1880s which were as weak as they were short-lived.

The first attempt at labor organization took place in 1882 or 1883 among those workers whose knowledge of Western developments was greatest—the printers and typographers.[11] Their union affiliated with the International Printers' Association but soon withered as contact between the main Sofia and the smaller provincial branches was lost.[12]

In 1892 some workers of Sliven attempted to form a combination of a trade union and a consumers' cooperative which soon collapsed owing to the apathy of the workers, the opposition of the employers, and the weaknesses inherent in all such "one big brotherhood" systems of workers' organization undifferentiated by profession or industry. A more modest and practical attempt later in the year to found a textile workers' union succeeded[13] and in 1893 the unification of the Social Democratic Party and Union provided the stimulus for a spurt of labor organizing. That year witnessed the

[10] A graphic description of these police actions is given in *Progres*, I, No. 34 (July 3, 1893).
[11] Black, *The Establishment of Constitutional Government in Bulgaria*, p. 220 reports that most of these printers and typographers had, in fact, returned to Bulgaria only after the Liberation in 1877 from Bräila, Bucharest, and Vienna where they had produced the Bulgarian "exile press." They were thus by the nature of their work as well as in consequence of their residence abroad ideologically more advanced than the textile or tobacco workers who had spent their lives in Ottoman Bulgaria. Dellin, *Bulgaria*, p. 229 states that Czech printers working in Bulgaria initiated the founding of the printers' union.
[12] Rainoff, *Die Arbeiterbewegung in Bulgarien*, p. 87.
[13] *Ibid.*, p. 88.

first May Day demonstrations in Bulgaria as well as a few strikes—pitiful efforts, such as those of seven printers in Vidin who protested against the irregular payment of their wages, and of nine coppersmiths in Sofia who demanded higher pay.[14]

In the freer political atmosphere which followed the fall of the Stambolov regime in 1894, the printers' association was revived, other unions were founded, and a series of strikes broke out during the following two years among the textile workers of Sliven and Gabrovo, the tobacco processors of Plovdiv, the Oryakhovo woodworkers, and the printers in Sofia. The depression of 1897-1901, however, enfeebled the young labor movement and frightened into docility those workers who retained their jobs. The only strike in this period was that of forty tailors of Gabrovo in 1897. In the same year, when 200 workers were burned to death in a factory in Russe, the trade unions did not even dare to stage protest and sympathy demonstrations. The only new labor organizations founded during the depression were the shoemakers' union and the consumers' cooperative Rabotnik (Worker),[15] the latter a defensive reaction to the depression and unemployment.[16]

One of the most unfortunate consequences of the Socialist Party schism of 1903 was the splitting of this still undeveloped trade-union movement a year later on Blagoev's initiative. In general his group managed to win control of the provincial union locals while those of the capital supported Sakazov, just as the Sofia Party organization had done in 1903.[17] Rival locals were soon established throughout the country. The struggle between the two groups was fought on a level of viciousness which reinforced and in turn was reinforced by the low cultural and ideological standards of the workers over whose allegiance it was waged. The "raiding" or enticing of workers from one to the other group, the sacking of each other's union premises, and general brawls were frequent.[18] The struggle against the bourgeoisie became almost secondary.

[14] Ibid., p. 88.
[15] Ibid., pp. 89-91.
[16] For a fuller discussion of labor legislation and labor organization in Bulgaria before the First World War, see Appendix (pp. 305ff.).
[17] Assen Tsankov, "Der Sozialismus in Bulgarien," p. 629.
[18] Rainoff, Die Arbeiterbewegung in Bulgarien, p. 92.

In July, 1904, the trade unions controlled by the Narrow Party, with somewhat less than 1,500 members, assembled in congress at Plovdiv where they organized the Obsht Rabotnicheski Sindikalen Sayuz v Balgaria (General Workers Trade Union Federation in Bulgaria), explicitly subordinate organizationally as well as ideologically to the Central Committee of Blagoev's Narrow Socialist Party.[19] A month later the unions under the influence of the Broad Socialists held their constituent congress in Sofia, their stronghold, and founded the Free Trade Union Federation, then representing about 1,200 workers. Its declared aims were to educate the workers and to obtain for them better conditions of work and life. The affiliated unions were to be open to all workers irrespective of religion or political opinion, and the Federation was to be organizationally independent of all political parties, though its support would be given to that party which showed itself to be the most consistent protagonist of the workers' cause. This protagonist was envisaged by the Federation leaders as the Broad Socialist Party.[20] Blagoev, as was to be expected, denounced this statement as heretical because it did not declare the aims of the trade unions to be identical with those of the political socialist movement and because it regarded with indifference the political and ideological opinions of their individual members. In Blagoev's trade unions, every worker was methodically and persistently bombarded with Narrow Socialist propaganda[21] and the General Trade Union Federation was strictly controlled by the Narrow Party. Decisions on trade-union policy were taken by the Labor Council, composed of the already overlapping Central Committees of the Narrow Party and the General Federation. On the local level the same control by the party unit was exercised.[22] Georgi Dimitrov early emerged as the Narrow Party's most successful trade-union organizer and functionary.

Dimitrov was born on June 18/30, 1882, in the village of Kovachevtsi, near Radomir. His mother, who lived to see her son achieve

[19] Blagoev, *Die Sozialistische Arbeiterbewegung in Bulgarien,* pp. 565-66. The first secretary was Nikola Kharlakov. He was succeeded by Georgi Kirkov who resigned in 1909 and was replaced by Georgi Dimitrov.

[20] "Rundschau: Gewerkschaftsbewegung: Bulgarien," p. 853. The leaders of the Free Federation were supporters of Sakazov and usually belonged to the Broad Party.

[21] *Ibid.,* p. 853.

[22] Blagoev, "Die Sozialistische Arbeiterbewegung in Bulgarien," p. 568.

world renown at the Reichstag fire trial in 1933, was one of that small band of Bulgarian Protestants which had emerged after the middle of the nineteenth century as the result of American missionary activity. His father, like Stalin's, was a ruined artisan driven by industrialization into becoming a factory worker.[23] Though Georgi Dimitrov himself was one of the very few prominent Bulgarian Narrow Socialist (and later Communist) leaders who had not spent his revolutionary apprenticeship in the Russian socialist movement, this connection was provided by his brother Nikola who was arrested in an underground printing plant in Odessa in 1908 and banished to Siberia where he died in 1916 or 1917.[24] Georgi Dimitrov's mother, like Stalin's, wanted her son to become a cleric and in 1892 enrolled him in an American missionary school. Expelled, like the Georgian who subsequently became his chief in the Communist world, after two years, Dimitrov, again like Stalin, who became a clerk in the Tiflis astronomical observatory, joined the ranks of the quasi-intelligentsia as a typographer in Sofia. Here he achieved some notoriety in connection with the May Day demonstrations of 1898. At this time Dimitrov was a typesetter in the office of the Liberal Party's paper *Narodni Prava* (People's Rights). On the day following the workers' demonstrations, Radoslavov, leader of the Party, wrote an article abusing the paraders as "street loafers, drunkards, robbers." Dimitrov refused to set the type until Radoslavov deleted these words.[25]

Following in the footsteps of his older brother Konstantin, who

[23] Official accounts of Dimitrov's life are numerous. In addition to those in the two editions of the *Bolshaya Sovetskaya Entsiklopedia* and the obituary article in *Bol'shevik,* XXVI, No. 13 (July 15, 1949), 8-15, there is the biography by Dimitar Blagoev's daughter, Stella Blagoeva, *Dimitrov: A Biography,* most of which consists of excerpts from the subject's testimony at the Reichtag fire trial. In 1952 the Bulgarian Academy of Sciences published a monumental 800-page adulatory chronicle of Dimitrov's life compiled by Elena Savova, who had five years earlier completed a similar though shorter portrait of Vasil Kolarov. Her compilation is entitled *Georgi Dimitrov: Letopis na zhivota i revolyutsionnata mu deinost.* For a briefer work see *Georgi Dimitrov: A Short Biographical Sketch* (Sofia, 1948).

[24] Blagoeva, *Dimitrov: A Biography,* p. 10; *Georgi Dimitrov,* p. 8.

[25] Dimitrov, "A First of May and its Consequences," *Inprecorr,* XIV, No. 29 (May 11, 1934), 774. The incident had an amusing sequel seventeen years later. When in 1915 Dimitrov, then a Narrow Socialist deputy in the Sobranie, protested against the press censorship of Radoslavov, who was then prime minister, the latter railed across the floor, "You want to speak about censorship; of all people—*you,* Dimitrov. Can you remember, when you worked for me as a typesetter, you even tried to censor my article?" Dimitrov, apparently, had been the only typographer in the office able to decipher Radoslavov's handwriting.

had been secretary of the printers' organization,[26] Georgi Dimitrov threw himself into trade-union activities from the moment of his entry into the printing trade. In 1897 his first article, demanding better working conditions, appeared in the union's newspaper *Pechatarski Rabotnik* (Printing Worker), and three years later, at the age of eighteen, he was elected secretary of the union's Sofia organization. Dimitrov joined the Socialist Party in 1902 on the eve of its schism, sided with the Narrow faction, and in the spring of the following year was elected secretary of that fifty-member Sofia splinter group whose recognition by the Blagoev-dominated Central Committee as the official Party organization of the capital was the issue occasioning the Party split.[27] In 1904 he played a leading part in extending the Party schism to the trade unions, and by 1909 his reputation as an energetic organizer and a ruthless "splitter" was such that when Georgi Kirkov resigned as secretary-treasurer of the Narrow-affiliated General Trade Union Federation, Dimitrov was chosen as his successor, a post he was to occupy uninterruptedly until the cessation of legal Communist activity after the September debacle of 1923. In 1909 Dimitrov was also elected to the Central Committee of the Narrow Party, four years after Vasil Kolarov, who was to be his life-long colleague and to whom he was always subordinate in the international Communist movement though he stood in the limelight of the Comintern after the Reichstag fire trial. In 1913 Dimitrov was one of the sixteen Narrow Party candidates elected to the Sobranie in the Socialist avalanche of that winter and was the first worker to be elected to any Balkan parliament. He retained his seat for Sofia in the elections of February 23/March 8, 1914, despite a fall in Socialist representation and served as a deputy uninterruptedly until the September insurrection of 1923, when he fled the country, not to return until November, 1945. He was also for many years a member of the Sofia municipal council.

[26] Konstantin was killed at the front during the Second Balkan War. Nikola died in Siberia and a third brother, Todor, who had taken part in the Communist uprising of September, 1923, was arrested by the Bulgarian police on the eve of the Sofia cathedral outrage of April, 1925, and killed in the subsequent White Terror. In that same year Dimitrov's sister Lena escaped to the USSR. A nephew fell fighting with the partisans in 1943.

[27] "Vydayushchisya deyatel' mezhdunarodnogo rabochego dvizhenia," p. 9. He headed the Narrow organization in Sofia for ten years. For the split in the capital see p. 31.

Dimitrov's role in the international activities of the Bulgarian Narrow Socialist Party was always subordinate to those of Kolarov and Kabakchiev. He attended the First Balkan Socialist Conference in Belgrade in 1910 as well as the Budapest Congress of the International Federation of Trade Unions in 1911 without making any notable contributions. Expelled in 1912 from Rumania whither he had gone as a fraternal delegate to the congress of that country's Socialist Party,[28] he returned to Bucharest in July, 1915, to attend the Second Balkan Socialist Conference and was once again expelled, this time permanently.[29]

It was not to international Socialist politics but to the internal battle against the Broad-controlled Free Federation that Dimitrov devoted his main energies. He was a tireless organizer, constantly traveling from town to town, everywhere splitting the Broad-controlled Free union locals, marshalling the Narrow supporters, maneuvering to take over the control of strikes declared by the Free unions. "How can our organizations grow," complained Sakazov, "if whenever a strike is declared anywhere Dimitrov inevitably turns up there?"[30] Communist propaganda claims that in 1910 Broad trade-union leaders sought to assassinate Dimitrov when he attempted to persuade the striking ore miners of Plakalnitsa to desert the Free for the General Federation.[31] In 1911 he served a month's prison sentence for libeling a rival trade-union official with the charge of strikebreaking.[32]

In 1908, on the eve of his accession to the secretaryship, Dimitrov centralized the hitherto loosely organized General Federation, power henceforth being concentrated in the secretariat which, together with the Central Committee of the Narrow Socialist Party, composed the Labor Council. The only information on the strike activity of this tightened General Federation between that year and the outbreak

[28] Blagoeva, *Dimitrov: A Biography*, p. 27.
[29] For the resolutions of this Balkan Socialist Conference calling for an end to the First World War and the formation of a Balkan Federation, see p. 65. Dimitrov's permanent exclusion from Rumania was recalled in 1920 when the sailboat on which he was traveling from Varna to Odessa to attend the Second Comintern Congress was blown onto the Rumanian shore and he was imprisoned, to be released only on the energetic representations of Chicherin. See *Le Bulletin Communiste*, I, No. 25 (August 19, 1920), 14-15.
[30] Quoted by Blagoeva, *Dimitrov: A Biography*, p. 23.
[31] *Basler Rundschau*, IV, No. 73 (December 12, 1935), 2828.
[32] *Bolshaya Sovetskaya Entsiklopedia*, 1935, s.v. "Dimitrov."

of the war in 1912 comes from Communist sources, which put the number of strikes organized by Dimitrov's now centralized secretariat as high as 680 for the four years.[33] As this estimate was made in Dimitrov's triumphal year, 1935, when, with the Reichstag fire trial behind him, he was hailed at the Seventh Comintern Congress as the pride of the Communist International, the symbol of the United Front, whose every action since conception had been the political master stroke of one of Stalin's best pupils, the figure is probably exaggerated, or at best a half-truth. Far more plausible is Dimitrov's own statement made in 1921 that between the split of 1904 in the trade-union movement and the end of the Balkan Wars in 1913, his General Federation led 630 strikes of 32,519 men.[34] This gives an average of 52 strikers for each of these actions—yet another indication of the primitive state of Bulgarian industry and the weakness of the trade unions. Nor did the ratio of successful to unsuccessful strikes greatly improve in the years following Dimitrov's centralization of the General Federation. In 1910, for example, he called out a total of 8,543 strikers in 163 strikes of which 97 were "offensive" and 67 "defensive." Of these strikes, in which 52 (again a small figure) was the average number of participants, 65 failed utterly, 39 were partially successful, and only 60 resulted in the acceptance of all the workers' demands.[35] In 1914, up to the outbreak of the First World War, the two Federations (the Proletarian Federation of the Liberal Socialists having merged with the Free Federation in June, 1908) called out 1,900 workers in 30 strikes of which 16 failed, 12 met with partial success, and only 2 achieved their goals.[36]

In the meantime, the membership of both Federations had continued to expand: [37]

[33] Blagoeva, *Dimitrov: A Biography*, p. 23.

[34] Dimitrov, "Die Gewerkschaftliche Bewegung in Bulgarien," p. 328.

[35] Rakovski, "Der Sozialistische 'Allgemeine Gewerkschaftsbund' in Bulgarien," p. 278.

[36] *The American Labor Year Book, 1916*, p. 170.

[37] Compiled from Rakovski, "Der Sozialistische 'Allgemeine Gewerkschaftsbund' in Bulgarien," p. 277; Rakovski, "Aus Bulgarien," p. 688; Trotsky, "In den Balkanländern," p. 73; *Rapport du Parti Ouvrier Social Democrate Bulgare (Unifié) au Bureau Socialiste International*, p. 12; Dimitrov, "Die Gewerkschaftsbewegung Bulgariens," *Inprekorr*, III, No. 24 (February 5, 1923), 183; *The American Labor Year Book*, 1916, p. 170.

Year	Membership of Free Federation (Broad)	Membership of General Federation (Narrow)
1908	—	2,080
1909	3,020	3,420
1910	—	4,600
1911	4,020	5,400
1912	4,850	—
1913	—	—
1914	3,170	6,560
1915	4,900	7,590

It is hazardous to draw conclusions from a comparison of these figures as the bases of enumeration vary. Were only those who had fully paid their dues counted, a sharp decline in membership would have to be recorded for the mobilization years 1912 and 1915.[38] An additional difficulty arises from the General Federation's inclusion of state employees in the transport and teaching professions, whereas the Free Federation, under whose influence most of these employees actually stood through their nominally neutral unions, did not include them in its lists.

The ideology of the Bulgarian teaching profession, as of the intelligentsia as a whole, was socialism. Before the founding of the Socialist Party the creed had been nurtured in the teacher-student *krazhotsi*. Blagoev had founded a teachers' association and journal in 1889 while director of the Vidin gymnasium.[39] In 1894 this poorest of the professions organized its union. The split of the Socialist Parties was in time reflected in its ranks. Small fractions affiliated in 1905 with the Proletarian (Liberal Socialist) and General (Narrow) Federations, while the largest bloc formed the officially neutral but actually Broad-influenced Union of Teachers, which published its own paper *Saznanie* (Consciousness). In 1906-7 the Liberal Petkov government persecuted and temporarily dissolved this union because it supported a great railway strike.[40] By 1911 the Union of Social Democratic Teachers adhering to the Narrow-

[38] Thus *The American Labor Year Book, 1916,* estimates that the membership of the General Federation declined from 8,500 to 5,350 in the course of the Balkan Wars and that of the Free Federation from 4,850 to 4,000.

[39] See p. 17, footnote 30.

[40] Rainoff, *Die Arbeiterbewegung in Bulgarien,* p. 95.

controlled General Federation numbered 954 members while 4,826 members of the profession belonged to the Union of Bulgarian Teachers, which stood under the Broad Party's influence.[41]

The Narrow Party had forfeited the support of the railway men by virtue of the ambiguous attitude it had taken toward their strike in 1906-7 (see Appendix, pp. 309-11). In 1911 it could muster only 1,000 railway, postal, and telegraph workers in its General Federation whereas 14,000 of these were members of the General Transport Workers' Union, which, though organizationally independent of the Free Federation, cooperated closely with the Broad Party.[42] In 1909 all these unions of state employees banded together in a loose Union of Unions which always stood under the Broad Party's influence.[43]

In view of this affiliation of the railway men, one cannot accept Dimitrov's reiterated assertion that the "real" proletarians adhered to his General Federation while only the semi- and the *lumpen*-proletarians of the pigmy sweatshops and the merchant firms joined the unions of the Free Federation.[44] Furthermore, Dimitrov's own average of 52 men involved in each of the 630 strikes led by his Federation indicates that it did not dominate the large, modern (mostly textile) plants where the "true" proletarians worked. Nor do the facts support the later Communist claims that the workers of the General Federation had all been trained to be thorough Marxists.[45] In 1911 there were 13,000 marchers in the May Day parade but only 1,560 workers subscribed to the orthodox Marxist *Rabotnicheski Vestnik*,[46] and this after a decade of Narrow exhortations to the workers to consider this "their own" paper and at a time when General Federation membership was 5,400. The strength of the

---

[41] Rakovski, "Aus Bulgarien," p. 688. The extent to which the nominally non-political Union of Bulgarian Teachers permitted itself to take up political positions is illustrated by the fact that its congress in July, 1911, at Sofia sent expressions of support to all the parties which at the Constituent Assembly held in Tirnovo that year had opposed the constitutional amendment permitting King Ferdinand to conclude secret treaties.

[42] *Ibid.*, p. 689.

[43] "Rapport . . . au Bureau Socialiste International," p. 12.

[44] Dimitrov, *Der Kampf um Arbeiterschutz in Bulgarien*, p. 3; Dimitrov, "Die Gewerkschaftsbewegung Bulgariens," *Inprekorr*, III, No. 24 (February 5, 1923), 183.

[45] See, for example, Kabakchiev, Boshkovich, and Vatis, *Kommunisticheskie Partii Balkanskikh Stran*, p. 52.

[46] Rakovski, "Der Sozialistische 'Allgemeine Gewerkschaftsbund' in Bulgarien," p. 278.

Socialist movement in economically backward Bulgaria on the eve of the First World War still lay not in a strong army of proletarians but in the small, though growing, Socialist Parties dominated by a circle of intellectuals who were committed to the Marxist ideology.

III

THE INTERNATIONAL
MOVEMENT
AND THE WARS

Within the Socialist International the Bulgarian Socialist Parties were given an importance quite disproportionate to their small membership by virtue of the increasing preoccupation of the International after 1905 with the danger of war in the Balkan Peninsula. This was one of the factors prompting the frequent efforts of the International to reconcile the two wings of Bulgarian socialism. The Narrow Party stood usually on the left of the International, at times with a doctrinairism irritating even to Lenin. At the Stuttgart Congress of the International in August, 1907, its delegates had, like Lenin, supported Rosa Luxemburg's amendment sharpening the resolution on the proper policy of Socialist Parties in the event of war with instructions to utilize the ensuing crisis to overthrow the capitalist system.[1] A year later, when the International Socialist Bureau in Brussels discussed the application for admission of the British Labour Party, the Narrow delegate, a certain Avramov, then a student in Brussels, alone voted with Hyndman against the admission of these "opportunists." [2] Kautsky and Lenin were both exasperated by such bigotry and Blagoev, sensitive to the criticism of the German Socialist, subsequently rebuked Avramov.[3] At the International's Copenhagen Congress in 1910, the contribution of

---

[1] For the full text of the resolution, see Grünberg, *Die Internationale und der Weltkrieg*, pp. 10-12. For the position of the Narrow delegation, see Kabakchiev, "Lenin i bolgarskie Tesnyaki," p. 176.

[2] V. I. Lenin, *Sochinenia*, 3d ed., Vol. XII (Moscow, 1931), p. 348.

[3] *Novo Vreme*, No. 11 (1908). Avramov, like so many others of the intelligentsia, shortly thereafter left the Socialist fold.

the Narrow delegation, consisting Blagoev, Kirkov, Kolarov, and Kabakchiev, was to demand the ouster of the rival Broad Party.[4] The Congress was little inclined to accept this suggestion, for, whatever might be the deviations of the Broad Party in internal Bulgarian politics from standard Socialist policy, as regards the International its conduct was orthodox, supporting Kautsky against Bernstein.[5] In any event, the International was far more concerned to effect a closing of Socialist ranks than to administer punishments, for war clouds now loomed ever more ominously on the Balkan horizon.

At the October, 1908, session of the International Socialist Bureau Avramov had been able to announce that the proclamation earlier in the month of complete Bulgarian independence from Turkish suzerainty (a proclamation which preceded by two days the official announcement of Austria-Hungary's annexation of Bosnia-Herzegovina) had been condemned by the Bulgarian Socialists as endangering even more the already precarious peace of the Balkans. The Bureau decried King Ferdinand's proclamation and Aehrenthal's annexation for the same reason.[6] When the storm finally broke over the Peninsula in October, 1912, the various Balkan Socialist Parties, as well as the International, all denounced the war.

On September 17/30, 1912, the day of Bulgarian mobilization, the Narrow Party's *Rabotnicheski Vestnik* printed an editorial so anti-war in tone that the paper was suspended for five months.[7] A few days later when Sakazov, at that time the only Socialist deputy in the Sobranie, denounced the war, he was howled off the tribune and assaulted by a mob of chauvinistic students on leaving the parliamentary buildings.[8]

The International met in Extra-Ordinary Congress at Basel on November 24-25 with no agenda other than the war danger. Kabak-

---

[4] Kabakchiev, Boshkovich, and Vatis, *Kommunisticheskie Partii Balkanskikh Stran,* p. 71.

[5] Tchitchovsky, *The Socialist Movement in Bulgaria,* p. 18. An exception was its support of Jaurès against Guesde. This was given because Jaurès had been Sakazov's foreign champion during the critical pre-split years 1900-1903. See p. 35.

[6] Lenin, *Sochinenia,* 3d ed., XII, 351-52.

[7] Trotsky and Kabakchiev, *Ocherki politicheskoi Bolgarii,* p. 137. In August the Narrow Party had at its Russe Congress condemned the war preparations. Toward the end of September it issued more antiwar manifestoes and scheduled protest rallies. See Stavrianos, *Balkan Federation,* p. 190.

[8] *Yanko Sakazov yubileyen sbornik,* p. 14.

chiev and Sakazov attended for the rival Bulgarian parties. When the former attempted the usual Narrow tirade against the Broad Party, he was quickly silenced by the presiding officer, Viktor Adler;[9] the Congress was too conscious of the world crisis to tolerate the squabbles of the Bulgarian delegations. Kabakchiev's suggestion that the Congress adopt as its resolution the editorial from the *Rabotnicheski Vestnik* of September 17/30 was also rejected by Adler.[10] The manifesto then issued unanimously by the Congress began by quoting the resolutions of the Stuttgart Congress that the several Socialist Parties should work for the speedy termination of the war and utilize the crisis to hasten the abolition of class rule. It praised the Socialist Parties of the belligerent states for their united opposition to the Balkan War and called on the working classes of the Great Powers to impress upon their governments the duty of limiting and ending the Balkan War. The manifesto closed with a bold and, as the First World War was later to demonstrate, **exaggerated threat**:

> Let the governments . . . recall that the Franco-German War was followed by the . . . Commune, that the Russo-Japanese War set in motion the revolutionary forces of the peoples in the Russian Empire . . . . A world war would inevitably call forth . . . the revolt of the working class.[11]

The antiwar policy of the two Bulgarian Socialist Parties earned them the imposing electoral gains of December, 1913,[12] as well as considerable governmental persecution. In the spring of 1913, when

[9] Kabakchiev, "Lenin i bolgarskie Tesnyaki," p. 178. When Kabakchiev thereupon attempted to distribute several hundred printed copies of his planned speech, Huysmans, secretary of the International Socialist Bureau, threatened to expel him.

[10] Trotsky and Kabakchiev, *Ocherki politicheskoi Bolgarii*, p. 137.

[11] Grünberg, *Die Internationale und der Weltkrieg*, pp. 21-25. Karl Kautsky, in his analysis of the accomplishments of the Congress, "Der Baseler Kongress und die Kriegshetze in Oesterreich," did claim that it was the united voice of Social Democracy at Basel which frightened the Great Powers into preserving the peace. Particularly in Vienna, he insisted, where the decision whether or not to intervene was balanced on a thin edge, the manifesto was decisive. These claims are at best exaggerated. From the opening of hostilities, responsible statesmen in the major capitals had sought, without prompting by the Socialist International, to localize and end the war.

[12] See p. 44. When the two Balkan Wars were over and the Treaty of Bucharest had been signed in August, 1913, Bulgaria had gained 8,918 square miles of new territory, lost in the Southern Dobruja 2,960 square miles of old territory, acquired 400,000 new subjects and lost 170,000. "From the economic point of view the game was certainly not worth the candle, while from the nationalistic point of view the outcome of the great venture was a terrible catastrophe. The war had been [fought] for Macedonia . . . but there Bulgaria had failed." R. H. Markham, *Meet Bulgaria*, p. 73. Defeat and disillusion after an unnecessary war benefited the antiwar parties.

relations between Bulgaria and its erstwhile allies had become increasingly tense and Kabakchiev, as editor of one of the Narrow Party's subordinate journals in Sofia, again took up his pen to warn against a renewal of hostilities, he was summoned to the headquarters of the Sofia garrison and threatened with a lashing. The paper was suspended.[13] The electoral gains of December, 1913, however, reflected a revulsion against the war policy, particularly against King Ferdinand's deliberate provocation of the Second Balkan War in June, 1913, and not any mass conversion to socialist principles. This is indicated not only by the decline of the Socialist vote in the election of February 23/March 8, 1914, once the first spasm of anger had passed, but also by the failure of party membership to grow even proportionately with the vote. In the autumn of 1915 Narrow Party membership was still only 3,400, and early in 1916 that of the Broad Party stood at 5,800.[14]

The balance of power between the two armed camps at the outbreak of the First World War in August, 1914, was so fine that the position of even small states assumed great importance. Though King Ferdinand and his Liberal government had stood aside at the opening of the conflict, they never intended to remain permanently neutral but simply waited to see which side would emerge the stronger and offer them more. For Bulgaria the World War was an opportunity to resume the pursuit of her frustrated aims in Macedonia. With the entry of Turkey on the side of the Central Powers in November, 1914, the bridge between that state and her new allies became of crucial importance to both sides, and Bulgaria's price rose accordingly. Paralleling the efforts of the diplomats of the two alliance systems to woo the Bulgarian government, the Socialists who supported their countries' war efforts sought to convince the Bulgarian Socialists of the "objectively progressive" role being played by their own states in the great crusade against the "feudal" or "militaristic" foe, hoping to persuade the Bulgarian Socialists to influence the Bulgarian government's decision to enter the war on the side of their respective countries. The two leading

[13] Trotsky and Kabakchiev, *Ocherki politicheskoi Bolgarii,* p. 33.

[14] B., "Die Kommunistische Bewegung in Bulgarien," p. 136; *The American Labor Year Book, 1916,* p. 170. In 1912 the Narrow Party had 2,900 members and in 1911 the Broad 3,100.

Socialist pleaders in this campaign were Plekhanov for the Entente and Parvus-Helfand for the Central Powers.

On July 12/25, 1914, when it was evident that the Sarajevo assassination would have serious consequences, Blagoev arose in the Sobranie to insist that the country and the Peninsula needed peace and to assert that peace could be assured only through a federation of Balkan states. A few days later the Narrow Sobranie deputies issued antiwar manifestoes, and toward the end of October the Party organized public demonstrations against Bulgarian participation in the war.[15] In November the eleven Narrow deputies tendered a motion in the Sobranie, which only they supported, calling on the government to consult with other neutrals with a view to mediating the war and to initiate measures for common defense and federalization with the other Balkan states.[16]

To the August, 1914, issue of *Novo Vreme* Blagoev contributed an article, written before he learned of the vote for war credits by the German and French Socialists, confidently proclaiming that the only victor of a European war would be "the European revolution." The September number of the journal, prepared after the war-credit votes, is confused and hesitant.[17] Plekhanov, interpreting this reluctance as well as that of the Broad Socialists to denounce the major Western Socialist Parties as calculation in preparation for opting for one of the warring sides, invited the Bulgarian Socialists, in a letter from San Remo of October 14/27, to follow his example and join the fight against German imperialism.[18] On the previous day Blagoev had rebuked the French and Belgian comrades for entering the war cabinets of their countries[19] and in the *Novo Vreme*

---

[15] Kabakchiev, "Der Weg zur Kommunistischen Internationale," p. 620.

[16] For the text of this motion, see Walling, *The Socialists and the War*, p. 211.

[17] Among the explanations of the policy of Western Socialist Parties which Narrow leaders presented were that the governments had tricked the Socialist Parties with the "fatherland in danger" cry and that the Socialists had been moved to vote for war credits by the thought that a large proportion of these moneys would pay the allowances to the dependents of the mobilized. Thus Blagoev, unlike Lenin, was not yet willing to level the charge of "treason" against the Social Democratic leaders though, like Lenin, he ascribed primary responsibility for the failure to declare "The Revolution" to the German Party.

[18] This letter is reprinted in Plekhanov, *O Voine*, pp. 7-33.

[19] Kabakchiev and Karakolov, "Bolgaria v Pervoi Mirovoi Imperialisticheskoi Voine," p. 65. Blagoev was, however, far more gentle with the French than the Russian and German "social patriots." It was part of the Socialist tradition to consider republican France the mainspring of revolution in Europe (and Russia that of reaction) and therefore deserving of Socialist support in a struggle for survival

issue of December, in an article jeeringly entitled "Magister Dixit," he lashed out against Plekhanov. The conduct of the German, French, and Belgian Socialists, he thundered, while deplorable, was at least explainable but that a Socialist could bring himself to champion the war effort of Tsarist Russia and even to invite Balkan Socialists to support the ambitions of that power, which wanted only to enslave the peoples of the Peninsula, was apostacy, all the more disgraceful for coming from the teacher and guide of the Narrow Socialists. Germany, too, had imperialist ambitions in the Balkans and for this reason not the victory of either side but the socialist revolution alone could guarantee the liberty and progress of the peoples of the Peninsula. To these Russia represented the most ancient and dangerous threat.[20]

This vehement attack upon Tsarist Russia encouraged the German "social patriot" Parvus to hope that the Narrow Socialists might be induced to support the Central Powers. When he went to Sofia for this purpose in January, 1915, however, he too was rebuffed.[21]

By then the Narrow leaders were becoming uneasily aware that the war soon threatened to engulf Bulgaria. In February, 1915, they summoned Serbian and Rumanian Socialists to a conference in Sofia at which the Balkan governments were called upon collectively to defend the Peninsula against invasion.[22] These Socialists were, apparently, under the illusion, which Turkey's joining the Central Powers ought to have shattered, that the Balkan nations could still isolate themselves from the war. The conference repeated the previous Socialist admonitions to the Balkan governments to consult with other neutrals in order to mediate and end the conflict. A few days earlier Secretary-General Kirkov of the Narrow Party had

---

against "Prussian militarism." Socialist apologists for Germany, on the other hand, reverted to Engels's defense of that country as the home of Europe's most powerful Social Democratic movement. Her geographic role as "bastion" of European civilization against Russia's "Asiatic hordes" and "Cossack barbarians" would also be cited.

[20] Blagoev's hatred of Tsarist Russia as the main enemy of international Socialism, a belief general among prewar Socialists and deriving from the writings of Karl Marx, had led him in the 1890s to cheer Stambolov's Russophobe policies while denouncing the internal activities of his government. See Blagoev, *Prinos kam istoriata na sotsializma v Balgaria,* pp. 102-6. Marx's essays on Russian foreign policy, mostly written for the New York *Daily Tribune,* were collected by his daughter and son-in-law and published as *The Eastern Question* (London, 1897).

[21] Kabakchiev and Karakolov, "Bolgaria v Pervoi Mirovoi Imperialisticheskoi Voine," p. 65.

[22] *Ibid.,* p. 65.

protested strongly to the International Socialist Bureau in The Hague against the support given to the national war efforts by the German and French Socialists and against the inactivity of the International in the face of the crisis.[23] At about the same time, in the mid-February issue of *Novo Vreme*, Blagoev lauded the policy of the "international" wings of the Russian Bolshevik and Menshevik parties led by Lenin, Martov, Aksel'rod, and Trotsky, whose Paris-published *Nashe Slovo* (Our Word) was influential in securing the adherence of Balkan Socialists to the antiwar camp.[24]

Some Bulgarian Communist apologists[25] have subsequently claimed that this article of Blagoev's, in which he first used such terms as "opportunist" to abuse the Socialists supporting the national war efforts and seemed to consider dispassionately the possibility of a split in the ranks of the International, denoted agreement with Lenin's thesis that the old International had shown itself "bankrupt" by its failure to "transform the imperialist war into a civil war" and that a new, purified International must be founded. The fact is, however, that subsequently the Narrow Party consistently took a moderate and anti-Leninist stand within the Socialist antiwar camp, the Zimmerwald Movement. Kirkov's letter to the International Socialist Bureau had demanded not the organization of a new International but the convening of a peace-and-reconciliation conference of the old one.

At the antiwar International Conference of Socialist Youth, held in Berne, Switzerland, April 5-7, 1915, and attended by German, Polish, Dutch, Swiss, Russian, Italian, Scandinavian, and Bulgarian (Narrow) delegates, the lone representative from Bulgaria voted for the resolution proposed by the Swiss Grimm which condemned the war. He opposed the Bolshevik demand for a complete rupture with all Socialists unwilling to unleash a civil war.[26] Moreover, in

---

[23] Kirkov's letter was reprinted in *Rabotnicheski Vestnik*, February 21, 1915. It closed with a demand that the International Socialist Bureau convoke a conference to reestablish the disunited International. Huysmans, who had several times been berated by Blagoev for the inactivity of the Bureau in the war, dismissed the Narrow Socialists as "the old incorrigibles."

[24] See Trotsky, *My Life*, p. 215.

[25] For example, Kabakchiev, Boshkovich, and Vatis, *Kommunisticheskie Partii Balkanskikh Stran*, p. 84; Kabakchiev, "Der Weg zur Kommunistischen Internationale," p. 624.

[26] *Kommunismus* (Vienna), I, No. 33 (August 24, 1920), 1159; Fainsod, *International Socialism and the World War*, p. 58.

July, 1915, the Narrow Party was represented at the Second Balkan Socialist Conference in Bucharest where, together with the Greek, Rumanian, and Serbian Socialist Parties, it issued a manifesto denouncing the "imperialist war," the predatory ambitions of the Great Powers, the oppressive Balkan "ruling classes and dynasties" and once again calling for federation as the only safeguard for the liberty and integrity of the Balkan peoples.[27] This Conference, at which the Broad Socialist Party was not represented, did not raise the question of founding a new International.

While the Narrow leaders were exhorting the International Socialist Bureau to summon a socialist peace conference, for Lenin the International had ceased to exist since he learned in August, 1914, that the Western Socialist Parties had voted for war credits. In the *Seven Theses on the War*, composed in Switzerland during the first week of September, 1914,[28] he had announced the death of the old International, and on November 1, in the first number of his revived *Sotsial Demokrat*, he issued a call for a new one, dedicated to revolution and civil war.[29] After the antiwar Socialist Women's Conference in Berne on March 26-28, 1915, and the one of Socialist Youth there a week later, Lenin was able, with the cooperation of the Italian and Swiss Socialist Parties and in defiance of the International Socialist Bureau, to muster a general conference of antiwar Socialists at Zimmerwald, Switzerland, September 5-8, 1915. Though the great names of prewar international Socialist congresses were absent, the delegations were sufficiently imposing to drive a permanent wedge into the previously cohesive ranks of European Socialism. As Karl Liebknecht was in jail at the time for his antiwar agitation, the German delegation included Ledebour, Borchardt, Ernst Mayer, and Bertha Thalheimer. Merrheim and Bourderon, two trade-union leaders, came from France. Aksel'rod and Martov represented the Menshevik and Lenin and Zinoviev the Bolshevik "international" wings of Russian Social Democracy, while Natanson-Bobrov and Chernov attended for the Social Revolutionaries. Trotsky, of the *Nashe Slovo* (Our Word) group of antiwar

---

[27] *La Fédération Balkanique*, March 1, 1927. The Narrow delegation consisted of Blagoev, Kirkov, Kolarov, and Dimitrov. A central office to coordinate the antiwar activities of the participating parties was established. It was ineffectual.

[28] Wolfe, *Three Who Made a Revolution*, p. 635.

[29] Lenin, *Sochinenia*, 3d ed., XVIII, 89.

Mensheviks and some Bolsheviks then living in Paris, played the role of mediator between the conference factions. Closely associated with the Russian Socialists were the Lettish Social Democrats, represented at Zimmerwald by Berzin-Winter. Attending for various Polish Socialist groups were Radek, Hanecki, Warski, and Lapinski. The Jewish *Bund* sent an observer. Dutch, Italian, Norwegian, Swedish, and Swiss Socialists also attended, some officially representing their parties, others coming in a private capacity or on behalf of splinter groups. The Bulgarian Narrow delegate was Vasil Kolarov. Christian Rakovski attended for his Rumanian Social Democratic Party.[30]

Lenin demanded that the Zimmerwald Conference then and there break with the "traitor" International and found a new body dedicated to revolutionary civil war, but he could rally only seven or eight of the thirty-eight delegates to support this idea.[31] Kolarov, though sympathizing with Lenin's bitterness against the socialists supporting the war, was not prepared to sever connections with the International Socialist Bureau. Rakovski also pleaded for the preservation of organizational unity within the old International.[32] Trotsky worked out a compromise by which a "Zimmerwald Secretariat" was established to keep the sympathizing parties and groups informed of developments so as to enable them to act in unison. At the time none but Lenin and Zinoviev regarded the Secretariat as the seed of a new International, though Blagoev, in the first issue in 1916 of *Novo Vreme*, wrote that if the Zimmerwald Conference did indeed portend a split in the Socialist International, then it was probably an inevitable and necessary schism.[33]

After the entry of Bulgaria into the war on the side of the Central Powers in October, 1915, an action against which the Narrow Party

---

[30] Gankin and Fisher, *The Bolsheviks and the World War*, p. 320. Altogether thirty-eight delegates, some of them nonvoting observers, attended.

[31] Lenin's position was supported only by the Lettish and Polish representatives who were in any event wards of the Bolshevik Party, by the Swedish and Norwegian delegations whose countries were neutral and who could allow themselves to indulge in brave phrases about turning the imperialist war into a civil war, and by one German and one Swiss participant. For full details see Balabanoff, "Die Zimmerwalder Bewegung," p. 321. The author was secretary of the conference and subsequently of the "Zimmerwald Secretariat."

[32] *Ibid.*, p. 318.

[33] This article is discussed by Kabakchiev in Kabakchiev, Boshkovich, and Vatis, *Kommunisticheskie Partii Balkanskikh Stran*, p. 85.

and the Peasant Union had fought with the utmost vigor, the Party's freedom of maneuver and propaganda was restricted. The Austrian authorities, probably with the approval of the Bulgarian government, refused to grant transit visas to Kirkov and Kolarov, designated to represent the Narrow Party at the second conference of the Zimmerwald Movement which met in Kienthal, Switzerland, April 24-30, 1916,[34] and thus it was not until the involved episode of the Stockholm Conference in the summer of 1917 that Narrow delegates again appeared on the international Socialist stage.

The February Revolution in Russia galvanized the hitherto inactive and patriotic Socialists into international action. In the spring of 1917 the neutral Dutch-Scandinavian Socialist Committee invited all European Socialist Parties to meet in Stockholm in May in order to "discuss the international situation." [35] Initially the patriotic Socialist Parties of the Western Allied powers hoped to utilize the conference to persuade their Russian comrades to continue the war, but, after a number of them had visited Petrograd in the spring, they suggested that peace negotiations be initiated at Stockholm. The French government thereupon refused passports to its nationals wishing to attend the conference and Havelock Wilson, head of the British Seamen's Union, forbade his men to man ships carrying Socialists to Stockholm.[36] The conference thus degenerated into what Friedrich Adler called a "reunion of the commercial travelers of the Central Powers."

The parties and groups making up the Zimmerwald Movement were committed to consult together and act in unison in such a situation. The February Revolution had greatly increased the power of the Bolshevik Party, and Lenin, now no longer merely the leader of a band of refugees dependent upon the Socialists of little Switzerland but the head of a powerful party in one of the Great Powers, was quite prepared to split the Zimmerwald Movement as well as

[34] Kabakchiev, "Lenin i bolgarskie Tesnyaki," p. 180. About one third of the expected participants, including the British, Austrian, Rumanian, Swedish, Norwegian, as well as the Bulgarian delegations, were prevented from attending by passport difficulties. The full attendance was 43 or 44, of whom 12 now belonged to Lenin's camp and 7 more voted with him on some crucial questions, leaving him only 3 short of a majority. Fainsod, *International Socialism and the World War*, p. 90.

[35] The invitation is reprinted in an anniversary issue of *Inprekorr* (VII, No. 42 [April 19, 1927], 881). The conference was originally scheduled for May 15, 1917, but was repeatedly postponed until the late summer.

[36] Fainsod, *International Socialism and the World War*, p. 136.

the Socialist International and to cast off those moderates not yet prepared to found a new International. He was, however, overruled by his own party.[37] Two more years were to pass before the Comintern was founded. At a conference of "left-Zimmerwaldians" in Petrograd in May, 1917, Rakovski, representing his Rumanian Socialist coterie, together with the Swiss Grimm and the Russians Martynov and Natanson-Bobrov, even sought, though unsuccessfully, to persuade Trotsky, Zinoviev, Kamenev, Ryazanov, and Angelica Balabanoff that the Bolshevik Party should be reconciled to the "social patriots" and attend the Stockholm Conference, since, they argued, the conference had been endorsed by the "revolutionary" Petrograd Soviet as well as by the "opportunist" International Socialist Bureau.[38]

The Bulgarian Narrow Party had, in the meantime, moved to the left, partly because of the stimulus of the February Revolution in Russia. Blagoev was the first protagonist of the new orientation within the Central Committee.[39] Kabakchiev soon also took up his pen to advocate in the pages of *Rabotnicheski Vestnik* the formation of a new International,[40] and when Kirkov and Kolarov were in Stockholm in the late spring and summer of 1917, the former signed with the Bolshevik, Lettish, Polish, and Swedish Left representatives a joint manifesto in the Swedish press denouncing the proposed general Stockholm Conference as the last effort of the "social patriots" to save the war for their bourgeois overlords in the face of increasing popular discontent. Not by such fraudulent discussions but only through proletarian revolution, the manifesto proclaimed, would the peoples obtain peace and liberation from enslavement.[41] When another conference of Zimmerwald delegates assembled in Stockholm early in September to define the organization's attitude toward the later conference called by the Dutch-Scandinavian Committee, Kirkov and Kolarov had already returned home, but before leaving they had approved Lenin's policy of boycotting the general conference.[42] Though no Zimmerwald Social-

[37] *Ibid.*, pp. 162-63.
[38] Balabanoff, "Die Zimmerwalder Bewegung," p. 365.
[39] Kabakchiev, "Der Septemberaufstand in Bulgarien," p. 2125.
[40] Vladimirov, "Nekrolog: Kh. S. Kabakchiev," p. 159.
[41] Balabanoff, "Die Zimmerwalder Bewegung," p. 381. The manifesto was first published on July 20, 1917.
[42] Fainsod, *International Socialism and the World War*, p. 159.

ists from the Entente countries other than Russia had been able to reach Stockholm, the decision not to participate in the general conference, taken after vigorous debate and against the opposition of the Mensheviks Aksel'rod and Panin, who walked out, was declared binding upon all the groups in the Zimmerwald Movement. It was endorsed by the Narrow Party as well as by Nikola Kharlakov and Koika Tineva, the former Liberal and Progressive Socialists who had broken with Blagoev in 1905 and 1908 and had subsequently joined the Broad Socialists. Now in 1917 they had left that Party in protest against its endorsement of Bulgarian war aims and had come to Stockholm—too late to participate in the deliberations of early September.[43] Kharlakov and Tineva claimed to represent respectively the antiwar opposition within the Broad Party and Free Trade Union Federation.[44]

The Stockholm episode of the summer of 1917 was a watershed for the Broad Socialist Party as well as for its Narrow rival. A short discussion of its wartime policy is therefore in order.

Though he had denounced the Balkan Wars in his Sobranie speech of October, 1912,[45] Sakazov, after Bulgaria's defeat in the second of the wars, allowed himself to be tempted by that cardinal sin of pre-World War Socialism—ministerialism—and participated in a Crown Council called to discuss the country's future policy.[46] He declined, however, to serve in the cabinet and in May, 1914, in an address to the congress of the Serbian Socialist Party, roundly attacked the diplomats and "despotic dynasties" who had involved the Balkan brothers in fratricidal war.[47]

Sakazov's espousal of Balkan brotherhood did not prevent his believing strongly that Bulgarian claims to Macedonia were legitimate. He had expressed this conviction even in his Sobranie speech of October, 1912. Once the World War had broken out, he supported the government's wait-and-see policy, designed to obtain Macedonia at the lowest price. Furthermore, he dissociated the

---

[43] Balabanoff, "Die Zimmerwalder Bewegung," p. 397.
[44] *Ibid.*, p. 397. See also Lenin, *Sochinenia*, 3d ed., XXX, 358, and Gankin and Fisher, *The Bolsheviks and the World War*, p. 675.
[45] See p. 59.
[46] *Yanko Sakazov yubileyen shornik*, p. 7.
[47] Excerpts from the speech are reprinted by Walling, *The Socialists and the War*, p. 107.

Broad Party both from the Narrow Sobranie motion of November, 1914, calling upon the government to consult with other neutrals with a view to ending the war and with other Balkan states to initiate measures for common defense and federalization,[48] as well as from the resolution of the Second Balkan Socialist Conference at Bucharest in July, 1915, which denounced the war, the Great Powers, and the Balkan dynasties and again demanded a Balkan federation.[49]

Sakazov initially opposed Bulgarian entry into the war, and on August 13/26, 1915, on the eve of this event, he joined the Peasant and other opposition leaders in protesting against King Ferdinand's conclusion of an offensive alliance with the Central Powers against Serbia and in vainly demanding the convening of the Sobranie to discuss the situation before the irrevocable step was taken.[50] After Bulgaria had entered the war in October, however, the Broad Party endorsed the government's territorial ambitions, and a strong section of it, led by the staff of the Party paper *Narod* (People), became openly chauvinistic. Though the Party's Sobranie fraction, led by Sakazov, always abstained from the votes for war credits,[51] Broad Socialists helped draw up plans for economic mobilization[52] and accepted, with Prime Minister Radoslavov's thanks, important positions in the administration.[53]

As the war dragged on, Sakazov developed misgivings about supporting it. These, like the similar regrets of Bernstein and Kautsky in Germany, were rejected by his followers. He lost much of his influence to the rabid war-supporters in the Party, who were led by the editors of *Narod*. This paper followed the example of the German "social imperialists" in equating the war against the British side with the struggle against capitalism.[54] It also took its cue from German Socialist apologists in rationalizing support of the war effort with the spurious argument that the war economy

[48] See p. 62. Sakazov emphasized that his party was a loyal *national* opposition.
[49] See p. 65.
[50] See the despatch of August 14/27, 1915, from Savinski, the Russian ambassador in Sofia, to Sazonov, in Savinski, "La Declaration de guerre de la Bulgarie aux Alliés," p. 34.
[51] Yanko Sakazov, "Die Wahrheit ueber Makedonien," p. 161.
[52] Kuhne, *Bulgaria Self-Revealed*, p. 202.
[53] *The American Labor Year Book, 1917-18*, pp. 235-36.
[54] *Narod*, October 23 and 24, 1916. Citations from *Narod* are from Kuhne, *Bulgaria Self-Revealed*.

was an approach to Socialism.[55] The paper frequently demanded the "rounding off" of Bulgaria with the acquisition of Macedonia and the reannexation of the Southern Dobruja, ceded to Rumania after the Second Balkan War of 1913, and consistently omitted Serbia from its list of states "having an objective right to live." [56]

These were comments for Bulgarian internal consumption but the conduct of the Broad delegation to the abortive Stockholm Conference in the summer of 1917 was no less chauvinistic. Though Sakazov was a member of the delegation, and though he also believed in the justice of Bulgaria's claims to Macedonia,[57] he was reluctant in his support of the war policy. The leadership of the delegation devolved upon Nikola Sakarov, the former Progressive Socialist who had joined the Broad Party in 1908 after his break with Blagoev and was now its most enthusiastic war patriot. The delegation also included Assen Tsankov, Krastyu Pastukhov, P. Djidrov, and Y. Yanulov. Before leaving Sofia the latter had declared that the formula "peace without annexations" recently accepted by the Russian and German Socialists must be submitted to correction insofar as it concerned Bulgaria. On May 3, the day of its departure, the delegation issued the following statement:

We shall demonstrate that Bulgaria's right must be recognised to rule Macedonia, the Dobruja and all the areas which we have gained at so great a sacrifice, which are peopled by Bulgars, which crown our national unity and without which our economic development would be uncertain.[58]

This could perhaps be regarded as a demand for no more than lands inhabited by Bulgarians, a demand which a Socialist could in good conscience advance. But the Broad delegation did not stop there. Assen Tsankov demanded the entire Timok valley in Serbia.[59] At one of the halts on the journey Yanulov declared that Serbia must be truncated to give Bulgaria a common frontier with Austria-

---

[55] *Narod*, October 18, 1916.

[56] Kuhne, *Bulgaria Self-Revealed*, p. 65.

[57] Passing through Berlin on his way to Stockholm in May, 1917, Sakazov ruefully told a reporter of the *Internationale Korrespondenz*, "The Entente would never have purchased our neutrality at the price of Macedonia. . . . Thus we have lost the basis on which we founded our opposition to Radoslavov's policy." Quoted by Logio, *Bulgaria: Problems and Politics*, p. 155 and by Kabakchiev and Karakolov, "Bolgaria v Pervoi Mirovoi Imperialisticheskoi Voine," p. 65.

[58] Quoted in *The New Europe*, III, No. 32 (May 24, 1917), 184.

[59] *The New Europe*, IV, No. 40 (July 19, 1917), 18.

Hungary,[60] while Sakarov insisted that at least the Negotin district be given Bulgaria as a corridor to the Habsburg Empire.[61] Yanko Sakazov was throughout more reluctant to echo such demands.[62]

The Stockholm Conference ultimately came to naught because the Zimmerwald groups boycotted it and the delegates from the Western Entente states were prevented from attending.[63] As the fortunes of war turned against Bulgaria, the territorial claims of her Broad Socialists became more modest. By the spring of 1918 the Party had already sent a reasonably conciliatory, if vague, reply to the request of the Third Inter-Allied Labor and Socialist Conference, which had met in London in February, for a statement of peace terms which it would be prepared to accept, a reply which the Fourth Inter-Allied Labor and Socialist Conference, meeting in London in September, found satisfactory.[64] Early in September a Broad Party conference in Sofia advised the abandonment of pretensions to territories "forming an integral part of neighbouring states" and recommended that henceforth Bulgaria's policy be based not on conquest but on the projected League of Nations.[65] At the Berne Conference, which met in February, 1919, for the purpose of resurrecting the Socialist International, the Broad Party was reconciled to its Socialist comrades of the Entente states.[66] By then the Narrow Party had accepted Lenin's rejection of any attempts to reconstitute the old International. Together with the Bolshevik, Spartacist, Italian, Swiss, Serbian, and Rumanian Socialist Parties, it denounced the Berne Conference as reactionary and refused to attend.[67]

Though the Narrow Socialists had supported the Bolshevik demand that the Zimmerwald groups boycott the Stockholm Conference,[68] the Party was not yet prepared to follow Lenin's lead in all

[60] *The New Europe*, III, No. 32 (May 24, 1917), 184.

[61] *The New Europe*, III, No. 36 (June 21, 1917), 316.

[62] This was remarked in the Narrows' *Rabotnicheski Vestnik*, June 9, 1917.

[63] The collapse of the Stockholm Conference may have helped bring the Bolsheviks to power in Russia, for it convinced the war-weary masses that the Provisional Government could not or would not bring them peace.

[64] Fainsod, *International Socialism and the World War*, p. 119.

[65] This resolution is quoted at length by Logio, *Bulgaria: Problems and Politics*, p. 7.

[66] Lazitch, *Lénine et la IIIe Internationale*, p. 95.

[67] Fainsod, *International Socialism and the World War*, p. 193.

[68] See p. 68.

matters. Not until after the Bolshevik seizure of power in October, 1917, did it adopt Lenin's slogan of transforming the imperialist into a civil war. Even then, as its boycott of the Radomir peasant-soldier mutiny in September, 1918, demonstrated, it had no inkling of how to implement this phrase.[69] But regardless of its ineptitude in political action, the Party had burned its bridge to moderate socialism and had by the end of the war committed itself to the Leninist camp. When invitations were sent from Moscow on January 24, 1919, to thirty-eight "left" Socialist groups and parties to join in organizing a new International, Rakovski signed the invitation on behalf of the "Executive Committee of the Revolutionary Social-Democratic Federation of the Balkans." [70] He represented the Narrow Party at the first Comintern Congress which met in Moscow in March, 1919, as no delegate from Bulgaria could get to Moscow and Rakovski was already in Russia. He disposed of three deliberative votes on behalf of the Rumanian and Bulgarian parties.[71] Rakovski warmly advocated founding a new International then and there in spite of the objections of Rosa Luxemburg's deputy, Eberlein.[72] At the close of the Congress he was elected to the Bureau of the Executive Committee of the new Communist International together with Zinoviev (chairman), Lenin, Trotsky, and Fritz Platten.[73] Blagoev in Bulgaria heartily approved the founding of the new International, and in May, 1919, the Narrow congress changed the Party's name to The Bulgarian Communist Party and affiliated it, without serious defections, to the new Comintern, bringing into that organization its only mass party, other than the Bolshevik one, of a truly "Russian" complexion.[74]

[69] See the next chapter.

[70] Fainsod, *International Socialism and the World War*, p. 201.

[71] *Der Erste Kongress der Kommunistischen Internationale: Protokoll der Verhandlungen*, p. 5. Another Bulgarian named Djorov, who also happened to be in Moscow, was given a consultative vote as was the Serb Milkić. The Congress was timed to offset the Berne Conference of the moderate Socialists.

[72] *Ibid.*, p. 131.

[73] *Ibid.*, p. 205.

[74] *Balgarskata Komunisticheska Partia v Rezolyutsii i Reshenia*, Vol. II, pp. 1-3.

IV

THE RADOMIR REBELLION

The newly-founded Comintern was intended to be the general staff of the world revolution which Lenin and the other Communist leaders were certain was about to sweep over Europe with the end of the war. Ironically, the immediate prelude to the 1918 debacle was not what Lenin had throughout the war demanded—civil war in the industrial countries, initiated by the proletariat and led by the Socialist Parties—but a peasant-soldier mutiny in backward Bulgaria in which the Socialists declined to participate.

On the morning of September 14, 1918, the Allied armies on the Macedonian front launched their long-prepared offensive against the Bulgarian positions at Dobropolé and on the following day achieved a break-through. Their advance was maintained throughout the following week and on September 28, General Lukov, commander of the Bulgarian Second Army, Finance Minister Lyapchev, and Simeon Radev, the historian, presented themselves at Franchet d'Espérey's headquarters to sue for an armistice, which was signed the next day at Salonika. Thus was Bulgaria knocked out of the war to which her King had committed her three years earlier and obliged to renounce the purpose of her entry—the acquisition of Macedonia and the Dobruja. With this defeat the southeastern phalanx of the Central Powers caved in.

The war against the Liberator of 1877—Russia—had never been popular with the peasants. Even as early as the period of the mobilization in September, 1915, there had been an abortive mutiny in an infantry regiment, encouraged by Narrow and Peasant Union agitators, and troop trains to the Serbian front had to be sealed and guarded by picked Macedonian detachments to prevent desertion.[1]

---

[1] Savinski, "La Declaration de guerre de la Bulgarie aux Alliés," p. 52. The author was Russian ambassador to Bulgaria. See also Pravdin, "Revolutionäre Taktik und revolutionäre Phraseologie," p. 691; Logio, *Bulgaria: Problems and Politics,* p. 146.

After the Balkan conflicts of the recent past, neither the country nor the army was prepared for a long war. Medical and supply conditions at the front were chaotic, and within a year of the country's entry into the war army pay was six months in arrears.[2] Officers and ranks alike resented the better conditions and arrogant behavior of the German and Austrian armies which swarmed into the Balkans in the autumn of 1915 and stripped Bulgaria of food.[3] When pro-Russian demonstrations occurred in Plovdiv, Yambol, and Stara Zagora in the summer of 1916, the government, not considering its own army sufficiently reliable, called upon German units to suppress them.[4] Though the "redemption" of Macedonia and the Southern Dobruja was popular with the people, the price being paid for it in terms of casualties, poverty, and inflation was too high. The two Balkan Wars had already cost Bulgaria 58,000 dead and 105,000 wounded, and in this third and longer struggle she was to pay with another 101,224 known dead (exclusive of influenza deaths and those killed in the final retreat from Macedonia) and 300,000 seriously wounded—a price beyond the means of a nation of 5,000,000 in which the number of males in 1915 between the ages of twenty and fifty was only 713,419.[5] Though German voracity for Bulgarian grain initially gave the peasants large paper profits, the illusion of war prosperity soon evaporated even for those to whom it had seemed most real—the producers of marketable surpluses. The illusion was shattered by the grim reality that in the war period 1912-18 fully one third of the country's livestock and farm inventory was destroyed, and a cutback of 25 percent

[2] *The Times* (London), August 29, 1916.
[3] At the trial of the Radoslavov Cabinet after the war, it was revealed that 18,000 German troops stationed on the Macedonian front after the occupation of Serbia drew rations for 100,000. Each German soldier, had, furthermore, permission to send home to his hungry family five kilogram of food per week.
[4] *The Times,* August 29, 1916.
[5] The estimates of Balkan War casualties were those of the reliable Director of the Bulgarian Statistical Institute, Kiril Popov, cited by Kabakchiev, "Bulgarien nach dem imperialistischen Kriege," p. 155. The estimate of the number killed and wounded during the First World War is that prepared by Professor Ernest L. Bogart for the Carnegie Endowment for International Peace, cited in his book *Direct and Indirect Costs of the Great World War,* p. 272. None of these statistics include the considerable number of indirect casualties—civilians who died in the typhus and influenza epidemics. That these were serious and extensive is indicated by the death rate, which rose from 21.8 per 1000 in 1905 to 23.8 per 1000 in 1915 and to 36.5 per 1000 by 1918. Kabakchiev, "Bulgarien nach dem imperialistischen Kriege," p. 156.

in the area under cultivation occurred.[6] Moreover, this was not a "good war" for the villagers because the vast majority of the killed and disabled were their sons and husbands.

For the towns the war was a catastrophe. The throngs of arrogant, overpaid Germans, the contrasting clusters of Bulgarian maimed and wounded, the fantastic inflation and shortage of food,[7] led in 1916 to a series of "women's revolts," or bread riots.[8] In September of that year, following the pro-Russian demonstrations of August in other towns, a mass meeting held in Sofia in spite of police prohibitions cheered demands that Bulgaria withdraw from the war. It ended in disorder.[9]

The morale of the troops inevitably reflected that of the villages; shaky enough, at the start of the war, it deteriorated rapidly in 1918, owing to hunger as well as to corruption in official circles, and affected no doubt by events in Russia. The Narrow paper *Rabotnicheski Vestnik*, which harped upon these two themes, became popular reading matter at the front,[10] where the Peasant Union's *Zemedelsko Zname* (Peasant Banner) was prohibited. In June, 1918, soldier deputies from three regiments on the Salonika front held a meeting, with which the officers dared not interfere. They discussed arresting the officers and opening the front to the enemy. The most moderate, and revealing, suggestion made at this ostensibly secret conclave, as subsequently reported by a Bulgarian deserter,[11] was that the army should compel the government to alleviate the famine among the civilian population and to improve the lot of the troops. Though no drastic consequences resulted, the affair was illustrative of the advanced state of unrest in the army.

---

[6] Tsonev and Vladimirov, *Sentyabr'skoe vosstanie v Bolgarii 1923 goda*, p. 41. The 1917 harvest was a particularly bad one, and only the emergency importation of food stocks from Bessarabia, the Ukraine, and Germany itself saved the situation. Logio, *Bulgaria: Problems and Politics*, p. 220.

[7] For some illustrative price statistics comparing the 1905 and 1917 costs of staple food stuffs, see Logio, *Bulgaria: Problems and Politics*, p. 196. The author, an Englishman, lived for many years in Bulgaria.

[8] Tsonev and Vladimirov, *Sentyabr'skoe vosstanie v Bolgarii 1923 goda*, p. 24.

[9] *Daily Telegraph*, September 25, 1916.

[10] *The Times*, July 12, 1918. The evidence of large-scale corruption was brought out at the postwar trial of the Radoslavov Cabinet. For details, see Logio, *Bulgaria: Past and Present*, p. 418. They were earlier discussed by the German minister General von Stein (*Erlebnisse und Betrachtungen aus der Zeit des Weltkrieges* [Leipzig, 1919], pp. 172-73, 183).

[11] *The Times*, August 26, 1918.

The replacement of Radoslavov by Malinov as Prime Minister in mid-June, 1918, was assumed, despite official denials, to herald Bulgaria's early retirement from the war. Many soldiers vowed not to fight after September 15, if the new government did not conclude peace by then.[12] This deadline, by coincidence, was the day on which the break-through at Dobropolé occurred. In the last few months of the war desertions increased to a steady flow.[13]

When the Allies rolled up the Bulgarian front in September, several thousand soldiers decided that they had had their fill of war and, like the Russian "peasants in uniform" the year before, "voted for peace with their feet." But instead of dispersing to their homes, a column marched on Sofia to overthrow the government. In desperation King Ferdinand on September 25, called upon the only man who might possess sufficient influence with these peasant soldiers to pacify them—Alexander Stamboliski, leader of the Peasant Union, then completing his third year in jail for his vehement opposition to the war—and asked him to go to Kyustendil to persuade the mutineers to re-form ranks.

Stamboliski agreed, unwisely, not only to undertake this mission but even to announce his readiness to forget his "bad recollections" of Ferdinand and to exhort everyone to do his civil and military duty at this moment of crisis so as to prevent the front from collapsing and to facilitate the conclusion of an honorable armistice.[14] This conciliatory statement of the reputed fire-eater quelled an incipient panic in Sofia, and on September 26 Stamboliski went with his colleague in the Peasant Union, Raiko Daskalov, the War Minister General Savov, the Broad Sobranie deputy Sakarov, and other deputies to Radomir, whither the mutinous tide had rolled, to seek to turn it.

On the morning of September 27, he addressed the soldiers in the town square of Radomir from the back of a truck—with that inelegant, passionate rhetoric which never failed to impress his peasant listeners.[15] This time, however, his appeals, as well as those

---

[12] Madol, *Ferdinand of Bulgaria,* p. 251.

[13] The Balkan correspondent of *The Times* estimated that during the three years of fighting about 6,000 Bulgarian soldiers were tried by court martial for insubordination, mutiny, or desertion; see Bourchier, "Alexander Stambolisky," p. 788.

[14] Stamboliski's proclamation is reprinted in Gentizon, *Le Drame bulgare,* pp. 15-16.

[15] For this speech see Gentizon, *Le Drame bulgare,* p. 16.

of Sakarov, to return to the front fell on deaf ears. What was the sense of getting oneself killed now that he war was obviously lost and over? When a noncommissioned officer named Aronov followed these speeches with a harangue urging the men on to revolutionary action, they were far more impressed. At this point General Savov saved the day by entreating the soldiers to disperse to their villages after stacking their arms in the town of Radomir. This compromise was accepted by a show of hands, and Savov returned to Sofia, confident that a revolt had been averted. Without his commanding presence, however, the revolt flared up anew. Stamboliski was then induced by his erstwhile prison mate, Raiko Daskalov, to put himself at its head. A republic was declared, with Stamboliski as president and Daskalov as commander-in-chief of the army, and the march on Sofia resumed.[16]

The capital was defended by two German artillery battalions and special contingents of Macedonians, ready to continue the war against Serbia to the bitter end. The latter were under the command of General Protogerov, who was later destined to play a key role in relations between the Communist Party and the Internal Macedonian Revolutionary Organization (IMRO).[17] The two armies met at Vladaya, about ten miles south of Sofia, and fighting went on intermittently for three days, rolling ever closer to Sofia. On September 29 Protogerov halted the rebels at Knyazhevo, a village less than three miles from the capital. Between Radomir and Knyazhevo, the "republican army," initially 10,000-15,000 strong, had suffered about 3,000 casualties and of the survivors all but 3,000 to 4,000 had dwindled away.[18] That night news was received that an armistice had been signed. The rebels, their basic aim satisfied, thereupon dispersed to their villages leaving Stamboliski and the wounded Daskalov without an army and with death sentences hanging over their heads.[19]

[16] Today's Communist historiography asserts that just prior to the proclamation of the republic, Stamboliski had gone to nearby Kyustendil and that Daskalov acted on his own initiative, in Stamboliski's name, at Radomir. See Birman, "Narastanie revolyutsionnoi situatsii v Bolgarii v 1917-1918gg. i Vladaiskoe Vosstanie," pp. 58-59.

[17] See pp. 76-92.

[18] "Die Tätigkeit der Sozialdemokratie (der 'Tesnjaki') in Bulgarien," p. 786; Kabakchiev, "Die Balkanpolitik der Entente," p. 112.

[19] Lebedev, *Novym putem*, p. 117. The entire episode is narrated in detail by Gentizon, *Le Drame bulgare*, pp. 16-18 and, from a Communist point of view, by Birman, "Narastanie revolyutsionnoi situatsii v Bolgarii v 1917-1918gg. i Vladaiskoe

What was the attitude of the self-proclaimed greatest revolutionaries of Bulgaria, the Narrow Socialist Party, towards this abortive but highly significant Radomir revolt? The Party's propaganda and the actions of some of its leaders during the three years that Bulgaria had been in the war would have led one to expect that, like Lenin's Bolshevik Party in Russia, it would place itself at the head of such a movement and seek to extend it into a general revolution. On the day of Bulgarian mobilization, a clandestine manifesto of the Party, extending a "brotherly hand" to the workers of the neighboring states and denouncing the war, had been distributed in thousands of copies throughout the land,[20] and leaflets had been broadcast urging the reservists to defy the mobilization orders.[21] When the Sobranie reassembled in December, 1915, Blagoev, in announcing the Narrow faction's vote against war credits, delivered a stirring speech, protesting against the war in general, the dismemberment of Serbia in particular, and calling again for the federation of the Balkan states.[22]

The Narrow Party's antiwar stand was not determined by the country's late entry into the conflict. The increasing hardship and loss of life in the following three years, however, and the fact that, without provocation and after calculated bargaining, Bulgaria had been committed by her government to a war from which she could have remained aloof, brought the party much of the mass support which it enjoyed. The *Rabotnicheski Vestnik* had tens of thousands of readers, even at the front, despite, or because of, the fact that it was banned ten times between 1915 and 1918 for varying periods, that its editors were repeatedly arrested, that issues were often confiscated and columns deleted by the censor.[23]

In June, 1916, Georgi Dimitrov won approval for his conduct in

---

Vosstanie," pp. 46-72. Stamboliski went into hiding, and Daskalov fled to the French lines. Both were pardoned by King Boris after the abdication of his father and the end of the war.

[20] The manifesto is reprinted in Trotsky and Kabakchiev, *Ocherki politicheskoi Bolgarii*, p. 147, as well as in Tsonev and Vladimirov, *Sentyabr'skoe vosstanie v Bolgarii 1923 goda*, p. 20. The Narrow Sobranie delegation which issued this manifesto was indicted for inciting to sedition, but the government quickly dropped the matter.

[21] Logio, *Bulgaria: Problems and Politics*, p. 146.

[22] The important passages of this speech are quoted by Stavrianos, *Balkan Federation*, p. 200.

[23] Trotsky and Kabakchiev, *Ocherki politicheskoi Bolgarii*, p. 149.

refusing as a Sofia municipal councilor to participate in the ceremonies of welcome for a visiting delegation of German Reichstag deputies because they were, in his words, "partisans of the prolongation of the war . . . to the total victory of German imperialism" and their visit was "but a link in the chain of measures forged to dominate the Balkans, especially Bulgaria, economically and perhaps also politically." [24] The Germans were by this time quite unpopular, and here Dimitrov spoke for many Bulgarians. As a Sobranie deputy he took advantage of an ostensible investigation into the conditions of the Drama tobacco workers in October, 1917, to call a conference of Narrow Party members in the army in that area and to found an illegal workers' group in Drama.[25] Earlier, in August, 1917, Dimitrov had won popularity in another typical incident. He had encouraged a wounded soldier to disobey an officer's order to vacate a first-class railway compartment. Deprived later of his parliamentary immunity for this episode, Dimitrov was sentenced in 1918 to prison "for inciting to mutiny." He was released toward the end of the year.[26] Todor Lukanov, another Sobranie deputy and member of the Narrow Central Committee, was also sentenced to imprisonment on similar charges.[27] As for less important members of the Party, 1,000 of them had been jailed by January, 1917, and another 600 sent to the front though they were too old to be liable to conscription.[28]

It was in the last year of the war, when hardship and discontent were most acute and the news of the two Russian revolutions by contrast most exhilarating, that the influence of the Narrow Party grew spectacularly. The circulation of *Rabotnicheski Vestnik* climbed from 5,000 in 1914 to 30,000 in 1918.[29] The Party also made amazing gains in membership. Whereas in 1912, at the beginning of the war period, it had 2,500 members and in 1915, at the time of Bulgaria's entry into the World War, only 3,400, by the

---

[24] *Rabotnicheski Vestnik,* June 24, 1916, quoted in Kuhne, *Bulgaria Self-Revealed,* p. 110.

[25] Blagoeva, *Dimitrov: A Biography,* p. 29.

[26] He was, however, rearrested later in December at a meeting of Pernik miners. Brought to Sofia for trial in the confusion of the end of the war, he was torn from the police by a mob at the railway station.

[27] Trotsky and Kabakchiev, *Ocherki politicheskoi Bolgarii,* p. 148. See also Dimitrov, "The European War and the Labour Movement in the Balkans," p. 102.

[28] *The American Labor Year Book, 1917-1918,* p. 236.

[29] Kabakchiev, "Balgaria v Pervata Imperialisticheska Voina," p. 52.

spring of 1919, it could boast over 21,000,[30] many of whom were demobilized peasant soldiers.

In September, 1918, the very month in which the Radomir rebellion was later to erupt, deputy Kosta Tsiporanov and a number of other Socialist agitators and soldiers were tried by a court-martial in Stara Zagora on charges of distributing revolutionary leaflets among the troops.[31]

When the Radomir rebellion broke out, however, the Narrow Party remained passive. The official defense of this inaction states:

Stamboliski also had a conversation with Blagoev [on September 25] and suggested to the latter that the Communist Party [actually this name was adopted only in May, 1919], together with the Peasants' Party, should take part in the insurrection. His first and last basis of negotiation was merely the bourgeois democratic republic. . . . Of course, Blagoev declined to give any kind of support. This entire insurrection was ultimately reactionary. It was a rising of the peasantry against the urban population and against King Ferdinand. In the light of the circumstances the Communist Party did not take part in the insurrection, for quite apart from the fact that the foreign situation . . . made direct revolutionary action impossible . . . the Peasant Party was much stronger [than the Narrow Party] so that every joint action with the Peasant Party—which would, furthermore, have been a compromise—was accompanied by the risk of our being suffocated by the reactionary masses. . . . The "Bulgarian Revolution" in September, 1918, was not a fight of the proletariat and its party against the bourgeoisie but rather a fight within the bourgeoisie. . . . The insurrection was the work of ambitious and glory-hunting leaders and of the reactionary propertied peasant masses against the incompetence of the bourgeois parties. They wanted to wrest power to themselves in order to brake by force the process of history.[32]

This is an extremely interesting statement and reveals as much about Blagoev and his Party as about the insurrection. The pupil of Plekhanov had lost none of his mistrust of the "reactionary peasantry." Apart from the reference to the "foreign situation" and to the Narrow Party's relative weakness, the justification for his boycott of the rebellion is quite fraudulent. As Franz Borkenau

---

[30] B., "Die Kommunistische Bewegung in Bulgarien," p. 136; *Balgarskata Komunisticheska Partia v Rezolyutsii i Reshenia*, II, 1.

[31] *Vasil Kolarov: Important Dates of His Life and Work*, p. 26. Kolarov was the defense attorney. For further details, see Koren'kov, "Internatsionalistskaya pozitsia Bolgarskikh Tesnykh Sotsialistov v period Pervoi Mirovoi Voiny 1914-1918gg.," pp. 385-86.

[32] Pravdin, "Revolutionäre Taktik und revolutionäre Phraseologie," p. 692.

pointed out,[33] the very fact that Stamboliski proposed an alliance to Blagoev demonstrates that his original intention was more than simply to lead a crusade of the peasants against the towns. It was precisely Blagoev's rebuff which forced Stamboliski to rely exclusively on the peasant soldiers at Radomir. Had Blagoev possessed an iota of Lenin's imagination he would have cooperated with Stamboliski to secure a democratic republic as the first step toward a socialist state. But Blagoev, an opaque dogmatist, sneered at a movement to establish a "mere democratic bourgeois republic." Lenin, to whom such a situation would have been child's play, bubbled over with enthusiasm when the confused reports of the Radomir insurrection reached him. In his exhilarated mood of the moment, he believed this to be the spark which would set all of the Balkans afire, consume Austria-Hungary, and ignite the Allied occupation armies with the flames of mutiny.[34]

In the final analysis, Blagoev was probably right *malgré lui*. An "objectively revolutionary situation" did not exist at the time in Bulgaria. The mutineers wanted an end to the war, not a social revolution. Once an armistice was signed, they dispersed to their villages. Unlike their Russian counterparts, the Bulgarian peasant soldiers had no landlords to dispossess. In any event, the Entente occupation armies, which reached Sofia a few days after the insurrection, would have suppressed anything remotely resembling a Bolshevik regime—a term then used very loosely by Western politicians and generals—even if, as seems unlikely, the German and Macedonian contingents had not been able to crush a combined Peasant-Narrow insurrection. This was, however, a minor consideration in Blagoev's rejection of Stamboliski's invitation. Nor did the Narrow Party, whose proud boast it was ever after to be the only prewar party other than Lenin's to have entered the Comintern as a unit, alter its dogmatically contemptuous attitude toward the peasant movement until the time was too late. Five years later it was once again to exasperate the Russian Communist leaders by standing aside when a military coup overthrew Stamboliski's "mere bourgeois peasant republic" and established a regime which also

[33] Borkenau, *The Communist International,* p. 97.
[34] See Lenin's speech to the Sixth All-Russian Congress of Soviets on November 8, 1918; also his earlier speech of October 22, 1918 to a joint meeting of VTsIK, the Moscow Soviet, and the trade-union committees. Lenin, *Sochinenia,* XXIII, 266, 229.

decapitated the Communist Party and drove it underground for twenty long years, whence it emerged only after the entry of the Red Army into Bulgaria in September, 1944.

Lenin made it clear that as far as he was concerned, the Narrow Party's boycott of the rebellion was unforgivable.[35] Yet for almost a decade after the event the Bulgarian Communist leaders continued to insist on the essential correctness of their conduct at the time, basing their defense on the relative weakness of their Party[36] and on the subsequent "treachery" (by Communist definition) of Stamboliski who ceased to fight for a republic as an immediate aim and became in October, 1919, Prime Minister to the new King Boris.[37] It is ironic to see the Communists wax indignant over Stamboliski's alleged "betrayal" of an ideal upon which they themselves had spat at the time of the rebellion. When in 1920 the antiparliamentarian ultraleft Bulgarian Communist Workers' Party, in alliance with the German and Dutch groups of the same persuasion, attacked Blagoev's Radomir policy as unrevolutionary and opportunistic, the orthodox Bulgarian Communist Party was able to win an endorsement of that policy from a special commission of the Third Comintern Congress in 1921.[38] As late as 1924 Vasil Kolarov justified the Narrow Party's abstention from the insurrection by pleading its insufficient experience in maneuvering large masses.[39] Only in 1927, as one aspect of an overhauling of the party leadership, did the process of "self-criticizing our Narrow heritage" and breast-beating for the great Radomir error begin.[40] Though Kolarov, always Blagoev's closest disciple and most fervent apologist after the master's death in 1924, was more reticent than his colleagues in

[35] See Kabakchiev's report of his interview with Lenin after the Second Comintern Congress in 1920. Kabakchiev, "Lenin i bolgarskie Tesnyaki," p. 184.

[36] "B" ("Die Kommunistische Bewegung in Bulgarien," p. 135) claimed that only 600 Party members were not in the army in September, 1918, and of these only 50 were in Sofia. Author "B" was probably Blagoev. The "weakness argument," which was genuine in the sense that Blagoev feared his Party would be smothered by an alliance with Stamboliski—the same fear that had led him to reject Sakazov's "common action" policy in the 1890s—was also emphasized in the account in *Kommunismus* by Pravdin and in "Die Tätigkeit der Sozialdemokratie (der 'Tesnjaki') in Bulgarien," p. 787.

[37] Trotsky and Kabakchiev, *Ocherki politicheskoi Bolgarii,* p. 149.

[38] Kabakchiev, "Lenin i bolgarskie Tesnyaki," p. 184. The Left Communist criticism of the policy was expounded by Sidarov, "Die Revolutionäre Bewegung in Bulgarien."

[39] Kolarov, "Die Taktik der K.P. Bulgariens im Lichte der Ereignisse," p. 256.

[40] Kabakchiev, "Der Septemberaufstand in Bulgarien," p. 2126.

condemning his teacher's policy and more inclined to excuse it,[41] the critical "line" hardened, and it was maintained even after 1935 when the old guard of Kolarov and Dimitrov wrested control of the Party back from the younger critics. It has remained the official one to this day.[42]

[41] See, for example, Kolarov's introduction to Kabakchiev, Boshkovich, and Vatis, *Kommunisticheskie Partii Balkanskikh Stran*, p. 16. For Kolarov's general defense of the Narrow heritage against the younger critics who controlled the Party between 1928 and 1933, see his *Protiv lyavoto sektantstvo i Trotskizma v Balgaria*. This is a reprint of three speeches he delivered to the Bulgarian *émigrés* in Moscow in 1934 and 1935. It was he who was chosen by Blagoev to make the motion at the Tirnovo Congress in 1902 which crystallized the split (see p. 29), who was hand-picked to succeed Blagoev as Party leader in Plovdiv when the latter transferred his headquarters to Sofia in 1904 (see *Vasil Kolarov: Important Dates of His Life and Work*, p. 13), and who defended Blagoev's refusal to conclude electoral alliances when it evoked murmurings within the Party in 1911 (see p. 44).

[42] Dimitrov, *Politicheski otchet na Ts.K. na BRP(k)*, p. 16. Earlier condemnations of the policy are those of Bazhenov, "Sentyabr'skoe vosstanie v Bolgarii," p. 263; Tsonev and Vladimirov, *Sentyabr'skoe vosstanie v Bolgarii 1923 goda*, p. 28; Kabakchiev, "Glavnie etapi i osobenosti razvitia fashizma v Bolgarii," p. 45.

V

STAMBOLISKI AND THE
COMMUNISTS

Alexander Stamboliski (1879-1923) was the virtual dictator of Bulgaria from his accession to the premiership in October, 1919, until his overthrow and murder in June, 1923. The most striking peasant leader of postwar Eastern Europe, he evoked the fervid devotion of the village masses, whom he organized into a private army of club-wielding Orange Guards, and incurred the deathless hatred of the smaller urban bourgeoisie, whom the guards were used to overawe. Brutal, violent, domineering, corrupt, possibly dishonest,[1] Stamboliski was neither better nor worse than his predecessors and successors in Bulgarian politics. He was, however, uniquely different from them as well as from most of the agrarian leaders of other Eastern European countries in his determination to implement politically his conviction that the peasants, hitherto abused and exploited by politicians and usurers, were the noblest, purest, and wisest of God's children in whose exclusive interests Bulgaria, 80 percent of whose population they composed, must be governed. Though he continued in the direction set by Radoslavov and Ferdinand, brutalizing and demoralizing Bulgarian political life, Stamboliski was at least partially redeemed by his devotion to the cause of Balkan peace and union, and by his determination to create

---

[1] When he emerged from jail in September, 1918, and embarked on the career which was to take him to the premiership, Stamboliski was a poor man. Though he continued to insist upon his virtuous poverty, asserting that "his goods were not of this world," a vast hoard of foreign currency was claimed by the Tsankov government to have been found on his farm at Slavovitsa after his overthrow. See Gentizon, "Stamboulisky et le peuple bulgare," p. 599. Though this charge of personal dishonesty comes from an obviously prejudiced source, and though apologists for Stamboliski claim that the money was a fund, from which he drew no gain, for bribing members of the Inter-Allied Control Commission to relax the enforcement of the terms of the peace treaty, detached observers agreed that Stamboliski at least was aware of and tolerated corruption on the part of his colleagues and subordinates.

in Bulgaria an egalitarian utopia for his peasants, free from the domination of merchants and usurers and the competition of "The City." His ultimate attachment was to his Peasant Union, the strongest of the agrarian parties in Eastern Europe after the First World War, and he unashamedly stated that as long as he remained in power, the real constitution of Bulgaria would be the *tsepenitsa*, the peasant's club with which the Orange Guard was armed.[2]

Stamboliski's hatred of the city as such, of the "Sodom and Gomorrah" whose disappearance he said he would welcome,[3] his failure to recognize, or at least to draw logical conclusions from, the fact that peasants are most prosperous precisely in those countries where their economic and cultural life is closely integrated with that of cities, his refusal to concede that the Bulgarian peasantry could achieve a better life only if the excess rural population were to find employment in the cities—all these were the typical, if irrational, manifestations of an outlook widespread among the peasants of Eastern Europe. Observers who discuss the Eastern European peasant ideology and Stamboliski's implementation of it as either the quintescence[4] or the negation[5] of democracy miss the point, for terms such as democracy and dictatorship imply a political context whereas the peasant ideology was in essence antipolitical. The backward peasant, no matter how egalitarian his outlook, is not a "natural" democrat, and the history of peasant movements and rebellions, from Wat Tyler's in the fourteenth century through the German ones of the sixteenth, those of Razin and Pugachev in the seventeenth and eighteenth centuries, the French and Polish *jacqueries* of 1789 and 1846, to the peasant stirrings in Russia and Eastern Europe in the twentieth century, demonstrates only that the peasant is, if anything, a "natural" anarchosyndicalist. He has neither respect for, nor patience with, orderly politics. He prefers burning down a manor house to casting a ballot, and looting a merchant's shop to conducting parliamentary discussions.[6]

---

[2] Tchitchovsky, *The Socialist Movement in Bulgaria*, p. 24.

[3] Quoted by Gentizon, *Le Drame bulgare*, p. 104. The author was the special Balkan correspondent of *Le Temps*.

[4] Lebedev, *Novym putem*, and X.Y.Z., "Le Peuple bulgare et l'Union Paysanne," pp. 236-56.

[5] Gentizon, *Le Drame bulgare*, and Logio, *Bulgaria: Past and Present*.

[6] For the theory that the peasant is fundamentally a democrat, see Hodža, *Federation in Central Europe: Reflections and Reminiscenses*, pp. 110ff., and Mitrany,

Stamboliski's antiurban ideology and policy resulted in ambivalence and confusion in his attitude toward the Communist Party while the latter, tied by its Russian masters to the typology—fallacious for Bulgaria—of kulak, middle, and poor peasants as the sole correct vehicle for "bringing the class struggle into the village," never came to grips with the basic challenge presented by this peasant movement whose militancy, enthusiasm, and chiliastic self-righteousness matched its own. Stamboliski was prepared to differentiate between the urban middle classes, whom he hated, feared, and wished to destroy, and the proletariat, which he scorned and pitied for the dehumanization to which it was subjected in the factory. Of the middle class he wrote, "This band of parasites says: 'We want to live . . .' Lice and bugs also ask to live, but we don't listen to them. We kill them in order that we may live." [7] About the proletariat he mused:

I was in . . . Manchester . . . [and] went through dozens of great plants where I saw workers who had been going through the same mechanical motions for twenty years. I sympathize with the workers; but can people accustomed to nothing but mechanical work be expected to reason wisely and direct the affairs of a nation? . . . I don't like these workers with the narrow [sic] ideas of the West; they have little culture. . . . With peasants it is different. . . . In the peasant are the seeds of a fully developed human personality. . . . The experience of the peasant assures him an incontestable advantage over the worker for nature, who is his master, took it upon herself to round off his education.[8]

To rationalize his conviction that the peasants are the most productive and cultured and valuable element of the community, Stamboliski elaborated a theory of society in which classes are replaced by *saslovie*, or estates, listed in descending order of their

---

Marx Against the Peasant: A Study in Social Dogmatism, pp. 118-30. The irrational, antipolitical temper of the Bulgarian peasant can be discerned from the following demands raised by various peasant speakers at their Union's congress in 1921: the legal profession to be outlawed; judges who have sentenced peasants to be dismissed; intermarriage between peasants and townspeople to be prohibited; the foresters to be removed and the peasants permitted unlimited exploitation of the woods; all peasants to enjoy free railroad travel; all joint-stock companies to be expropriated; last, and perhaps most justifiable, doctors to be prevented from exploiting the poor by being transformed into state functionaries with fixed salaries.

[7] Stamboliski in the *Zemedelsko Zname*, September 17, 1920, quoted by Gentizon, *Le Drame bulgare*, p. 90.

[8] Stamboliski, quoted by K. Todorov, *Balkan Firebrand*, p. 142 and Gentizon, *Le Drame bulgare*, p. 155.

productiveness and social usefulness as agricultural, artisanal, hired labor, industrial, commercial, and bureaucratic. Only the artisans can be considered reliable allies of the peasants, while the commercial and bureaucratic estates must ultimately be liquidated. Socialism and Communism, he claimed, by denying the primacy of the peasantry, warp the basic human instincts and pervert the essence of society.[9]

Stamboliski's ultimate fate was to prove the superior power of the city over the village even in a country as overwhelmingly rural as Bulgaria, for it was by the city that he was overthrown. Until that moment came, however, he submitted Bulgaria to a series of social and political experiments which were a reflection of his peasant ideology and an attempt to implement it.

The peasant's loathing for the supposed arch-parasite, the lawyer, was manifested in a law enacted in the spring of 1921 prohibiting members of that profession from practicing it while serving as Sobranie deputies, mayors, or municipal councilors.[10] Then the operations of the opposition press were restricted, protests being drowned in jeers that "censorship against the bourgeoisie doesn't stop the grain from growing." [11] To eliminate speculation in grain, the formation of a state-controlled Cereal Consortium was voted by the Sobranie in November, 1919, amidst much peasant enthusiasm. Administrative difficulties, internal opposition, and pressure from the Entente powers, however, obliged a reluctant Stamboliski to restore free trade in grain in September, 1921.[12] Nevertheless, the Peasant Union Congress of May, 1922, called for a restoration of the Consortium. The Law Concerning Those Responsible for the National Catastrophe, originally voted in December, 1919, to authorize the punishment of the Radoslavov cabinet with up to five years' imprisonment at hard labor as well as all others "who profited from the war through speculation or . . . who, for purposes of gain, contributed in any manner towards the preparation, declaration, or prolongation of the war" was used arbitrarily by Stamboliski to

[9] Stamboliski, *Politicheski partii ili saslovni organizatsii?* For the Communist reply to this social theory, see Kolarov, "Bauernparteien und Verbände," and "Der 'Agrarismus' als Theorie des 'Sozialen Friedens.' "

[10] Kazasov, *Burni godini: 1918-1944,* p. 83.

[11] Gentizon, *Le Drame bulgare,* p. 152.

[12] For details see Kirshevskaya, "Reformi pravitel'stva Zemledel'cheskogo Soyuza v Bolgarii i ikh krakh," pp. 23-31, 63-66.

victimize opposition merchants. Once again the intervention of the Inter-Allied Commissioners was required to force a cessation of these excesses and to bring about an emendation of the law in September, 1921.[13]

In his theoretical work on society Stamboliski had predicted the ultimate elimination of both the governmental-bureaucratic and the free professional intelligentsia, as well as of the commercial middle class, as the spirit of cooperation ripened.[14] He was not hesitant in giving history a push. The governmental bureaucracy was filled with inexperienced and often corrupt hangers-on of the Peasant Union, whose abuse of power, particularly during Stamboliski's extended trips abroad, was scandalous.[15] In his educational policy, Stamboliski also lashed out at the "superfluous" intelligentsia by reducing instruction in the Sofia University—at one time in 1922 closing it down for six months[16]—while simultaneously bending every effort to encourage peasant education through the construction of a thousand new primary village schools and the development of agronomic and veterinary institutes.[17]

The most remarkable of Stamboliski's efforts to transform Bulgaria into a peasant's paradise, which demonstrate that with all his faults, his intolerance, his brutality, he was genuinely devoted to the ideal of a prosperous, egalitarian village society, were the land-limitation law and the compulsory labor scheme. Believing that no man is genuinely free unless he owns a plot of land and equally convinced that such property must be small if all men are to be free,

[13] Lazard, *Compulsory Labour Service in Bulgaria,* pp. 26-27.
[14] Stamboliski, *Politicheski partii ili saslovni organizatsii?,* p. 84.
[15] Woods, "The Bulgarian Revolution," p. 298. One of the most bizarre of these lieutenants was Prutkin, a Russian anarchist, smuggler, and spy whom Stamboliski met in the Sofia jail during the First World War and whom he appointed police commissioner of Sofia in 1919, a position which Prutkin abused for purposes of blackmail and violence. Prutkin's speciality was the staging of provocations and false attempts at assassination as pretexts for further suppression of the bourgeois opposition. Ultimately he went too far and had to be dismissed after it was established that he had ordered the dynamiting of the Odeon Theater on a night in March, 1920, when many bourgeois political leaders were expected to attend a lecture. His efforts to persuade Stamboliski of his innocence by arranging a bogus assassination attempt against himself failed. Thereafter Prutkin vanished from the Bulgarian political stage for over twenty years, only to make a spectacular reappearance in January, 1942, when he was tried for sabotage and espionage as an agent of the USSR and shot in Varna. See Swire, *Bulgarian Conspiracy,* p. 144 and K. Todorov, *Balkan Firebrand,* p. 93.
[16] Lamouche, "La Bulgarie et l'Entente Démocratique," p. 237.
[17] X.Y.Z., "Le Peuple bulgare et l'Union Paysanne," p. 242.

Stamboliski had the Sobranie enact legislation in April, 1921, limiting the size of a peasant holding to 30 tilled hectares (75 acres) with an extra 5 hectares for every member of the family above four, and sharply curtailing the amount of farmland which a city-dweller might own. In the case of wood- or pasture-land, the basic maximum over which property rights were recognized was 20 hectares in the plains and 50 hectares in the mountain districts. Land not cultivated by the peasant's own family was liable to indemnified confiscation.[18] Under the terms of this law about 70,000 hectares of land were expropriated from individual landowners and about 20,000 from parish lands for distribution among 18,000 dwarf holders.[19] As a final measure for the implementation of the Peasant Union's slogan of "the land to those who till it," 4 hectares of every peasant's holding were made inalienable. Though the law was altered after Stamboliski's overthrow, and some of the expropriated land returned to the previous owners, his successor Tsankov retained the general principle that holdings should not surpass 30 hectares and by 1934 only 1 percent of the total number of farms in the country exceeded this acreage and these occupied only 6 percent of the land.[20] Though Bulgaria had been a country of small holders long before Stamboliski's advent to power and would probably have remained so regardless of his measures, this legislation crystallized both the ideology of the movement and the devotion of the peasants to Stamboliski.

The compulsory labor law, enacted in June, 1920, and amended in October, 1921, required a physically fit male to undertake at some time between his twentieth and fortieth birthdays an eight-month period of manual labor for the benefit of the state and to

[18] For the detailed provisions see Yotsov, "Upravlenieto na Zemledelskia Sayuz," p. 255 and *The Times,* May 15, 1921. As a cure for Bulgaria's chronic economic illness, rural overpopulation, and underemployment, Stamboliski's land reform was ineffective. At best is was a short-term palliative. The rate of population growth was steep, and most of this increase accumulated on the already overcrowded countryside. The primitive small farms remained primitive because the peasants were too poor to invest in machinery and live-stock. The result was a vicious circle of overpopulation, underemployment, underconsumption.

[19] Roucek, *Balkan Politics,* p. 46; Yotsov, "Upravlenieto na Zemledelskia Sayuz," p. 255.

[20] Seton-Watson, *Eastern Europe between the Wars: 1918-1941,* p. 87. The remaining large holdings were in the northeastern corner of the country bordering on the Dobruja. In 1924 the Tsankov government exempted the country's few mechanized farms from limitations on size.

be liable to perform in his own district up to twenty-one days of labor for the state every year until the age of fifty. For unmarried women the age span was sixteen to thirty, and the duration of the extended term of service four months. Married women were exempt from service. At the insistence of the Inter-Allied Control Commission, Stamboliski permitted after November, 1921, the purchase of exemptions at a fee of 12,000 to 48,000 leva provided that in any year no more than 20 percent of those designated for the call-up could purchase exemption. This was Stamboliski's ingenious substitute for military conscription, prohibited Bulgaria by the Treaty of Neuilly, and the psychological and physical results achieved were considerable.[21] By the end of 1925, about 800 bridges had been constructed, 600-700 miles of railroad track laid, 1,800-1,900 miles of road built, swamps drained, canals dug, telephone lines strung, and forests planted.[22] The scheme was retained in altered form by subsequent governments.

Stamboliski also used the banks and cooperatives to favor the peasant and hamper the middleman. Compulsory crop insurance had preceded his coming to power, but the credit system of the National Bank was radically revised. Whereas in 1911 over 73 percent of the credits it extended had been to companies and other banks and only 0.7 percent to peasants, by 1922 the proportions were 20 percent and 52 percent respectively.[23] The peasants had additional sources of credit, notably the Agricultural Bank and their own cooperatives—the most efficient in Eastern Europe and through which Stamboliski hoped to eliminate the merchant class altogether.

Stamboliski did not limit himself to economic legislation or to

[21] Stamboliski clearly stated that the scheme was intended to replace conscription. He also stressed, in introducing the bill in the Sobranie, the moral value of the program which would result in "Improving education and preparing youth for practical life. . . . Socialising human labour, the source of all wealth. . . . Fostering the sentiments of social duty and interest in national and social resources." Quoted by Lazard, *Compulsory Labour Service in Bulgaria*, pp. 30-31.

[22] X.Y.Z., "Le Peuple bulgare et l'Union Paysanne," p. 241. In five years over six million labor days had been worked under the scheme, mainly for the Ministries of Public Works and Transport. For the detailed accounts see *Le Service obligatoire du travail en Bulgarie*, pp. 8-14. Compulsory service for women was abolished by the Tsankov government on June 15, 1923, a few days after the seizure of power.

[23] Kolarov, "Die Sozialen Grundlagen des Zankowregimes," p. 888. Industry's share of credits from the National Bank remained relatively stationary during this period. In June, 1924, after Stamboliski had been overthrown, the National Bank extended credits of 785 million leva to industry and only 63 million to peasants. See Ordon, "Bemerkungen über die Bauernbewegung in Europa," p. 273.

petty prescriptions in his determination to liquidate the urban bourgeoisie. He did not shrink from using his club-wielding Orange Guards to crack opposition heads and break up bourgeois political gatherings. The most serious of such cases and the one which decided the bourgeois parties to overthrow him, if necessary by a *coup d'état*, occurred in September, 1922, while he was abroad, and was managed by his erstwhile colleague of the Radomir rebellion and then Minister of the Interior Raiko Daskalov.

In June, 1922, the bourgeois opposition parties, confederated in a constitutional bloc, scheduled a rally of protest against the government's arbitrary and unconstitutional acts. It was to be held on Sunday, September 17, in the ancient capital city of Tirnovo. Stamboliski replied by summoning his Orange Guards to a counterrally to be held at the same time in the same city and ordering the railways to transport his supporters thither free of charge. On the night preceding the scheduled rallies the train carrying the opposition leaders Malinov, Danev, Todorov, Majarov, and others to Tirnovo was halted and boarded at Dolni Dabnik by a mob of Orange Guards. The mob was preparing to lynch the unfortunate politicians, having already torn out their beards, when Daskalov, traveling on the same train, persuaded it not to murder the victims by promising to try them as "war criminals" guilty of the catastrophes of 1913 and 1918.[24] The opposition leaders were taken into "protective custody" in Shumen jail,[25] and, on November 19, a referendum was held to determine whether twenty-two of them, who had served in the wartime cabinets of Geshov (1911-13), Danev (1913), and Malinov (1918) should be placed on trial, Stamboliski having previously intimated that the reparation debt, then still fixed at £90,000,000, would be geographically apportioned according to the number of negative ballots cast in the various districts.[26] The result of the plebiscite was 650,000 votes for and 225,000 against the trial.[27] Though the trial never took place, the prospective defendants simply being kept in jail until the overthrow of Stamboliski in June

[24] *The Times*, September 19, 1922.
[25] Majarov and Burov managed to escape abroad.
[26] Gentizon, *Le Drame bulgare*, p. 120.
[27] Yotsov, "Upravlenieto na Zemledelskia Sayuz," p. 271. The Broad Socialist Party instructed its supporters to cast blank ballots, of which there were 56,000. The affair made a poor impression in the West where Stamboliski lost much of the favor he had won by his scrupulous adherence to the terms of the Neuilly Treaty. November,

of the following year, the affair marked a turning point in Bulgarian politics, for the bourgeois opposition, realizing that Stamboliski would stop at nothing to destroy it, decided that it too must use all means to bring about his downfall. The conviction deepened further when in December, 1922, the Orange Guard, assembling for a skirmish against IMRO detachments at Kyustendil, marched on Sofia, sacked bourgeois party headquarters and newspaper offices, and filled the hospitals with battered victims.[28]

The Bulgarian Communists viewed the Dolni Dabnik incident as an opportunity for coming to power through the back door. They had so often repeated to themselves and to Moscow the refrain that Stamboliski was but a more stupid Bulgarian version of Kerenski, who could be shouldered aside at will,[29] that they had come to believe it, and a few days after the near-lynching at Dolni Dabnik the Central Committee of the Communist Party confidently authorised Vasil Kolarov, who had replaced the dying Georgi Kirkov as Secretary-General at the first congress in May, 1919, to suggest to Daskalov that the Communist Party be armed in order that a new Kornilov-type bid for power by the bourgeois parties could be suppressed.[30] The Communists were dismayed to learn that the supposedly stupid Daskalov was as familiar as they with recent Russian history and refused to act the part to which they assigned him. Amused at being taken for a fool, he assured Kolarov that should there arise the danger of a bourgeois coup which the Peasant Union and the government felt unable to suppress by themselves, his own Ministry of the Interior would supply the Communists with arms in good time—say, about fifteen minutes before the event.[31] Shocked out of their smug overconfidence, the Communist leaders, though instructing Party members to vote for the trial of the alleged

---

1922, was a rather late date for suddenly discovering that the cabinets of 1913 and 1918 had been criminal, especially since, in 1919, Stamboliski had served in the same cabinet with some of the alleged criminals without objection. This was clearly a different matter from the question of the war guilt of the Radoslavov cabinet.

[28] Swire, *Bulgarian Conspiracy*, p. 254; Logio, *Bulgaria: Past and Present*, p. 44.

[29] This was the theme of the Party's fourth congress held in the summer of 1922. See Pieck, "Der Vierte Bulgarische Parteikongress," pp. 597-601. That it was also a standard Bulgarian boast to the Comintern is reported by Serge, *From Lenin to Stalin*, p. 58.

[30] This was first revealed by Kolarov a quarter of a century afterwards in *Rabotnichesko Delo*, September 26, 1947.

[31] *Ibid.* Cf. Yotsov, "Upravlenieto na Zemledelskia Sayuz," pp. 266-67.

war criminals in Shumen jail as a matter of principle, henceforth regarded Stamboliski and the Peasant Union as their main enemy. He, in turn, was encouraged by the "victory" of Dolni Dabnik and his party's tremendous success in the elections of April 23, 1923 (which gave the Peasant Union 212 deputies in a 245-member Sobranie, the Communists holding 16 seats and the Broad Socialists only 2) [32] to regard his power as absolutely secure and great enough to warrant a final campaign to crush all other political forces. The Communists and Stamboliski were both to be proven wrong, but the stage was set for the events of June 9, 1923, in which the Communists stood by as passive and approving spectators to the overthrow of Stamboliski and the seizure of power by a regime which was to persecute them far more severely than he had ever done. This, however, was only the final act of a complicated drama in which the relations between Stamboliski and the Communists underwent many changes, determined on Stamboliski's part by election results and Western diplomatic pressures and on the Communists' part also by internal political developments and by the external discipline of oscillations in the Comintern line.

The aftermath of the war found Bulgaria in a catastrophic condition, crushed by inflation,[33] gripped by food shortage, burdened with a reparations' load of £90,000,000,[34] and saddled with over 276,000 refugees from the lost territories.[35] Prospects for a Communist seizure of power were considered ideal, both by the Party and by its enemies. In this atmosphere of uncertainty and crisis Stamboliski became Prime Minister on October 6, 1919, his Peasant Union having emerged from the elections of August 17 as the largest party, with 85 seats in a Sobranie of 236.[36] In foreign policy

[32] Kazasov, *Burni godini: 1918-1944*, p. 127.

[33] If the cost of the primary necessities of life in 1914 is taken as an index value of 100, then by 1919 it had risen to 1,754 and in January, 1920, stood at 2,577. Buchan, ed., *The Nations of Today: Bulgaria and Romania*, p. 152.

[34] This was revised in 1923 with a series of annuities to extend over thirty-seven years at an average annual payment of £1,320,000. In 1930 the total debt was reduced to £22,000,000.

[35] This was the official figure. Inflated estimates were issued for propaganda purposes.

[36] In the previous Sobranie, elected in February/March, 1914, the Peasant Union had 49 deputies. Stamboliski had been pardoned for his role in the Radomir Rebellion by the new King Boris and in January, 1919, was appointed Minister of Public Works in the cabinet of Todor Todorov. (*The Times*, February 3, 1919). The Broad So-

he was pledged to fulfillment of the severe Treaty of Neuilly, which he signed on November 27, thereby arousing the resentment of the nationalists, and to the establishment of a "Green International" of peasant parties to be the nucleus of a federation of Eastern European peasant states.[37] In internal affairs he was determined to inaugurate the peasant millenium, which could only be achieved by crushing all opposition. The Communists, in their turn, were convinced, as all Communists were required to be during the two years between the founding of the Comintern in March, 1919, and the Kronstadt mutiny of March, 1921, that the world revolution and their own accession to power were imminent. Both their numerical strength and their reading of the international situation in the apparently revolutionary summer of 1919 had hardened this conviction.

At the congress in May, 1919, at which the Narrow Party changed its name to the Bulgarian Communist Party and entered the Comintern en bloc, 21,577 members were represented—a tremendous gain over the prewar figure and one largely reflecting the weariness of a people which now rewarded the antiwar parties with its membership and votes. Though only 2,215 members were industrial workers and though as many as 9,421 were of the bourgeoisie,[38] the optimism of the congress was unclouded, for was not the Party's influence over the proletariat assured by its control of thirteen trade unions with 13,000 members?[39] Scornfully rejecting any intermediate form of government, the congress called for the formation of soviets as the only genuine expression of the will of the masses.[40] On July 27, accordingly, the Party sought to

---

cialist Sakazov held the portfolio of Commerce, Industry, and Labor and his party colleague, Djidrov, that of Justice in the Todorov cabinet, which had been formed in November, 1918, to replace that of Malinov, who had assumed the premiership after the fall of Radoslavov in June, 1918. Sakazov had entered the Malinov cabinet in October, 1918, shortly after the armistice and Ferdinand's abdication, and was retained by Todorov. In May, 1919, Krastyu Pastukhov, another Broad Socialist, became the all-important Minister of the Interior. See *The Times,* December 16, 1918, and Varga, *Sotsial-demokraticheskie partii,* p. 239.

[37] Early in 1921 Stamboliski visited Prague, Warsaw, and Bucharest to solicit support for his scheme of a Green International. A permanent bureau was in fact established at Prague. He entertained high ambitions for it, hoping that the Green International of peasant parties would lead to a Green Entente of peasant states as a counterpoise to both the West and Russia.

[38] For a detailed breakdown of the membership list by classes and professions, see *Balgarskata Komunisticheska Partia v Rezolyutsii i Reshenia,* II, 1.

[39] "Die Tätigkeit der Sozialdemokratie (der 'Tesnjaki') in Bulgarien," p. 787.

[40] *Balgarskata Komunisticheska Partia v Rezolyutsii i Reshenia,* II, 7. A German

"take over" the streets of Sofia and other towns, but its demonstrations were vigorously suppressed by the Socialist Minister of the Interior, Pastukhov, backed by the Inter-Allied Control Commission. A number of demonstrators were killed, many arrests made, and freedom of assembly and the press temporarily restricted.[41]

The Communists' appetite was only further whetted by the results of the election of August 17, 1919, from which the Party emerged as the second strongest in the country with 47 Sobranie deputies and 119,000 voters. The antiwar activities of the Narrow Party were bearing fruit. Stamboliski, backed by 85 Peasant deputies elected on 198,000 ballots, suggested a coalition cabinet to the Broad Socialist Party, which could claim 36 deputies returned by 83,000 supporters.[42] Had these talks succeeded, the resulting government would have had a small majority in the 236-member chamber. Agreement was in fact reached on a six-to-four division of portfolios, but the negotiations collapsed over the allocation of the Ministry of the Interior, which controlled the police. This assignment was considered the key post in Eastern European countries long before the Communists were to make it so notorious after the Second World War. Though the Socialists eventually agreed to accept the War Ministry instead of that of the Interior, Stamboliski's confidence in them had been shaken by the protracted negotiations, and on October 6, 1919, he took the premiership, heading a coalition government of five Peasant Unionists, two Nationalists, and one Progressive-Liberal, the latter being ex-premier Danev, whom Stamboliski was later to charge with war criminality after the Dolni Dabnik incidents of September, 1922.[43]

---

translation of the congress's resolution appeared in *Die Kommunistische Internationale,* No. 5 (September, 1919), pp. 729-36.

[41] Trotsky and Kabakchiev, *Ocherki politicheskoi Bolgarii,* p. 156. Violence erupted also in the Pernik mines, in Vidin, Lom, Nova Zagora, and Ferdinand. A Communist estimate of the number of killed and wounded is 100. Tsonev and Vladimirov, *Sentyabr'skoe vosstanie v Bolgarii 1923 goda,* p. 33. In September, 1919, six Communists were killed in disorders in Plovdiv.

[42] For these statistics, see Kazasov, *Burni godini: 1918-1944,* p. 33. The bourgeois parties received only 233,000 votes, good for 68 seats. The Liberal Party, hitherto the dominant force in Bulgarian politics, was almost wiped out.

[43] Assen Tsankov, "Bulgarien nach dem Umsturz," p. 115; Yotsov, "Upravlenieto na Zemledelskia Sayuz," p. 312. Stamboliski's coalition partners were Bulgaria's two most reactionary parties. In November, 1920, they fused to form the National-Progressive Party. The Nationalists had received 58,000 votes and the Progressive-Liberals 37,000 in August, 1919.

Today the Communist "line" berates Stamboliski for not having formed a united-front government of the four "republican" parties —Peasant, Communist, Socialist, and Radical—after the 1919 elections.[44] At that time, however, the Communists, intoxicated by their vision of the impending world revolutionary explosion, were no more prepared to enter a bourgeois coalition than Stamboliski was to accept them.[45] Only a soviet government would do for them. Were not 119,000 Communist votes—more than twice as many as the Narrow Party had received in 1913—proof that the policy of permanent opposition was bearing fruit? With the Communists in this mood, one only hardened by the Party's startling success in the communal elections of December 7, 1919,[46] it is not surprising that the leadership was tempted to push the great railroad strike of December, 1919-February, 1920, to the limits of insurrection.

On December 25, the Sofia railway men struck in support of wage demands submitted five days earlier. The Communist and Socialist Parties appear to have been momentarily taken by surprise, but on the evening of December 26, a Communist delegation of Nikola Penev and Ivan Bakarjiev informed the Socialists, under whose influence the majority of the railway men stood, that the Communist Party would on the following day proclaim a general strike which the Socialist trade unions were invited and expected to join. The latter agreed and on December 28, all the railway, telegraph, and telephone workers under their control were ordered to strike. A united strike committee consisting of three Socialists and one Communist—a proportion reflecting the two parties' respective degrees of influence over the railway men—was formed.[47] About 20,000 railway, postal, and telegraph workers were involved. Simultaneously the Communists ordered the 13,000 workers in unions under their control to strike.

[44] Kazasov, *Burni godini: 1918-1944*, p. 88.

[45] This was admitted and defended two years later by Kolarov, "Die Taktik der K.P. Bulgariens im Lichte der Ereignisse," p. 257. The Inter-Allied Control Commission would not in any event have tolerated a government including "Bolsheviks."

[46] Though these were but local elections, the Communist vote not only climbed to 140,000, but in the large cities it was nearly double that cast in the national Sobranie elections of August 19. In Sofia, for example, there were 3,758 Communist votes cast in August, 6,031 in December; in Varna, 2,613 in August, 3,849 in December; in Russe, 1,450 in August, 3,224 in December.

[47] The three Socialists were Dimo Kazasov, a politican and journalist, Petar

The reaction of the government was vigorous. Stamboliski returned from Paris on December 26. Five thousand Orange Guards were brought into Sofia, and Daskalov organized an emergency rail service manned by those supporters of the Peasant Union who had served in the army's transport command during the war. Though it was midwinter, the families of the striking railway men were, as in 1906-7, evicted from their state-owned flats. Three thousand railway men were dismissed. Stamboliski was prepared to consider the demand for higher wages to keep up with the spiraling cost of living but not before the cessation of what he regarded as a political strike intended to embarrass and ultimately to overthrow his government. In this position and in all the measures which he took to break the strike, Stamboliski had the support of his cabinet colleagues and of the Inter-Allied Control Commission.

As regards the Communists' intentions, Stamboliski's charge was correct, namely that the strike was political—as every general strike is objectively. He showed them no quarter. The arrest of the strike strategists on their Central Committee was ordered, and Todor Lukanov was caught and imprisoned, though Kolarov, Kabakchiev, and Dimitrov managed to slip underground.[48] The Party press was suppressed. Ten strike "terrorists" were killed.[49]

In the face of these energetic measures the Communist Party leadership lost its nerve and, to the disgust of its militant wing, decided that discretion was the better part of valor. The general strike was called off eight days after it had been declared, and the 13,000 Communist-led workers in private industry ordered to return to their jobs. "Restraint" became the Party's watchword. The railway men remained on strike until February 25, 1920, but the revolutionary momentum of the movement had petered out, and

---

Alekov, an officer of the telegraph and postal workers' union, and Nikola Isaev, a railway man. The Communist was Nikola Penev.

[48] *Le Bulletin communiste,* I, No. 2 (March 18, 1920), 12-13. In connection with violence committed during the strike, 230 railway men were arrested in Sofia, 350 in Plovdiv, and 300 in Plevna. In Plovdiv and Gorna Oryakhovitsa the Communist Party had greater influence over the railway men than in the capital. K. Todorov (*Balkan Firebrand,* p. 131) says that after the conclusion of the strike Dimitrov's wife, Lyuba, came to Todorov to beg that the order for her husband's arrest be rescinded so that he might emerge from hiding. Her request was granted. Todorov was a close friend of Stamboliski.

[49] Kabakchiev, "Die Ereignisse in Bulgarien," p. 88.

the government was master of the situation after the first week.

Though the militant dissidents heaped the burden of blame for the retreat on the shoulders of Anton Ivanov,[50] secretary of the Sofia Party organisation, the Central Committee accepted full responsibility and ever afterward defended the policy of caution by pleading the absence of an objectively revolutionary situation in Bulgaria at the time.[51] Blagoev was a strong advocate of prudence, his constant admonition being "save the movement from provocation." [52] As hopes of international revolution had already faded with the suppression of the Bavarian and Hungarian Communist regimes in 1919 and as Lenin himself was soon to exorcise the "infantile disorder" of left-wing Communism from the body of his movement,[53] the Bulgarian Central Committee's policy of discretion was endorsed by the Comintern against its more militant critics. The latter, numbering about a thousand and led by a certain Ivan Ganchev, broadened their attack into a general crusade against "parliamentarism," which they considered the source of the Central Committee's "softness." They founded a separate "Left" Communist Workers' Party to advance their cause and in April, 1922, joined with German and Dutch groups of the same persuasion to form a new Communist Workers' International, dedicated to pursue the struggle for pure communism against both the allegedly degenerate capitalist West and the corrupted bureaucratic Soviet Union.[54] The vituperative journal of this Bulgarian sect was *Rabot-*

[50] A vitriolic Left Communist attack upon Ivanov was that of Sidarov, "Die Revolutionäre Bewegung in Bulgarien," pp. 565-66.

[51] For the official defense see Kolarov, "Die Taktik der K.P. Bulgariens im Lichte der Ereignisse," p. 259. He accuses the ultraleftists of inability to distinguish between provocation and revolutionary action and of playing into the government's hands by terrorist acts. *The Times* of January 8, 1920, did in fact report the blowing up of a railroad bridge on the Varna-Sofia line in consequence of which 200 suspects were arrested and 4 shot.

The Central Committee was correct in its judgment that no revolutionary situation existed. Isolated violence by Communist extremists could not cloak the fact that the railway men had struck not for political demands but for typical trade-union ones. such as seniority guarantees, easier conditions of work, a cheaper bread ration, and an adjustment of wages. For the original memorandum of demands presented by the strikers, see Kazasov, *Burni godini: 1918-1944*, p. 52.

[52] Klincharov, *Dimitr Blagoev*, p. 278.

[53] Lenin, *"Left-Wing" Communism: An Infantile Disorder* (London, 1920). This pamphlet, which Lenin wrote in April, 1920, was published in May.

[54] Reichenbach, "Zur Geschichte der KAPD," p. 139. See also the pamphlet of this Communist Workers' movement: *Zur Frage der Internationale.*

nicheska Iskra (Labor Spark) which survived at least until the spring of 1923 and perhaps longer.[55]

The strike and its aftermath also resulted in a leftward swing in the Broad Socialist Party. In June, 1920, the Socialist Party Congress decided by 140 votes against 125 to disaffiliate from the Socialist International as a form of pressure to bring about a reconciliation between it and the Communist International.[56] Earlier, in February, when the passions of the strike and resentment against Stamboliski's policy of force were still hot, the Socialist Party's Central Committee had approached the Communists with an offer of common action leading to unification.[57] The Bulgarian Communists replied in a memorandum of February 29, 1920, that unity could take place only within the Comintern and after the expulsion of those who were then leaders of the Socialist Party, especially of Pastukhov, the former Minister of the Interior.[58] These terms were rejected by a vote of 106 to 28 at a special Socialist Party congress in October.[59] The next Communist move—later to be standard procedure—was to split the Socialist Party by requiring those within it who were prepared to accept the Communist terms to secede and pass over to the Communist Party. This occurred in Bulgaria in October, 1920,[60] the same month in which Zinoviev split the Unabhängige Sozial-demokratische Partei Deutschlands (USPD) at Halle[61] and three months before the Bulgarian Khristo Kabakchiev and the Hungarian Matyas Rákosi were to splinter the Italian Socialist Party at Leghorn.[62] The leaders of the new converts to Communism were none other than Nikola Sakarov, the former Progressive Socialist

[55] An incomplete file of *Rabotnicheska Iskra* is available at the Internationaal In-stituut voor Sociale Geschiedenis in Amsterdam. The last issue there is Volume III, No. 6, of March, 1923. It was published in Varna.

[56] Kazasov, *Burni godini: 1918-1944*, p. 68. The account of the abortive attempt to reunite the two Internationals is: *The Second and Third Internationals and the Vienna Union: Official Report of the Conference between the Executives Held at the Reichstag, Berlin, on 2nd April 1922 and Following Days.* In May, 1923, the would-be mediators of the "2½ International" rejoined the Socialist International.

[57] *Narod*, February 23, 1920. The offer was debated at the Communist Party's Party Council session of February 27-29, 1920.

[58] *Balgarskata Komunisticheska Partia v Rezolyutsii i Reshenia*, II, 58-63.

[59] *The American Labor Year Book, 1921-1922*, p. 250.

[60] *Rote Fahne*, No. 239, November 20, 1920. See also Zinoviev, "Die Lage in der Kommunistischen Internationale," p. 566.

[61] See Zinoviev, *Twelve Days in Germany.*

[62] See Kabakchiev, *Die Gründung der Kommunistischen Partei Italiens.* Kabakchiev had learned the technique at Halle, whither he had accompanied Zinoviev.

rebel against Blagoev in 1908 and ultrapatriot at Stockholm in 1917, and Georgi Bakalov, the smuggler of *Iskra* into Russia and Liberal Socialist defector from the Narrow Party in 1905.[63] Their cohorts probably numbered fewer than 2,000, of whom many were industrial workers. The Socialist Party of Sakazov and Pastukhov, left with only 8,000 members,[64] was never again able, despite its subsequent recovery in numbers, to match the Communist Party's political power. The latter henceforth considered the Socialist Party a corpse and did not bother to apply to it the united-front line adopted by the Enlarged Plenum of the Executive Committee of the Communist International in February, 1922. Only after the bourgeois *coup d'état* of June, 1923, did the Communists address frantic but vain appeals to the Socialists for common action to overthrow the new government.

Stamboliski's reaction to the collapse of the strike was to seize the moment of his triumph to consolidate his power. The Sobranie was dissolved on February 20, 1920, and elections scheduled for March 28. Prutkin, the irresponsible Sofia police chief, did his bit to evoke an atmosphere of fear and terror by arranging the dynamiting on March 3 of the Odeon Theater when it was packed with political and cultural leaders attending a lecture by a Russian sociologist. Five people were killed and many injured.[65] Throughout the country the opposition parties' meetings were assaulted. The extremist agrarian Daskalov, who had replaced the Socialist Pastukhov as Minister of the Interior, replied to protests in the Sobranie against this campaign of intimidation with a cynical "We beat and shall continue to beat; we imprison and shall continue to imprison." [66]

The elections indicated that the pendulum was still swinging

---

[63] Yotsov, "Upravlenieto na Zemledelskia Sayuz," p. 251. A colleague was Genko Krastev, also a heretic of 1908.

[64] *The American Labor Year Book, 1921-1922*, p. 250. The number of those who followed Sakarov and Bakalov into the Communist Party is nowhere stated. A rough estimate can be made on the basis of a comparison of the number of members represented at the second and third congresses of the Communist Party in June, 1920, and May, 1921, which were, respectively, 35,478 and 37,191. See *Balgarskata Komunisticheska Partia v Rezolyutsii i Reshenia*, II, 66 and 93. The resulting figure will, however, be highly speculative for the turnover in Communist Party membership was considerable, and new adherents quite distinct from Socialist defectors were being constantly recruited.

[65] Kazasov, *Burni godini: 1918-1944*, p. 63.

[66] Quoted in Buchan, *The Nations of Today: Bulgaria and Romania*, p. 153.

toward the two extremist parties, the Peasants and Communists, who between them received almost 60 percent of the votes. From a total of 894,000 ballots cast, the share of the former was 347,000 and that of the latter 182,000. No other party polled more than 100,000 votes, the Socialists' declining to 55,000 while the five bourgeois parties shared the remaining 310,000.[67] That the Peasant Union would emerge as the largest party had been a foregone conclusion— only twice since the Liberation had the government party managing the electoral machinery failed to win. Yet the extent of its triumph was imposing. To guarantee victory, Stamboliski had made voting compulsory, thus ensuring that the politically ignorant and indifferent peasants who might otherwise not have voted cast ballots for him.[68] He could also count on the "dowry" of Moslem votes which invariably went to the government party.

Despite these stratagems, the Peasant Union's 39 percent of the total vote failed to provide that parliamentary majority which would have enabled Stamboliski to dispense with a coalition. His party received 110 seats in a Sobranie of 229. The Communist vote entitled the Party to 50 seats, a gain of only 3 over the previous Sobranie though its poll had risen by half—from 119,000 to 182,000. The Socialist Party's seats fell from 36 to 9 while the combined bourgeois representation was cut from 68 to 60. Nothing daunted, Stamboliski forcibly fashioned a majority by arbitrarily canceling 13 opposition seats and refusing to fill them through by-elections. Of the ejected deputies, 9 were Communists, 3 Democrats, and 1 a Nationalist.[69] Thenceforth Stamboliski ruled through a single-party government, convinced that the overwhelmingly peasant character of the country justified any and all measures to ensure his permanent rule.

Realizing that Stamboliski could not be overthrown by a scattered opposition, the bourgeois parties formed a Constitutional Bloc in 1921 to achieve this purpose. Fearing that he would never permit himself to be ousted by legal means, certain leaders of these parties

[67] *Ibid.*, p. 153, for the complete statistics. The Socialist vote receded to that polled by the Broad Party in 1913, whereas the Communist was four times the Narrow total of that year.

[68] For details of Stamboliski's alterations of the electoral regulations, see Vandervelde, *Les Balkans et la paix,* p. 51, and Assen Tsankov, "Bulgarien nach dem Umsturz," p. 115. Heretofore, at the most 60-70 percent of the electorate had voted.

[69] Yotsov, "Upravlenieto na Zemledelskia Sayuz," p. 249.

entered into collaboration with the reserve army officers, who despised Stamboliski for his acceptance of those terms of the Neuilly Treaty which limited the Bulgarian army to 20,000 men, and with IMRO, which hated him for his policy of friendship with Yugoslavia, and began planning to overthrow his government by a *coup d'état*. It was assumed that the success of such an enterprise would be greatly facilitated by—indeed, might even depend upon—the cooperation of the second most powerful armed body then in Bulgaria, namely, the 20,000-man remnant of Wrangel's White Russian Army which had been settled in Bulgaria. In such a coup the policy of the Communist Party might also be decisive.

In November, 1920, the Red Army had broken into the Crimea and the White Armies of General Wrangel were withdrawn, to be dispersed throughout the Balkans. Approximately 6,700 officers and 12,500 men were evacuated to Bulgaria where they maintained their organization and retained their 25,000 rifles and 156 machine guns, which, in view of the military clauses of the Treaty of Neuilly, made them virtually as strong a force as Bulgaria's own army.[70] The arrival of these contingents, commanded by General Kutepov, was met in late December, 1920, by mass protest demonstrations organized by the Communist Party.[71] Just as the Communists were prepared to resort to any and all means to bring about the disintegration or expulsion of this army which had fought against Lenin's regime in Russia, so many of the White officers were willing to use their units in any venture directed against "bolshevism"—the term in which Stamboliski's government was described to them by the bourgeois politicians.

Toward the end of March, 1922, the Communist Party obtained documents taken from the former Russian embassy, where Wrangel's staff had established itself, indicating that the White officers were engaged in intrigue with Bulgarian bourgeois politicians to overthrow Stamboliski by force. On March 26 and 30 the Party organized more protest demonstrations.[72] A few days later, on April 3, the (Soviet) Ukrainian Commissariat for Foreign Affairs protested to the Bulgarian government against the activities of the White

[70] Kazasov, *Burni godini: 1918-1944*, p. 93.
[71] See the report of the Bulgarian Communist Party to the Second Comintern Congress in July, 1920, in *Die Kommunistische Internationale*, No. 15 (1921), p. 470.
[72] Tsonev and Vladimirov, *Sentyabr'skoe vosstanie v Balgarii 1923 goda*, p. 60.

officers in Bulgaria. Stamboliski, convinced that the Communist allegations were true, expelled 150 of the officers, including General Kutepov, whereupon in mid-May, Wrangel, then in Belgrade, warned Stamboliski that this action had brought close "the specter of struggle" between the White Russian Army and Stamboliski's Bulgarian supporters.[73] Nevertheless, with the backing of the Inter-Allied Control Commission supervising the application of the Neuilly Treaty, Stamboliski persevered and confiscated most of the arms of the Wrangelite contingents.

On April 12 and 13 the Communist Party Council had met in Sofia to discuss, among other items, this episode, then approaching a climax. A resolution was adopted stressing that the Communist Party must oppose every attempt at a bourgeois coup, even though it be directed only against the Peasant government. Significantly, however, this resolution was kept secret so that Stamboliski should be uncertain of Communist policy. It was felt that the Party's reaction to a clash between Stamboliski and the bourgeois parties was its ace, not to be revealed before the critical moment.[74] The public statement issued by the Party on May 16 warned against the imminent danger of another attempt at a bourgeois-military coup but, instead of offering to collaborate with the Peasant Union to ward off this threat, simply called upon all "right-thinking" ele-

[73] Kazasov, *Burni godini: 1918-1944*, p. 92. The Communist Party subsequently organized a campaign to persuade the enlisted men of the Wrangel Army to return to Russia. A Soviet Red Cross Mission of three hundred men came to Bulgaria to organize the repatriation of those willing to return. After the overthrow of Stamboliski, the Tsankov government expelled this mission on the grounds that it engaged in espionage. Chicherin's protests were rejected. For a bizarre account of these alleged espionage activities, see Bashmakov, *Mémoire sur le mouvement communiste en Bulgarie durant les années 1921 et 1922.* After the expulsion of the Mission and the rejection of Chicherin's protests (see *The Times,* July 23 and September 17, 1923) the Nansen Office of the League of Nations took over the repatriation and welfare work. In May, 1926, it reported 30,000 Russian refugees still in Bulgaria, of whom 14,400 were gainfully employed. U. Timescu, "Die Flüchtlingsfrage in Bulgarien vor dem Völkerbund," *Inprekorr,* VI, No. 82 (June 8, 1926), 1310.

[74] The resolution was first published in 1924 by Kolarov, "Die Taktik der K. P. Bulgariens im Lichte der Ereignisse," p. 265. It is reprinted in *Balgarskata Komunistischeska Partia v Rezolyutsii i Reshenia,* II, 160-61. The fact that the Communist Party took this affair so seriously as to discuss it in such great secrecy casts doubt on the claim of Stamboliski's colleague Kosta Todorov (*Balkan Firebrand,* p. 185) that the entire "Wrangelite plot" was a Communist forgery "planted" with the assistance of Stancho Trifonov, assistant chief of the Sofia police. Todorov is, however, careful to state that the alleged forgery was the work of the Russian Red Cross Mission itself. Such a Mission would, of course, keep the Bulgarian Communist leaders in ignorance of its clandestine activities. The truth will probably never be known.

ments in the Union to desert Stamboliski for the Communist Party.[75]

The psychological effect upon both the Communist and the Peasant leaders of this "Wrangelite plot" incident, combined with that of the near-lynching and subsequent imprisonment of the leading bourgeois politicians in September, was deep and disastrous. Each group chose to regard the cumulative results of these two episodes as evidence that the bourgeois parties' strength had been irretrievably undermined, that the balance of power in Bulgaria henceforth rested with itself, and that the chief obstacle to the consolidation of this power was the other of these two extremist parties. When Kolarov approached Daskalov after the Dolni Dabnik riot to ask that the Communist Party be armed by the government and was refused, both negotiators used the alleged "bourgeois danger" purely as a pretext, both felt that it was already secondary and that the real battle would be with each other, and both probably knew that these were the thoughts of the other.

The Communists, ever ready to draw dubious parallels with Russian events, persuaded themselves that in the "Wrangel affair" they had rescued the Bulgarian Kerenski from a Kornilov putsch.[76] Since, by definition of the precedent cited, Kornilov was more powerful and dangerous than Kerenski, the policy of opposing a bourgeois coup recommended in the Party Council's secret resolution of April 13 was logical. When in the autumn, however, Stamboliski and Daskalov declined to play Kerenski and shook the Communists out of their "Russian" dreams by proceeding against the "danger from the right" without appealing for their aid, the Communist leaders were confused and alarmed. Already on September 18 the *Rabotnicheski Vestnik* had protested against the Orange Guard's ruthlessness at Dolni Dabnik on the previous day,[77] and in the following weeks the conviction hardened among the Communist leaders that the main threat came no longer from the supposedly weakening bourgeois parties and military groups but was represented by Stamboliski himself. Orthodox balance-of-power

[75] Vasilev, *Vaorazhenata saprotivata sreshtu fashizma v Balgaria*, p. 38.

[76] See the "Introduction," by Kolarov to Trotsky and Kabakchiev, *Ocherki Politicheskoi Bolgarii*, p. 4, where the claim is made that the Communist Party had rescued Stamboliski. The Kerenski-Kornilov comparison appears constantly not only in Bulgarian Communist propaganda but as often in the remarks of the leading Russian Communists on Bulgarian developments.

[77] Kazasov, *Burni godini: 1918-1944*, p. 111.

theory now dictated that the Communists favor any small third force opposing the Peasant colossus, and when in December, 1922, Stamboliski's government was embarrassed by a successful IMRO raid upon the town of Kyustendil, the Communists cheered,[78] little realizing that they, like Stamboliski himself, greatly exaggerated his power and underestimated that of the now semiunderground bourgeois and revisionist forces. This crystallization of the Communist attitude toward Stamboliski, which was to prove so fateful to both in June, 1923, was the terminus of a constantly weaving ideological path, the twists and turns of which were dictated by the Bulgarian Communist leaders' periodic appraisals of the strength of their party as well as by variations in the official line of the Comintern in Moscow.

Numerically, the Communist Party, after a spectacular initial expansion, continued to grow slowly throughout the Stamboliski era. Its membership, however, was hardly proletarian in character as is shown in the following list, giving by years the number of members and, respectively, the number of "wage workers" among them: [79]

Year	Number of Members	Number of "Wage Workers"
1919	21,577	9,281
1920	35,478	11,177
1921	37,191	10,654
1922	38,036	12,546
1923	39,000	12,000

The Party's electoral fortunes prospered not only in the Sobranie

[78] The Communist Party's reaction to this event is candidly discussed by Vladimirov, "Zum 15. Jahrestag des Septemberaufstandes in Bulgarien," p. 1038. The raid was intended as a warning to Stamboliski to desist from his policy of *rapprochement* with Yugoslavia. The Bulgarian army had probably connived at the raid and in any event did not resist it. The IMRO units withdrew on the arrival of Stamboliski's Orange Guard, who used the occasion to terrorize Sofia to such an extent that the diplomatic corps protested. Ancel, "La Politique bulgare: Union Paysanne et Entente Démocratique," p. 301; Kazasov, *Burni godini: 1918-1944*, p. 113.

[79] These are the statistics presented by the Central Committee to the annual summer congress of the Party. They refer to Party membership at the beginning of the respective year. The category of "hired workers" (*naemni rabotnitsi*) unfortunately lumps together industrial and agricultural proletarians as well as salaried employees. See *Balgarskata Komunisticheska Partia v Rezolyutsii i Reshenia*, II, 1, 66, 93, 167. Another source states that the number of genuine industrial proletarians who belonged to the Party in 1922 was only 1,563. Pandov, *Grazhdanskata voina*, p. 100. The figures for 1923 were prepared for the congress of that year, which never met owing to the *coup d'état*, and were published in: *From the Fourth to the Fifth World Congress: Report of the ECCI*, p. 44.

but also in municipal and departmental elections to which other parties paid less attention. In the municipal elections of December, 1919, the Communists scored a striking victory,[80] and the town and village elections of October, 1920, once again revealed that, though the Peasant Union could easily outdistance the Communists, no third force came within shouting distance.[81] The Communists had won control of 22 municipal and 65 village councils. Stamboliski, however, simply dissolved them and scheduled new elections for 1921.[82] After these the Communist Party controlled 9 municipal and 104 village councils, and a total of 3,623 Communists sat on such councils throughout the country.[83]

The Party's literary and "front" activities were also thriving. In the summer of 1922 the circulation figures of some of its thirteen publications were: [84]

Rabotnicheski Vestnik (Workers' Newspaper), general, daily	25,000
Novo Vreme (New Time), theoretical, semimonthly	5,000
Selski Vestnik (Village Newspaper), special paper for the peasants	12,000
Ravenstvo (Equality), for women	10,000
Mladezh (Youth), weekly for the young	14,000
Bratstvo (Brotherhood), for the Jews	1,400
Nov Svyat (New World), for the Armenians	1,000
Osvobozhdenie (Liberation), for the Macedonians	500
Cherven Smyakh (Red Laughter), humor	4,000

Between 1919 and the end of 1922 the Party publishing house had issued 1,500,000 copies of Communist books and brochures—both translations and original works.[85] These well-organized activities were made possible by a subsidy from Moscow which,

[80] See p. 97, footnote 46.

[81] As reported in the *New York Times* of November 28, 1920, the Ministry of the Interior issued the statement that the total number of votes cast were 100,811, of which 52,097 were for the Peasant Union, 29,992 for the Communist Party, 2,711 for the Socialist Party, and 16,011 for the bourgeois parties.

[82] *Le Bulletin communiste*, III, No. 24 (June 8, 1922), 456; Dimitrov, *Politicheski otchet na Ts. K. na BRP(k)*, p. 19.

[83] T. Lukanov, "Die Lage der K.P.B.," *Inprekorr*, II, No. 158 (August 10, 1922), 1016. Three cities in which the Communists were particularly strong and in which they controlled the municipal government for several years were Varna, Burgas, and Samokov (known as the "Samokov commune").

[84] Ibid., p. 1016. In view of the presence of thousands of indigenous and refugee Macedonians in Bulgaria, the low subscription to *Osvobozhdenie* is striking. There was also a paper for the Turkish-speaking minority with a circulation of 1,800.

[85] Kabakchiev, "Die Lage in Bulgarien und die K.P.B.," *Inprekorr*, II, No. 216 (November 9, 1922), 1527.

according to one agrarian politician in close touch with the Communists, amounted to twenty million leva annually.[86]

Much attention was paid to "front" organizations, of which the General Trade Union Federation with 29,000 members in 1922 [87] was the most important. Special Communist organizations of refugees, of war veterans, and of reserve and noncommissioned officers were formed. The Party's cooperative Osvobozhdenie (Liberation) grew from 13,560 at the time of the 1920 Party Congress to 57,000 when that of 1922 assembled.[88] Propagandizing and organizing the young was considered particularly important. By the end of 1921 the Communist Youth League had 13,216 members and a year later 15,000.[89]

The considerable Communist electoral successes in the villages, the relatively large numbers of peasants who joined the Party, and the strong sale of *Selski Vestnik* encouraged the Party leaders to dream of weaning the peasantry from Stamboliski and bringing it under their own influence. A party founded, shaped, and led by Blagoev would have been unlikely to develop a sober policy toward the peasant movement and the agrarian government even if it had not been further handicapped by Moscow's imposition of the unrealistic kulak-middle-poor peasant typology and quixotic injunction to "take the class struggle into the villages" in a country without great landlords. Between the tradition of Blagoev's mania for "proletarian purity" on the one hand and on the other the Comintern's fatuous instruction, imposed until the Fourth World Congress in November, 1922, to detach the peasant masses from Stamboliski's influence and bring them under Communist control, the Bulgarian Communist Party's peasant policy fell into ineffectiveness.[90]

The Comintern instructions were applied with vigorous crudity. From the first meeting of the Party Council in September, 1919,

---

[86] K. Todorov, *Balkan Firebrand*, p. 179.

[87] Lukanov, "Die Lage in der K.P.B.," *Inprekorr*, II, No. 158 (August 10, 1922), 1016.

[88] "Bericht der K.P. Bulgariens," p. 472 and Lukanov, "Die Lage in der K.P.B.," *Inprekorr*, II, No. 158 (August 10, 1922), 1016.

[89] Lukanov, "Die Lage in der K.P.B.," *Inprekorr*, II, No. 158 (August 10, 1922), 1016, and Kolarov, "Die Taktik der K.P. Bulgariens im Lichte der Ereignisse," p. 254.

[90] Only Vasil Kolarov dared to reproach the Comintern with at least partial responsibility for this failure and even his censure is phrased very obliquely. See his "Die Taktik der K.P. Bulgariens im Lichte der Ereignisse," p. 261.

after Stamboliski's electoral victory of the preceding month, through every subsequent Party Congress and Council session the endless refrain went up that Stamboliski represented but the kulak element, that his radicalism was fraudulent, or only the reflection of a reactionary utopianism, that he had been installed in power by the old ruling classes as a sop to popular resentment against their disastrous war policy and as a fig leaf behind which they could hide until the storm of the people's righteous anger had blown over. After the riots of September, 1922, and the subsequent imprisonment of the bourgeois politicians, a new stanza was added explaining this clash between the alleged peasant puppet and his bourgeois masters as a reflection of the decision of the latter to resume power openly since Stamboliski had failed in his assigned task of destroying the Communist Party. The "Radomir line" was taken up again with the assertion that Stamboliski's "is and remains a government of the village bourgeoisie," in the outcome of whose struggle with the urban bourgeoisie the class-conscious toiling peasantry has as little stake as the proletariat and its Communist Party.[91] This in effect canceled the proposed policy of the secret memorandum of April 13, 1922.

The Communist attempt to pry the peasants away from Stamboliski could not but fail. The charge of "kulakism" leveled at the Peasant Union made no impression.[92] No more successful was the Communist attempt to play on the patriotic string of resentment against the traitor Stamboliski, who allegedly had thrown away at Neuilly the national aspirations of Bulgaria and transformed her into a colony of Britain and France.[93]

Shortly after the critical events of September, 1922, in Bulgaria, the Russian Communist leaders decided that the generalization of the New Economic Policy (NEP) on the international level required the adoption by the Comintern of the slogan "Workers' and Peasants' Government," which they then imposed upon the Fourth

[91] Kabakchiev, "Die Letzten Ereignisse in Bulgarien," *Inprekorr*, II, No. 197 (October 10, 1922), 1319.
[92] In 1921 the membership of the Peasant Union consisted of 3,268 landless peasants; 97,798 peasants owning up to 5 hectares (12.5 acres) of land; 27,176 peasants owning between 5 and 10 hectares; 3,839 peasants owning more than 10 hectares.
[93] Resolutions passed at the various congresses. See *Balgarskata Komunisticheska Partia v Rezolyutsii i Reshenia*, II, *passim*.

World Congress of the Comintern in November, 1922.[94] The Bulgarian Party leaders had by now, however, convinced themselves that the campaign to undermine Stamboliski's control of the peasantry could, with a little extra effort, be carried to success. In any event, they reasoned, a "worker and peasant" party alliance made sense only where both classes were faced by a strong reactionary movement. In Bulgaria, however, this had been eliminated in September, 1922, and Stamboliski was now, in fact, the greatest threat to the Communist Party which therefore could not ally itself with him. The Bulgarian Communist leaders, pleading unique circumstances, declined to apply Moscow's new united front policy "from above," that is, in the form of an agreement between the leaders of the two parties, and insisted upon implementing it only "from below," which meant simply to continue the attempts to subvert Stamboliski's control of the peasants by appealing to local Peasant Union cells to transfer their allegiance to the Communist Party's Central Committee. Such was the explicit decision of the Party Council session of January 21-22, 1923, summoned to discuss the new Comintern line.[95]

Thus the Communists' underestimation, after September, 1922, of the strength of the urban bourgeois forces, their fear of Stamboliski, and their exaggerated notion of their own influence over the peasantry, and therefore of their power to decide the outcome of any political crisis,[96] combined to set the stage for the disastrous neutrality policy of June 9, 1923, when the Communist leaders greeted the overthrow of Stamboliski with almost spiteful glee and instructed their followers not to resist the imposition of the Tsankov dictatorship. The Communist leaders refused to believe that any

---

[94] For the background to this development see Borkenau, *The Communist International,* pp. 221-31.

[95] For the resolution adopted by the Council see *Balgarskata Komunisticheska Partia v Rezolyutsii i Reshenia,* II, 248-51. This policy was strongly defended by Kabakchiev in Trotsky and Kabakchiev, *Ocherki politicheskoi Bolgarii,* pp. 187-200. The Comintern leaders did not publicly object to it until after the overthrow of Stamboliski, when they criticised it severely. See *From the Fourth to the Fifth World Congress: Report of the ECCI,* p. 45.

[96] The Party Council of April 25-26, 1923, for example, called upon the toilers of town and village to be prepared at the decisive moment to strike against both the urban and rural bourgeois parties, to seize power, and thereupon to establish a Workers' and Peasants' Government. See *Balgarskata Komunisticheska Partia v Rezolyutsii i Reshenia,* II, 261.

government could be more repressive than Stamboliski's. They were quickly to learn otherwise.

Stamboliski himself also misread the political situation in Bulgaria in the spring of 1923. Like the Communists, he entertained an inflated impression of his own strength and considered it sufficiently great to warrant simultaneous crusades against both the bourgeois remnant and the Communists in an ultimate effort to institute the agrarian millenium in Bulgaria. An appreciation of his position in the fateful months before the June cataclysm requires some familiarity with the oscillations of his policy toward the Communists in his years of power.

Stamboliski, like Mustafa Kemal, pretended to accept Moscow's assurances that the Soviet State and the Communist International were completely distinct political entities and that the former had no control over and could not accept responsibility for the actions of the latter. This fiction enabled Stamboliski to be on friendly terms with the Soviet Union while claiming a free hand in his dealings with the Bulgarian Communist Party. Though sufficiently aware of his defeated country's dependence upon the goodwill of France and Britain to heed their warnings not to recognize the Bolshevik government, Stamboliski still took care to demonstrate to the Soviet leaders his anxiety not to be counted among their enemies.[97] He granted permission for a Soviet Red Cross Mission to come to Bulgaria to seek to persuade the Wrangelite troops to be repatriated, and at the Genoa Conference he had several talks with Rakovski which suspicious Western observers viewed as ominous indications of an alliance.[98] Though such fears, if real, were vain, Stamboliski, as the theorist of East European "agrarianism," did believe that the best policy for the Central and Eastern European peasant states was one of balance between the industrial West and the Bolshevik East, both alien to "peasantism." Indeed, in its diplomatic aspect, his pride and joy, the Green International, was intended to be an entente of peasant states able to hold their own against both Russia and the West through united action.

<hr />

[97] That this was understood in Moscow is indicated by Louis Fischer, *The Soviets in World Affairs*, II, 516. In 1921 Stamboliski sent wheat to alleviate the Russian famine.
[98] *Daily Telegraph*, June 7, 1922. For Stamboliski's denial that he had concluded a secret pact with the Russians at Genoa, see *The Observer*, June 18, 1922.

The large extent to which his regime rested on the good will of Britain and France, where he initially enjoyed high regard for his frequently reiterated determination to fulfill the terms of the Neuilly Treaty, also introduced an element of ambivalence into Stamboliski's policy toward the Bulgarian Communists. On his frequent trips to the West he assured the journalists of France and England that "peasantism" was the greatest barrier to the spread of Bolshevism in the Balkans [99] and promised the statesmen to take more vigorous action to suppress the Bulgarian Communist Party.[100] Once home, however, he always relented, influenced perhaps by his more radical advisers and certainly by his naïve conviction that any group of men as strongly "antibourgeois" and "antiparasite" as were the Communists could not be altogether evil. Did not Communism, despite its disordered principles, at least have the energy to fight bourgeois decadence? Stamboliski was fond of saying that in his opinion only two interesting social experiments had been attempted in modern Europe—his own and Lenin's—and that if he were ever forced to relinquish power, he would hand it over to the Communists who would at least keep Bulgaria in a state of revolution.[101] Even their addled proletarian-industrialist theories seem initially to have aroused in Stamboliski only that pitying indulgence toward the Communists which is usually shown toward backward children or well-meaning eccentrics. They were "school-boys [who] . . . having read too many pamphlets," could always be usefully manipulated as shock troops against the bourgeoisie.[102] The Communists, however, had only to attempt to undermine his authority in the villages and to seek to break his control of the peasants for Stamboliski's benevolent toleration to turn into fierce resentment. When the Communist Party received 230,000 votes out of a total of 994,000 in the local departmental elections of January 14, 1923, many of which were polled in the villages, he decided to smash it.[103]

[99] *Manchester Guardian,* October 11, 1920; *La Revue Internationale,* February, 1922, pp. 87-88.

[100] Collins, "Bulgaria," p. 705.

[101] Gentizon, "Stamboulisky et le peuple bulgare," pp. 598, 600.

[102] Quoted in the *Morning Post,* April 14, 1923. In the fight against the bourgeoisie, he said, the Communists were his "faithful hounds." See Logio, *Bulgaria: Past and Present,* p. 444.

[103] Kabakchiev, "Ein Neuer Erfolg der K.P.B.," *Inprekorr,* III, No. 26 (February 9, 1923), 201. Stamboliski's Peasant Union received 437,000 votes. His speeches indicate that he was already considering measures against the Communists in the previous sum-

After the Dolni Dabnik riots of the previous September the Communists were in any event no longer necessary to him as a club with which to beat the bourgeoisie. Accordingly, the campaign preceding the municipal elections of February 11, 1923, was marked by acts of Orange Guard terror against the Communist Party in which the Communist mayor of Dupnitsa, a certain Kosta Petrov, was murdered. The Communist Party nevertheless recaptured control of Samokov, Lom, Dupnitsa, Kalofer, Yambol, Nova Zagora, Gorna Djumaya, and a score of lesser towns.[104] Stamboliski now decided, once and for all, to crush this nuisance as well as all other opposition in the Sobranie elections scheduled for April. On December 15, 1922, an attempt had been made, probably by IMRO, on the life of his favorite colleague, Daskalov, followed on January 28, 1923, by one on Tsanko Bakalov, the Minister of Public Works and a leader of the Orange Guard, and on February 5 by one on Stamboliski himself. All three were unsuccessful.[105]

Stamboliski prepared for the Sobranie elections of April 22, 1923, by purging the Peasant Union of its moderate wing, led by Turlakov and Tomov, the Ministers, respectively, of Finance and War.[106] The campaign proceeded in an atmosphere of considerable intimidation, of which these erstwhile colleagues were the victims equally with the Communist and bourgeois parties. Stamboliski let it be known that after his victory—a foregone conclusion—the property of those peasants who had voted for the Communist Party would be confiscated.[107] His Minister of Justice demanded that the Orange Guard break up Communist meetings and beat up the speakers, assuring the Guard that they would not be prosecuted. Kolarov, Gabrovski, and other Communist deputies were jailed during the

---

mer. Thus he announced early in September, 1922, that he might apply to the Bulgarian Communists Lenin's methods of dealing with opposition parties. Cf. Kazasov, *Burni godini: 1918-1944*, p. 101.

[104] Kabakchiev, "Die Bürgerliche Reaktion in Bulgarien," *Inprekorr*, III, No. 43 (March 9, 1923), 320.

[105] The opposition claimed that the attempt to assassinate Stamboliski in the National Theater on February 5 was a sham arranged to give Stamboliski a pretext for new measures against the opposition. See Kazasov, *Burni godini: 1918-1944*, p. 119.

[106] *The Times*, March 2, 1923. Relations within Stamboliski's cabinet had long been strained, and charges of attempted mutual assassinations were levied. Once Minister of Education Omarchevski threatened Stamboliski with a revolver during a cabinet discussion. See *The Times*, March 15, 1923, and Logio, *Bulgaria: Past and Present*, p. 443.

[107] *The Times*, April 12, 1923, quoting a speech by Stamboliski of April 10.

campaign.[108] The electoral law was again altered, this time proportional representation being abolished, and voting was again made compulsory in order to mobilize the inert peasants behind the government. The votes in the election were as follows: [109] Peasant Union, 569,000; Communist Party, 204,000; Socialist Party, 28,000; bourgeois parties, 275,000.

The Communist percentage of the total vote had remained roughly stationary since March, 1920, but in consequence of the new electoral law the Party's representation fell from 50 [110] to 16 deputies. The Socialists received 2 places, the bourgeois parties 15, and Stamboliski filled 212 of the 245 seats with his own Peasant Unionists, though his party's share of the vote was only 53 percent.[111]

Stamboliski now lost all sense of political reality and felt himself strong enough, by virtue of his unchallengeable control of the Sobranie, to proceed against all other political institutions and inaugurate the final drive for the establishment of the agrarian Arcadia in Bulgaria. Rumors circulated that a constitutional convention would be convoked to declare a republic, or at least to deprive the king of real authority.[112] On May 6, a fortnight after the elections, a reshuffle of army commands took place, and, to add insult to the officers' injury, a column of mounted Orange Guards commanded by Tsanko Bakalov paraded through Sofia.[113] Two days later, on May 8, a number of Macedonian organizations were declared illegal, their journals confiscated, and their leaders arrested.[114] On May 9, it was announced that a Peasant Union rally would be held in Sofia in September at which 200,000 participants would be "guarded" against the city's population by 10,000 mounted

[108] O. Stiglic, "Parlamentswahlen in Bulgarien unter dem Weissen Terror," *Inprekorr*, III, No. 79 (May 14, 1923), 671-72.

[109] Kazasov, *Burni godini: 1918-1944*, p. 127.

[110] This was actually reduced to 41 after Stamboliski's arbitrary invalidation of 9 Communist Sobranie mandates. See p. 102.

[111] *The Near East*, May 31, 1923. Among those elected were the still imprisoned ex-Premiers Malinov and Danev.

[112] Swire, *Bulgarian Conspiracy*, p. 156. Stamboliski's actions and attitude toward King Boris had always been highhanded. For some examples, see Kennedy, "A Peasant Statesman," p. 181. See also the slighting remarks about the King in Stamboliski's speech to the Peasant Union congress in 1922, quoted in the *Daily Telegraph*, June 6, 1922.

[113] Kazasov, *Burni godini: 1918-1944*, p. 131.

[114] *The Times*, May 9, 1923. This action had been preceded by the signing on March 23 of the Nish Convention for joint Bulgarian-Yugoslav action against the Macedonian border raiders. It was to come into force on May 12.

Orange Guards and an equal number on foot armed with pikes. This ominous bulletin was followed on May 15 by an editorial in Stamboliski's paper, *Zemedelsko Zname*, warning that if a single peasant participant came to harm at the rally, Sofia would be surrounded and starved out.[115] Though this threat was rather hysterical, the depredations of the Orange Guard in Sofia during the previous December on the occasion of the expulsion of IMRO from Kyustendil and the record of police provocations made it anything but idle. On May 13, Stamboliski predicted that while other parties would come and go, his regime would last for decades.[116] The bourgeois parties, the Crown, the army, and the powerful Macedonians saw themselves threatened with annihilation by this peasant, whose removal from office by constitutional electoral procedures had become impossible after the elections of April, 1923. The stage was set for the violent upheaval of June 9. When that moment came, the Communists had also been alienated. Acting from sheer resentment and political myopia, they refused to come to Stamboliski's aid. Like him, they underestimated the bourgeoisie's power and overestimated the significance of the election statistics.

Stamboliski could not forgive the Communists their considerable inroads upon the peasant vote[117] or their boast that in a crisis their own authority in the villages would be greater than his. If he expected a *coup d'état* it was less from the bourgeois than from the Communist quarter and when early in May, 1923, a Soviet ship was caught running arms from Odessa to Varna, Stamboliski's fears were confirmed, and he pounced on the Party. The entire leadership in Varna was arrested and the Party members of a number of towns brutally beaten. Throughout the country Communist functionaries were arrested.[118] Now Stamboliski thought himself free of all dangers and dismissed the Communists as "toothless bears."[119]

Stamboliski's position was in fact far weaker than he or the Communists realized, for it rested only on the ill-armed Orange Guard, which could not compete in power or mobility with the

---

[115] Kazasov, *Burni godini: 1918-1944*, p. 133.

[116] *Ibid.*, p. 132.

[117] A leading Communist estimated that 75 percent of the Communist votes in the elections of April, 1923, were cast by peasants. See Kabakchiev, "Glavnie etapi i osobenosti razvitia fashizma v Bolgarii," p. 45.

[118] *The Times*, May 18, 1923.

[119] Quoted in the *Daily Herald*, May 16, 1923.

army, quartered in the towns. Every other political institution or force had been antagonized. Mesmerized by the fact that 80 percent of the population of the country consisted of "his" peasants, Stamboliski, with a purely arithmetical appreciation of power, assumed that this figure automatically provided both the justification and the guarantee of his agrarian dictatorship. The bourgeois parties were miserable exploiters in his eyes, and the Communists, though recognized as a "left" party, were ideologically suspect for their theory of industrialism and socialism in opposition to ruralism and private property, and they were considered particularly dangerous as opponents whose ruthlessness matched Stamboliski's own.

Though he did much for Balkan peace, Stamboliski's experiment in Bulgaria was a disappointment. The moral objects of some of his legislation were highly sympathetic, but they were debased in practice by his irrational antiurban demogoguery and the approved ruffianism of his Orange Guards. From Stambolov and Radoslavov and Ferdinand he had inherited a political tradition of brutality, corruption, and violence, and he failed to rise above it. That his successors maintained and deepened this tradition does not absolve Stamboliski from responsibility. Much of his legislation was but the codification of the frustrated resentments of the exploited peasant. His vision of society was static. Instead of establishing a model peasant democracy in Bulgaria, he dealt a stunning blow, felt throughout the Balkan Peninsula, to the concept of government by the rural masses.

VI

THE JUNE COUP

At three o'clock on Saturday morning, June 9, 1923, army units
under the direction of General Lazarov, president of the Reserve
Officers' League, occupied the police, government, and communications buildings of Sofia. Provincial town centers were simultaneously seized. The operation required half an hour in the capital
and forty-five minutes in the country. When daylight broke, the
political leader of the putsch, Alexander Tsankov, professor of
economics at the University of Sofia, went to the palace and was
appointed by King Boris to be the new Prime Minister of Bulgaria.[1]
Within six weeks of his stunning electoral triumph Stamboliski's
government was thus effortlessly toppled and he himself outlawed.
Resistance was slight and ineffective. Alexander Botev, the Peasant
President of the Sobranie, and Alexander Obbov, the Minister of
Commerce, mobilized the Orange Guard in the districts of Radomir
and Pleven, respectively,[2] but although in the past these gangs had

---

[1] Whether or not King Boris was aware of the plans to stage a *coup d'état* against
his Prime Minister has been hotly argued. The refugee Peasant Union representatives
abroad insisted that he was. See *La Bulgarie sous le régime de l'assassinat.* Dimo
Kazasov, the Socialist who participated in the conspiracy and became Minister of
Transport in Tsankov's government, has given two flatly contradictory answers to
this question. In his monograph on the putsch, *V tamnite na zagavora,* he claimed
(p. 130) that the King was taken completely unawares by the coup. After World
War II Kazasov became one of the leading fellow-traveling propagandists for the
Bulgarian Communist regime and as such found it expedient to execrate Boris as not
only party to the conspiracy but veritably one of its leading spirits. See Kazasov,
Burni godini: 1918-1944, pp. 148-52. One might be inclined to accept the earlier,
pre-Communist version were it not for the fact that Kazasov had always been a
careerist. About the only definitely established fact is that as late as June 7, on the
Thursday before the coup, the King and his sisters went to Stamboliski's farm at
Slavovitsa to visit him. This may have been an act of friendship or a ruse. In view
of rumors after the April, 1923, election to the effect that a republic might be
declared or the King's powers curtailed, it would not be surprising if Boris had come
to the conclusion that the Crown was in jeopardy under Stamboliski. In any event
he accomodated himself to the putsch with alacrity.

[2] *The Times,* June 11, 1923; Swire, *Bulgarian Conspiracy,* p. 166.

been effective enough in terrorizing the civilian population of the towns with their armory of clubs, rakes, and scythes, now they were no match for the army. The Guards were dispersed in a few skirmishes in which 70 peasants and 30 soldiers lost their lives.[3] Obbov fled to Rumania.

The coup took Stamboliski, who was spending the week end on his farm at Slavovitsa, by surprise. He, too, tried hastily to mobilize the Orange Guard of the Tatar-Pazarjik vicinity but his pitiful column of 1,200 faithful but virtually unarmed peasants was quickly routed. Captured on June 14, he was beheaded the next day, after having suffered horrible tortures and mutilations. His Macedonian murderers, though known, went unpunished on the grounds that he was an outlaw.[4]

The coup was accompanied by a roundup of leaders and functionaries of the Peasant Union. Colonel Volkov, the new Minister of War, stated in the Sobranie on June 12 that 3,000 political prisoners had been arrested. The actual number was probably larger. General Lazarov and Colonel Damyan Velchev, commander of the Military Academy, who had organized the technical aspect of the coup, had hoped to keep it bloodless but bands of the IMRO committed atrocities and murders.

The active participants in the coup consisted of the numerically small organization of intellectuals and politicians known as the Naroden Sgovor (National Entente), founded early in 1922,[5] the

---

[3] *Manchester Guardian,* June 22, 1923. Obbov's 6,000 Orange Guards at Pleven disposed of 300 rifles. The military units sent against them were armed with artillery and supported by the 600-man local detachment of the Wrangel Army. There was almost no resistance to the coup in the Stara Zagora district, where Stamboliski's purged Peasant Union rivals, Turlakov and Dragiev, had their personal following, nor in the Burgas district where the expelled Radolov enjoyed local influence. In Tirnovo resistance was offered by the anarchists led by Georgi Popov and the Balkhov brothers. Everywhere the *gendarmerie* surrendered without a struggle. The active army officers sympathized with their reserve colleagues who organized the coup. Those few officers and army units loyal to Stamboliski were at the time stationed in Petrich Department on the Yugoslav frontier to implement the Nish Convention for the disarming of IMRO detachments attempting raids across the border. They were thus unable to thwart the coup in Sofia.

[4] Before killing Stamboliski, the Macedonians cut off his hands—"the hands that had signed the Nish Convention." For details of Stamboliski's last days, see Swire, *Bulgarian Conspiracy,* pp. 167-68 and Kazasov, *Burni godini: 1918-1944,* pp. 156-58. Officially, he was "shot while attempting to escape." *The Times,* June 16, 1923.

[5] The original leader of the Naroden Sgovor was the journalist and former diplomat Alexander Grekov and it was only after his murder on May 21, 1922, that Alexander Tsankov became its candidate for the premiership.

Reserve Officers' League, with which the Sgovor maintained close connections,[6] and IMRO detachments. The intelligentsia, the Socialists, and indeed virtually the entire urban population of the country were sympathetic.[7] Stamboliski had alienated them all by the violence of his regime and by his acquiescence in the territorial provisions of the Bucharest and Neuilly treaties. Friendship towards Yugoslavia and acceptance of her annexation of a major part of Macedonia outraged the army and IMRO. Stamboliski had looked forward to a *rapprochement* and even ultimate unification with Yugoslavia in order to form one peasant state stretching from the Julian Alps to the Black and Aegean Seas. Pašić and King Alexander in Belgrade, however, were too shortsighted to realize that in allowing Stamboliski's government to be overthrown, they were conniving at the downfall of the one Bulgarian statesman whose primary aim was peace and unity with Yugoslavia.[8] They were not, however, alone in their blindness.[9]

On the morning of June 9, 1923, the Central Committee of the Bulgarian Communist Party issued a proclamation "To the Workers and Peasants of Bulgaria" which read:

[6] The military clauses of the Treaty of Neuilly limited the Bulgarian army to 20,000 volunteers. Thousands of the active officers in the wars from 1912 to 1918 were forced into retirement. About 2,000 of the younger ones had enrolled in the law faculty of the Sofia University, and their resentment against Stamboliski was doubled by his closing of political careers to lawyers. The Reserve Officers' League, re-formed after 1918 to preserve professional solidarity, was treated tactlessly by Stamboliski, and the Orange Guard even provoked brawls against it. By 1923 about 90 percent of all the retired officers had joined it.

[7] The veteran Socialist leader Pastukhov had declared before the coup: "With the devil I can be friends, but the Peasant Government must be destroyed." See Swire, *Bulgarian Conspiracy*, p. 156. The participation of the Socialist journalist Kazasov in the camp has already been cited (p. 117, footnote 1). In addition to abhorring Stamboliski's violence, the Socialists were also motivated by lingering resentment against his smashing of the great railroad strike of 1919-20.

[8] In a stormy session of the Yugoslav Skupština a few days after the *coup d'état* in Bulgaria, the Democratic politician Svetozar Pribičević and the Agrarian leader Jovan Jovanović bitterly reproached the government for its failure to intervene in support of Stamboliski. See the *Morning Gazette,* June 19, 1923. That they would have acted differently had they been in power in Belgrade is, however, unlikely. In its international implications the Bulgarian coup was a blow to France's eastern position. The new government rapidly associated itself with Italy, which Stamboliski had always declined to do. For the story of the Italian overtures to Stamboliski, see the two accounts by K. Todorov ("The Macedonian Organization Yesterday and Today," p. 478 and *Balkan Firebrand,* pp. 137-38).

[9] For a general account of the coup by a fervent admirer of Stamboliski, see Lebedev, "Bolgarski perevorot," pp. 49-56, 71-89.

Last night the government of the Peasant Union was overthrown by a military putsch. . . . The government of Stamboliski, which maintained its power . . . by terror and coercion has been overthrown. The government of the peasant bourgeoisie which . . . used its power to defend its class and clique interests has been overthrown. The government of the Peasant Union . . . suppressed the rights of the toiling people and waged a merciless crusade against their only protector, the Communist Party. . . . Therefore, the workers and peasants must not today come to the aid of this government. . . . The working masses in town and village will not participate in the armed struggle . . . between the urban and rural bourgeoisies, for by such participation the toilers would be pulling the chestnuts out of the fire for their own exploiters and oppressors.[10]

It closed with the usual Communist demands for lower taxes, peace, freedom of press, speech, and assembly. As the broadsheets bearing this manifesto appeared, Communist agitators, driven through the streets of Sofia on trucks, were calling on the people to remain calm and passive. When the local Communist leaders of Plevna, Plovdiv, Karlovo, Kazanlak, and Tirnovo, unaware of the Central Committee's decision for neutrality, mobilized their comrades to cooperate with the Orange Guard in armed resistance to the coup, Todor Lukanov, one of the two secretaries of the Central Committee, telegraphed them orders to desist from this course of action.[11] Khristo Kabakchiev, on behalf of the Central Committee then gloated in the international Communist press that the *coup d'état* "had been met

[10] The proclamation is reprinted in its entirety in *Inprekorr*, III, No. 102 (June 20, 1923), 858-59.

[11] Lukanov sent this telegram after an interview with General Russev, the new Minister of the Interior. See the minutes of the Party Conference in exile of December 8, 1927, in *Balgarskata Komunisticheska Partia v Rezolyutsii i Reshenia*, II, pp. 349-50. In later years the unfortunate Lukanov was burdened with the full blame for a policy which was that of the entire Central Committee and of which he was but the chief executor. The other Secretary, Vasil Kolarov, had gone to Moscow on May 2 and thus enjoyed the good fortune of being able to deny all responsibility for the neutrality policy. Lukanov was purged in 1927 while Kolarov went on to become one of the Stalinist stalwarts in the Comintern and was Prime Minister of Communist Bulgaria at the time of his death on January 23, 1950. For the detailed account of Communist resistance in Plevna and the discussions among the local Party leaders on correct policy before the arrival of Lukanov's instructions, see Dilovska, "Borbata sreshtu voenno-fashistkia prevrat na 9 Yuni 1923 v Plevenski Okrag," pp. 63-84. In Plevna the chief Communist advocate of resistance was a certain Assen Khalachev while in the Karlovo area it was the Communist Sobranie deputy Pencho Dvoryanov who set about mobilizing resistance. When early in August the trial of those Communists charged with resisting the coup in Plevna took place, the Central Committee did not shrink from disavowing them. Four were sentenced to hang; 2 to life imprisonment; 7 to 12 years and 73 to 3 years imprisonment; 9 were acquitted. See *The Times*, August 13, 1923.

by the urban toiling masses with indifference and even with a certain amount of relief," a comment which Georgi Dimitrov repeated almost word for word a few days later at a trade-union meeting.[12]

In Moscow the Enlarged Plenum of the Executive Committee of the Communist International (ECCI) assembled three days after the *coup d'état* in Bulgaria. Toward the end of his interminable presidential report on June 12, 1923, Zinoviev announced that a message had just reached him that in Bulgaria a bourgeois *coup d'état* had occurred in the face of which the Communist Party had remained neutral. He hoped that the second part of this dispatch was untrue. The Bulgarian comrades were surely aware that the only correct policy in such a situation would be that of the Bolsheviks at the time of the Kornilov putsch, the policy of resistance. Passivity could lead only to annihilation, to the end of influence over the masses, or to a party schism—in any event, to catastrophe.[13]

Shortly thereafter a telegram arrived in Moscow from Prague, sent by Raiko Daskalov, whom Stamboliski had made ambassador to Czechoslovakia earlier in the spring. He demanded that the Comintern order the Bulgarian Communists to cooperate with the Orange Guard in resistance to the Tsankov *coup d'état*.[14] Within the next two days confirmation of the Communist Party's neutrality policy arrived from Bulgaria; it was a sheepish Kolarov who mounted the rostrum at the ECCI session on June 14 to attempt to explain how his party, which had always boasted of being the second best in the Comintern—second only to the Bolsheviks themselves—could have committed such a blunder.[15] Kolarov not only conceded the enormity of the error—an admission which was to make him henceforth the Comintern's chief agent for correcting deviations in the Bulgarian Party—but even advanced the rueful claim that had the Bulgarian Central Committee acted correctly four days earlier,

---

[12] Kabakchiev, "Der Bürgerlich-Militaristische Umsturz und die K.P. in Bulgarien," *Inprekorr*, III, No. 105 (June 25, 1923), 886. Georgi Dimitrov's statement was reported in the *Rabotnicheski Vestnik* of June 28, 1923.

[13] *Rasshirennyi Plenum Ispolnitel'nogo Komiteta Kommunisticheskogo Internatsionala (12-13 Iyunya 1923 goda)*, pp. 100-102.

[14] Gentizon, *Le Drame bulgare*, p. 165. Daskalov was shortly thereafter assassinated in Prague on August 26, 1923.

[15] For an account of this Bulgarian arrogance within the Comintern, see Serge, *Mémoires d'un révolutionnaire*, p. 195.

Bulgaria would now have a "Workers' and Peasants' Government" of the pattern sketched at the Fourth Comintern Congress in the preceding November. In concluding, however, Kolarov could not resist appealing for special consideration on grounds which have since become the standard explanation for the great lapse of June 9. He begged the assembled comrades to remember that the Bulgarian Party had been engaged in a life-and-death struggle with Stamboliski whose persecutions had aroused fierce and justified resentment —resentment so bitter, it was now demonstrated, as to blind the Central Committee to a yet greater danger.[16]

By June 14 news had reached Moscow that the Bulgarian Central Committee had not only counseled passivity on June 9 but had subsequently even halted the resistance in Plevna, which, it was asserted, might have captured control of the town. Zinoviev could not believe this report. He and Kolarov, in the name of the ECCI, sent to the Central Committee in Sofia a demand for immediate clarification. They admonished the Bulgarian Communists to ally themselves with the lesser evil of Stamboliski, in spite of his past repression of the Party, and once again recommended the Bolsheviks' "Kornilov policy."[17] Simultaneously, Karl Radek was instructed to make a thorough study of the Bulgarian Communist Party's policy and present recommendations for its correction.

Radek managed to gather the facts and prepare his report in time for delivery at the last session of the ECCI Plenum on June 23.[18] He was vitriolic. The events of June 9 were "the greatest defeat ever suffered by a Communist Party." (Radek was speaking a few weeks before the autumn catastrophe in Germany but several months after Mussolini's coming to power in Italy.) The second largest party in Bulgaria, one enjoying the support of one fourth of the

[16] "Rede des Genossen Kolarow am 14. Juni," Inprekorr, III, No. 103 (June 21, 1923), 872.

[17] This message to Sofia of June 14 from Zinoviev and Kolarov was first made public by the latter in 1925, in the course of the anti-Trotsky campaign within the Comintern, set off by the appearance in October, 1924, of Trotsky's The Lessons of October, 1917. See Kolarov, "Die 'Lehren des Oktober' und die K.P.B.," Inprekorr, V, No. 6 (January 9, 1925), 71. Zinoviev had given the ECCI the gist of the message on June 15, 1923. In 1924 Trotsky charged both the Bulgarian Communist Party and the Comintern leadership with political incompetence during the events of June and September, 1923. See Trotsky, The Lessons of October, 1917, p. 14.

[18] Rasshirennyi Plenum Ispolnitel'nogo Komiteta Kommunisticheskogo Internatsionala (12-23 Iyunya 1923 goda), pp. 254-62.

voters, had opted for a policy of servile inactivity and spineless surrender when the manifestly correct reaction would have been immediate fighting support for Stamboliski who, though not a Communist, nevertheless represented a genuinely radical, anti-bourgeois social force. In a country where 80 percent of the population were peasants, the Communist Party's understanding of the peasant movement and appreciation of the peasant temper had been proven completely deficient. The plea that the international situation precluded Communist resistance was a shallow subterfuge. At a time when Great Britain was the main foe of Soviet Russia and the leading protagonist of a policy of crusades against her, any event strengthening Britain's diplomatic position in the Balkans was not a triviality but a matter of utmost gravity in the Communist world.[19] The excuse that a neighboring state would have intervened to crush a Communist-inspired resistance movement was a cowardly evasion; Tsankov had not allowed himself to be deterred from his coup by the possibility of Yugoslav action in support of Stamboliski. With a little intelligence and vigor and courage the Central Committee could have rallied the Peasant Union and IMRO [sic] into a fighting coalition. We in Moscow, Radek concluded, have now been rudely disillusioned of our faith in the Bulgarian comrades. Never again will we be deflected from ruthless purge measures by a squeamish reluctance to apply "the Moscow hatchet" to an "old and tried" party.

The ECCI Plenum shared Radek's indignation and, as one of its last acts unanimously demanded that the Bulgarian Communist Party reverse its policy, effect an alliance "from above" with the Peasant Union and IMRO, and go "forward into the battle" against the Tsankov government with the battle cry of "Long live the Workers' and Peasants' Government."[20] On July 2 Zinoviev repeated and amplified these instructions in a message to the Central Committee.[21] He demanded thorough self-criticism, preparation for

---

[19] The Lausanne Conference was at this moment drawing to a close. It marked the success of Lord Curzon's efforts to detach Kemalist Turkey from exclusive dependence upon Soviet Russia. In May, 1923, Anglo-Russian relations had been subjected to acute strain by Curzon's ten-day ultimatum of May 2, demanding the discontinuation of Communist activities in the Central Asian buffer states. See Nicolson, *Curzon: The Last Phase,* pp. 356-60.

[20] *Rasshirennyi Plenum Ispolnitel'nogo Komiteta Kommunisticheskogo Internatsionala (12-23 Iyunya 1923 goda),* pp. 300-304.

[21] Parts of Zinoviev's letter were published in Kolarov's reply to Trotsky's *The Lessons of October, 1917.* See above, p. 122, footnote 17.

underground activity in view of the probability that the Party would be outlawed, and active approaches to the surviving leaders of the Peasant Union in place of the fatuous tactic of "united front from below," which in practice amounted to maligning Stamboliski and exhorting the peasants to desert this "kulak." Vasil Kolarov had already left Moscow for Bulgaria on June 17, when the reports of the neutrality policy had been substantiated, with instructions from Zinoviev to bring about its reversal. Shortly after landing illegally at Varna on June 23 or 24, he was recognized and arrested at Gorna Oryakhovitsa. Released after several weeks, he did not arrive in Sofia until August 5.[22]

Though the Central Committee thus did not learn the most detailed and secret directives of the Comintern until August, it had for some time been aware of the general criticism to which its neutrality policy had been subjected in Moscow. The telegram of June 14 from Zinoviev and Kolarov had been received in Sofia a day later[23] and was followed by further reports of the dissatisfaction with the Party's policy voiced at the ECCI meeting. To discuss this predicament, the Party Council met in Sofia July 1-6. At the end of its deliberations it adopted two highly important resolutions. The first of them, "On the Position of the Bulgarian Communist Party to the Events of June 9," defended the neutrality instructions sent out by the Central Committee on June 9 as the only correct ones in the given circumstances.[24] A revolutionary situation, it declared, had not existed, and the masses could not have been rallied to

---

[22] *Vasil Kolarov: Important Dates of His Life and Work,* p. 39.

[23] See Dimitrov's report of December 8, 1927, to the Party Conference held in Berlin, first published in *Balgarskata Komunisticheska Partia v Rezolyutsii i Reshenia,* II, 352.

[24] Translated in *Inprekorr* (Wochenausgabe), III, No. 29 (July 21, 1923), 696-97, from the *Rabotnicheski Vestnik* of July 10, 1923. The resolution is reprinted in *Balgarskata Komunisticheska Partia v Rezolyutsii i Reshenia,* II, 270-72. A few days later the Bulgarian delegate to the conference of the Communist Youth International, which met in Moscow July 10-18, also defended the June 9 neutrality policy. See "Die Vierte Bürositzung der K.J.I.," *Inprekorr,* III, No. 130 (August 8, 1923), 1132.

The Party Council was a smaller version of the annual Congress. It consisted of the Central Committee, the Control Commission, and a delegate from each geographical Department who had been chosen by the previous Congress. The Council met regularly every three months and could be called into extraordinary session by the Central Committee. It made decisions on the most important questions of party policy. For the statutes of the Bulgarian Communist Party adopted at its First Congress in May, 1919, see *Balgarskata Komunisticheska Partia v Rezolyutsii i Reshenia,* II, 22-29.

resistance against the coup. The misgivings of Comrade Zinoviev and of the ECCI are attributed to insufficient familiarity with the situation in Bulgaria, and confidence is expressed that when the ECCI had all the relevant information at its disposal, it too would acknowledge the correctness of the neutrality policy, which was not, as alleged in Moscow, a policy of spineless passivity but one of independent struggle. The Comintern's proposal of an alliance "from above" with the Peasant Union leaders is declared unsound, for these leaders are alleged to have lost all credit with the peasant masses, who now begin to realize that they have been betrayed by them, and to flock to the banner of the Communist Party. Yet, the resolution concluded, the Communist Party does not exclude co-operation with the Peasant Union under the slogan of "Workers' and Peasants' Government" if the remaining Peasant Union leaders are prepared to accept the Communists' terms. So ends this remark-able resolution. It was adopted by 42 votes against 2, the pair in the minority being supported in their disapproval by four members having only consultative voices. They represented Plevna and the other provincial organizations which had spontaneously decided to resist the coup.[25] Zinoviev's supposition that the opposition to the neutrality policy was sufficiently powerful within the Bulgarian party to make a split possible was thus shown to be unfounded. Whereas this resolution reveals an almost courageous naïveté in its appeal to the ECCI to respect a policy which had the well-nigh unanimous approval of the entire Bulgarian Party, the second resolution adopted by the Party Council on July 6 manifests a complete misreading of the political significance of the *coup d'état* and of the nature of the Tsankov government.[26]

Opening on a note of typical pseudo-Marxist casuistry with the confident assertion that the bourgeois coalition must speedily dis-integrate as a consequence of its inherent contradictions, the reso-lution continues with an expression of regretful surprise at the failure of the new government to restore full civil and political democracy. Descending into the realm of specific demands, the resolution then appeals to this new government for lower taxes,

[25] See Kabakchiev, "Die Ereignisse in Bulgarien," p. 91, and, by the same author, "Dmitri Blagoev i bolgarskie Tesnyaki," p. 53.

[26] This second resolution was published in the German edition of *Inprekorr*, III, No. 120 (July 18, 1923), 1052.

higher wages, more houses, and a shorter work day. Although Stamboliski had been dead for three weeks, the Council found it fitting to continue the resolution with a more than usually violent torrent of abuse upon the government of the murdered peasant leader which merged into the expected appeal to the poor peasants to rally around the Communist banner instead of mourning this "bankrupt" and "incompetent" spokesman of the village exploiters (*chorbaji*). The resolution concludes with an attempt to enlighten the people on one of the previously mentioned contradictions within the bourgeois camp, namely, the Macedonian issue. The Macedonian organizations are implicitly derided for their trusting support of Tsankov, who, once he was in power, had speedily agreed to abide by the Nish Convention with Yugoslavia negotiated by Stamboliski. In contrast, it is pointed out, the Communist Party remains a reliable champion of the cause of the oppressed Macedonians as well as of the Thracians and Dobrujans.

The resolution was adopted unanimously. One of its more significant clauses expresses regret at the insufficiently liberal policy of the new Tsankov government. That this disappointment was genuine is indicated by the pronouncements of the Communist leaders in the hours immediately following the coup. Though on June 9 the Party leaders had declared that the current clash was fundamentally one between two wings of the bourgeoisie in the outcome of which the Communists had no stake, the *Rabotnicheski Vestnik* of the next morning commented more hopefully: "We do not know the plans of the new government . . . . The new government has declared that it will strengthen the constitutionally guaranteed rights and freedoms. This is its declaration. The toiling masses must endeavor to ensure that these words will be turned into facts." [27] The Communists were, of course, interested only in their own rights and freedoms, and initially Tsankov encouraged their passivity policy by refraining from persecuting the Party. While the Orange Guard was being suppressed, government credits were extended in June and July to the Communist Party's cooperative federation, Osvobozhdenie (Liberation), as well as to the

---

[27] Quoted by Bazhenov, "Sentyabrs'koe vosstanie v Bolgarii," p. 271. The article contains many similar quotations from this newspaper in the days immediately following the June 9 coup. An entire editorial from the *Rabotnicheski Vestnik* of June 11 is reprinted in *Inprekorr*, III, No. 107 (June 27, 1923), 915-17.

Socialist Party's cooperative, Napred (Forward).[28] Cabinet ministers gave private assurances to Communist leaders that the putsch was in no way directed against the Communist Party, that they would take measures to halt the molesting of Communists in the provinces by overenthusiastic followers of the new regime, and that when once the Orange Guard had been crushed, a reversion to strictly constitutional government would be instituted.[29] On the appeal of the Central Committee, Tsankov even freed Vasil Kolarov on August 5, though he knew that the Communist leader had returned from Moscow clandestinely and must have suspected that he carried instructions to reverse the neutrality policy. Tsankov probably took the calculated risk that by restraint on his part the position of the advocates of passivity in the Communist Party would be strengthened to a point where orders from Moscow to abandon that policy would be defied.[30] Such a presumption could ultimately be naught but vain in regard to so dictatorial an organization as the Comintern. The illusion that Moscow could be defied by the Sofia Central Committee was, however, temporarily shared by the Bulgarian Communist leaders themselves, as is indicated by the correspondence which passed between them and the Comintern secretariat during July and August.

Radek's denunciation of the Bulgarian comrades' bankrupt policy of June 9 together with the ECCI's critical resolution of June 23, were particularly disturbing and galling to the Bulgarian Communist chiefs. To the Party's theoretician and propagandist, Khristo Kabakchiev, who had been the *rapporteur* on the neutrality policy to the Party Council at the beginning of July, fell the task of

---

[28] Kazasov, *Burni godini. 1918-1944,* p. 182.

[29] Bulatsel', *Ocherki sotsial'no-politicheskoi zhizni sovremennoi Bolgarii,* p. 101.

[30] Tsankov's own remark that no measures would be taken against the Communist Party as such but that disturbers of the peace would be dealt with drastically is mentioned in *The Times,* July 19, 1923, where the comment is added that such statements were intended to affect the clash between the Moscow ECCI and the Sofia Central Committee. Tsankov's hopes in this matter were encouraged by Moscow's fears to the same effect. In July the government claimed to have intercepted a secret message from Zinoviev to the Bulgarian Central Committee, subsequently published in the official white paper on the Bolshevik conspiracy, in which Zinoviev, as if afraid that Kolarov might be converted to the neutrality position, takes care to state that "up to his departure [from Moscow on June 17] Comrade Kolarov had in all respects the same opinion as ourselves concerning these events" of June 9. See *La Conspiration bolchéviste contre la Bulgarie,* p. 41.

refuting them. His voluminous defense of the June 9 tactic, published by the Comintern leaders as proof of their charge of the political imbecility of the Bulgarian comrades,[31] is one of the most interesting records available of a genuine quarrel within the Comintern, strikingly different from the later staged condemnations of "Trotskyism," or "right-" or "left-deviationism." After the Stalinization of the Comintern, such a rejoinder as Kabakchiev's would have been unthinkable.

It begins with a candid review of the past relations between Stamboliski and the Communist Party and a description of the steady worsening of these relations in 1922 and 1923. Stamboliski's April electoral triumph and subsequent preparation of measures against the Communist Party, Kabakchiev continues, had made it impossible for the Party to adopt toward him any attitude other than one of total hostility. It is, thus, perfectly true, as charged, that the Central Committee issued its orders to the Party not to rise in defense of Stamboliski's government early on June 9, without first informing itself of the extent of resistance to the coup in the country. Subsequently, however, it was revealed that this resistance was so light that even the Communist Party's weight could not have turned the scales against the putschists.[32] The day after the coup, resistance continued only in Shumen and Plevna, and these two trouble spots were pacified on June 11. By the following day only isolated shots were being fired in the country. There was therefore at no time any objective reason to reverse the original neutrality orders of June 9. The Central Committee's intervention to terminate the resistance in Plevna had been motivated by an even more serious consideration than the probability of failure, namely, by the paramount necessity of maintaining a single party front. The charge (made by Radek) that June 9 represented a colossal defeat for the Party is nonsense, for not only is the Party's organization intact and its striking power unimpaired, but its influence with the peasant masses is greater than ever, now that these have been disabused of their illusions about

[31] Kabakchiev, "Die Ereignisse in Bulgarien," pp. 74-103.

[32] This assertion came to be considered Kabakchiev's cardinal theoretical sin. In subsequent litanies of self-criticism, beginning with those of Dimitrov and Kolarov in the following year, there was included the confession that the Tsankov coup could have been defeated had the Communist Party energetically resisted it. See Dimitrov, "Die Kommunistische Internationale und die K.P. Bulgariens," pp. 135-36, and Kolarov, "Die Taktik der K.P. Bulgariens im Lichte der Ereignisse," pp. 253-71.

Stamboliski's strength. Since the peasants cannot support the bourgeois government, they are obliged henceforth to rally behind the Communist Party. Of course, Kabakchiev continues, contradicting himself, now the Communist Party need no longer hesitate to establish a united front with the remnant of the Peasant Union and even with its surviving leaders,[33] who, after all, must by the nature of recent events have been pushed to the left.[34]

Kabakchiev then takes up and rejects in turn each of Radek's reprimands and the ECCI's admonitions and in doing so, recites once again the standard tirade against Stamboliski. He then dares to lecture Zinoviev on lessons of the Bolshevik Revolution and rejects as irrelevant the comparison between Kornilov and Tsankov and the conclusions which Zinoviev drew therefrom.[35] The reproach that the Party lost a rare opportunity to sabotage the coup by its failure to call the railroad workers out on strike is also dismissed as baseless since, Kabakchiev insists, the railroad workers with their memories of 1919-20 were more fiercely resentful of Stamboliski than was any other group and could not possibly have been mobilized in defense of his regime. In any event, Kabakchiev admits, the vast majority of the 27,000 railway men stand under moderate Socialist

[33] This gesture and the identical one at the close of the Party Council resolution of July 6 were probably sops to the Comintern "line" of the moment.

[34] Kabakchiev's memory is here as short as his confusion is profound. The claim that the peasantry must flock to the Communist banner now that its own party has been smashed is directly followed by the statement that the Communist Party can henceforth cooperate with a radicalized Peasant Union. Kabakchiev had, apparently, forgotten that in January the Party Council had adopted a resolution, for which he had himself been *rapporteur,* characterizing any move to the left on the part of the Peasant Union or the development of a left wing within it, as meaningless and fraudulent and that he had himself praised the wisdom of this position throughout the international Communist press during the spring. For the resolution, see *Balgarskata Komunisticheska Partia v Rezolyutsii i Reshenia,* II, 248-51, and, for Kabakchiev's enlargements upon it, *Inprekorr,* III, No. 57 (April 3, 1923), 459-65; *Le Bulletin communiste,* IV, No. 18 (May 3, 1923), 210; and *Die Internationale,* VI, No. 11 (June 1, 1923), 345-52.

[35] Kabakchiev's audacity is the more breathtaking when one realizes that it was precisely the Bulgarian Communists who had put the Russians in mind of this comparison by ceaselessly juxtaposing Stamboliski with Kerenski. Kabakchiev here objects to the comparison on the grounds that: (*a*) Kerenski's regime was the product of a revolution (while Stamboliski's was not), and therefore had deserved Bolshevik support; (*b*) in fighting Kornilov the Petrograd workers were defending their Soviets, but these did not exist in Bulgaria and the proletariat therefore had nothing to lose by Tsankov's triumph; (*c*) the reaction in Russia was one of large-landed magnates, nonexistent in Bulgaria where the kulaks of Stamboliski's party were the reaction; (*d*) there was genuine *spontaneous* opposition in Petrograd to Kornilov's march which did not exist in Sofia to Tsankov's putsch.

influence and only about 3,500 belong to the Communist-controlled union. Even had it been feasible, he continues, a railway strike ought not to have been called for the events of three years before had shown that this is a critical weapon, one to be used only in a really desperate struggle for political power. Since that was precisely the policy which Zinoviev and Radek maintained ought to have been initiated on June 9, this assertion discredited Kabakchiev even further in Moscow's eyes.

Kabakchiev then suggests once again that Zinoviev's and the ECCI's interpretation of the meaning of the events of June 9 rests on inadequate information. Should the Comintern leaders, however, now that they are in receipt of more facts and of this, the Bulgarian Central Committee's apologia for its conduct, continue to demand the reversal of the Bulgarian Party's policy, they are assured by Kabakchiev that his Party, as a loyal member of the Comintern, will obey such orders. Only, he continues, the Party will insist on preserving its unity—a veiled warning that Moscow, in demanding a reversal of the Party line, would do well not to insist on a purge of those responsible for the faulty tactics of June 9.

In Moscow the Party Council's resolutions of July 6 and Kabakchiev's memorandum of the end of the month aroused well-nigh apoplectic anger. Even as early as the end of June, Zinoviev had scornfully rejected Kabakchiev's earlier nimble assertion that the toiling masses had met the coup with indifference and relief. Bitterly, Zinoviev had replied that "the masses, as is well known, have a broad back; anything can be loaded on it" and contended that the real reason why the Central Committee had adopted a policy of passivity on June 9 was that, despite two earlier warnings from the ECCI, it had allowed itself to fall victim to the deadly diseases of excessive caution and legalism. It feared to risk its imposing People's Houses, its flourishing cooperatives, its extensive press, in an armed struggle. It wanted revolution, but only a revolution with guarantees.[36]

On the receipt of the Party Council's two resolutions of July 6 in Moscow, the Hungarian Communist Matyas Rákosi, who had been

[36] Zinoviev, "Die Lehren des bulgarischen Umsturzes," *Inprekorr,* III, No. 115 (July 9, 1923), 1007-10. The presidium of the ECCI drew the attention of "all section of the Comintern" to this article.

Kabakchiev's accomplice in splitting the Italian Socialist Party at Leghorn in January, 1921,[37] was commissioned to refute the claims presented in them—a task which he executed with brutal bluntness.[38] Finally, as a warning to the Bulgarian leaders that, though they had so far been regarded in Moscow as the best of the Balkan Communists, this favoritism could not survive such blunders, the Yugoslav Communist leaders Sima Marković and Mikhailović, bitter rivals of the Bulgarians, were invited to join the ranks of the critics of the neutrality policy. This proposal they accepted with relish, Marković, in particular, gleefully enumerating to the Bulgarian leaders all their brave old pledges that, at the moment of an attempted bourgeois coup, the Bulgarian Communist Party would resolutely fight and conquer.[39]

All these criticisms of the course of action adopted by the Central Committee on June 9 are interesting, though, with the exception of Zinoviev's article on "The Lessons of the Bulgarian Coup," they add little of substance to Radek's original report. Zinoviev's reproach of "legalism" as the possibly unconscious reason for the failure to resist the *coup d'état* undoubtedly contains much truth. The Central Committee's pronouncements, on the other hand, suggest that it had also been blinded by jealousy and resentment of Stamboliski.[40] Finally, this indifference to the outcome of a struggle "within the bourgeois camp," while it may have been, in the given situation, "bad" Leninism, reflected a lack of discrimination virtually inherent in Communist doctrine. It had been evident in Germany during the Kapp putsch in 1920 and was to reappear there in the years immediately preceding Hitler's coming to power. In the period between the two World Wars, Communists seemed consistently to be incapable of appreciating the significance of a military-reactionary

[37] See Kabakchiev, *Die Gründung der Kommunistischen Partei Italiens.*
[38] Rákosi, "Die Neue Stellungnahme der K.P.B.," *Inprekorr* (Wochenausgabe), III, No. 29 (July 21, 1923), 698-99.
[39] S.M. (Sima Marković), "Der Bürgerlich-Militaristische Umsturz und die K.P. in Bulgarien," *Inprekorr,* III, No. 124 (July 27, 1923), 1086-87, and Mikhailović, "Die K.P.B. und der 9. Juni," *Inprekorr,* III, No. 134 (August 17, 1923), 1171. For the history of the rivalry between the Bulgarian and Yugoslav Communist Parties and Moscow's position toward it, see Chapter XI, pp. 227-29; 241-56.
[40] Surprise at the coup may also have paralyzed the Central Committee. At the Fifth Comintern Congress in the summer of 1924, Kolarov admitted that the coup had taken unawares the Central Committee which, like Stamboliski, had persuaded itself that the April, 1923, elections had destroyed the urban bourgeoisie as a political force. See *Fünfter Kongress der Kommunistischen Internationale: Protokoll,* p. 290.

attack on a non-Communist "bourgeois" government. Just as the Communists of Germany could assert in 1920 and 1933 that bourgeois democracy was no concern of theirs and could attack Legien and Hilferding more violently than Kapp and Hitler, so the Bulgarian Communists could dismiss the overthrow of the peasant government as well-deserved retribution and vilify the murdered Stamboliski more than the triumphant Tsankov, while declaring that the replacement of the agrarian regime by a military-bourgeois government was an affair in which the proletariat had no stake. Truly they deserved the appelation of "Narrow-minded."

It now remains to attempt to assign responsibility for the decision to remain neutral on June 9. Three years afterwards, Kabakchiev stated that, with the exception of Kolarov, who had been in Moscow from where, as has been noted, he advised resistance when news of the coup reached him, the entire Central Committee had advocated neutrality and supported its defense against Moscow's initial protests.[41] In June, 1923, however, Blagoev was already too old and ill to be considered answerable for the Party's activities. Though he undoubtedly approved the neutrality policy, the primary responsibility for it lay with the three senior active leaders, Secretary Todor Lukanov, propagandist Khristo Kabakchiev, and labor organizer Georgi Dimitrov.[42] Notable as was the unanimous decision of the Sofia leaders to adopt a policy of passivity, yet more significant is the fact that when Moscow persisted in its demands to reverse that policy, all members of the Central Committee, with the exception of the wavering Lukanov, obediently reversed themselves and committed the entire Party to the hopeless September uprising. The *Kadavergehorsam*, or zombi-like obedience, of the Bulgarian Communists to Moscow was to become unique even in the Comintern and is the real reason why, despite their frequent blunders, the Bulgarians were always Moscow's favorite Balkan disciples and its regular gendarmes and purgers within the Comintern.

[41] Kabakchiev, "Der Septemberaufstand in Bulgarien," p. 1966.

[42] In the 1930s, when he had become the bright ornament of the Comintern, Dimitrov would frequently lament that the two unforgivable sins which he and the other Bulgarian Communist leaders had committed were their passive attitudes at the time of the Radomir rebellion and the June coup. See, for example, his article on the tenth anniversary of Blagoev's death in *Inprecorr* (English edition), XIV, No. 36 (June 22, 1934), 947-48.

VII

THE SEPTEMBER INSURRECTION

On June 23 or 24, Vasil Kolarov secretly stepped ashore on the Bulgarian coast near Varna from a motorboat which had brought him from Odessa. His instructions were "to straighten the erroneous line of the Party."[1] On his way to Sofia he was recognized and arrested at Gorna Oryakhovitsa on the technical charge of not carrying an entry permit,[2] and was held in prison for several weeks, during which time the Party Council, evidently unaware of the importance which Moscow attached to Kolarov's mission, adopted its two unfortunate resolutions of July 6 and authorized Kabakchiev to write its ill-received apologia. On his release and arrival in Sofia on August 5, Kolarov immediately summoned an emergency meeting of the Central Committee. Confronting it with Moscow's orders, he forced the Committee to reverse the policy pursued since June 9 and resolve to prepare an armed insurrection to overthrow the Tsankov government and replace it with one of "Workers and Peasants."[3] The Party organizations at Vidin and Stara Zagora, it was later claimed, had already previously entertained second thoughts about the wisdom of the policy of benevolent neutrality toward the Tsankov government and welcomed the new line,[4] but within the Central Committee there seems to have been considerable reluctance to adopt it, as is indicated by the otherwise unexplained fact that at this emergency session a highly irregular cooption of

[1] Savova, *Vasil Kolarov: Bio-Bibliografia*, p. 43.
[2] "Zur Verhaftung des Genossen Kolarow," *Inprekorr*, III, No. 115 (July 9, 1923), 1014. In his absence, the ECCI Plenum elected Kolarov one of its three secretaries together with Pyatnitski and Neurath.
[3] Savova, *Vasil Kolarov: Bio-Bibliografia*, p. 43. The secret resolution of the Central Committee accepting this imposed policy appears not to have been published until 1951 when it was included in the collection *Balgarskata Komunisticheska Partia v Rezolyutsii i Reshenia*, II, 275-76.
[4] Bazhenov, "Sentyabr'skoe vosstanie v Bolgarii," p. 275.

four members to the Committee took place.[5] Blagoev disapproved of the new policy but was too old and ill to prevent its adoption.[6] Once the decision had been taken, Communist discipline asserted itself, and the only member of the Central Committee subsequently to be accused of persistent opposition to the new policy was Secretary Todor Lukanov.

On August 6 a military committee was set up by the Central Committee to work out the technical arrangements for an insurrection. More important, however, was the political preparation, the formation of a united front with the Socialist and Radical parties, with IMRO and the refugee organizations, and above all with the remnant of the Peasant Union whose adherence alone would lend plausibility to the slogan of "Workers' and Peasants' Government" under which the uprising was to be launched. That the Central Committee sincerely believed in the possibility of recruiting these organizations as allies in an armed rebellion is shown by the secret resolutions of August 5-7 [7] and its disappointment on the refusal of the Socialist, Radical, and Macedonian organizations to participate in it was genuine.[8] The Socialist Party met the Communist overtures with the sarcastic response that this invitation to all "progressive" forces to join to overthrow the "reactionary" government apparently indicated that the Communists had now come to accept the policy which Sakazov had advocated a quarter of a century before in his *Obshto Delo* and for which Blagoev had at that time expelled him and his Broad followers from

---

[5] *Balgarskata Komunisticheska Partia v Rezolyutsii i Reshenia*, II, 355.

[6] In public statements, such as the obituary article on Blagoev in *Inprekorr* (IV, No. 54 [May 13, 1924], 653-54) and regularly thereafter, the Communists would deny that the old leader had opposed the insurrection. In a secret report delivered to the Bulgarian Communist Party Conference in Berlin on December 8, 1927, however, Georgi Dimitrov did admit to the assembled comrades that Blagoev had held "a negative opinion" of the decision taken by the Central Committee in August, 1923, to launch an armed uprising. This report was not, apparently, made public until 1951 when it was appended to *Balgarskata Komunisticheska Partia v Rezolyutsii i Reshenia* (II, 358). The fact of Blagoev's dissent had been revealed as early as 1926 by the then ex-Communist Ivan Klincharov in his *Dimitr Blagoev*, p. 278. The old leader's objections were ignored, explained Dimitrov in 1927, because, owing to his ill health, he had not been properly informed about the situation. Blagoev died on May 7, 1924, and his funeral on May 9 developed into an imposing workers' procession.

[7] *Balgarskata Komunisticheska Partia v Rezolyutsii i Reshenia*, II, 275-77.

[8] See "Another Onslaught Upon the C.P. of Bulgaria," *Inprecorr* (English edition), III, No. 62 (40) (September 27, 1923), 702.

the movement. Such a policy, the Socialists replied, could still be considered but only if based on constitutional methods and only after assurances were received that the Communists would not only abandon the policy of violent revolution but also liquidate all their illegal activities.[9] This answer was, in effect, a refusal, and the Socialist Party furthermore authorized Dimo Kazasov to continue to serve as Minister of Transport in the Tsankov government. The tiny Radical Party likewise declined to ally itself with the Communists though its well-meaning but naïve leader Kosturkov testified in 1924 at the trial of Kabakchiev that the Communists' uprising had been provoked by Tsankov's terror.[10] IMRO also refused to participate in an insurrection though afterwards the Communists claimed to have been assured that it would at least remain neutral in the event of a revolt against the Tsankov government.[11] Finally, responsible Peasant Union leaders also turned a deaf ear to the Communist overtures though a small group of extremists, led by a certain Dimitar Grancharov, did respond.[12]

[9] Karakolov, "Kharakterni momenti ot borbata na Balgarskata Rabotnicheska Partia—Komunisti," p. 147. See also the *Daily Herald,* September 3, 1923.

[10] Willard, *Was ich in Bulgarien gesehen habe,* p. 31.

[11] See Georgi Dimitrov's report of December 8, 1927, to the Party Conference in *Balgarskata Komunisticheska Partia v Rezolyutsii i Reshenia,* II, 361 and Vladimirov, "The 15th Anniversary of the September Uprising in Bulgaria," *World News and Views,* XVIII, No. 48 (October 10, 1938), 1109. If the Communists launched their insurrection in the expectation that IMRO would remain passive they were due for a heavy disappointment. IMRO units helped the government to hunt down rebel bands during and after the uprising. There seems, however, to have been confusion even within IMRO as to the policy to be adopted. Some of its local chiefs in the Razlog area aided the Communists and after the suppression of the insurrection, Aleko "Pasha" Vasilev, IMRO boss of Petrich Department in Bulgarian Macedonia, sheltered the rebels. The Communists subsequently claimed, however, that, apart from these isolated acts of aid, IMRO doublecrossed them in September in violation of a pledge to remain neutral. These charges were elaborated by the Communist Berlow, "Zu dem bewaffneten Aufstand in Bulgarien," *Inprekorr,* III, No. 159 (October 10, 1923), 1357, and "Die Mazedonische Konterrevolutionäre," *Inprekorr,* III, No. 160 (October 12, 1923), 1367. The reluctance of Vasilev and the IMRO leaders in Razlog to aid the government in September probably reflected their dissatisfaction with Tsankov's endorsement of the Nish Convention concluded between Stamboliski and the Yugoslav government and their suspicion that Tsankov was not interested in Macedonia or the Macedonian movement except as pawns in Bulgarian diplomacy. In the following months these misgivings were felt by the chief IMRO leaders as well, and in May, 1924, the IMRO Central Committee sought a *rapprochement* with the Communists in the hope of receiving Soviet Russian support enabling them to end IMRO's exclusive dependence upon Tsankov's toleration and Mussolini's subsidies. See pp. 180-88.

[12] Grancharov was even wilder than Stamboliski in his anticapitalism. His brochure, "The Bloc of Toiling Democracy," called for the confiscation of all land not cultivated personally by its owner, nationalization of all banking, large industry, and

This angling for alliances had been suggested to the Central Committee by the ECCI which had also insisted upon the replacement of extremist Communist phraseology by the slogan of "Workers' and Peasants' Government" as the battle cry of insurrection.[13] In their subsequent accounts of the events of 1923, the Communists have written indignantly about the rebuff administered to their advances, above all by the Peasant leaders. This resentment was genuine and is an excellent illustration of the inability of Communists to entertain the conception of a "missed opportunity" in history or appreciate the fact that their own "errors" react upon the conduct of other groups. The Bulgarian Communists were outraged at the "treasonable" refusal of the Peasant Union leaders, whom a few weeks before they were showering with insults, to accept the proffered hand of friendship. That their own conduct on and after June 9, their malicious joy at the overthrow of Stamboliski, might have shaken Peasant Union confidence in themselves is a thought which either had not occurred to the Communists or had been rejected. That their conduct on June 9 had made later successful insurrection impossible, had enabled their opponents to pass through the critical danger period and consolidate power, had allowed the "revolutionary situation" to melt away, is again a view of events which Communists are apparently unable to entertain. They are the least Marxist of political parties in their refusal or incapacity to understand the objective nature and fluidity of political history insofar as they are involved in it. They prefer to persuade themselves that simply by a subjective act of will, by the reversal of an

---

foreign trade, and an eternal struggle against capitalism in general. For a discussion of Grancharov's theories, see Kabakchiev, "Die Nationale- und die Agrarfrage auf dem Balkan," pp. 1780-81. He had been a Broad Socialist until 1921 and was killed in the White Terror following the dynamiting of the Sofia Cathedral in April, 1925. *Inprekorr,* V, No. 87 (May 26, 1925), 1197.

[13] *Rasshirennyi Plenum Ispolnitel'nogo Komiteta Kommunisticheskogo Internatsionala (12-23 Iyunya 1923 goda)*, pp. 300-304. This resolution was adopted on June 23. On the same day the function of the term "Workers' and Peasants' Government" was explained in another ECCI document. It was "a propaganda slogan . . . a tactic of manoeuvre." The ECCI further stressed the "self-evident" fact that it must under no circumstances be interpreted as implying the transformation of a Communist Party into a Worker and Peasant Party, as this would neutralise the very purpose of the maneuver, the domination by a tight Communist Party of a flabby "toilers" front. See "Resolution on the Term 'Workers' and Peasants' Government' Adopted by the Enlarged Executive on 23rd June 1923," *Inprecorr* (English edition), III, No. 52 (July 23, 1923), 538-40.

erroneous "line," and a purge of party cadres, they can again conjure up a missed opportunity for political action. And later, when this gamble has failed, they will again evade an objective analysis of the effect of their actions and errors upon the course of events with the pious pronouncement that all this was a "lesson," a "purifying experience," a "turning point" in the path toward the "Bolshevization" of the Party.[14]

The Central Committee, in its deliberations of early August, had provisionally concluded that arrangements for an armed uprising could not be completed before late October or early November.[15] The assumption that such measures could be kept hidden from the government for so long was unrealistic. Tsankov's police intercepted instructions from Moscow to the Bulgarian Party concerning the planned insurrection.[16] Tsankov, claimed the Communists, was supplied with other pertinent information by IMRO,[17] and he took energetic measures to cripple the Communist Party, forcing it to launch its uprising before preparations were even remotely near completion.

Tsankov, like the Communists, was eager to recruit political allies and he, too, initiated negotiations with other parties for a broad coalition which, unlike those of the Communists, were successful. On August 10, four days after the Communist decision to prepare an insurrection and solicit Socialist, Radical, Peasant, and Macedonian support, the Democratic, Radical, and National-Progressive Parties joined with Tsankov's own *Naroden Sgovor* (National Entente) to form the *Demokraticheski Sgovor* (Democratic Entente) as a permanent governing league. On October 15 the Socialist Party also adhered to this alliance which, despite the defection of Malinov and Kosturkov, the leaders respectively of the Democratic and

[14] See, for example, Dimitrov, *Politicheski otchet na Ts.K. na BRP(k)*, p. 17, and Kolarov, *Protiv lyavoto sektantstvo i Trotskizma v Balgaria*, p. 176.

[15] This was first publicly revealed in 1932 by Bazhenov, "Sentyabr'skoe vosstanie v Bolgarii," p. 276. In his secret report of December 8, 1927, to the Party Conference in Berlin, Dimitrov had stated that until the arrests of September 12, 1923 (see below, p. 138), the insurrection had been foreseen as occurring some time between October, 1923, and January, 1924. See *Balgarskata Komunisticheska Partia v Rezolyutsii i Reshenia*, II, p. 361.

[16] See the government's White Paper, *La Conspiration bolchéviste contre la Bulgarie*.

[17] Berlow, "Zu dem bewaffneten Aufstand in Bulgarien," *Inprekorr*, III, No. 159 (October 10, 1923), 1357.

Radical Parties, enjoyed an impregnable position of power both in the Sobranie and in the country, supported as it was by the army and IMRO and including as it did all parties other than the discredited Liberals, the Peasants, and the Communists.[18] Having thus consolidated his political position, Tsankov was ready to forestall the expected Communist attack. On August 21 a draconic draft Law for the Defense of the Realm was submitted to the Sobranie. (It became law in January, 1924.) At three o'clock on the morning of September 12 about 2,000 Communist functionaries were rounded up and imprisoned in a spectacular police swoop.[19] Though the majority of the Central Committee escaped, the only member caught being Kabakchiev, the editor-in-chief of *Rabotnicheski Vestnik*,[20] the second and third echelons of the party apparatus, which would be of critical importance in an insurrection, were shattered. In its secret deliberations of early August the Central Committee had naïvely resolved to meet such a mass roundup with a 24-hour protest strike, excluding the railway men and telegraph

[18] For the history of these negotiations leading to the formation of the Democratic Entente, see Ancel, "La Politique bulgare: Union Paysanne et Entente Démocratique," pp. 302-3, and Kazasov, *Burni godini: 1918-1944*, pp. 176-77. Both these accounts are critical of Tsankov, Ancel mourning Stamboliski and Kazasov now toeing the Communist line. A sympathetic discussion of the Democratic Entente is that of Lamouche, "La Bulgarie et l'Entente Démocratique." In their refusal to join the Democratic Entente, Malinov and Kosturkov were joined by twenty-one other deputies of their two parties. Dimitrov's appeal of August 24 to these dissenters to ally themselves with the Communist Party was rejected. Tsankov also sought to neutralize peasant hostility. He sent functionaries of the Democratic Entente into the villages to participate in the harvest festivals but they were rebuffed. See Bazhenov, "Sentyabr'skoe vosstanie v Bolgarii," p. 276.

[19] The Communist organizations of those towns which, like that of Plevna, had resisted the June 9 coup had been smashed earlier. The forty-member Soviet Red Cross Mission had also previously been expelled. Simultaneously with the mass arrests, Communist Party locals were closed, assets frozen, and journals, which had been heavily censored for some time, suppressed. The government claimed that the police action of September 12 was prompted by the interception of Communist plans to launch a revolt on September 17 but did not publish this alleged document in the later White Paper, and the Comintern heatedly denied its existence. See the statement of the ECCI in *Inprecorr* (English edition), III, No. 64(41) (October 4, 1923), 717. Plans for an uprising certainly existed but it is unlikely, in view of the conclusions reached by the Central Committee in early August, that they scheduled its launching for September 17.

[20] Kolarov, "Sabitiata prez 1923 god i poukite ot tyakh," in *25 Godishninata na Septemvriiskoto Vastanie*, p. 36. Kabakchiev was held incommunicado for almost two years until he was tried in June, 1925, together with Tina Kirkova, Anton Ivanov (formerly secretary of the Metal Workers' Union and of the Communist Party organization in Sofia), Nikola Penev (the chief of the small Communist railway men's union—as such he had opposed an insurrection), Kolarov, Dimitrov, and Lukanov—the latter three in absentia—for planning the September insurrection. Ka-

operators, and also with mass meetings and demonstrations, the further course of the struggle to depend on circumstances.[21] As might have been foreseen, this intended course of action proved ineffectual and the general strike called on September 14 in reply to the "provocation" of September 12 aborted.[22]

On September 15, consequently, a Central Committee thoroughly disabused of its illusions about the ease with which it could seize the initiative from Tsankov and overthrow him met to consider whether a revolt was still feasible. It was decided to send couriers into the provinces to reconnoiter the political and technical situation. The final decision, to be made on the return of the scouts, was entrusted to a special committee consisting of Kolarov, Dimitrov, Todor Lukanov, and Todor Petrov. By this time police vigilance was hampering the activities of the Communist leaders still at large, and this Committee of Four could not meet as scheduled on September 17 because neither Petrov nor Lukanov dared venture to the assigned place. On that same day the Communist organizations of three isolated villages in the districts of Kazanlak, Pazarjik, and Peshtera in central and south central Bulgaria revolted, probably in consequence of a misunderstanding, for they had been instructed only to stand by for action. Kolarov and Dimitrov thereupon agreed

bakchiev played an evasive role at the trial, denying that the uprising had been planned at all and insisting that it had been provoked by the "objective conditions" of the Tsankov dictatorship. It is true that the final decision to unleash the rebellion had been taken by the other leaders after Kabakchiev's arrest, but he knew full well that his Party was responsible. The only document produced by the prosecution was an alleged confession made to the examining magistrate by Petko Enev, who had led the insurrection in Stara Zagora and had, said the police, been shot while attempting to escape after making his confession—a rather sinister explanation of a prisoner's death and one given with ominous frequency at that time. Many defense witnesses had "disappeared." Ivanov, Penev, and Kirkova were acquitted and Kabakchiev, Kolarov, Dimitrov, and Lukanov sentenced to twelve and a half years at hard labor. Le Temps, July 4, 1925; Inprekorr, V, No. 98 (June 23, 1925), 1321. Kabakchiev was released in 1926 and joined Dimitrov, Kolarov, and Lukanov in the Soviet Union where one of his first acts was again to self-criticize his sins of June, 1923, though he had already done so once in a letter from prison in November, 1923. See his article "Der Septemberaufstand in Bulgarien," p. 1965. These self-flagellations did not, however, save him from being dropped from the Central Committee in 1928. He was allowed to survive the Yezhovshchina as a writer for the Kommunistische Internationale and the Istorik Marksist and died in the USSR in 1940. In his last years he was a member of the CPSU(b), i.e., the Communist Party of the Soviet Union (bolsheviks). See the obituary in Istorik Marksist, XI, No. 87 (1940), 158-59 and Karakolov, "Revolyutsionniat i tvorcheski pat na Khristo Kabakchiev," pp. 194-213.

[21] Balgarskata Komunisticheska Partia v Rezolyutsii i Reshenia, II, 277.

[22] Le Bulletin communiste, IV, No. 45 (November 8, 1923), 813.

that, despite the incomplete state of preparations, the outbreak of the insurrection would have to be advanced to September 22. When Petrov and Lukanov were consulted on September 18, the former asked for a delay to September 23, while Lukanov replied despondently that, while he was in favor of calling off the entire venture, he would bow to the will of the majority.[23] Instructions were immediately dispatched to all Party organizations to rise in revolt on the night of September 22-23 under the slogan "Down with the Fascist Dictatorship! For the formation of a Workers' and Peasants' Government." These orders reached the most distant organizations of Varna and Burgas on September 19.

On September 20 the Central Committee secretly assembled in a chemical laboratory in Sofia to approve the decision of its Committee of Four. Absent were the imprisoned Kabakchiev, Todor Petrov, who was ill, Tina Kirkova, who could not be informed in time of the meeting place, and, for unexplained reasons but probably because of his poor health, Dimitar Blagoev.[24] Todor Lukanov, whose misgivings were increasing daily, pleaded for delay, citing both the inadequacy of the preparations and his belief that if the Party refrained for a while from violence, it stood a good chance of achieving great success in the parliamentary elections which Tsankov would be obliged to hold shortly. Lukanov was overruled, the others probably reasoning that, after the mass arrests of September 12, it was foolish to expect Tsankov to permit the Communists to reap the fruits of any electoral victory, even assuming, though they thought it unlikely, that genuinely free elections would be permitted. The instructions to revolt were confirmed and a special Supreme Revolutionary Committee, consisting of Kolarov, Dimitrov, Gavril Genov, and any Peasant Union leaders whom these three might coopt to it, was appointed to direct the military operations. The fact that these elementary measures were taken only three days before the scheduled outbreak of the insurrection demonstrates the deficiency of the preparations. On September 21 the Supreme Revolutionary Committee established its headquarters

---

[23] A detailed account of the discussions at all these meetings and consultations was given by Dimitrov to the Party Conference in Berlin on December 8, 1927. His report was published as an appendix to *Balgarskata Komunisticheska Partia v Rezolyutsii i Reshenia*, II, 342-61.

[24] Kazasov, *Burni godini: 1918-1944*, p. 184. Tina Kirkova was the widow of the Narrow Party Secretary Georgi Kirkov.

in Ferdinand, a town near both the Yugoslav and Rumanian borders in the Vratsa District of northwestern Bulgaria. There the three Communists on the Committee were joined by two Peasants.[25] At the same time a "leak" enabled the police to arrest the designated local revolutionary committee for the Sofia District and to learn the military plan of the insurrection two days before it was launched.[26]

The plan was simple. As the Bulgarian army was limited to 20,000 men and the gendarmerie to 10,000 by the Treaty of Neuilly —a force clearly insufficient to defend simultaneously all towns and localities as well as the long frontier—the plan envisaged scattered but simultaneous risings in a maximum number of towns and villages throughout the country, excepting only Sofia. The rising in the capital was to be held off for a few days until all the troops barracked there had been drawn into the provinces at which moment the local Communist cadres could effortlessly take control of the centers of government and power.[27]

The plan failed. The element of surprise had been eliminated by the premature risings of September 17 and the government's capture of the plans in Sofia. The main insurrection was staggered in its eruption through about fifty towns and villages, beginning with Stara Zagora on the night of September 19-20,[28] so that the government, which, thanks to the Socialist Minister of Transport Dimo Kazasov's influence over the railway workers, retained complete control over the communications system, was able to shift its troops

[25] Vasilev, *Vaorazhenata saprotivata sreshtu fashizma v Balgaria*, p. 65. The triumvirate of Kolarov–Dimitrov–Genov held together for a decade and was terminated only by the death of Genov from tuberculosis in January, 1934. After 1923 Kolarov and Dimitrov were active in the Comintern, whereas Genov became a functionary of its peasant auxiliary, the Krestintern. See his obituary in *Basler Rundschau*, Vol. III, No. 12 (February 1, 1934).

[26] Savova, *Vasil Kolarov. Bio-Bibliografia*, p. 40; also *The Struggle of the Bulgarian People Against Fascism*, p. 20. The former source refers to a "leak" as responsible for the arrest of the committee; the latter alleges deliberate betrayal on the part of some comrades. One of those arrested was Anton Ivanov, ex-metal-worker, Sobranie deputy, member of the Central Committee, and Secretary of the Sofia party organization. Tried with Kabakchiev in 1925 on the charge of having organized the September insurrection, he was acquitted and emigrated in the same year to the USSR. During the Second World War he returned illegally to Bulgaria to organize the resistance movement, was arrested early in 1942 and shot with five comrades on July 23, 1942.

[27] Berlow, "Zu dem bewaffneten Aufstand in Bulgarien," *Inprekorr*, III, No. 159 (October 10, 1923), 1357.

[28] The entire committee of the Stara Zagora party organization had been arrested on September 12. It was an emergency committee of young and inexperienced mem-

in time from one incendiary point to another as each ignited in its turn. The rebels, claimed by Communist sources to have been about 20,000 strong,[29] were poorly armed and easily routed by the army aided by the Wrangelite and IMRO detachments. In no major city did an uprising occur, and only the towns of Ferdinand, where the Supreme Revolutionary Committee had established its headquarters, and its neighbor Berkovitsa, both in the northwest, were captured on September 23 and 24 respectively and held for a few days by the insurgents. Everywhere the rebel columns were overwhelmingly peasant in composition and in most cases the uprising took the form of hopeless charges by scythe-armed villagers upon the towns and their garrisons. Indeed, the Communist Party district committees of the advanced and presumably more sophisticated centers of Russe and Burgas refused to obey the order to revolt.[30] No doubt these local leaders regarded the premature launching of an insufficiently prepared insurrection as suicidal, as indeed it was.[31] In view of the fact that calm reigned throughout the period of the uprising in the great Communist agglomeration of Sofia, it is not without interest to note that a month earlier the secretaryship of the Communist Youth League in the city and province of Sofia had been conferred upon Valko Chervenkov, then twenty-three years old.[32] The arrest of the local revolutionary committee was, of course, of primary importance in accounting for the absence of an uprising in the capital.

The center of the insurrection was the Vratsa district of northwestern Bulgaria, though outbreaks also occurred in Plovdiv and Stara Zagora of the south central part. In Bulgarian Macedonia, the towns of Razlog and Bansko were affected. Vratsa had neither strategic nor industrial importance, and Kolarov, Dimitrov, and Genov had probably chosen to establish their headquarters here because it afforded the quickest route of retreat into Yugoslavia.

bers which prematurely unleashed this hopeless rising against the 14,000-man garrison. Bazhenov, "Sentyabr'skoe vosstanie v Bolgarii," p. 281.

[29] Kabakchiev, Boshkovich, and Vatis, *Kommunisticheskie Partii Balkanskikh Stran,* p. 103.

[30] Vladimirov, "Zum 15. Jahrestag des Septemberaufstandes in Bulgarien," p. 1043.

[31] The final panicky advance of the date of the insurrection from November or October to September 23 had aroused surprise and misgivings even in Moscow. See Zinoviev, "La Signification des événéments de Bulgarie," *Le Bulletin communiste,* IV, No. 43 (October 25, 1923), 782-83.

[32] *Informatsionni Byulletin,* Vol. IV, No. 6 (June, 1950).

This surmise, if correct, is eloquent testimony of their expectations of the outcome of this rebellion, which at Moscow's injunction they were inflicting on the Party.[33] Their defeatism was justified and their caution in ensuring themselves an escape corridor amply rewarded when on September 28 they were enabled to retire with 1,000-2,000 followers into Yugoslavia, where the not unfriendly government, ignoring a Bulgarian request for extradition,[34] accepted them as political refugees. The next month Kolarov transferred the Party's headquarters and the offices of *Rabotnicheski Vestnik* to Vienna, the center of Communist operations in Central Europe, though most of the Bulgarian exiles remained in Yugoslavia.[35] About 3,000 insurgents allegedly escaped to Rumania.[36]

[33] Primary consideration should, of course, have been given to the capture of the political and administrative hub of the country, Sofia. The Central Committee later sought to defend the selection of the remote northwest as the base of the uprising by claiming that from there Sofia could be dominated strategically. This was nonsense for not only do the Balkan Mountains shelter Sofia from the north, but at the time it was connected with Vratsa by only one railway line and one highway, both of which were uninterruptedly controlled by the government forces. For a detailed analysis of the military aspects of the September uprising, see Bazhenov, "Sentyabr'skoe vosstanie v Bolgarii," and Tsonev and Vladimirov, *Sentyabr'skoe vosstanie v Bolgarii 1923 goda.* Tsonev is the pseudonym of Gavril Genov, one of the three leaders of the insurrection.

The Bulgarian Anarchists have claimed that it was their own and not Communist units which led the risings at Berkovitsa and Nova Zagora. See Svobodin, "El Movimiento Anarquista en Bulgaria," p. 155. Though it is possible that Anarchists participated, the main effort in both localities appears to have been Communist-organized. The Nova Zagora uprising, in fact, according to one report (*Daily Telegraph*, September 24, 1923) was led by the reluctant Todor Lukanov. Since this unfortunate man was subsequently purged and cannot therefore be given credit in Communist historiography for any positive actions, this report has not been corroborated by Party publications.

[34] For this request, see *The Times,* October 1, 1923.

[35] *From the Fourth to the Fifth World Congress: Report of the ECCI.* In 1949 an organization calling itself La Commission d'Aide aux Anti-Fascistes de Bulgarie, which had headquarters in Paris and apparently was composed of refugees supporting the Bulgarian Peasant and Anarchist movements, published a brochure entitled *Les Bulgares parlent au monde* in which it is suggested (p. 6) that Kolarov and Dimitrov had in fact crossed into Yugoslavia before the outbreak of the insurrection and directed it in safety from across the border. Such an assertion had not previously been published, and it is flatly contradicted by all Communist accounts of the insurrection. It is in all likelihood false. Not only would it have been practically impossible to direct the hour-by-hour tactical operations of the uprising from across the closed and heavily guarded Yugoslav frontier, but the only "evidence" presented in the Paris pamphlet is that no one consulted by the author could recall having seen the two Communist leaders during the uprising. That is hardly conclusive proof and the episode serves as a warning of the reserve with which all politically motivated accounts of the Bulgarian Communist movement must be treated.

[36] *Inprekorr,* III, No. 167 (October 29, 1923), 1426.

The number of rebel casualties which, if it could be established, would serve as an index of the extent of the insurrection, is difficult to determine. In the first figures published immediately after the uprising, the Communists, striving to impress the world with their strength, claimed that 5,000 insurgents had been killed,[37] but at about the same time they asserted, in a protest to the International Red Cross at Berne against the alleged brutality of the victorious government, that only 500 had fallen in the actual fighting while the remaining 4,500 victims had been murdered in a white terror unleashed after the collapse of the insurrection.[38] The allegations of a white terror are supported by non- and anti-Communist sources. One of the better informed foreign correspondents was told by Colonel Marinkov, who had commanded the government forces in the main skirmishes in northwestern Bulgaria, that 4,200 rebels had been killed of whom only a fraction had fallen in combat,[39] while *Nezavisimost* (Independence), the journal of the militantly anti-Communist but nongovernmental National Liberal Party also admitted shortly afterwards that nine tenths of those killed in connection with the insurrection had not fallen in actual battle.[40] When Émile Vandervelde visited Bulgaria in September, 1924, he was given highly discrepant estimates of the number killed in the insurrection. Government spokesmen insisted that it was only 1,500, Peasant leaders held out for 16,000, while informants from the diplomatic corps told the Belgian Socialist statesman that 10,000 might be a reliable estimate.[41] By the first anniversary of the insurrection the Communists had settled on 20,000 as a convenient round figure for the number of victims to be charged to Tsankov for the insurrection and its immediate sequel, and to this estimate they adhered with occasional variations.[42] These "estimates" appear quite

[37] *Ibid.*, p. 1426.

[38] Letter of the Emigrant Committee of Aid for the Victims of the White Terror in Bulgaria (a Communist 'front' organization) to the International Red Cross published in *Inprekorr*, III, No. 169 (November 2, 1923), p. 1442.

[39] *Daily Telegraph*, October 6, 1923.

[40] *Nezavisimost*, October 18, 1923, cited in *Spisanie na Sayuza na Balgarskite Studentski Druzhestva v Germania* (Review of the Union of Bulgarian Student Societies in Germany), No. 3-6, September-December, 1923. *Manchester Guardian* of October 1, 1923, prints a similar report from its correspondent.

[41] Vandervelde, *Les Balkans et la paix*, p. 53.

[42] *Inprekorr*, IV, No. 124 (September 23, 1924), 1642; *La Fédération Balkanique*, III, No. 65 (April 1, 1927), 1254; Maus, *What Is Happening in Bulgaria?*, p. 14; *Les Traitres à la cause macédonienne*, p. 60.

preposterous, and Communists admitted privately that the total number of victims of the June coup, the September insurrection, and the government terror following the bombing of the Sofia Cathedral in April, 1925, was not over 5,000.[43] The number killed in and immediately after the uprising of September might therefore be reasonably placed at 1,500 to 2,500. That the government and especially the paramilitary forces which supported it indulged in a white terror after the collapse of the insurrection is true.

The peasantry provided most of the participants and casualties of the rebellion which, though organized by the Communist Party, had been fiercest in the areas which were once Stamboliski's strongholds.[44] Indeed, the chief item of self-criticism listed by the Communists in their post-mortem on the insurrection was the lack of revolutionary action in the cities. This, characteristically, was ascribed to opportunism and treason within the Party, especially on the part of Todor Lukanov and the leaders in Burgas and Russe who had countermanded the order to revolt.[45] Even in those towns in which the fighting reached serious proportions, the major effort was made not by the local proletariat but by invading hordes of peasants from adjacent villages, frequently led by schoolteachers[46] and as often as not bent on plunder as much as on political revolution.[47] These peasants had been assured by the Communists that Yugoslavia would go to war in their support, and, when their

[43] Information from a former Bulgarian journalist who had contacts with Communist leaders, among them Traicho Kostov.

[44] Realizing this, the government issued a proclamation in the course of the uprising, promising to maintain all of Stamboliski's important legislation on agrarian matters, especially the law on land holding, to grant subsidies to peasants, and to declare a moratorium on their debts to the banks.

[45] Kabakchiev, "Der Septemberaufstand in Bulgarien," p. 2122; also see the article by Vladimirov, "Zum 15. Jahrestag des Septemberaufstandes in Bulgarien." The passivity of the cities has remained to this day the main item of self-criticism. See Chervenkov, "Septemvriiskoto vastanie prez 1923 goda," in 25 Godishninata na Septemvriiskoto vastanie, p. 55.

[46] Logio (Bulgaria: Past and Present, p. 362) states that over 1,000 schoolteachers led the uprising. Teaching was a depressed profession, and a teacher's pay was considerably lower than that of other civil servants with the same educational qualifications. He was also much subjected to governmental interference. The number of elementary school teachers dismissed in 1923 and 1924 was 1,533. Twenty-nine were killed in these two years and eleven in 1925. Many schools were closed, and this resulted in much unemployment for teachers quite apart from individual dismissals. A teachers' union and certain student groups were dissolved by the government as politically dangerous. See F. Challaye, "Le Corps enseignant sous la dictature du Fascisme bulgare," La Fédération Balkanique, IV, No. 94 (June 15, 1928), 1992.

[47] Logio, Bulgaria: Past and Present, p. 450.

Jacquerie was allowed to collapse unrescued by Pašić, they turned on the Communist leaders of their bands and murdered a number of them.[48]

Official Communist historians and propagandists have nevertheless sedulously fostered the myth that the uprising was a joint worker-peasant effort aiming at the establishment of a "wide democratic ... government ... [representing] the huge majority of the Bulgarian people—the toiling masses." Not soviets, as Tsankov has alleged in order to alarm the West, but, protest the Communists, revolutionary committees were set up.[49] This is, of course, a quibble, for the Russian soviets were orginally also committees of workers', peasants', and soldiers' deputies, and the Supreme Revolutionary Committee in Ferdinand did in fact "decree" the nationalization of banking and industry and the confiscation of business establishments.[50]

While most of the rebels were peasants, it is not true that the majority of the peasant population joined in the uprising. Had that been the case, the result might well have been different. The readiness of the railroad workers, who were thoroughly disillusioned with Communist adventurism after the winter strikes of 1919-20 and whose union remained under Socialist control until 1933, to transport the troops to the trouble spots also doomed Communist hopes. Nor did the hoped-for mutinies of the peasant soldiers materialize. The Communist Party's own effort was also inadequate and unenthusiastic. Repeated admonitions from Moscow during the preceding years to prepare an underground apparatus and collect arms had been ignored.[51] The incompleteness and inadequacy of

[48] *The Times,* September 25, 1923.

[49] This line was laid down immediately after the insurrection by Kolarov and Dimitrov in their famous "Open Letter to the Workers and Peasants in Bulgaria," first published in *Inprekorr,* III, No. 161 (October 15, 1923), 1376-77 and reprinted in the anniversary anthology *25 Godishninata na Septemvriiskoto vastanie* (the above quotation from their letter is on p. 240). In the letter Kolarov and Dimitrov also launched the myth that the insurrection had been "provoked" by the arrests of September 12. The apotheosis of worker-peasant friendship required a sharp twist in the Communist line in regard to the peasants' hero Stamboliski. From a stalking horse of the bourgeoisie and a rabid persecutor of Communists he became a vigorous if erratic foe of capitalism who was overthrown because of his toleration of Communists. Compare the two articles of Kabakchiev, "Die Letzten Ereignisse in Bulgarien," *Inprekorr,* II, No. 197 (October 10, 1922), 1319 and "Der September-aufstand in Bulgarien," 1965-73.

[50] Bazhenov, "Sentyabr'skoe vosstanie v Bolgarii," p. 288.

[51] For the text of one such warning, see "Die Exekutive der Kommunistischen

the technical arrangements for the insurrection were not compensated for by an element of surprise, and psychologically the Moscow-ordered switch from a policy of passivity to one of armed rebellion was too abrupt and too confusing to carry the entire Party with it. Hence the "treason" of some Party leaders and the inactivity of many members. Their reluctance to revolt in large measure reflected the feeling that the Party had too much of a stake in legal existence, in its bulging membership files, its modern club buildings, its thriving cooperatives, and its large electoral support to risk these in an adventure forced upon them by desperate men in Moscow. Lukanov's "soft" plea of September 20, before the insurrection, that the coming parliamentary elections be awaited on the chance that they might bring the Party success was probably more honest than his later "hard" rationalization of his position on the grounds that it was wrong to "water down" the ideals and slogans of "soviet government" and "dictatorship of the proletariat" for the sake of an alliance with the peasants.[52]

Though it failed, the insurrection had some lasting consequences. Within the Comintern it gave the small Bulgarian Communist Party a prestige second only to that of the Russians and Germans, and the readiness of the Bulgarian leaders to reverse their own policy with robot-like obedience ensured for them the lasting favor of the Russian masters. In the West, however, the effect of the insurrection was negative. There, where Stamboliski had won confidence with his policy of fulfillment of the Treaty of Neuilly, the June coup had initially been viewed with disquietude. The Communists came to Tsankov's rescue by enabling him to pose toward the West as the sole bulwark against the Bolshevik tide.[53] Within Bulgaria

Internationale an den Kongress der Kommunistischen Partei Bulgariens," pp. 421-23. No effort had been made by the Communists in June to secure the arms of the Orange Guard, and the insurrection had to be fought with insufficient guns, some of which had first to be stolen from government arsenals.

[52] That this was Lukanov's later defense is stated by Kolarov, *Protiv lyavoto sektantstvo i Trotskizma v Balgaria,* p. 140.

[53] This claim was acknowledged by even the sober English papers. See *The Observer,* September 30, 1923, and *The Times,* August 5, 1924. Tsankov took advantage of this temper in the West to press the claim that the September events had demonstrated the necessity of permitting Bulgaria to expand her army beyond the Neuilly limitations. See his propaganda organ *Selections de la presse Bulgare,* No. 5 (1923), p. 5.

the uprising made the Communist Party the leading opposition force, though it also crystallized the support of the frightened bourgeoisie around the Democratic Entente government as the supposed only alternative to Communism. This polarization of political attitudes was to give the Communists a great advantage over other opposition groups when public opinion swung again to the left in the Popular Front era of the 1930s and the anti-Nazi struggle of the following decade. Tsankov's terror facilitated this success by preventing the moral isolation of the Communists.

That the forces of the insurrection commanded considerable sympathy in the country is shown by the results of the balloting of November 18, 1923, for a new Sobranie. Though the elections were held in an atmosphere of intimidation, though Tsankov retained Stamboliski's electoral law, which favored the government in power and against which the bourgeois parties had protested during their years in the wilderness, though campaigning and canvassing by the left opposition was not allowed, though neither Peasant nor Communist candidates were permitted to stand in their party strongholds (namely, the districts of Vratsa, Plevna, and Plovdiv),[54] yet the Communist-Left Peasant bloc received 217,607 votes, good for 31 Peasant and 8 Communist seats in the Sobranie.[55] Many of the new Peasant Union deputies were young townsmen who had joined the Union in a burst of conscience-stricken idealism after the war. Such, for example, were Petko Petkov, son of the assassinated prewar Liberal Prime Minister and brother of the Nikola Petkov martyred by the Communists in 1947, and Lieutenant Nikola Petrini.[56] The strong showing of this united front frightened

---

[54] *Manchester Guardian*, June 1, 1925; Kazasov, *Burni godini: 1918-1944*, p. 219.

[55] *II. Kongress der Sozialistischen Arbeiter-Internationale ... Tätigkeitsbericht ... Vorgelegt vom Sekretariat der SAI*, p. 151. In twelve electoral districts joint Peasant Union–Communist Party lists were filed, and these received about 89,000 ballots. In thirty other districts arrangements were made whereby the Communist Party instructed its followers to vote the Peasant Union ticket. See Kazasov, *Burni godini: 1918-1944*, p. 219.

[56] Shortly after the elections of November 18, Petko Petkov was accused by the government of being a Yugoslav agent. The public prosecutor dismissed the evidence against him as worthless, it having been extracted by torture from a number of peasants. On June 14, 1924, the first anniversary of Stamboliski's murder, Petkov met the same fate in a Sofia street. The murderer, a Macedonian police agent named Karkalashev, was tried in October, 1924, condemned to death, reprieved, and released in time to participate in the White Terror following the Sofia cathedral outrage of April, 1925, in which he took part in the murder of Dr. P. Mikov, the lawyer

Tsankov into postponing municipal and district elections for several months, but when these were finally held in May, 1924, the government failed to get the customary majority.[57]

The parliamentary elections of November 18 contributed to the polarization of Bulgarian politics, for in the course of the pre-election campaign the Socialists destroyed their claim to be considered a party of the left. Kazasov's independent participation in the June 9 *coup d'état* had earlier been endorsed by the party leadership and now, for the sake of retaining their parliamentary representation, a deal was arranged between the Socialists and the Democratic Entente whereby thirty-seven Socialist candidates were accepted on joint voting lists with the Democratic Entente. This coalition received 638,675 votes, 61 percent of the total, and 202 seats, of which the Socialist share was 29. The only condition set by the Socialists to their entering into an alliance with the Democratic Entente was that no similar arrangement be made by the latter with the National Liberals. This party's vote trebled to 136,507, entitling it to 7 parliamentary seats. A "right" Peasant Union group led by Dragiev which rejected the alliance with the Communist Party received 42,737 votes and 19 seats, while a communist deviationist splinter group, also opposing this united front as opportunist, polled 5,809 votes but was unrepresented in the chamber.[58]

When the Communist Party turned to survey the insurrection, it was only natural that some members should ask themselves why Moscow had ordered the venture. (How this skepticism was soon

---

who had been instrumental in securing his conviction. Petkov's murder made an impression similar to that of Matteotti in Italy, which occurred in the same week. A railroad strike was called, and the funeral procession developed into a political demonstration against the government. See *La Bulgarie sous le régime de l'assassinat* (published by the Representation de l'Union Paysanne Bulgare à l'Étranger), pp. 105-7; *Manchester Guardian,* June 25, 1924; *Daily Herald,* June 27, 1924. Petrini was also killed by the police in the White Terror following the dynamiting of the Sofia Cathedral in April, 1925.

[57] The votes were divided as follows: Democratic Entente, 389,747 (or 49 percent); Peasant Union–Communist Party bloc, 238,207 (or 30 percent); National Liberal Party, 52,667; Social Democratic Party, 46,918; Radical and Democratic dissidents from Democratic Entente, 44,860; National Liberal dissidents, 13,390. In Sofia the government received only a third of the ballots cast, and in Vratsa, Sliven, Khaskovo, and other areas it received less than the Peasant Union–Communist Party bloc. For further statistics, see Dimitrov, "Die Lage in Bulgarien," *Inprekorr,* IV, No. 57 (May 23, 1924), 687-88.

[58] *Fünfter Kongress der Kommunistischen Internationale: Protokoll,* p. 72; Assen Tsankov, "Bulgarien nach dem Umsturz," p. 119.

to turn into heresy will be discussed in the next chapter.) Their question is important. The possibility of Moscow's decisions having been influenced by the results of the Lausanne Conference and the crisis in Anglo-Russian relations has been mentioned. It is also not unlikely, as Trotsky hinted, that the current Ruhr crisis encouraged the Russian leaders to hope that the revolutionary tide was again in flow throughout Europe. A successful Bulgarian uprising would be an excellent prelude to "the German revolution." [59] Finally, one must not overlook the possibility that Zinoviev, the Russian leader most directly involved in the September insurrection, felt that such a success for "his" Comintern, which at the time had little prestige in the Soviet Union, would strengthen his position in the jockeying within the Bolshevik Party for the succession to Lenin, then a dying man. The tone of his post-mortem inquest on the uprising, a concoction of hysteria and inane optimism, suggests that he was held personally responsible for the affair by his colleagues on the Politburo.[60]

The stakes for which the Communists played were high and seemed to justify the gamble. Had the Bulgarian insurrection succeeded, Rumania could have been crushed between two Communist powers, Turkey would have been caught in similar encirclement, while Yugoslavia and Greece would have been subjected to Communist-manipulated campaigns for Macedonian and Thracian independence. The task assigned to the Bulgarian Party was, however, a hopeless one. Though Communist propaganda must perforce insist that the "insufficient degree of Bolshevization" of the Bulgarian Party was the reason for the defeat of the insurrection,[61] in fact objective conditions, of which the dilettantism of the Party in revolutionary action was but one, precluded victory.

The September insurrection has, however, become the great myth of the Bulgarian Communist Party, the sacred fire in which

[59] Trotsky, *The Lessons of October, 1917*, p. 14. Among the Russian leaders Stalin was skeptical of the wisdom of revolutionary action by the Communists in Germany in the autumn of 1923. For his letter of August, 1923, to Zinoviev and Bukharin on his subject, see Carr, *The Interregnum, 1923-1924*, p. 187, and Souvarine, *Stalin: A Critical Survey of Bolshevism*, pp. 335-36.

[60] Zinoviev, "La Signification des événements de Bulgarie," *Le Bulletin communiste*, IV, No. 43 (October 25, 1923), 782-83.

[61] This is the reason which Dimitrov gave during his testimony at the Reichstag fire trial in Leipzig in 1933 and again in his *Politicheski otchet na Ts.K. na BRP(k)*, pp. 23-24.

it was steeled and hardened into a "truly Bolshevik" party, "the Bulgarian 1905." [62] From the morrow of the uprising unending libations of gratitude have been poured by Bulgarian leaders to the deities in Moscow who turned the Party from the evil ways of the June neutrality policy and directed it to the straight path of revolutionary activism.[63] There were, however, some doubters, some who were outraged over the sacrifice of the Bulgarian Party at the behest of Moscow. Their rebellion followed close upon the defeat of the ill-starred September insurrection.

[62] From Dimitrov's twelfth anniversary message of September 23, 1935, to the Bulgarian Communist *émigré* colony in the USSR, reprinted in *25 Godishninata na Septemvriiskoto vastanie*, pp. 23-24.
[63] Dimitrov, "The Bulgarian Communist Party and the Communist International," pp. 191-92. This ritual was performed at almost every Comintern Congress or ECCI Plenum and continues to this day in Bulgarian Communist literature. In the early years Kolarov would address his adulation to Zinoviev. Later its object became the anonymous "leadership of the Comintern."

VIII

DEFECTORS AND ALLIES

On December 24, 1923, in the Sobranie debate on the reply to the speech from the Throne, Nikola Sakarov, the leader of the Progressive Socialist deviation from Blagoev's Narrow Party in 1908, the arch-chauvinist of the World War, and the chief of that wing of the Socialist Party which in 1920 went over to the Communists, who was then chairman of the parliamentary group of eight Communists, elected on November 18, arose to disavow the September insurrection and to insist that it had been imposed on an unwilling Communist Party against the better judgment of the Central Committee by Vasil Kolarov and Georgi Dimitrov acting at the behest of the Comintern. He then sent a letter to the Speaker, signed by seven of the newly elected Communist deputies (the eighth, Khristo Kabakchiev, was still in jail), pledging themselves henceforth to pursue exclusively legal political activities. On December 26, these deputies constituted themselves a new Independent Labor Group, which they declared to have no connection with the Communist International and to be committed to constitutional-parliamentary methods of political struggle.[1] On December 27 a number of Communist leaders in Sofia not members of the parliamentary group, among them Ivan Klincharov, Sider Todorov, and Stefan Manov (who were to play important roles in the later crises of Trotskyism and deviation in the Communist Party), issued a statement which also deprecated the insurrection as an irresponsible act.[2]

The government, unaware of the seriousness of the strains which the tactic of violence and especially the fact of its imposition by Moscow had caused within the Communist Party, suspected that all

---

[1] *The Times*, December 29, 1923; Kostov, "Borbata na Balgarskata Komunisticheska Partia protiv likvidatorstvoto sled Septemvriiskoto vastanie v 1923 godina," p. 137.

[2] Kostov, "Borbata na Balgarskata Komunisticheska Partia protiv likvidatorstvoto sled Septemvriiskoto vastanie v 1923 godina," pp. 136-37.

this activity was but a ruse of the Communist leaders to avert from their Party the retribution consequent to a miscarried revolution, but the *émigré* Central Committee, then in Vienna, knew better and immediately expelled from the Party Sakarov and any one supporting his views[3]—a formula probably left deliberately vague in the hope that those who initially followed the chief renegade would recant, thereby sparing the Party a major internal crisis and the *émigré* Central Committee acute embarrassment at a difficult moment. This, however, was not to be. Though the Sofia Party Organization did formally approve Sakarov's expulsion and ejected from its own ranks those who had supported him on December 27, Kharlambi Stoyanov, an old railway worker, was at first the only deputy to repudiate, early in March, 1924, his support of Sakarov's "treasonable" declaration and liquidationist activities.[4] Kabakchiev, in prison, retracted his defense of the June neutrality policy and also submitted to the wise men of the Comintern.[5] In June, 1924, Dimo Haji Dimov, a Communist, was elected to the Sobranie to fill the seat of the murdered Peasant leader Petko Petkov. He too adhered to the Central Committee and Moscow as did one other deputy, Todor Strashimirov, brother of one of Bulgaria's leading men of letters, who "solidarized" with the "true" Communists in 1924.[6] The other Communist deputies refused to recant, including

[3] "Erklärung der K.P.B.," *Inprekorr,* IV, No. 2 (January 4, 1924), 16.
[4] "Unsere Märtyrer: Haralambi Stoyanov," *Inprekorr.* V, No. 33 (March 10, 1925), 492-93. In a letter of March, 1924, to the Speaker of the Sobranie he repudiated his signature to the joint letter of December, 1923, which Sakarov and the other six Communist deputies had then sent to the Speaker. Before this letter of March to the Speaker, he sent one to *Zvezda* (Star), a paper then at Sakarov's disposal, explaining that he had originally adhered to Sakarov's position because he had assumed that it was merely a ruse designed to mislead the government and save the Communist Sobranie delegation from expulsion. He had not then realized that Sakarov was defying Party and Comintern leadership. See Panaiotov, "Borbata na Balgarskata Komunisticheska Partia (T.S.) protiv likvidatorite sled Septemvriiskoto vastanie (1923-1925)," pp. 389-90.
[5] *From the Fourth to the Fifth World Congress: Report of the ECCI.* p. 47.
[6] All these men except Kabakchiev were later murdered either by IMRO or by the police. Dimov was involved in the abortive negotiations, described in a later chapter, to effect an alliance between the Communists and IMRO. He was murdered on September 13, 1924, in a Sofia street by the IMRO gunman Vlado Chernozemski, who ten years later was to assassinate King Alexander of Yugoslavia. See "Nachruf: D. H. Dimov," *Inprekorr,* IV, No. 122 (September 19, 1924), 1621. Todor Strashimirov was shot down in a Sofia street on February 17, 1925, and on March 6, 1925, the same fate overtook Kharlambi Stoyanov. See "Die Bilanz einiger Wochen Weissen Schreckens in Bulgarien," *Inprekorr,* V, No. 38 (March 20, 1925), 573-75, and *Le Temps* of March 7 and 8, 1925.

the veteran Nikola Maksimov, who had been one of those delegated to represent the Party at the Second Comintern Congress in 1920 and who represented on the central Party Council the local organization of Burgas, which had refused to participate in the September insurrection.[7]

Though Sakarov's cardinal sin was his denunciation of Moscow's forcing the insurrection policy upon a reluctant party through Kolarov and Dimitrov—a complaint which indicates that he had never grasped the meaning of the twenty-one conditions of affiliation to the Comintern—his deviation had also an ideological content. Sakarov objected both to the specific electoral league with the Peasant Union of November, 1923, as well as to the general alliance with that "petit-bourgeois" movement. He had, in fact, emphasized in his campaign speeches that if elected he would consider himself in no way bound by the policies of the Peasant partner of the alliance.[8] Both communist-defectionist and socialist writers have asserted that Sakarov enjoyed the sympathy of Blagoev,[9] and though this is vehemently denied in official Communist Party literature, it is not improbable that Blagoev, the old doctrinaire who had fought before the war to protect the Marxist purity of the Party from contamination by the "petit-bourgeois" agrarian movement, and who in his last year had opposed the insurrection on the grounds that the Party must be guarded against provocation and that the fate of socialism in Bulgaria depended in any case primarily upon events in the industrial Western Europe of which the Balkan Peninsula was but a semicolony,[10] did wish well to one who now proclaimed these principles as still valid. In any event, Blagoev died a few months later, and by the end of the year Sakarov was active in the publication of a new semimonthly journal entitled *Proletarii* (Proletarian). The editorial columns of the first issue identified this paper as an organ of the Bulgarian branch of the Communist

---

[7] A year later Maksimov was tried and acquitted of the charge of having been an organizer of the September insurrection. See *Inprekorr*, V, No. 35 (March 13, 1925), 529. Subsequently he settled in the USSR.

[8] Panaiotov, "Borbata na Balgarskata Komunisticheska Partia (T.S.) protiv likvidatorite sled Septemvriiskoto vastanie (1923-1925)," p. 386.

[9] Klincharov, *Dimitr Blagoev*, p. 278, and Tchitchovsky, *The Socialist Movement in Bulgaria*, p. 28. For the orthodox denials of these allegations, see the obituary on Blagoev in *Inprekorr*, IV, No. 54 (May 13, 1924), 653-54, and the eulogy by his favorite disciple Vasil Kolarov, "Dimitry Blagojew—der Gründer und Führer der Bulgarischen K.P."

[10] Klincharov, *Dimitr Blagoev*, p. 278.

Workers' International founded in 1922 with other branches in Germany and the Netherlands.[11] Readers were exhorted to struggle for the preservation of the principles of Marx and Engels in all their pristine purity, to despise equally both the Socialist and Communist Internationals, both the capitalist West and Soviet Russia ("a second edition of capitalism"),[12] and particularly to recognize that workers, peasants, and artisans form three distinct classes with conflicting social interests which make any policy of forging them into a united front both ineffectual and a betrayal of Marxism.[13]

The polemic between the defectors and the orthodox was fought out in the pages of *Lach* (Ray), founded in October, 1923, by Ivan Ganchev, who had in 1920 led that heretical Communist Workers' Party with which Sakarov now associated himself, had edited its journal *Rabotnicheska Iskra* (Labor Spark) [14] but, motivated by sentiments of proletarian solidarity had led a small group of his followers back into the official Communist Party after the June coup. The Central Committee in Vienna at first welcomed *Lach* as a legal platform for Communist propaganda. Ganchev initially tried to facilitate a *rapprochement* between the *émigré* Central Committee and its critics by opening the pages of *Lach* to both sides and maintaining editorial neutrality. After a short time, however, this policy was abandoned, and *Lach*, though not supporting Sakarov's sectarianism and not denouncing the Communist International in principle, became increasingly critical of the Central Committee. Whereas the latter, from the safety of Vienna, continued to claim that a revolutionary situation persisted and further insurrections ought to be prepared,[15] Ganchev tended to sympathize with the theory, argued in his paper by Klincharov, Sider Todorov, and

[11] *Proletarii*, I, No. 1 (November 28, 1924). The first, second, and fifth issues of the paper are filed at the Internationaal Instituut voor Sociale Geschiedenis in Amsterdam. General accounts of this Workers' International are *Zur Frage der Internationale*, and Reichenbach, "Zur Geschichte der KAPD."

[12] *Proletarii*, I, No. 5 (February 1, 1925).

[13] As has been mentioned, a number of Sakarov's partners in deviation subsequently became Trotskyists and will reappear in a later chapter. This, however, is an appropriate place to eliminate Yordan Yordanov, who in December, 1923, not only had endorsed Sakarov's public denunciation of the insurrection but had drafted the statement of aims of the Independent Labor Group. In 1925 Yordanov joined the National Liberal Party, traditionally the most hated enemy of the Socialists, and became an editor of its newspaper.

[14] See pp. 99-100.

[15] Panaiotov, "Borbata na Balgarskata Komunisticheska Partia (T.S.) protiv likvidatorite sled Septemvriiskoto vastanie (1923-1925)," p. 404.

Yordan Yordanov, that events had bipassed such policies and that they must be abandoned if the Party was to be saved from destruction by police persecution. The editorial columns of *Lach* also became critical of the alliance with the Peasant Union politicians who, it was feared, would desert to the bourgeois camp at the first offer of a bribe.

What particularly angered Ganchev, however, was the temerity of Kolarov and Dimitrov in simply declaring themselves and a handful of "coopted" members who had also fled from Bulgaria to be the legitimate Central Committee of the Party. He insisted that a Party Congress or Conference be convened, clandestinely if necessary, to elect a representative Central Committee.[16] Kolarov and Dimitrov, unable to oppose this demand, were obliged to agree that a Party Conference be convened soon inside Bulgaria at which recent events would be examined and the leadership judged.[17]

Kolarov and Dimitrov lost little time in seeking to meet one of the major demands of their critics, namely, the resumption of some legal activity, and simultaneously to neutralize the dissident Independent Labor Group, by authorizing the formation on January 14, 1924, of a front party, The Party of Labor, officially led by Svetoslav Kolev, Avram Stoyanov, and Todor Pavlov, the latter serving also as chief editor of its daily newspaper, *Zname na Truda* (Banner of Labor) which made its first appearance on January 26.[18] By the end of March this new party claimed to have 13,961 members, of whom 7,137 were in the towns and 6,824 in villages, while

---

[16] *Ibid.,* p. 396. In August, 1923, the policy of insurrection had been adopted only after Kolarov had managed to secure the cooption of four new members who supported it to the Central Committee.

[17] Ganchev, shortly afterwards reexpelled from the Communist Party, was killed in the White Terror following the dynamiting of the Sofia Cathedral in April, 1925. He was a brilliant journalist and the translator of Goethe's works into Bulgarian. *Lach* ended with him.

[18] Panaiotov, "Borbata na Balgarskata Komunisticheska Partia (T.S.) protiv likvidatorite sled Septemvriiskoto vastanie (1923-1925)," p. 404. Todor Pavlov has had an interesting career. He first became a member of the Party's Central Committee in 1924. In the later 1920s he spent some years in prison where he made several unsuccessful suicide attempts. In the autumn of 1939 he wrote a book "demonstrating" that the Molotov-Ribbentrop pact was dialectically an historical necessity. Again imprisoned during the Second World War, he was appointed one of the three regents for King Simeon by the Fatherland Front government in 1944. Today he is President of the Bulgarian Academy of Sciences. His philosophical specialty is aesthetics.

Avram Stoyanov is not to be confused with the deputy Kharlambi Stoyanov who repudiated Sakarov in March, 1924, and was murdered a year later (see p. 153). Avram Stoyanov became a Sobranie deputy for the Workers' Party, a Communist

Pavlov boasted a circulation of 10,000 for his paper.[19] On April 4, however, this venture came to an end when the Court of Cassation ruled that the Party of Labor, the Communist-controlled cooperative federation Osvobozhdenie (68,000 members), the Communist-controlled trade union federation (35,000 members), as well as the Communist Party proper and its Youth League were illegal organizations under the terms of the Law for the Defense of the Realm of January, 1924.[20] Only the parliamentary fraction, consisting mainly of dissidents, escaped dissolution by virtue of the constitutional immunity of the deputies.

The Communist Party, however, was able to adapt itself to a clandestine existence with remarkable facility. At a meeting of surviving leaders held in Sofia immediately after the court's ruling, a cell system of "fives" was chosen as its organizational pattern, arrangements were improvised for smuggling and hiding weapons, instructions issued to infiltrate youth, athletic, and cultural organizations, and to assemble secret printing presses.[21] Two days after the court's ruling, a secretly printed Communist newssheet was being distributed on Sofia's Tsar Samuel Avenue,[22] and within little more than a month the Party was able to convene, without police discovery, the full-dress Party Conference to which Kolarov and Dimitrov had been obliged to consent by pressure from within Bulgaria. The Conference, attended by delegates from most districts of the country, was held on Mount Vitosha, a massif located a few miles south of Sofia, and lasted for two days.[23]

'front,' in the late 1920s and in this capacity agitated ceaselessly for an amnesty for all Communists. He was frequently arrested on charges ranging from disorderliness during May Day demonstrations to conspiracy against the state. See *La Fédération Balkanique,* June 1, 1928; December 1, 1928, and *Manchester Guardian,* December 17, 1929.

[19] Panaiotov, "Borbata na Balgarskata Kommunisticheska Partia (T.S.) protiv likvidatorite sled Septemvriiskoto vastanie, (1923-1925)," p. 404.

[20] *The Times,* April 5, 1924. Shortly afterwards, on April 23, an amnesty was decreed for the "small fry" involved in the insurrection. It covered also those on the government's side who had committed excesses in the course of suppressing the revolt.

[21] Vasilev, *Vaorazhenata saprotivata sreshtu fashizma v Balgaria,* p. 86.

[22] Kazasov, *Burni godini: 1918-1944,* p. 233. The Party was also able to use the following legal or semilegal front journals for its propaganda: *Trud* (Labor), *Otziv* (Review), *Nashi Dni* (Our Days), and, in the later 1920s, *Novini* (News).

[23] The exact date is in doubt. The official account of the resolutions (not of the discussions) of the conference appeared months later in *Inprekorr,* IV, No. 111 (August 22, 1924), 1438, and stated simply that the conference had taken place "a short time ago." Panaiotov, "Borbata na Balgarskata Komunisticheska Partia (T.S.) protiv likvidatorite sled Septemvriiskoto vastanie (1923-1925)," p. 406, says that the

Fortunately for the Vienna *émigrés*, the chief organizer of the conference was their supporter Stanke Dimitrov, who operated under the code name of Marek. (Henceforth the name Marek will be used in these pages to avoid confusion with Georgi Dimitrov.) Marek was assisted by two other adherents of the *émigré* Central Committee, Yako Dorosiev and Valcho Ivanov.[24]

In two days of discussions the dissidents were defeated. The conference rejected an attempt by Todor Lukanov and Georgi Popov to induce it to express reservations concerning the correctness of the Party's policy in September[25] and not only endorsed that policy but, as a gesture to emphasize its absolute condemnation of those who had, unlike Lukanov and Popov, actually left the Party, claiming that the abandonment of the legal-parliamentary path of political activity had been a mistake, it even resolved that a "revolutionary situation" still existed in the country and that further insurrections must be contemplated and prepared.

Kolarov, Dimitrov, and Kabakchiev—the latter having acknowledged his errors of June and July and announced his endorsement

---

most probable date was May 16-17, a week after the burial of Blagoev. The publication of the Soviet Academy of Sciences *Istoria Bolgarii* (II, 136), gives the date as May 17-18. Dimitrov's memory appears to have been in error when he stated in his report to the Fifth Party Congress in 1948 that the conference took place in April. See Dimitrov, *Politicheski otchet na Ts.K. na BRP(k)*, p. 25.

[24] Ivanov and Dorosiev were assassinated in Sofia respectively in February and March, 1925. See *Inprekorr*, V, No. 28 (February 24, 1925), 422 and No. 54 (April 10, 1925), 758. Marek survived to become in 1936 one of the chief purgers together with Traicho Kostov and Georgi Damyanov, of the "left-sectarian" opposition within the underground Party in Bulgaria to Dimitrov and Kolarov abroad. See *Izvestia na Instituta za Balgarska Istoria*, III-IV, 57.

[25] What Lukanov and Popov demanded of the conference is not clear. The official account in *Inprekorr* does not mention them at all. In the ECCI's report on the world-wide activities of the Comintern, published under the title: *From the Fourth to the Fifth World Congress,* there is an ambiguous allusion (p. 47) that "while recognising and defending the September Uprising as a mass action [they] made certain reservations with reference to the correctness of the policy of the party in Sepember." A decade later Kolarov in a report to the Bulgarian *émigrés* in the USSR published in 1949 in his *Protiv lyavoto sektantstvo i Trotskizma v Balgaria* (p. 140), said that the main tenor of Lukanov's open criticism was that it had been wrong to "water down" the ideals and slogans of "soviet government" and "dictatorship of the proletariat" in September for the sake of a peasant alliance. A postwar account goes further and states that Lukanov and Popov sought to have the Vitosha Conference declare the insurrection as such to have been a mistake. See Karakolov, "Kharakterni momenti ot borbata na Balgarskata Rabotnicheska Partia—Komunisti," p. 150. In any event, Lukanov and Popov were expelled from the Party at its next conference, held in Berlin in December, 1927, and January, 1928. See Dimitrov's report to the Sixth World Congress of the Comintern in *Sechster Weltkongress der Kommunistischen Internationale*, I, 241.

of the September policy in a letter from jail in November, 1923—were reelected to the Central Committee, the first two being confirmed as heads of the Foreign Bureau. Marek, previously only a member of the Party Council, was elevated to the Central Committee and made Organizational Secretary in place of Lukanov. Ivan Manev, one of those coopted to the Central Committee after Kolarov's delivery of Moscow's ultimatum in August, 1923,[26] and one Kosta Yankov were selected to function with Marek as the Internal Bureau of the Central Committee, paralleling the Foreign Bureau of Kolarov and Dimitrov. Marek and Manev were to be responsible for the political and Yankov, a lieutenant-colonel in the army, for the military aspects of the approved policy of preparing further revolutionary activity. Others elected to the Central Committee were Yako Dorosiev, one of the organizers of the conference, Todor Pavlov, who had led the Party of Labor during its brief existence,[27] and Dimo Haji Dimov, destined to be elected a few weeks later to the Sobranie seat of the murdered Petko Petkov.[28]

The Vitosha Conference thus delivered a rebuff to the dissidents and defectors. The latter were isolated from the rank and file and drifted either into sectarianism, like Sakarov and Sider Todorov, or, like Yordanov, to the bourgeois parties. Kolarov and Dimitrov, whose policies had already been endorsed by the Comintern leadership in February, 1924,[29] and favored by the fact that the conference had been arranged, organized, and controlled by their henchmen, were given a vote of confidence which fortified them in their current political campaign—the attempt to harness, with the aid of funds from Moscow, the Peasant and Macedonian movements to the Communist chariot.

There are, preached the Communists, three revolutionary forces on the Balkan Peninsula which, if combined, could be the lever with which the bourgeois order might be overthrown. They are the labor movement, the peasant movement, and the nationalist movement—

[26] See pp. 133-34.
[27] See p. 156.
[28] For the detailed account of the selection of this new Central Committee, see Panaiotov, "Borbata na Balgarskata Komunisticheska Partia (T.S.) protiv likvidatorite sled Septemvriiskoto vastanie (1923-1925)," pp. 406-8.
[29] *From the Fourth to the Fifth World Congress*, p. 48.

all three, but especially the latter two, interconnected both ideologically and sociologically.[30] To bring about this coalition was the task of the Communist parties, a task facilitated by the bitter rivalries of the Balkan governments, often verging on and supposedly inevitably resulting in war, and by the absence of strong Social Democratic parties whose existence would have complicated the problem of an alliance of the Communists with the revolutionary peasants. To effect this combination of forces and to forge these alliances was the task which Kolarov and Dimitrov set themselves in their exile.

A strong part—and not only the right wing—of the Bulgarian Peasant Union rejected the approaches of men who bore so great a responsibility for the defeat of Stamboliski and whose comrades then ruling Russia so rigorously suppressed the political peasant movement of that country.[31] One radical section of the Union, however, headed by some of Stamboliski's ministers who had fled to Yugoslavia after the June coup, was prepared to accept Communist aid in its bid to return to power, and these leaders, thinking no doubt that they could make use of the Communists—the same sentiment which the latter in their turn entertained toward these disciples of Stamboliski—responded to the Communist overtures.

The senior Peasant Union leaders abroad, after the murder in Prague on August 26, 1923, of Stamboliski's closest collaborator Raiko Daskalov by an IMRO gunman,[32] were Alexander Obbov, who had held a number of cabinet posts under Stamboliski, and Kosta Todorov, who had been Undersecretary of Foreign Affairs to Stamboliski. They had established a "Revolutionary Committee" in Prague to which the Czechoslovak Agrarian Party contributed 500,000 crowns and published their paper *Zemedelsko Zname* (Peasant Banner) with the aid of a subsidy from the Czechoslovak

---

[30] Stalin, "Zur nationalen Frage in Jugoslawien," *Inprekorr*, V, No. 76 (May 8, 1925), 1013-14, and, by the same author, "Noch einmal die nationale Frage," *Inprekorr*, V, No. 120 (August 11, 1925), 1730-32. These two contributions by Stalin are reprinted in his *Sochinenia* (Works), VII, 69-76 and 216-26. See also Dimitrov, "Die Lage auf dem Balkan und die Aufgaben der Kommunistischen Balkanföderation."

[31] For informative analyses of the various groupings within the Peasant Union, see *The Near East*, November 24, 1924, and the *Deutsche Allgemeine Zeitung*, February 13, 1925. For the statement of those who rejected the Communist connection, see X.Y.Z., "Le Peuple bulgare et l'Union Paysanne," p. 246.

[32] *Manchester Guardian*, November 15, 1923.

Social Democratic Party. Considerable sums were also received from French and Yugoslav sources. Bulgarian Peasant Union adherents abroad, 4,000 of whom resided in Yugoslavia, were "taxed" 10 percent of their incomes. [33] To preserve bourgeois connections while knitting new ones with the Communists was eventually to prove impossible even for the artful Todorov but the attempt to do so covered the activities of the Peasant Union *émigrés* with a net of mystery and conspiracy which to this day has not been completely unraveled.

Early in January, 1924, Todorov went to Vienna for consultations with Georgi Dimitrov and Gavril Genov, who had come for this meeting from Yugoslavia where he was in charge of the Bulgarian Communist *émigrés*. Dimitrov suggested an alliance of the two movements with the aim of overthrowing the Tsankov government and replacing it with one of "Workers and Peasants" in which the Peasant Union would hold six portfolios, including the premiership, and the Communists four, among which must be those of the Interior, Communications, and War. As a preliminary, the Peasant Union's "Revolutionary Committee" in Prague would have to be widened to include a Communist delegation. If these proposals were accepted, arms would be forthcoming from the Soviet Union.

Todorov claims to have rejected these conditions on the grounds that they amounted to Communist domination and that such open participation of Communists in a future revolutionary government would only provoke Bulgaria's neighbors to intervene and smash it, as Rumania had done with Bela Kun's. Dimitrov declined to accept Todorov's rejection as final and suggested that further discussions be held in Moscow. Todorov was urged to accept this proposal by Obbov, by the Peasant Union exiles in Yugoslavia, and even, he claims, by Eduard Beneš who allegedly advised him to turn to the Czechoslovak Trade Mission in Moscow if difficulties were placed

---

[33] Unless cited otherwise, the information contained in the following pages is taken from the memoirs of Kosta Todorov, *Balkan Firebrand: The Autobiography of a Rebel, Soldier and Statesman,* pp. 198ff. Whenever possible it has been checked against the relevant publications of the Bulgarian government, i.e., its white paper *La Conspiration bolchéviste contre la Bulgarie,* and the daily information and propaganda paper *La Bulgarie,* which was the organ of its Ministry of Foreign Affairs. The procommunist account of Kazasov, *Burni godini: 1918-1944,* contains references to these events on pp. 285-87. The Western European papers have also been consulted.

in the way of his departure from the Soviet Union in the event of a breakdown of negotiations.[34]

Accompanied by a colleague,[35] Todorov traveled to Russia by way of Berlin where he was given a Soviet passport by Krestinski. He arrived in Moscow on January 28, 1924, the day after Lenin's funeral. Kolarov now replaced Genov as the second Communist negotiator, and initially he and Dimitrov advanced once more the Vienna conditions which were again rejected. Invited to make counterproposals, Todorov suggested that the revolutionary struggle be organized by a committee consisting of an equal number of representatives of the two parties in Bulgaria and abroad. Once Tsankov was overthrown the Peasant Union would form a Provisional Government, restore civil liberties, permit the Communist Party to reemerge as a legal party, and conduct democratic elections.

"According to you, then, we're not even to be represented in the government?" Dimitrov exploded.

"Of course not. That would result in foreign occupation . . . ."

"In other words, you want us to fight to bring you to power?" sneered Dimitrov.

"True. But it's in your interest to do so because we'll give you full freedom."

"We know all about your freedom," said Kolarov. "Dimitrov and I spent several months eluding your police."[36]

Mistrust was mutual and the inconclusive discussions went on for several days. Finally, Dimitrov advanced a modification of his proposals. The Communists would "surrender" the portfolio of either the Interior or of War if, in return for this "big concession" (and for Communists the yielding of the Ministry of the Interior certainly would be that), the Peasant Union would enter the newly organized International Peasant Council. Though Dimitrov also promised that twenty million French francs would be placed at the disposal of the joint revolutionary committee which Todorov would

---

[34] K. Todorov, *Balkan Firebrand*, p. 201.

[35] There is no mention of this companion in Todorov's account. A year later, however, Georgi Dimitrov, in a letter from Moscow published on April 27, 1925, in the Sofia *Slovo* (Word), stated that Todorov had been accompanied to Moscow by a colleague. The government, in its *La Conspiration bolchéviste contre la Bulgarie*, p. 19, identifies him as a certain S. Tsanov. The Dimitrov letter is reprinted on p. 73 of this government white paper.

[36] K. Todorov, *Balkan Firebrand*, p. 204.

head with Genov as his assistant, Todorov continued adamantly to insist that his own proposals represented the only possible basis for an understanding. The negotiations were on the verge of collapse when Kolarov suggested a few days' recess to give him an opportunity to discuss the matter with Zinoviev and Bukharin. Todorov agreed to remain in Moscow until February 15 and in the interval applied for an interview with Chicherin, naïvely hoping that the Foreign Affairs Commissar could be persuaded to commit the Comintern to the Peasant Union's terms.

He was quickly disabused. At the Foreign Commissariat Sandomirski of the Balkan Division confessed that he was dependent on the Comintern for all his information concerning the Peninsula, and Chicherin advised Todorov not to count on Soviet Russian intervention should Rumania move to suppress a Bulgarian revolution. To Todorov's protests against the unreasonable demands of Kolarov and Dimitrov, Chicherin replied that he was powerless to interfere in the affairs of the Comintern.

At this point the various accounts of the negotiations become contradictory. Todorov insists[37] that when his negotiations with Kolarov and Dimitrov were resumed it quickly became apparent that neither side was prepared to make concessions of substance, that he thereupon announced he would return to the West, that he was then confronted with the threat of forcible detention in Russia which was averted only through the intercession of Henri Rollin, the Moscow correspondent of *Le Temps*, who threatened to expose the story in his paper, that he returned to Yugoslavia, where the greatest number of Peasant Union refugees from Bulgaria resided, to find that the Communists were conducting a whispering campaign against him, that after deposing those leaders of his organization who had become infected with this Communists virus, he went to the West on a fund-raising tour which was highly successful thanks to the influence and aid of Vandervelde, Švehla, Beheny, and Mme. Ménard-Dorian.[38]

The Communists have never published their account of the Moscow negotiations. Dimitrov's letter of April 17, 1925, published

---

[37] *Ibid.*, pp. 209-11.
[38] Vandervelde was the Belgian Socialist statesman. Švehla and Beheny were leaders respectively of the Czechoslovak Agrarian and Social Democratic Parties.

in *Slovo* on April 27,[39] reveals nothing about them. In a chronological account of the life of Kolarov published after the Second World War, however, there is a cryptic statement that Kolarov and Todorov agreed "to wage a common fight against the Bulgarian fascist dictatorship."[40] This hints at a more positive conclusion to the negotiations than Todorov asserts was the case. A year later, after a bitter quarrel within the Peasant Union in exile, which will be discussed presently, one of Todorov's rivals sent to the Yugoslav weekly *Politički Glasnik* (Political Herald) an account of the Moscow negotiations in which he asserted that agreement was reached on the following program: [41]

1. The Tsankov government must be overthrown by an armed uprising organized and led by the two parties.

2. A suitable occasion for unleashing this uprising would be a war between Bulgaria and Yugoslavia.

3. In the meantime, in their activities against the Tsankov government, both parties should take care that they do not become instruments of the Yugoslav government.

Though proof is lacking, this last account is probably correct. Todorov did not repudiate it. It is supported by the brief Communist reference to the affair in the biography of Kolarov. In the later 1920s the Obbov-Todorov group was denounced in Communist publications as one of the betrayers and double-crossers who had sold themselves to the Yugoslav, Czechoslovak, and French governments[42]—language which suggests that Todorov had indeed agreed to a program such as that described and had subsequently reneged on its third clause (a clause which could have relevance only to the Peasant partner of the proposed alliance) by continuing to accept outside subsidies. That Todorov was accepting subsidies from both the Communists and the governments of Prague and Belgrade was also the charge made against him at the time of the Peasant Union

[39] See p. 162, footnote 35.

[40] *Vasil Kolarov: Important Dates of His Life and Work,* p. 43. The date of Todorov's visit is here incorrectly given as August, 1924.

[41] This article in the *Politički Glasnik* of March, 1925, was translated and printed in the Bulgarian Foreign Office journal *La Bulgarie* on May 21, 1925. *La Bulgarie* is filed at the Internationaal Instituut voor Sociale Geschiedenis in Amsterdam.

[42] See, for example, *La Fédération Balkanique,* III, No. 59 (January 1, 1927), 1081, and IV, No. 90-91 (May 1, 1928), 1900; also Ordon, "Bemerkungen ueber die Bauernbewegung in Europa," p. 273.

schism later in 1924. There is also a later passage in Todorov's own account which does not agree with the assertion that the Moscow negotiations broke down, for here Todorov admits that in the summer of 1924 he again met Dimitrov in Vienna, where the Communist "expressed dissatisfaction because of Genov's reports that all the arms I received went exclusively to our [Peasant Union] organization." [43] This suggests that some agreement existed on the sharing of weapons. Finally, Todorov fails to account adequately for the vast sums of money which he disposed of and which must certainly have far exceeded those supplied him by Czech politicians and French friends. After the schism in his organization his rivals accused Todorov of having in fact accepted a subsidy of twenty million dinar from Moscow. [44]

The rupture within the Peasant Union was provoked by the next move of the Communists. By the summer of 1924 the Communists were finding their relations with the Obbov-Todorov group to be unsatisfactory. Whether this was because the Moscow negotiations had ended in a deadlock or because Todorov had reneged on an agreed understanding is here immaterial. The Communists, accordingly, arranged through their underground organization in Bulgaria for the escape from that country of two former ministers of Stamboliski, then awaiting trial, whom they expected to be more malleable. These men, Nedelko Atanasov, who had served as Minister of Railways and Vice-President of the Sobranie under Stamboliski, and Khristo Stoyanov (not to be confused with the Communists Kharlambi and Avram Stoyanov), who had replaced Daskalov as Minister of the Interior during the last few months of the agrarian regime, joined Todorov and Obbov in Yugoslavia early in August, 1924, [45] and immediately insisted on closer collaboration with the Communists. Todorov then went again to Vienna to arrange with Dimitrov a new series of negotiations to be held in Prague. At these, which took place later in August, Dimitrov alone represented the Communist Party while the Peasant Union dele-

---

[43] K. Todorov, *Balkan Firebrand*, p. 215.

[44] Letter of Atanasov and Stoyanov in the Sofia paper of the National Liberal Party, *Nezavisimost*, April 3, 1925, published in *La Conspiration bolchéviste contre la Bulgarie*, pp. 71-73.

[45] *The Times*, August 6, 1924.

gation consisted of Obbov, Atanasov, and Stoyanov. Todorov did not participate and withdrew to Belgrade.

Todorov alleges that on the return of his three colleagues to Yugoslavia, he was confronted by Atanasov and Stoyanov with the *fait accompli* of their having assented to modified but to him still unacceptable terms. Dimitrov, they explained, had agreed to yield the ministries of both War and Interior, and had consented that the Peasant Union should lead a titular revolutionary government provided it was in fact subordinated to a joint extragovernmental bureau of three Communists and two Peasant Unionists. "Obbov and I," continues Todorov, "at once repudiated this absurd agreement. Still, the two former ministers seemed sincere and I agreed to turn over to Stoyanov the organizational work on the frontier and to Atanasov the care of the exiles. This left me free to concentrate on our general plans and to handle foreign contacts." [46] Atanasov and Stoyanov then allegedly conspired with the Communist Genov to oust Obbov and Todorov altogether from the leadership of the *émigré* organizations. Such is Todorov's account. It is supported by the pro-Communist version of Kazasov, who states simply that Atanasov and Stoyanov, in contrast to Obbov and Todorov, wanted to remain loyal to the united front with the Communist Party.[47] The true story seems, however, to be more complicated and an attempt to unravel it must now be made.

In March, 1925, after a winter of bitter dispute among the Peasant Union exiles, news of the negotiations with the Communists was leaked to the Belgrade paper *Politički Glasnik*,[48] which thereupon reproached the Peasant Union exiles with abusing Yugoslav hospitality. Obbov and Todorov thereupon rushed to repudiate the Communist contacts in *Vreme* (Time), another Belgrade paper, and to accuse Atanasov and Stoyanov of having become tools of the Communists.[49] The editor of the Bulgarian National-Liberal journal *Nezavisimost*, eager to embarrass the Belgrade government by insinuating that it was interfering in Bulgarian internal affairs by aiding rebels, thereupon opened its pages to a rejoinder by Atanasov

---

[46] K. Todorov, *Balkan Firebrand*, p. 218.

[47] Kazasov, *Burni godini: 1918-1944*, p. 285.

[48] See p. 164, footnote 41.

[49] Their letter in *Vreme*, March 30, 1925, is reprinted in *La Conspiration bolchéviste contre la Bulgarie*, pp. 69-71.

and Stoyanov.[50] They accused their erstwhile colleagues of double-crossing all supposed allies. While receiving subsidies from and professing friendship for the Yugoslav government, Obbov and Todorov are alleged to have accepted twenty million dinar from Moscow in direct violation of their understanding with the Yugoslav government. To receive this subsidy, Todorov had promised the Communists to sever connections with Yugoslav and Czechoslovak allies, a promise which again he did not honor. Todorov and Obbov even maintain secret contacts with and receive funds from the very Bulgarian ruling circles against whom they noisily profess to be preparing a revolution.[51] Now they accuse us, Atanasov and Stoyanov, of having sold out to the Communists, but the fact is that at the Prague talks with Dimitrov our chief spokesman was Obbov, who wanted to have those negotiations kept secret in order to facilitate the continued betrayal of our Yugoslav and Czechoslovak hosts and supporters. We, Atanasov and Stoyanov, objected to such duplicity and informed Nešić, the Yugoslav ambassador in Prague, as well as the Czechoslovak ministers Petar and Hodža. Todorov and Obbov are just a pair of unscrupulous embezzlers and adventurers.

At this point the curtain was rung down on the unpleasant drama by the intervention of the Communists in the form of a letter from Dimitrov in Moscow, dated April 17, 1925,[52] to the Sofia *Slovo* and published in it on April 27. After a cursory reference to the Moscow negotiations of February, 1924, Dimitrov proceeds to discuss those which he held in Prague with Obbov, Atanasov, and Stoyanov in August. At these, writes Dimitrov, I insisted on absolute secrecy and on the severing of all Peasant Union ties with the Yugoslav and Czechoslovak bourgeois governments and parties. I am, therefore, surprised and indignant to read now that Atanasov and

[50] The letter of Atanasov and Stoyanov in the *Nezavisimost* of April 3, 1925, is reprinted in *La Conspiration bolchéviste contre la Bulgarie*, pp. 71-73. Their charge that twenty million dinar were made available by Moscow to Obbov and Todorov is supported by an article in the *Deutsche Allgemeine Zeitung*, April 22, 1925.

[51] Todorov's own memoirs lend support to this accusation. He admits having accepted 500,000 francs (then about $25,000) from a leading Bulgarian banker but defends this action with the claim that he gave no political commitments in return for the sum, which was only personal "protection money" paid by the banker against the day when the Peasant Union would return to power. K. Todorov, *Balkan Firebrand*, p. 218.

[52] Also reprinted in *La Conspiration bolchéviste contre la Bulgarie*, p. 73.

Stoyanov have divulged information about the negotiations to Yugoslav and Czechoslovak ministers. In the name of the Bulgarian Communist Party, I hereby declare that we wash our hands of this affair and of these people.[53]

Later Communist remarks about the Peasant Union exiles denounce primarily Todorov and Obbov.[54] These were considered double-crossers while Atanasov and Stoyanov were regarded simply as willing but unreliable supporters. Their subsequent careers are interesting. As Obbov and Todorov, supported by the Yugoslav government, retained control of the Peasant Union organization in exile, the rival pair were isolated and ceased to play an important role in Bulgarian politics, though Stoyanov returned home and became a Sobranie deputy after the amnesty of 1933. He was arrested in 1935 in connection with the so-called Velchev conspiracy against the Crown and again in 1938 on the charge of being a member of a political group. (Political parties were illegal after May, 1934.) [55] Todorov became the confidant of King Alexander and protégé of Gavrilović in Belgrade.[56] In 1931 the moderate and right-wing Peasant Union forces in Bulgaria once again entered the government and when an amnesty was declared in January, 1933, Obbov also returned to Bulgaria where he took an active part in organizing the opposition Alexander Stamboliski Peasant Union, generally called, after the name of its newspaper, Pladne (Noon). It had been founded in November, 1932. Todorov supported it from Belgrade. This new party was pledged to a radical program of "peasant democracy" in internal affairs and close association with Yugoslavia in external affairs. It claimed 128,000 members and its president within Bulgaria was Dr. G. M. Dimitrov.[57]

[53] On March 7, 1926, all the principals—Dimitrov, Genov, Kolarov, Todorov, Obbov, Atanasov, and Stoyanov were condemned to death *in absentia* by a Bulgarian court which had found them guilty of revolutionary activities. See *The Times,* March 10, 1926, and *Inprekorr,* VI, No. 62 (April 23, 1926), 903.

[54] See p. 164, footnote 42.

[55] For the activities of the Peasant Union Sobranie fraction after the amnesty of 1932, see the publication of the British Foreign Office, *Bulgaria: Basic Handbook.*

[56] He also referred to Stojadinović as his "friend" (*Balkan Firebrand*, p. 248). He was, in fact, thought by many to have become a Yugoslav agent. In Bulgaria it was also rumored that in return for a Greek subsidy of five million drachmae, Todorov and Obbov had agreed to renounce Bulgarian claims to an Aegean outlet in Western Thrace if and when they should come to power. This was asserted in the Sobranie in November, 1927. See Logio, *Bulgaria: Past and Present,* p. 460.

[57] K. Todorov, *Balkan Firebrand,* pp. 240, 248. In September, 1939, though

All this, however, lay in the future when Georgi Dimitrov wrote the letter to *Slovo* which marked the end of the abortive attempt of the Communists to make use of the Peasant Union movement in exile. The policy of united front had, however, other facets. Within Bulgaria the radical Peasant Union groups became increasingly dependent on the superior Communist underground organization for arms and supplies.[58] An ambitious Communist effort to recruit allies was, furthermore, directed at the disaffected nationalist movements. The attempts to forge an alliance with IMRO and to stimulate Dobrujan and Thracian national-revolutionary movements must now be examined.

-----

political parties had been dissolved, the Pladne agrarians attempted to rally all opposition elements against the pro-German orientation of the government. They failed and in the Sobranie elections of December, 1939, and January, 1940, the government was returned with an even greater majority (140 vs. 20) than before (104 vs. 56). See *Bulgaria: Basic Handbook*, p. 9.

During the Second World War Todorov and Dr. G. M. Dimitrov, who was smuggled out of Bulgaria in a packing crate, worked with the British authorities in the Middle East. With the end of the war and the imposition of Communist domination upon Bulgaria, the Pladne agrarians split. Dr. G. M. Dimitrov, who returned to Bulgaria in September, 1944, was forced by Communist pressure to resign as Secretary General of the Peasant Union in January, 1945. The Communists could not forgive his having fled to British rather than Russian-controlled territory during the war and his subsequent advocacy of a more independent Peasant Union policy than the Communists would tolerate. He had repeatedly refused to join the Communist-dominated Fatherland Front government. G. M. Dimitrov was succeeded as Secretary General by Nikola Petkov, son of the Liberal Prime Minister who was assassinated in 1907 and brother of the Peasant Union leader murdered in 1924. Nikola Petkov had led the Pladne forces within Bulgaria during the war and had cooperated with the Communists in the struggle against the government and the Germans. He also found himself unable to work with the Communists and at the Peasant Union congress of May, 1945, which had been packed with disguised Communists, was forced out of the Secretary Generalship. He was replaced by the almost forgotten Obbov, who now came forward as the champion of the closest collaboration with the Communists. Petkov resigned from the Fatherland Front government in August, 1945, and began to publish his own *Zemedelsko Zname*, the Obbov faction having seized control of the party organ in May. In April, 1947, Petkov's paper was suppressed by the sinister Communist device of a "printers' strike." He was arrested on June 5, 1947, tried for treason, condemned to death on August 16, and, despite British and American protests, executed on September 23, 1947. Kosta Todorov had died the year before. Obbov became the Peasant Union's leading Communist puppet and was rewarded with the Vice-Premiership. See the New York *Times*, February 15, 1947. A concise account of the consolidation of Communist control over Bulgaria is in Seton-Watson, *The East European Revolution*, pp. 211-19. The story of the Petkov trial is told by Michael Padev, *Dimitrov Wastes No Bullets*. The official account has also been published: *The Trial of N. D. Petkov: Record of the Judicial Proceedings, 5th-15th August 1947*.

[58] This was admitted by K. Todorov, *Balkan Firebrand*, p. 214.

IX

ALLIES AND DECOYS

The Internal Macedonian Revolutionary Organization[1] was founded in 1893 to fight for the liberation and independence of Macedonia, the misgoverned Ottoman province drained by the Vardar and Struma Rivers, bounded on the north by the upper valley of the Morava River and the Shar Range, on the west by the mountains extending along the left bank of the Drin River to lakes Okhrid and Prespa, on the south by a line running virtually due eastwards from Kastoria through Salonika to Kavalla (excluding the Chalcidice Peninsula) and on the east by the Rila-Rhodope mountains and the lower Mesta River. In its origins IMRO was a genuinely Macedonian movement, open to anyone, regardless of race or nationality, living in that province. Its propaganda stressed the "internal" qualification in its name to emphasize that the goal of "Macedonia for the Macedonians" was to be the achievement of the people themselves.[2]

Macedonia was, however, coveted by each of the neighboring Christian states and when a rival organization to IMRO, the Supreme Macedo-Adrianopolitan Committee,[3] was founded in 1895 by Macedonians living in Bulgaria, the Sofia government and court, still dazzled by the vision of the San Stefano boundaries, lost little time in seeking to capture control of it in order to manipulate it in

---

[1] Vnarechna Makedonska Revolyutsionerna Organizatsia. The abbreviation IMRO will hereafter be used.

[2] Gotsé Delchev, founder and ideologue of the movement, warned, "The liberation of Macedonia is possible only through an armed internal insurrection; he who thinks otherwise lies to himself and to others. Let us organize the masses." Quoted in "L'Anniversaire de la morte de Gotsé Deltcheff," *La Fédération Balkanique*, III, No. 69 (June 1, 1927), 1354. Delchev refused to accept any aid from the Bulgarian government. He fell in a skirmish with Turkish troops in the spring of 1903, a few months before the Ilinden Revolt.

[3] Varkhoven Makedoni-Odrinski Komitet. This organization will henceforth be referred to as the Supremists.

the interests of Bulgarian expansionism. This aim was achieved by 1901. In the meantime, the Ethniké Hetaerea, a secret society founded in 1894 by nationalistic young Greek officers to "redeem" Macedonia for their country, had been sending armed bands into the province since 1896 in order to provoke a war with the Ottoman Empire which, it was hoped, would result in Greek annexation of the province. Serbia developed similar aspirations. The governments of each of these three states encouraged their so-called scholars to "demonstrate" with historical, geographical, ethnic, and linguistic "evidence" that the Macedonians were a branch of their own respective nations. Most of the mass of books that have been published about Macedonia in the last half century are consequently misleading.[4]

In the summer of 1902 the Supreme Committee was split when General Tsonchev, dissatisfied with its dependence upon the Bulgarian government, led a splinter group which established itself in Serres, a town in the Salonika vilayet of the Ottoman Empire. The majority section led by Lieutenant Boris Sarafov and the then Captain Alexander Protogerov remained attached to the Bulgarian connection. Shortly afterwards IMRO, drastically weakened by the failure of its Ilinden Uprising against the Ottoman government in the summer of 1903,[5] became dependent for funds upon Macedonians living in Bulgaria. In time it lost its non-Slavic adherents. The defeat of the uprising, furthermore, had persuaded many members that the Macedonians could never liberate themselves unaided by outside support. With the death of the two founders, Gotse Delchev in 1903 and Damyan Gruev in 1906, the organization passed into the hands of protégés of the Bulgarian government, which was interested in Macedonia as an object of annexation. The Supreme Committee in Sofia, now superfluous, dissolved itself; its members entered IMRO.[6] At the time of the Balkan and World Wars IMRO was led by a triumvirate consisting of Todor Aleksandrov, Protogerov, and Petar Chaulev. They placed the organi-

[4] A useful neutral survey is Elisabeth Barker's *Macedonia: Its Place in Balkan Power Politics,* published by the Royal Institute of International Affairs, 1950.

[5] In this insurrection 20,000-30,000 Macedonian partisans were pitted against 300,000 Ottoman troops and irregular *bashi-bazouks* who laid waste the country and left 60,000 homeless at the approach of winter.

[6] *Les Traitres à la cause macédonienne,* p. 11.

zation at the disposal of the Bulgarian army in which Protogerov then held the rank of a general and Aleksandrov that of captain. Chaulev was police commandant of Okhrida during the Bulgarian occupation of 1915-18.[7]

The Serres group, however, opposed the pro-Bulgarian policy of the new IMRO leadership. Since it was from the ranks of this circle that in the 1920s pressure was to arise within IMRO for the conclusion of an alliance with the Communists, it merits some attention.

In the first decade of the century the ideological and organizational leadership of the Serres group came into the hands of Yané Sandanski.[8] He gathered around himself a cohort of young disciples which included Dimo Haji Dimov, Todor Panitsa, and Dimitar Vlakhov, all three of whom were subsequently to become key figures either within the Communist movement or in the united front with it. The Serres group, to which adhered also the IMRO cells in Salonika and Strumitsa, opposed the absorption of Macedonia by Bulgaria and advocated a federation of all the peoples of the Balkan Peninsula and of the Ottoman Empire. They accordingly welcomed the Young Turk revolt of 1908 which they hoped would lead to the renovation of the Ottoman Empire along these lines and formed the People's Federal Party on the strength of which Sandanski, Dimov, Panitsa, and Vlakhov were elected to the new Ottoman parliament in August, 1908.[9] Though quickly disabused of the illusion that the Young Turks would permit the decentralization of power in the empire, the members of the Serres group continued to

---

[7] During the World War Protogerov commanded for a time the Eleventh Division, notorious for its atrocities against Serbians. Later he was appointed Food Administrator for all of Bulgaria. In September, 1918, he commanded the contingents which smashed the Radomir rebellion (see p. 78). After the end of the war, the Allied governments demanded the trial of Protogerov and Aleksandrov as war criminals for the atrocities committed by their units in Serbia. Stamboliski had them arrested in November, 1919, but they escaped, Aleksandrov fleeing to the hills and Protogerov abroad where he lived on Italian subsidies. See K. Todorov, *La Vérité sur l'ORIM*, pp. 7-9.

[8] General Tsonchev suffered eclipse after the Ilinden Revolt and died in 1908.

[9] Planinsky, "Die Mazedonische Frage," *Inprekorr*, V, No. 138 (October 2, 1925), 2019 and Swire, *Bulgarian Conspiracy*, p. 112. The Supremists, on the other hand, did everything possible to hamstring and embarrass the Young Turks (*Les Traitres à la cause macédonienne*, p. 13). This suited Ferdinand and his government, who feared that the regeneration of the Ottoman Empire would doom all hopes of Bulgarian expansion at her expense. Ferdinand took advantage of the Young Turk

advocate federalism as the only solution to Balkan national problems.

Enmity between the Serres federalists and the annexationists was bitter. In December, 1907, Panitsa, acting on Sandanski's instructions, killed Boris Sarafov and Ivan Garvanov, the most pliant tools of Prince Ferdinand among the Macedonian leaders.[10] Sandanski, in turn, was murdered in April, 1915, possibly with the connivance of King Ferdinand, by gunmen of IMRO because of his opposition to that organization's raids into embattled Serbia.[11] He was succeeded as leader of the federalists by Dimo Haji Dimov.

During these early years of the Macedonian political movement, the Bulgarian Socialists sided with the federalist faction.[12] IMRO's Ilinden Revolt in the summer of 1903 occurred at the moment when the Socialist Party, already deeply divided by a decade of bickering, finally split. It was applauded by the Broad section but suspected by the Narrow one as possibly an Austro-Hungarian machination.[13] The Narrow Socialists' attitude toward the Macedonian liberation movement was not, however, negative in principle. Blagoev, himself a Macedonian, supported it actively while Nikola Kharlakov, a member of the Narrow Party until his defection in 1905, was an enthusiastic propagandist for the Macedonian movement in its early years. Indeed, it was he who was asked by Sandanski in 1908, the year of the Young Turk revolt, to draft a program for the Serres group.[14]

The Broad Socialist leaders' championship of the federalist

---

revolt and the Austro-Hungarian annexation of Bosnia and Herzegovina to declare Bulgaria completely independent of Ottoman suzereinty and to have himself crowned King. He had previously been only a Prince owing nominal allegiance to the Porte. See Yanko Sakazov, "Das Unabhängige Bulgarien," pp. 1379-83.

[10] Ein Bulgare, "Gewitterwolken in Bulgarien," p. 590. For a sympathetic biographical sketch of Sarafov, see Christowe, *Heroes and Assassins,* pp. 64-69.

[11] Plantagenet, *Les Crimes de l'ORIM,* p. 11; Swire, *Bulgarian Conspiracy,* p. 134.

[12] Yanko Sakazov, "Die Makedonische Frage," p. 8.

[13] M. Popović, "Die Sozialdemokratie in den Balkanländern und die Türkei," pp. 153-58; B., "Die Kommunistische Bewegung in Bulgarien," p. 133.

[14] See the obituary article on Kharlakov in *La Fédération Balkanique,* III, No. 70-71 (July 1, 1927), 1370-71. Blagoev was a contributor to *Makedonski Glas* (Voice of Macedonia). There is an unconfirmed claim in the pamphlet *Les Bulgares parlent au monde,* p. 35, that Blagoev was prepared to join the Ilinden Revolt but was overruled at the urging of Georgi Kirkov by his own Central Committee. This account must be treated with great reserve in view of Blagoev's frequently demonstrated aversion to violent ventures (Radomir rebellion; September insurrection). In 1920, at

against the annexationist Macedonians did not, of course, survive their own metamorphosis into advocates of Bulgarian territorial expansion in the First World War. Deprived of the authority of the murdered leader Sandanski, some of his younger disciples of the Serres federalist group for a time also cast their lot with the Bulgarian government. Panitsa became an intelligence officer during the war while Vlakhov entered the civil service and rose to be District Commissioner of Priština in occupied Serbia.[15] Within a few years, however, both resumed connections with the revolutionary movement, this time as Communists.

After the war, Macedonians came to play an increasingly important part in Bulgarian public life[16] and exerted their considerable political power in the cause of revisionism. Not only did the 100,000 Macedonian refugees who fled into Bulgaria with her defeated armies in 1913 and 1918 or were expelled from Greece in 1923 [17] cherish hopes of returning to their homes in Greek or Yugoslav Macedonia, but the thousands of Macedonians living on both sides of the Yugoslav-Bulgarian frontier established by the Treaty of Neuilly resented this separation from their brothers. IMRO, which encouraged, organized, and profited from this resentment, became one of the dominant forces in Bulgarian political and economic life. In Petrich Department (the part of Macedonia lying within Bulgaria) it virtually established a state within a state.[18]

---

a time when he was still in complete control of the Communist Party, its propaganda proudly approved of the Narrow's "zealous agitation against this adventure." See B., "Die Kommunistische Bewegung in Bulgarien," p. 133. Author "B" may well have been Blagoev himself.

[15] Swire, *Bulgarian Conspiracy,* pp. 137, 148.

[16] According to Kazasov, *Burni godini: 1918-1944,* p. 252, the number of Macedonians holding key political and professional positions in Bulgaria in 1919 was as follows: 8 cabinet ministers, 14 diplomats, 54 Sobranie deputies, 11 metropolitans of the Orthodox Church, 12 professors, 90 writers and journalists, 100 judges and lawyers, 71 high civil servants, 262 active army officers, 453 reserve army officers. Hundreds of minor civil servants were also Macedonians.

[17] Figures released in 1926 by the reliable Bulgarian Statistical Institute, showed that the number of people living in that year in Bulgaria who had been born in what then was Greek Macedonia was 69,449 and the number from Yugoslav Macedonia was 31,695. The population of Petrich Department (Bulgarian Macedonia) was 220,000.

[18] IMRO not only ruled Petrich politically but also collected 5 leva on every kilogram of tobacco grown there. As the average annual yield of the crop in the Department in the 1920s was 3,000,000 kilo, IMRO became, in effect, one of the most powerful "business" units of Bulgaria. Subsidies were also paid it by Mussolini.

IMRO "sentenced" Stamboliski to death because he accepted the Neuilly frontier with Yugoslavia.[19]

It was during the Stamboliski era that the always complicated and often obscure story of relations between IMRO and the Bulgarian Communist Party began. The detailed and documented account of these contacts is contained in the book *Les Traitres à la cause macédonienne*, published anonymously in 1929 in Paris by an organization styling itself L'ORIM-Unifiée (United IMRO). The controversial nature of the contents of this now rare book[20] makes the determination of its author's identity a matter of importance. Careful examination has convinced the present writer that it could only be the work of Dimitar Vlakhov, mentioned above as a member of Sandanski's Serres group, as a deputy in the Young Turk parliament, then as a Bulgarian government official. Politically a radical, like his colleagues of the Serres group, a socialist even before the First World War, Vlakhov became convinced after its close that the Macedonian liberation movement could preserve its integrity only by severing all connections with the Bulgarian and Italian governments and allying itself with the Communists. While secretly urging this policy upon the leaders of IMRO, he accepted on appointment by the Tsankov government as Bulgarian consul in Vienna and used this position to establish contact with Comintern functionaries. In the spring of 1924 he was instrumental in bringing about a spectacular, if short-lived reconciliation between IMRO, the Federalists, and the Communists. Upon its collapse, he joined the Bulgarian Communist Party in 1925.[21] This, however, was kept secret and publicly denied in order to preserve his usefulness to the Communist cause as chief editor of the multilingual Communist front journal *La Fédération Balkanique* launched in Vienna on July 15, 1924.[22] In October, 1925, the year he joined the Bulgarian

---

[19] Just before he was murdered, "the hands that had signed the Nish Convention" for joint Bulgarian-Yugoslav action against IMRO border raiders were cut off. Swire, *Bulgarian Conspiracy*, p. 168. On October 22, 1921, IMRO had murdered the Minister of War, Alexander Dimitrov, on his return from a visit to Belgrade undertaken in order to work out a common Yugoslav-Bulgarian approach to the Macedonian problem. *The Times*, October 24, 1921.

[20] An uncatalogued copy was found at the Internationaal Instituut voor Sociale Geschiedenis in Amsterdam.

[21] See the introductory biographical sketch to his book *Iz istorije makedonskog naroda*, p. IX.

[22] An extensive but incomplete file of this journal is shelved at the library of St. Antony's College, Oxford.

Communist Party, Vlakhov founded in Vienna another Communist front organization, Obedinena-VMRO,[23] or L'ORIM-Unifiée, which published *Les Traitres à la cause macédonienne*. This book, together with the periodic resolutions on the Macedonian question adopted by the Bulgarian Communist Party, the Balkan Communist Federation, and the Comintern, is the main source for the following account of Communist-IMRO relations.

At the end of the First World War, Dimo Haji Dimov, a veteran of the Serres group, who, unlike some of his colleagues, had not in the course of the conflict supported the Bulgarian war effort or promoted the annexation of Macedonia by Bulgaria, issued a call for the creation of an autonomous Macedonia, to become one of the constituent states of an eventual Balkan federation. On March 9, 1919, Dimov sent a circular to all Macedonian clubs, lodges, organizations—including local IMRO groups—soliciting support for this revival of Sandanski's program, now modified in so far as the federal solution was to be transferred from the vanished Ottoman Empire to the Balkan Peninsula. Demanding a return to the old struggle for Macedonian independence and denouncing the existing Balkan governments as selfish and insincere in their interest in the Macedonian question, the circular, signed also by several of Dimov's collaborators, in effect called for the repudiation of the ruling triumvirate of Aleksandrov, Protogerov, and Chaulev, which had associated IMRO with the cause of Bulgarian expansionism. Dimov followed up this memorandum by launching a new journal. On the front page of each issue appeared the twin slogans "Independent Macedonia" and "Balkan Federation." When his campaign evoked no substantial response among the Macedonian organizations, Dimov abandoned his independent efforts and early in 1920 joined the Bulgarian Communist Party which authorized him to found a Union of Communist Refugees as a rival to IMRO for influence among the Macedonians in Bulgaria. It was a complete failure.[24] Another group of federalist Macedonians led by Georché

---

[23] Moissov, *Bugarska Radnichka Partia (Komunista) i makedonsko natsionalno pitanje*, p. 49.

[24] Its journal *Osvobozhdenie* (Liberation), edited by Dimov, had a circulation of only 500. See p. 107. The above account of Dimov's activities is condensed from *Les Traitres à la cause macédonienne*, pp. 26-34.

Petrov, joined the Peasant Union. Petrov was thereupon assassinated in Sofia on June 22, 1921. In 1921 Panitsa, who had broken off his wartime association with the cause of Bulgarian expansionism, together with a certain Philip Atanasov (not to be confused with Nedelko Atanasov of the Peasant Union), reorganized an independent federalist Macedonian organization.[25] The IMRO leaders, on the other hand, had flaunted their annexationist sympathies two years before by petitioning the Paris Peace Conference to award all of Macedonia to Bulgaria, "the mother country." [26]

The *rapprochement* between IMRO and the Communist Party was initially motivated by common opposition to Stamboliski and by IMRO's need of funds. Already toward the end of 1921 Protogerov, one of IMRO's ruling triumvirate, had sounded out the Bulgarian Communists on the possibility of obtaining financial support; King Ferdinand's prewar subsidy to the organization had been discontinued by Stamboliski, the funds which were later to be advanced by Mussolini had not yet begun to flow, and the "tobacco tax" in Petrich Department was still being collected by the federalist *cheta*-leader Aleko Vasilev with whom IMRO had not yet come to an understanding. As the response of the Bulgarian Communists to his approach was unsatisfactory, Protogerov went to Genoa in the spring of 1922 to negotiate directly with the Bulgarian-born Soviet diplomat Rakovski. Vlakhov, who played no part in this affair, asserts that Rakovski gave a noncommittal reply.[27] One is, however, inclined to doubt this as a few weeks later IMRO issued a policy declaration announcing that it now favored autonomy for Macedonia and would not henceforth allow itself to be used as a tool of Bulgarian policy. This was, in effect, a repudiation of its previous policy. Simultaneously Todor Aleksandrov made flattering remarks about the Bulgarian Communist Party.[28] While it is probably true that Rakovski did not definitely promise Protogerov a subsidy, it seems likely that this reversal of IMRO's propaganda was a preliminary price paid for an engagement by Rakovski on behalf of the Soviet government to consider supporting IMRO.

Since the Paris Peace Conference had awarded the lion's share of

[25] Swire, *Bulgarian Conspiracy*, pp. 145-48.
[26] *Les Traitres à la cause macédonienne*, p. 33.
[27] *Ibid.*, p. 71.
[28] *Ibid.*, p. 49.

Macedonia to Greece (34,600 square kilometers) and to Yugoslavia (26,776 square kilometers) and had left only a small slice of 6,798 square kilometers to Bulgaria, IMRO's new propaganda for a united autonomous Macedonia would continue to be as embarrassing to the two former states as its previous agitation for Bulgarian annexation of all of Macedonia. It would also provide a rationalization for the continued subversion by IMRO of the authority of Stamboliski's government in the Bulgarian slice of Macedonia. Stamboliski, who based his foreign policy on acceptance of the boundaries set by the Treaty of Neuilly between Bulgaria and Yugoslavia and on friendship with this neighbor, was anathema to IMRO. At about this time the Bulgarian Communists also began to regard him as their chief enemy and were thus inclined to favor opposition to him. From the Communist view, furthermore, an IMRO fighting for an autonomous Macedonia would be an IMRO working for the splintering of three "bourgeois" states, for the disruption of the Versailles settlement that was so hateful to Soviet Russia, and would, by fighting the centralist forces of these states, make itself dependent upon Communist support. The Bulgarian Communists, therefore, acted to remove the causes of friction between their party and IMRO. When an armed band using as its emblem a red hammer-and-sickle began to operate in Bulgarian Macedonia, the Party's Central Committee hastened to assure the IMRO leaders that it had not authorized this venture.[29] When IMRO units defied Stamboliski by ocupying Kyustendil in December, 1922, the Communists, whose fear of the peasant statesman had been increased immeasurably by the events surrounding and following the near-lynching of the bourgeois politicians at Dolni Dabnik in September, applauded.[30] In the same month of December the Fifth Conference of the Balkan Communist Federation, which was dominated by the Bulgarian Party, declared itself in favor of autonomy for Macedonia, Thrace, and Croatia within a future Balkan federation and stated that the task of the Communists was to "strive to free the national movement of Macedonia from the influence of the bourgeoisie of the neighboring countries and, rendering support to this movement . . . to direct it onto the path of revolutionary struggle."[31]

[29] Christowe, *Heroes and Assassins*, pp. 168-71.
[30] See p. 106.
[31] Kabakchiev, Boshkovich, and Vatis, *Kommunisticheskie Partii Balkanskikh Stran*, p. 221.

The Communists were not, however, the only ones to respond to IMRO's policy statement of 1922 favoring autonomy for Macedonia. It prompted Aleko Vasilev (called "Aleko Pasha" on account of his ample proportions), "king" of the Pirin Mountains and "collector" of the "tobacco tax" in Petrich Department, a man of federalist sympathies, to join IMRO, bringing with him his armed bands and his "revenue" organization.[32] Thus it came about that the IMRO declaration, the purpose of which had been to persuade the Comintern to grant the organization a subsidy, relieved IMRO of the need for Communist financial aid. Though both the IMRO and the Communist leaders were still interested in concluding an alliance against Stamboliski, and, though IMRO was shortly to be again in financial embarrassment, its immediate bargaining position vis-à-vis the Communists had been greatly improved by Aleko's adherence.

In the spring of 1923 IMRO approached the Bulgarian Communist Party to discover on what terms they could cooperate to overthrow Stamboliski. In May, however, IMRO once again went over the heads of the Bulgarian Communists when Todor Aleksandrov sent Vlakhov and another deputy to Moscow to solicit direct Comintern support. They were informed that it would be forthcoming only if IMRO "proved itself a really revolutionary organization," in other words, if it severed all ties with other parties or movements and accepted back into its ranks the federalists[33]—many of whom were, in fact, Communists. But while Vlakhov was being given these terms in Moscow, Aleksandrov was approached by "other parties," by those plotting the June coup against Stamboliski, with overtures for IMRO support which he eventually gave. Vlakhov's mission to Moscow was thus stillborn.

The June coup resulted in the replacement of the Orange Guard, large in numbers but equipped only with scythes and clubs, by IMRO, which disposed of about 8,000 well-armed *komitaji*,[34] as the private army of the ruling party. Petrich Department, with a population of 220,000, was virtually ceded to IMRO which established there its own financial and judicial administration and "appointed" the 8 (11 after 1926) deputies sent to the Sobranie. From these headquarters IMRO controlled and manipulated the large

[32] *Les Traitres à la cause macédonienne,* p. 48.
[33] *Ibid.,* p. 76. See also Swire, *Bulgarian Conspiracy,* p. 184. When Vlakhov arrived in Moscow, he found the federalist Philip Atanasov there.
[34] Bazhenov, "Sentyabr'skoe vosstanie v Bolgarii," p. 268.

Macedonian community spread throughout Bulgaria, becoming a veritable holding company with interests not only in the Petrich tobacco industry but in practically every business owned by Macedonians throughout Bulgaria. It should be noted that Macedonians occupied a dominating position out of all proportion to their numbers in the commercial and professional life of Bulgaria.[35]

Though IMRO had thus manifestly benefited from the establishment of the Tsankov government, the Bulgarian Communists nevertheless solicited its support when preparing the September insurrection. Whether they seriously expected IMRO thus to forfeit its manifest vested interest in the preservation of the Tsankov regime is problematical. In such matters the Communists' capacity for self-delusion is, of course, well-nigh unlimited. Furthermore, the ECCI had, on Radek's recommendation,[36] simply ordered the Bulgarian Party to recruit IMRO into the battle against the government.[37] Finally, the Bulgarian Communists probably counted, not without reason, on a favorable reaction from a number of local IMRO chiefs who, like Aleko Pasha Vasilev, were inclined to the political left, still believed in the cause of Macedonian autonomy or independence, and therefore felt conscience-stricken over IMRO's alliance with Tsankov.

The Communists had, however, nothing to offer IMRO in support of their appeal for an alliance against the government except the dissolution of Dimov's insignificant Union of Communist Refugees and the cessation of his trivial journal for Macedonians, *Osvobozhdenie*, neither of which had ever been a sufficiently serious embarrassment to IMRO to make their abolition a matter of weight to its leaders.[38] The Communists, who alone have published accounts of this episode,[39] nevertheless later claimed that the IMRO leaders,

[35] Gentizon, *Le Drame bulgare*, pp. 226-34; Logio, *Bulgaria: Past and Present*, p. 21.

[36] *Rasshirennyi Plenum Ispolnitel'nogo Komiteta Kommunisticheskogo Internatsionala (12-13 Iyunya 1923 goda)*, pp. 257-58.

[37] *Ibid.*, pp. 300-304.

[38] The abolition of these two institutions had been resolved by the Central Committee of the Communist Party on August 6-7, 1923. See *Balgarskata Komunisticheska Partia v Rezolyutsii i Reshenia*, II, 277. The Central Committee instructed Dimov and his followers to join Ilinden, the organization of survivors of the 1903 uprising.

[39] See Georgi Dimitrov's report of December 8, 1927, to the Party Conference in Berlin: *Balgarskata Komunisticheska Partia v Rezolyutsii i Reshenia*, II, 361; also Vladimirov, "The 15th Anniversary of the September Uprising in Bulgaria," *World News and Views*, XVIII, No. 48 (October 10, 1938), 1109.

though unwilling to render active aid to the insurrection, had promised to remain neutral. In view of the sympathies of such men as Aleko Pasha Vasilev, this allegation may be true. In any event, when the uprising broke out, IMRO units helped to suppress it,[40] except in Aleko's "kingdom" of the Pirin Mountains where he sheltered the defeated rebels. In Razlog, where Panitsa and Dimov enjoyed popularity, the local IMRO leaders even supported the insurrection, but this was an isolated exception.[41]

The success of the June coup and the suppression of the September insurrection brought about a reversal of the previous balance of strength between the Bulgarian Communist Party and IMRO. What had formerly been the second strongest party in the country and self-proclaimed heir to Stamboliski's power had been shattered and driven underground, its leaders either imprisoned or forced to flee abroad. Alexandrov, Protogerov, and Chaulev, on the other hand, who in the Stamboliski era had to hide in the hills or seek refuge abroad, now led an organization whose power in Bulgaria was second only to that of the army. The Bulgarian Communists, if left to themselves, would probably have considered enmity between themselves and the organization which had "betrayed" them in September to be inevitable and permanent. This, at any rate, is suggested by the tone of Berlow's two articles of October in *Inprekorr*.[42] The Comintern leaders in Moscow, however, more remote from the events and less likely to let resentment determine policy, were convinced that there still existed a leaven of genuine Macedonian nationalism in IMRO which might enable the Bulgarian Communist Party to detach that organization from the Bulgarian government. Recrimination quickly gave way to flattery in Communist pronouncements on IMRO.[43] Its struggle against

---

[40] Berlow, "Zu den bewaffneten Aufstand in Bulgarien," *Inprekorr*, III, No. 159 (October 10, 1923), 1357, and by the same author, "Die Mazedonische Konterrevolutionäre," *Inprekorr*, III, No. 160 (October 12, 1923), 1367. In the first of these articles Berlow charges that the mass arrest of Communists on September 12 had been the result of betrayal by IMRO to the government of Communist confidences.

[41] *Les Traitres à la cause macédonienne*, p. 60.

[42] See footnote 40, above.

[43] See, for example, the *Resolution on the Macedonian and Thracian Question*, adopted at the Sixth Conference of the Balkan Communist Federation in December, 1923, published in *The Communist International*, New Series, No. 4 (July-August, 1924), pp. 92-97. See also Bulatsel', *Ocherki sotsial'no-politicheskoi zhizni sovremennoi Bolgarii*, p. 104 (these essays were written January to March, 1924); and Aleksandri, *God uzhasov belogo terrora v Bolgarii*, pp. 33-34.

"Serbian imperialism" was particularly praised and its participation in the overthrow of Stamboliski partially excused on the grounds that he had allegedly wanted to sacrifice the Macedonian people to the Serb oppressor.[44] In March, 1924, Kolarov, then in Berlin, sent two letters to the party leaders in Bulgaria emphasizing particularly the importance of propaganda among the Macedonians which, he hinted, would soon bear fruit.[45]

The Communists, one may conclude, had decided that if they were to exercise any influence on the Macedonian question, with all its explosive potentialities and great importance, it could only be through IMRO, not through a separate organization of their own. IMRO had to be assured that its struggle against Yugoslavia, a struggle which had become its cardinal policy, far from being an obstacle to agreement with the Communists, enjoyed their approval. IMRO was being invited to ally itself, through the Bulgarian Communist Party,[46] with the Communist International behind which stood Soviet Russia—manifestly more powerful an ally than Tsankov. Nor did the other arguments which the Communists advanced lack plausibility.[47] For thirty years IMRO had fought to prevent the political dismemberment of Macedonia and had failed. Alone, it was too weak. Successive Bulgarian governments had either used, fought, or betrayed it. No sooner had IMRO helped Tsankov into the saddle than he confirmed the Nish Convention.[48] The Western Powers to whose sympathy IMRO was perpetually appealing would always support the existing Yugoslav and Greek states against a band of outlaws. Even Italy had now apparently abandoned IMRO,[49] and the League of Nations persistently ignored its pleas and memoranda. The Comintern and Soviet Russia, however, the Communists explained, champion as a matter of principle the struggle of national minorities for freedom and were prepared

[44] Aleksandri, *God uzhasov belogo terrora v Bolgarii*, pp. 33-34.

[45] *The Times*, May 2, 1924.

[46] The objections of leaders of the Yugoslav Communist Party to the policy of working for the dismemberment of their state were rejected by Moscow, which consistently supported the Bulgarian Communists.

[47] The substance of the Communist overtures is summarized by Christowe, *Heroes and Assassins*, pp. 170-71.

[48] See p. 114, footnote 114.

[49] On the signing of the Pact of Rome with Yugoslavia on January 27, 1924, Mussolini had suspended his subsidy to IMRO. It was later resumed when Italo-Yugoslav relations again deteriorated.

to support IMRO provided it severed all connections with other governments and committed itself to accept the integration of a future united and autonomous Macedonia in a Balkan Federation.

Aleksandrov and Protogerov did not reject these Communist overtures outright. They were indeed disquieted by Tsankov's reassurances to Yugoslavia, one aspect of which was the suppression of several Macedonian papers published in Bulgaria and the arrest of several hundred Macedonians. They were uneasy in their exclusive dependence on Tsankov. Sentiments of genuine Macedonian nationalism still animated many supporters of IMRO who could not be seduced simply by giving the organization a free hand in Petrich. Such powerful Macedonian leaders as Georgi Tsankov (not to be confused with the Prime Minister), president of the association of veterans of the Ilinden Uprising of 1903, and Arseni Yovkov, editor of the newspaper *Ilinden*, favored a move "to the left." A decision to associate IMRO with the Communists would, on the other hand, require the severing of all other connections. Not only did the Communists insist on this but Tsankov would turn against the organization should he learn of such an alliance. Collaboration with the Communists would, therefore, necessarily take the form of an offensive revolutionary pact directed against all the Balkan governments. Should such an endeavor succeed, IMRO could hope to become the ruling power of an autonomous Macedonia. Should it fail, the organization would be driven out of its last stronghold of Petrich. Both the prize and the risk were great.

Before accepting a Communist alliance Aleksandrov and Protogerov decided to make one more round of the European capitals in the spring of 1924, in a final effort to solicit the support of the Powers. Rebuffed everywhere, Aleksandrov went to Rome to consult with Chaulev, the third member of the IMRO Central Committee who, being in charge of IMRO activities in Western Macedonia and Albania, spent much time in Italy. Aleksandrov learned that Chaulev had been independently in contact with the Soviet legation in Rome.[50] As a result of the Rome consultations, Chaulev and Vlakhov were delegated to negotiate with representatives of the federalist and Communist organizations as well as to establish contacts with the Croatian, Montenegrin, and Albanian

---

[50] Christowe, *Heroes and Assassins*, p. 197.

separatist movements in order to fashion a wide coalition aiming at the formation of a Balkan Federation. At about this time the unsuspecting Tsankov government appointed Vlakhov its consul in Vienna and as this city was the regional headquarters for all Comintern activities in Central and Southeastern Europe, it was a conveninent setting for the ensuing negotiations.

The Vienna consultations lasted throughout the month of April, 1924. IMRO was represented by Chaulev and Vlakhov, the federalists by Philip Atanasov and Todor Panitsa. Dimo Haji Dimov, the veteran federalist who was shortly to be elected to the Communist Party's Central Committee at the Vitosha Conference,[51] and Nikola Kharlakov, who after an erratic political career had been reconciled to Communism, also had a hand in the negotiations.[52] When the talks were completed Aleksandrov and Protogerov came to Vienna to approve the agreed protocols and the proposed public declarations. Aleksandrov then left for London, possibly to confer with the Soviet ambassador Rakovski (though IMRO denied this),[53] and authorized Protogerov to sign the documents.[54]

The first of these, a statement of IMRO's future policy, was signed on April 29 by Protogerov and Chaulev and was probably not intended for publication.[55] It begins:

IMRO fights for the liberation and unification of the separated fractions of Macedonia into a completely independent political unit within its natural geographic and ethnographic boundaries. It considers that the political existence of Macedonia can be guaranteed only by a union of Balkan peoples . . . in the form of a Balkan Federation, alone capable of paralyzing the annexationist efforts of the Balkan states. . . .

2. As regards the realization of these tasks . . . IMRO counts exclusively on the moral support of the European progressive and revolutionary currents

[51] See p. 159.

[52] *Les Traitres à la cause macédonienne*, p. 84; "Erklärung des Z.K. der K.P.B.," *Inprekorr*, IV, No. 126 (September 26, 1924), 1677; *La Fédération Balkanique*, III, No. 70-71 (July 1, 1927), 1371. For Kharlakov's earlier activities, see p. 40, footnote 120.

[53] *The Times*, on July 19, 1924, reported that a meeting between Aleksandrov and Rakovski had taken place in London in May at which agreement is alleged to have been reached on the terms under which Moscow would finance IMRO's campaign against Yugoslavia in return for the organization's benevolent neutrality toward the Communist–Peasant Union alliance's struggle against Tsankov. On August 1, *The Times* published a denial from IMRO leaders in Sofia that such a meeting had taken place.

[54] *Les Traitres à la cause macédonienne*, p. 92.

[55] *Ibid.*, Appendix II, gives a photostatic copy.

and on the aid—moral, material and political—of the USSR which today shows itself to be the only state fighting for the liberation of all oppressed peoples. . . .

3. Consequently, the organization severs all liaison with the rulers of Sofia and resolves to oppose their policy.

4. Appreciating the immense importance of a united revolutionary front in the Balkans . . . IMRO will give its complete support to the formation, as soon as possible, of the united front. . . . IMRO will also establish contacts with the Communist Parties of the Balkan states.

Two final clauses express the intention of IMRO to cease the persecution of the federalists and to found a newspaper abroad which would propagate the principles here enunciated.

The next day, April 30, a Protocol of Unification of IMRO and the federalist groups was signed. It also covered the arrangements for establishing the proposed journal, to be named *La Fédération Balkanique*.[56]

Finally, on May 6 a Manifesto to the Macedonian People was signed. Beginning with a definition of the geographic position and boundaries of Macedonia, it continued with a strong statement of grievances against the Great Powers and Balkan states for their failure to secure the province's liberation despite thirty years of energetic revolutionary struggle on IMRO's part. It continued:

As long as these states . . . are not directed by governments who base their internal and foreign policy on the right of self-determination of the peoples, the Macedonian people cannot expect from them any aid in its liberation.

Deeply aware of this historic fact, IMRO arrives at the firm and decisive conclusion that in its revolutionary fight for the freedom of Macedonia, it can count only on the extreme progressive and revolutionary movements of Europe. . . .

None of the Balkan governments thinks of the liberation and reunion of the divided parts of Macedonia. . . . IMRO finds itself forced to declare that the policy of all the present Balkan governments is hostile to the free and independent political existence of Macedonia. The Organization will fight energetically, by all the means permitted by the revolution, against the conquering policy of these governments towards Macedonia and the Macedonian people. . . .

As regards Greece, IMRO will fight against every effort to restore the monarchy . . . and against every government which supports the present partition of Macedonia . . . and forcibly changes the ethnographic character of [Greek Macedonia] . . . by evicting the indigenous population in order

[56] *Ibid.*, Appendix III (photostat).

to replace it with settlers from Asia Minor and Thrace.

As regards Yugoslavia, IMRO will fight determinedly against all the Belgrade governments . . . which support the present Serb policy of arbitrary centralism, the denationalization and oppression not only of the Macedonian people but also of the people of Croatia, Bosnia-Herzegovina, Montenegro, Kossovo, Voivodina, Slovenia, and Dalmatia. . . .

As regards Bulgaria, IMRO declares that . . . the present Bulgarian government of Tsankov practices . . . a policy openly anti-Macedonian . . . a policy clearly Serbophile which not only perpetuates the partition of Macedonia but even prepares new territorial transformations at the expense of Macedonia. . . . It seeks to destroy IMRO and the Macedonian revolutionary movement, which are the most serious obstacles to the realization of its criminal intentions. . . .

IMRO declares that it is fighting and will fight with all the means permitted by the revolution:

i. For the liberation and reunification of the separated parts of Macedonia into a completely autonomous and independent political unit within its natural geographic and ethnic frontiers.

ii. For the democratization of the states bordering on Macedonia and their union into a Balkan Federation which alone can guarantee the political existence of an independent Macedonia and the independence of the other Balkan peoples, satisfy the economic and cultural interests of the Balkan nations . . . paralyze the annexationist aspirations of the Balkan states and the imperialist tendencies of the European states, guarantee a just solution of all national differences while promoting the development of the culture of all ethnic minorities.

The Manifesto ended with a warning of a fast-approaching Balkan war and a promise to cease IMRO attacks on other Macedonian groups. On the day it was signed, May 6, there was also drafted a declaration in the same vein to be sent to the eight deputies representing Petrich Department in the Bulgarian Sobranie.[57]

When the Manifesto was published in the first issue of *La Fédération Balkanique* in Vienna on July 15, 1924,[58] it aroused consternation in Sofia. Aleksandrov and Protogerov, who had in the meantime returned to the Petrich hills, were warned by the government to repudiate it, which they did on August 1, asserting that the signatures were forged and that Chaulev and Vlakhov had negotiated without authority.[59] Their claim to have had no connection

---

[57] *Ibid.*, Appendix V (photostat).

[58] It forms Appendix IV (photostat) to *Les Traitres à la cause macédonienne* and is reprinted in Barker, *Macedonia*, pp. 55-57.

[59] *The Times*, August 6, 1924. In 1927 Kosta Todorov announced that in return for the repudiation of the Manifesto, Aleksandrov and Protogerov had been promised

with this "fabrication" was, however, not convincing. "Even had we signed such a shameful document ten times over," they equivocated, "we should be guilty of a terrible crime if we did not withdraw it when we discovered its authors' true aims." [60] In the next issue of *La Fédération Balkanique*, that of August 15, Chaulev and Vlakhov, who had remained abroad, thereupon accused Aleksandrov and Protogerov of lying, exposed all the details of the negotiations and claimed that Aleksandrov had even amended the original text of the Manifesto to make the attack on Tsankov still sharper.[61] On September 10, 1924, Arseni Yovkov, the respected editor of *Ilinden* and co-leader of the organization of veterans of the 1903 revolt, wrote a letter to Chaulev in which, indicating his confidence that the Manifesto was genuine, he explained that he had printed 6,000 copies, most of which were confiscated by the police.[62] Had the Manifesto indeed been a "fabrication," the perpetrators would surely have forged Aleksandrov's name as well as the names of the others instead of resorting to the unnecessary device of having Protogerov "sign" for him. Even Christowe, the keen defender of IMRO, admits that Protogerov signed the Manifesto and concedes that "it is difficult to say whether Aleksandrov authorized his signature or not." [63] Dimo Kazasov, then the Socialist Minister of Transport, has since written that when he questioned Aleksandrov about the reliability of the Manifesto shortly after its publication, he was told that the document as such was genuine but that IMRO had never intended to implement its program. It was, Aleksandrov is alleged to have explained, but a maneuver to draw the attention of Paris and London to Macedonia and to IMRO by the threat of the extension of Communist, and thus of Russian, influence in Southeastern Europe.[64]

---

an annual subsidy of 12,000,000 leva by the government. K. Todorov, *La Vérité sur l'ORIM*, p. 11. As Todorov was a man of active imagination, if also of great sincerity, one need not necessarily accept this claim. The sum quoted is very large. As the Bulgarian government had Aleksandrov and Protogerov in its power and was stronger than IMRO, it would not appear to have been obliged to offer them such rewards for an action to which it could coerce them.

[60] Quoted by Swire, *Bulgarian Conspiracy*, p. 187.

[61] The Croatian Peasant leader Stjepan Radić, who had also flirted with the Comintern that summer on a visit to Moscow, joined in denouncing Aleksandrov and Protogerov for their repudiation of the Manifesto.

[62] *Les Traitres à la cause macédonienne*, Appendix VII (photostat).

[63] Christowe, *Heroes and Assassins*, p. 178.

[64] Kazasov, *Burni godini: 1918-1944*, p. 259.

This account is bizarre even by Balkan standards. IMRO's raids and assassinations in Yugoslavia had been drawing the anxious attention of London and Paris to Macedonia for several years. Sham dramatics were therefore quite unnecessary. There was, furthermore, no reason to assume that the Western powers would react to the threat of an IMRO-Communist alliance by appeasing IMRO rather than urging its destruction. That IMRO had never been sincere in the Vienna negotiations is denied by the fact that the third member of its Central Committee, Chaulev, continued to support the Manifesto even at the cost of his life.

A more plausible explanation than insincerity is that Aleksandrov had never thought out the consequences of an alliance with the Communists; he had not appreciated that, as a paramilitary organization dependent on the toleration of the government, IMRO could undertake the Vienna policy only if prepared for immediate revolution or civil war. It was not until his return to Bulgaria that he was overwhelmed by the dilemma, realized that revolt was impossible, and, on June 5 sent a panicky message to Vlakhov in Vienna forbidding the publication of the Manifesto or the launching of *La Fédération Balkanique*.[65] Disquieted by IMRO's exclusive dependence upon Tsankov, alarmed at the tendency of this dependence to reduce the organization to a mere private army of the government—a tendency starkly revealed in the September insurrection—apprehensive about Tsankov's policy towards Yugoslavia, vexed over the unreliability of Mussolini's subsidy, and probably urged by Macedonian public opinion in which elements of radicalism and Pan-Slavism survived, Aleksandrov had entered into negotiations for an alternative alliance without calculating all its implications. The requital for his several political somersaults came within a few weeks; he was assassinated on August 31, 1924.[66]

[65] A photostat of Aleksandrov's message of June 5 forms Appendix VI of *Les Traitres à la cause macédonienne*. The Sofia government subsequently claimed to have found documents purporting to prove that a Communist-Federalist revolt was planned to be launched in Petrich on September 15. The Communists vehemently denied this. See "Erklärung des Z.K. der K.P.B.," *Inprekorr*, IV, No. 126 (September 26, 1924), 1678.

[66] For the detailed circumstances surrounding Aleksandrov's murder see Christowe, *Heroes and Assassins*, pp. 178-86. It occurred while he was en route to a district congress of IMRO to be held in a village near Melnik in the Pirin Mountains, the same village in which Sandanski had been killed in 1915 by IMRO executioners (see p. 173). Three earlier district congresses held in the summer in different parts

The Communists had also miscalculated and underestimated Sofia's power over IMRO. The resolution of the Fifth Comintern Congress on the Macedonian question,[67] adopted in June, 1924, before Aleksandrov's repudiation of the Manifesto, and the various articles on this issue appearing in the Communist press in the spring all betray a high state of optimism and expectation in the revival of the revolutionary impetus in the Balkans as a consequence of IMRO's reconciliation with the "progressive" forces.[68] The Communists regarded IMRO as an ally against both the Tsankov government and the Yugoslav state. The Russian Communist leaders feared and hated Yugoslavia as an outpost of "French imperialism" in the Balkans and were convinced that it could and must be destroyed through the lever of its non-Serb nationalities. At about the time when the Vienna Manifesto announced the recruitment of IMRO into the ranks of the "progressive" and "anti-imperialist" forces, the Croatian peasant leader Stjepan Radić was persuaded in Moscow in June, 1924, to affiliate his party to the agrarian auxiliary of the Comintern, the International Peasant Council. In this case too, however, the Communists' hopes were dashed as Radić, on his return to Yugoslavia, also forsook the Communist connection and in No-

---

of Macedonia had been critical of Aleksandrov's repudiation of the Vienna Manifesto. At the coming congress he probably intended to justify his conduct as well as to discover and punish those responsible for several "unauthorized" assassinations, including that of Petko Petkov, by IMRO gunmen (see p. 148, footnote 56). Aleksandrov's murderers were his guides but these also were killed shortly. Several theories have been advanced as to the identity of the planners of the murder. Vlakhov and Swire both assert that the Bulgarian War Office, having lost confidence in Aleksandrov despite his repudiation of the Vienna Manifesto, instigated the murder. Whereas Vlakhov claims that the War Office's instrument was Protogerov (Vlakhov, "Das Mazedonische Drama," *La Fédération Balkanique*, V, No. 96-97 [August 1, 1928], 2068), Swire insists that it was Ivan Mikhailov, then IMRO's liaison with War Minister Volkov and subsequently Aleksandrov's successor as strong-man of IMRO (Swire, *Bulgarian Conspiracy*, p. 187). At the time of the murder both IMRO and Bulgarian government propaganda claimed that the Federalists and Communists had instigated it to avenge the repudiation of the Manifesto. The American Macedonian press still adhered to this version in 1932. See *Macedonia* (Indianapolis), I, No. 6 (June, 1932), 104. In 1928 Mikhailov had Protogerov killed and to justify this murder charged Protogerov with Aleksandrov's assassination. Two decades after the event Kosta Todorov, in his autobiography *Balkan Firebrand*, p. 213, again charged the Communists with responsibility for Aleksandrov's murder.

[67] Reprinted in *The Communist International*, New Series, No. 7 (December, 1924–January, 1925), pp. 93-95.

[68] Dimitrov, "Die Lage in Bulgarien," *Inprekorr*, IV, No. 57 (May 23, 1924), 688 and Aleksandri, *God uzhasov belogo terrora v Bolgarii*, pp. 37-38. Dimitrov trumpeted that as the scales were now dropping from the eyes of the Macedonians, "the days of the bourgeois-fascist government in Bulgaria are numbered."

vember, 1925, entered the Pašić government as Minister of Education. Even had IMRO implemented the Vienna Manifesto, it is difficult to see how the Bulgarian Communists could have maintained this alliance simultaneously with the one with the Peasant Union which they were also attempting to bring about at the time. IMRO could not have been reconciled to a party which they held responsible for the "betrayal" of Macedonia while the agrarians would never pardon the murderers of Alexander Dimitrov (October, 1921), Alexander Stamboliski (June, 1923), Raiko Daskalov (August, 1923) and many simple peasants during the June coup of 1923.

The murder of Aleksandrov evoked a vast massacre of IMRO leaders, federalists, and Communists who had either been involved in the Vienna negotiations or were suspected of supporting the Manifesto. It began on September 13, at a conference in Gorna Djumaya at which it had been hoped to effect a reconciliation between IMRO and Ilinden, the organization of veterans of the 1903 revolt against the Turks. Among those murdered were Arseni Yovkov, editor of the journal *Ilinden*, who had urged ending IMRO's exclusive dependence upon Tsankov and had endorsed the Manifesto, and Aleko Pasha Vasilev, the IMRO chief of the Pirin Mountains area, who had always harbored federalist sympathies and had protected Communist rebels after the September insurrection. Dimo Haji Dimov, the member of the Communist Party's Central Committee who had been a negotiator with IMRO, was shot dead in a Sofia street on September 13.[69] Chaulev, who had denounced the repudiation of the Manifesto and refused to return to Bulgaria, was pursued by IMRO to his hiding place in Milan and killed there on December 23, 1924.[70] Todor Panitsa, the veteran leader of the Serres federalists, who had also remained abroad after the Vienna

[69] "Nachruf: D. H. Dimov," *Inprekorr*, IV, No. 122 (September 19, 1924), 1621. Only a few months before he had been elected to the Sobranie seat of the murdered Petko Petkov. Dimov's assassin, Chernozemski, was the same IMRO gunman who ten years later was to kill King Alexander and Barthou at Marseilles. Dimov was born in 1878 and had participated in the Ilinden Rising of 1903. Like Delchev, Gruev, Aleksandrov, and many other leaders of the Macedonian movement, he was by profession a teacher.

[70] "Die Ermordung Peter Tschaulews," *Inprekorr*, IV, No. 169 (December 30, 1924), 2325. Born in 1880 at Okhrida, in what is today Yugoslav Macedonia, Chaulev joined the *komitajis* in 1898 and led a band in the Ilinden Rising of 1903. A man of federalist sympathies, he had vainly sought to cooperate with the Young

negotiations and had then established contact with the Yugoslav government through Žika Lazić, with the Peasant Union through Kosta Todorov, and with the Communists through Gavril Genov,[71] was shot dead in Vienna on May 8, 1925, by a young Vlakh woman, who as a reward for this deed[72] became the wife of Ivan Mikhailov, Aleksandrov's successor as leader of IMRO and the man who had organized this purge which is estimated to have claimed between 160 and 300 victims.[73] That the Tsankov government was content to see the left wing of the Macedonian movement thus shattered is indicated by the fact that the murderers were either never arrested or quickly released.

In February, 1925, Ivan Mikhailov and Georgi Pop-Khristov were elected to join Protogerov on the Central Committee in place of Aleksandrov and Chaulev. In March this trio issued a declaration on behalf of IMRO which reaffirmed the organization's ties to the Bulgarian government.[74] IMRO soon degenerated into a gangster band which ran a financial and extortion racket toward which successive Bulgarian governments, especially that of Lyapchev (1926-31), a Macedonian, showed remarkable tolerance. Protogerov's

---

Turks in 1908. Shortly before his murder he had been visited by Georgi Dimitrov who was then traveling through Europe to recruit allies for the Bulgarian Communist Party. In August, Dimitrov had negotiated with the Peasant Union in Prague. See pp. 165-66.

[71] Swire, *Bulgarian Conspiracy*, p. 195; K. Todorov, *Balkan Firebrand*, p. 212.

[72] "Die Ermordung des Mazedonischen Revolutionärs Panitza," *Inprekorr*, V, No. 82 (May 15, 1925), 1115; "Todor Panitsa—po sluchai dve godini ot smerta mu" (Todor Panitsa—on the Occasion of the Second Anniversary of His Death), *La Fédération Balkanique*, III, No. 68 (May 15, 1927), 1339. The murderess, Mencha Karnicheva, had ingratiated herself with Panitsa and shot him while attending, as his guest, a performance of *Peer Gynt* in the Burgtheater. Sentenced to eight years' imprisonment by an Austrian court, she was soon released for reasons of ill health and returned to Bulgaria. See Mermet, "Der Ausgang des Carniciu Prozess," *Inprekorr*, V, No. 139 (October 6, 1925), 2032. Panitsa was born in Oryakhovo (Rakhova), a town on the Danube, far from Macedonia, in 1877. When he was a boy of eleven, his father, an army major, was executed for being involved in a conspiracy against Prince Ferdinand. In 1907 Panitsa, having joined Sandanski's federalists on leaving the gymnasium, killed the rival leaders Sarafov and Garvanov. He was elected to the Young Turk parliament in 1908, served in the Bulgarian army in the World War, and, when Dimov joined the Communist Party at its conclusion, became co-leader with Philip Atanasov of the independent federalists.

[73] K. Todorov, "The Macedonian Organization Yesterday and Today," p. 480, opts for the higher figure. The lower one is an estimate in *La Fédération Balkanique*, IV, No. 74-75 (September 1, 1927), 1446.

[74] *Déclaration de l'Organisation Intérieure Révolutionnaire de Macédoine*. (This is a one-page broadsheet in the possession of the author. It is dated: Macédoine, Mars 1925).

murder by Mikhailov on July 7, 1928, ostensibly in retaliation for Protogerov's alleged connivance at Aleksandrov's death, removed the last genuine political figure among IMRO's leaders.[75] It was followed by another orgy of hundreds of murders among IMRO by opposing gangs of Protogerovists and Mikhailovists. As the latter enjoyed the protection of War Minister Volkov, it emerged victorious, the rivals having been decimated.[76] In April, 1929, Mikhailov arranged with Ante Pavelić, then visiting Bulgaria to place several experienced IMRO gunmen at the disposal of the Ustash, one of these being King Alexander's future assassin.[77] The Macedonian population of Yugoslavia had long since ceased to welcome the IMRO raiders from across the Bulgarian border who came ostensibly to "liberate" but actually only to terrorize Yugoslav Macedonia. In Bulgaria, Mikhailov transformed IMRO into a sheer gangster band. Its "executions" took place even in front of the Royal Palace. Still the government did nothing. In the summer of 1928 a joint Anglo-French *démarche*, with which Italy had significantly declined to associate itself, had been fruitless.[78] In 1932 Mikhailov launched IMRO into the illegal narcotics traffic.[79]

The end of IMRO finally came in May, 1934, when another *coup d'état* replaced the discredited parliamentary party system with a military government dedicated to a renovation of Bulgaria's internal affairs and a reconciliation with Yugoslavia in her foreign policy. The Protogerovists disbanded voluntarily. Mikhailov evaded imprisonment by fleeing to Turkey. His protector, General Volkov, for long War Minister and subsequently Ambassador to Rome, was dismissed from the government service. At the trial of those who had helped Mikhailov escape it was revealed that since 1924 IMRO assassinations had claimed 624 federalists and Communists, 220 Protogerovists, and 40 Mikhailovists.[80]

---

[75] Protogerov, as a general in the Bulgarian army, was given a state funeral.

[76] Ivanov, "Self-Extermination in the Camp of the Macedonian Fascists," *Inprecorr* (English edition), IX, No. 56 (October 4, 1929), 1216.

[77] Christowe, *Heroes and Assassins*, p. 216.

[78] *La Fédération Balkanique*, V, No. 98-99 (September 1, 1928), 2105.

[79] Swire, *Bulgarian Conspiracy*, p. 50.

[80] Londres, *Terror in the Balkans*, p. 234. In 1938 Mikhailov was expelled from Turkey (*The Times*, August 23, 1938). His whereabouts during the Second World War are not known to the author, though rumor had it that he was in Zagreb with Pavelić and being held in reserve by Hitler as a possible gauleiter of Macedonia should the Bulgarian occupation deteriorate. He survived the war. Bulgarian exiles

The main reason for IMRO's degeneration, as has been pointed out by Elisabeth Barker,[81] is that despite its efficient organization it lacked a definite political aim or a serious social program. Its propaganda catch phrases about "Macedonian freedom" were contradicted by its obvious dependence upon the Bulgarian and Italian governments and therefore had as little appeal to the people of Macedonia as the tactic of raids and murders had success in stimulating the Great Powers to redraw the Balkan frontiers. In any event, IMRO had never definitely decided how the Neuilly frontiers should be redrawn, had never resolved the ambiguity of whether it wanted Macedonia to be independent or annexed to Bulgaria.

Confusion and failure also characterized the Communists' Macedonian policy. Though they had carefully avoided overt participation in the negotiations of 1924 with IMRO—Dimov and Kharlakov acting ostensibly as federalist sympathizers and references to Soviet Russia being confined to the secret protocol of April 29 [82]—they had high expectations[83] for the success of this endeavor to draw IMRO into that "fellow-traveler" Balkan alliance system which they were simultaneously attempting to forge with the Bulgarian and Croatian Peasant Parties.[84] Aleksandrov's repudiation of the Vienna Manifesto was a cruel disappointment and confronted the Communists once again with the task of attempting to drive a wedge between IMRO and the Macedonian population. The failure of

in London understand that he was enabled to escape repatriation and punishment as a collaborator through the intercession of the Vatican. He has since had two worthless books published in the United States. The first, which appeared under the pseudonym "Macedonicus" is entitled *Stalin and the Macedonian Question* (St. Louis, Pearlstone Publishing Co., 1948). The second, issued by the same firm in 1950, is signed with his own name and entitled *Macedonia: A Switzerland of the Balkans.*

[81] Barker, *Macedonia,* p. 38.

[82] See pp. 184-85.

[83] See p. 189, footnote 68.

[84] The Bulgarian Communist Party's negotiations with the Bulgarian Peasant Union in exile, though still fruitless in the spring of 1924, had not collapsed and were about to be given a fresh impulse with the escape from Bulgaria of Atanasov and Stoyanov. Ultimately, as has been seen, this Communist effort to recruit an ally had as little success as those directed at IMRO and Radić. In retrospect, the year 1924 appears as one of high, if unfounded, Communist optimism in the Balkans. Significantly, it marked the creation of the Moldavian Soviet Republic on the left bank of the Dniester River in the Soviet Union, thus increasing the pressure on Rumania in the Bessarabian dispute.

Dimov's Union of Communist Refugees to win the support of more than a handful of Macedonians from its formation in 1920 to its dissolution in August, 1923, had, however, convinced the Communists of the futility of hoping to displace IMRO with a rival organization flaunting their own banner and had, in fact, persuaded them of the importance of coming to terms with IMRO. The problem which faced them at this point was, accordingly, to dissociate themselves from IMRO again and to seek to alienate from it the "betrayed" Macedonian "masses" without, however, appearing openly to intrude themselves into Macedonian politics. Front tactics were the order of the day, and their chief manipulator was to be Dimitar Vlakhov in Vienna.

Upon the publication and repudiation of the Vienna Manifesto in the summer of 1924, Vlakhov had been denounced by the Bulgarian government [85] in Vienna and, together with Chaulev, condemned to death by IMRO for "having betrayed the secrets of the Organization for the benefit of the Bolsheviks" and related offences.[86] Victor Serge, visiting him in Vienna some time afterwards, found Vlakhov suffering from "assassination tremors," [87] as well he might in view of the fate of the other participants in the negotiations. Yet he resolutely continued to bring out *La Fédération Balkanique*, taking over the editorship upon Nikola Kharlakov's retirement to the Soviet Union after the first five issues for reasons of ill health.

Vlakhov carefully avoided any overt association either of himself or of the journal with Communism. The fact that he joined the Bulgarian Communist Party in 1925 was kept strictly secret.[88] Suggestions that *La Fédération Balkanique* was financed from Communist funds were parried with the reply that it had been launched with 150,000 leva appropriated by Aleksandrov before his repudiation of the Vienna Manifesto and since then was being supported by sympathizers in Macedonia and America.[89] Patent appeals for Communism were eschewed in the journal's editorial

[85] Swire, *Bulgarian Conspiracy*, p. 182.
[86] *Les Traitres à la cause macédonienne*, p. 207.
[87] Serge, *Mémoires d'un révolutionnaire*, p. 198.
[88] It was openly admitted in the introduction to his book *Iz istorije makedonskog naroda*, p. IX.
[89] *La Fédération Balkanique*, July 15, 1925; *Les Traitres à la cause macédonienne*. p. 116.

policy, which Vlakhov confined to the program defined in its first issue of July 15, 1924, as follows:

> The main task of our journal is . . . to propagate the idea of the liberation and the right of self-determination of the Balkan peoples as well as that of federalization. . . . We want that they [i.e., the Balkan peoples] should cease to be the common prey of European imperialism and Balkan chauvinism. . . . Only Federation, which will destroy the roots of national conflict, which will guarantee the free cultural development of national minorities, which will secure to all its members free access to the sea and to the great rivers, which will ensure for everyone full political and economic freedom, will give the Balkans ultimate peace and permit the general cultural development of the peoples.

There was no mention of Soviet republics. To the observation that Federation was also the Balkan program of the Communists, Vlakhov retorted that it was advocated by European liberals and democrats as well [90] and in evidence presented endorsements of the policy from a brilliant galaxy of non-Communist intellectuals.[91]

In propagating the idea of Balkan federation, Vlakhov launched a series of journalistic crusades against Italian designs on Albania and Dalmatia as well as against British and French diplomatic influence in Yugoslavia, Rumania, Greece, and Bulgaria. Such opposition to "Great Power imperialism" in the Balkans corresponded, of course, to the interests of the Soviet Union at a time when she was still too weak to exert her own power on the peninsula. Vlakhov also attacked the Balkan governments which, like those of Belgrade and Bucharest, were charged with attempting to "denationalize" the minorities under their rule or, like Sofia's, with persecuting those of its subjects who favored federation and democracy.

An interesting aspect of the editorial policy of *La Fédération Balkanique* was that, simultaneously with its ceaseless propaganda for federation, it denounced attempts to bring about a *rapprochement* among the existing Balkan governments with a vehemence amounting at times to appeals to national xenophobia. The Bulgarian government, for example, was violently maligned for its "betrayal" of the Bulgarian minorities of the Dobruja, Thrace, and

---

[90] *La Fédération Balkanique,* July 15, 1925.
[91] *Ibid.,* 1926-28, *passim.* Many Western liberals, democrats, and intellectuals came to view Balkan problems almost entirely in the light in which these were presented in *La Fédération Balkanique.*

Macedonia to Rumanian, Greek, and Yugoslav oppression.[92] The
Communists, far from working for the pacification and reconciliation of the Balkan states, were interested, until the rise of National
Socialist Germany in the 1930s, in keeping the peninsula in a permanent condition of tension and disunity. The indirect encouragement
by *La Fédération Balkanique* of Bulgarian revisionism reflected not
so much Dimitar Vlakhov's sense of identity—for he readily
transferred his allegiance to Yugoslavia in the Second World War
—as the decision of the Russian Communist leaders to make Bulgaria the Balkan revisionist state par excellence, the *point d'appui*
of their Southeastern European policy.

In October, 1925, Vlakhov challenged IMRO by founding a new
organization named United-IMRO (*VMRO-Obedinena*) dedicated
to federation and the Vienna program. (In Communist nomen-
clature the term "united" always seems to identify a splinter group.)
It, too, was ostensibly non-Communist but other Macedonian federalists such as Philip Atanasov, who had participated in the Vienna
negotiations, no longer trusted Vlakhov's disclaimers about his
Communist connections and at about this time broke off relations
with him.[93] Since the Political Secretary of United-IMRO from its
inception to 1934 was Vladimir Poptomov, who had been a Sobranie
deputy for the Bulgarian Communist Party from 1920 to 1923,[94] it
is not surprising that Atanasov and other federalists refused to
accept Vlakhov's assurance that United-IMRO had no organizational
connection with the Communist Party. In 1928 Vlakhov expelled
from United-IMRO the old leader of Ilinden, Georgi Tsankov, for
being "too nationalist." [95] In that year the Communist Party
leaders, who until then had refrained from openly acknowledging
Vlakhov so as not to embarrass his front activities, for the first time
publicly endorsed United-IMRO.[96] Perhaps this was then considered
safe as Vlakhov's endeavors had manifestly failed.

[92] For example, see the issues of June 1, August 1, September 1, 1927 (III, No. 69,
IV, Nos. 72-73 and 74-75).
[93] Swire, *Bulgarian Conspiracy*, p. 195.
[94] See Poptomov's obituary in *Novo Vreme*, XXVIII, No. 5 (May, 1952), 14-16.
He became a member of the Central Committee of the Bulgarian Communist Party
in 1944 and a member of the Politburo in 1945. From that year until 1949 he was
editor-in-chief of the Party's daily *Rabotnichesko Delo* (Workers' Action). From August,
1949, to May, 1950, Poptomov was Minister of Foreign Affairs and from January,
1950 until his death in 1952 Vice-Chairman of the Council of Ministers.
[95] Swire, *Bulgarian Conspiracy*, p. 217.
[96] Kolarov, "Die Perspektiven des Klassenkampfes in Bulgarien," p. 1049. The

La Fédération Balkanique expired in April, 1931. Its circulation figures were never published but they were probably small, and it is unlikely that the paper had much influence in the Balkans. In November of the following year Vlakhov became a regular contributor to *Inprekorr* and in 1935 went to the Soviet Union.[97] United-IMRO failed so utterly to become a strong political force among the Macedonian population that in 1932 the Bulgarian Communist Party again considered coming to an agreement with the Proto-gerovist wing of IMRO.[98] Though the Communist violently opposed the military government which emerged from the Bulgarian *coup d'état* of May, 1934, they approved of its crushing of Mikhailov's IMRO band. In 1935 the Fifth Plenum of the Central Committee of the Bulgarian Communist Party, meeting in Moscow, adopted a resolution emphasizing the necessity of the Party's taking advantage of the elimination of IMRO to establish its own political control over Macedonia, especially over Petrich Department.[99] This, as the Second World War was to show, it failed to do.

Though Macedonia absorbed most of the Communists' interest in the Balkan national minority problem, they also sought to manipulate for their own benefit the Dobrujan and Thracian issues which bedeviled Bulgarian-Rumanian and Bulgarian-Greek relations.

In 1878 the Congress of Berlin had awarded the Northern Dobruja to Rumania as compensation for the cession of Southern Bessarabia to Russia. Though the province forms the historic southern invasion route into Rumania, the exchange was accepted only reluctantly by the Rumanians who protested prophetically that "geographically and ethnographically the Dobruja does not form

---

organization was also hailed in "Deklaration der Kommunistischen Balkanföderation zum Kroatisch-Mazedonischen Bündniss," *Inprekorr*, IX, No. 42 (May 14, 1929), 1023; D. Ivanov, "Self-Extermination in the Camp of the Macedonian Fascists," *Inprecorr* (English edition), IX, No. 56 (October 4, 1929), 1216; *Komunistichesko Zname* (Communist Banner), XII, No. 12 (1933).

[97] In the USSR Vlakhov worked at the Agricultural Institute and contributed articles on Balkan developments to the international Communist press. In 1943 he reemerged as a member of Tito's government in Yugoslav Macedonia and joined the Yugoslav Communist Party to which he remained loyal after its expulsion from the Cominform. Vlakhov became an important functionary and propagandist in the Macedonian People's Republic of Yugoslavia.

[98] "Declaration of the Central Committee of the Workers Party of Bulgaria," *Inprecorr* (English edition), XII, No. 56 (December 15, 1932), 1203.

[99] The text of this resolution is appended to Kolarov, *Protiv lyavoto sektantstvo i Trotskizma v Balgaria*, pp. 189-200.

a part of our territory . . . . In the future the Dobruja will be an open wound, a cause of discord between Rumania and Bulgaria which will be made use of by those who have an interest in embroiling the two countries." [100] In time, however, the Rumanians not only reconciled themselves to the acquisition of the Northern Dobruja but, for strategic reasons, came to covet as well the rich Southern Dobruja (Silistra) which the Congress of Berlin had assigned to the new Bulgarian principality but which Rumania forced Bulgaria to cede to her by the Treaties of Bucharest (1913) and Neuilly (1919). [101]

Bulgaria had protested to the Versailles powers that of a Southern Dobrujan population of 282,131 only 6,359, or 2 percent, were Rumanians while 48 percent were Bulgarians, 38 percent Turks, and the rest Gypsies, Tartars, and Jews. [102] In the 1920s, consequently, Bucharest sought to establish a Rumanian majority in the province by the settlement in it of Kutso-Vlakhs from Macedonia and by a program of land expropriation from the non-Rumanian population (Law of 1924). As a result, 40,000 Bulgarians and 20,000 Turks were obliged to leave the Dobruja and return as refugees to the lands from which their ancestors had come. [103] The Communists considered them fruitful objects of infiltration and manipulation.

The Drobujan question was, significantly, the responsiblity of the Bulgarian rather than the Rumanian Communist Party. The latter had been formed in 1920-21, partly through the intervention of Bulgarian Communists in the affairs of the Rumanian Social Democratic Party. The Socialist leaders from Transylvania and Bukovina,

[100] *Steaua României* (Star of Rumania), June 28, 1878, quoted by Logio, *Bulgaria: Past and Present,* p. 428.

[101] In 1918 the Central Powers imposed upon Rumania the temporary reversion of the Southern Dobruja to Bulgaria and established a four-power condominium over the northern province. See Radoslavov, *Bulgarien und die Weltkrise,* pp. 298ff. In September, 1940, the Southern Dobruja reverted to Bulgaria by the terms of the Treaty of Craiova.

[102] *Observations of the Bulgarian Delegation on the Conditions of Peace with Bulgaria,* Paris, 1919, pp. 22-34. In case the Western Powers doubted the objectivity of the Bulgarian census of 1910 upon which these figures were based, the Bulgarian delegation sought to reinforce its argument with the observation that even the most exaggerated Rumanian estimates had never claimed more than 27 percent of the Dobrujan population as being Rumanian.

[103] "Mémoire . . . présenté au IIIe Congrès des Minorités Nationales siégeant à Genève 22-24 Août 1927," *La Fédération Balkanique,* IV, No. 75 (September 1, 1927), 1447.

trained in the traditions of Hungarian and Austrian Social Democracy, had opposed association of the Rumanian Socialist movement with the Comintern. Nevertheless a Rumanian Socialist delegation was sent to the Soviet Union in 1920 to study the Comintern.
On the return of this group in January, 1921, it was revealed that
they had affiliated their party with the Comintern. The party thereupon split. Kolarov proudly claimed that the "directives" of the
Bulgarian Communists played a key role in the formation of the
Rumanian sister party.[104] Rakovski, then in the Soviet Union,
probably also had a hand in these matters. The Rumanian Communist Party remained of subordinate importance to the Bulgarian one
in the eyes of the Russian leaders. At their first Party Congress in
May, 1919, the Bulgarian Communists had called for the establishment of a Dobrujan Soviet Republic to form a constituent part of
that federation of Balkan Soviet Republics which they expected the
current "European revolution" soon to bring into being.[105]

At that time there were already a considerable number of Dobrujan refugees in Bulgaria, and when these assembled in a Grand
Dobrujan Congress in Sofia on November 21-25, 1919, the Communist-controlled left wing, led by a Dr. Peter Vichev, won control of
the organization and committed it to the Communist Party's program
of an independent Dobrujan republic. A later account of the deliberations reads:

This Congress found itself under the influence of the watchwords of the
Russian Revolution ... and in the USSR the Dobrujans saw [their] only
sincere ally for the realization of the liberty and independence of the
Dobruja. ... It was at this Congress also that it was decided to seek the
support of all the democratic forces of Bulgaria which, liberated from the
imperialistic influence of the bourgeoisie, would contribute to the achievement of the liberty of the oppressed peoples.[106]

The Communists, however, were unable to maintain their control
over the Dobrujan refugees. The province had been a fortress of the
Peasant Union from the time that the agrarian disorders at the turn
of the century had given birth to that party. Stamboliski retained

---

[104] Kolarov, "Die K.P. und die politische Lage Bulgariens," pp. 445-46. See also
Rakovski, "Die Kommunistische Bewegung in Rumänien," pp. 245-48; Kabakchiev,
"Die Neuen Ereignisse auf dem Balkan," p. 9; Roberts, *Rumania*, p. 247.
[105] *Balgarskata Komunisticheska Partia v Rezolyutsii i Reshenia*, II, 16.
[106] *La Fédération Balkanique*, III, No. 59 (January 1, 1927), 1078-79.

the support of many refugees by allocating 150,000,000 leva for their support. Others associated themselves with the bourgeois parties and supported the June coup. In March, 1925, and August, 1926, the Bulgarian police carried out a series of arrests among the left-wing refugees, thus crippling the Communists' efforts to dominate the refugee organization.

Peter Vichev, having thus lost the leadership of the refugee organization in March, 1925, remained an isolated figure on its steering committee. In September of that year, when Vlakhov was about to form his United-IMRO front group, Vichev, probably acting on the same Comintern instructions, also founded a new Dobrujan Revolutionary Organization to fight for the establishment of an independent Dobrujan republic. Though this group failed as dismally as did Vlakhov's to win the support of the refugees in Bulgaria, the Communists did control some underground revolutionary cells in the Dobruja until their local chief in the province, a certain Docho Mikhailov, was killed with six companions inside the Bulgarian frontier on August 26, 1926.[107] The Communists responded by reverting to legal front tactics. Vichev, who had covered himself by joining Malinov's Democratic Party, founded a journal named *Svobodna Dobruja* (Free Dobruja), the editorial policy of which was identical with that of *La Fédération Balkanique*, reflected the Communists' Balkan policy, and was calculated to exacerbate Bulgarian-Rumanian hostility.[108] These activities resulted in March, 1927, in his expulsion from the main organization of Dobrujan refugees, followed immediately by his arrest and that of ten colleagues on suspicion of maintaining contacts with Vlakhov in Vienna. Simultaneously *Svobodna Dobruja* was suppressed.[109] Released after eleven days, he was given a vote of confidence by the radical Sofia cell of the refugee organization.[110] In September, 1927, the Eleventh Congress of that organization rejected the program of Dobrujan autonomy and called for the reversion of the province to Bulgaria.[111] In December, 1930, Vichev organized in Sofia a new front organization, the Central Committee for Dobrujan

---

[107] *Inprekorr*, VI, No. 118 (September 24, 1926), 2009.
[108] *La Fédération Balkanique*, III, No. 59 (January 1, 1927), 1079.
[109] *Inprekorr*, VII, No. 33 (March 23, 1927), Chronik.
[110] *La Fédération Balkanique*, III, No. 67 (May 1, 1927), 1313.
[111] *Ibid.*, IV, No. 81 (December 1, 1927), 1634.

Action.[112] On his arrest two months later on the charge of treason for publishing a book by another author on the "national and colonial question" in which the Communist line was championed (Vichev was chairman of the Bulgarian section of the League Against Imperialism and for National Independence, an international Communist front organization), there was much agitation by the Labor Party (the legal cover for the underground Bulgarian Communist Party) and in the Communist press for his release.[113] This was achieved, but two years later, on June 16, 1933, Vichev was shot dead in the streets of Sofia by a gunman who allegedly confessed to having acted on the orders of IMRO chief Ivan Mikhailov.[114] In the Dobruja itself, persecution of the Communists was equally drastic. Docho Mikhailov's friend and successor Ivan Kunev committed suicide while being pursued by the police just inside the Bulgarian border on April 2, 1928.[115] The next year the Bulgarian Communist Party sent Dimitar Ganev into the province to take over the leadership of the Dobrujan Revolutionary Organization. He survived to become postwar Minister of Foreign Trade and a secretary of the Central Committee of the Communist Party in Bulgaria. Less fortunate was his colleague Dimitar Donchev, caught by the Rumanian Siguranţa, tortured, and shot on September 15, 1931.[116] Significantly all these men were Bulgarian.

The Rumanian Communists seem initially to have resisted the Bulgarian Party's control of Communist activities in a Rumanian province and even to have opposed its propaganda campaign for the detachment of the Dobruja from Rumania. This, at any rate, would appear to lie behind the oblique but categorical warning issued by Vasil Kolarov in the spring of 1924 that:

In the Southern Dobruja the nationalism of the Bulgarian peasants remains unshaken in spite of the terrorist methods employed by the Bucharest landowners. . . . In these circumstances it is obvious that the national question is of great and immediate importance for the Rumanian Communist Party. . . . To neglect it, to attempt to conduct the struggle solely on the

[112] *Ibid.,* VII, No. 141 (February, 1931), 23-24.
[113] *Inprekorr,* XI, No. 25 (March 17, 1931), 703.
[114] *Inprecorr* (English edition), XIII, No. 30 (July 7, 1933), 665.
[115] *Inprekorr,* VIII, No. 39 (April 18, 1928), Chronik; *La Fédération Balkanique,* IV, No. 90-91 (May 1, 1928), 1913.
[116] *Inprecorr* (English edition), XI, No. 52 (October 8, 1931), 954.

basis of class contradictions, would be to deprive oneself of a powerful instrument for gaining influence over the masses. . . . The Communist Parties should determine their relations towards these various [national] movements and strivings concretely in each individual case, basing themselves on the right of every nation to self-determination and guiding themselves by the interests of the revolutionary movement.[117]

As the Bulgarian Party's program of detaching the Dobruja from Rumania and forming it into an "independent" region suited the immediate tactical and propaganda interests of the Comintern, as it reflected Stalin's own doctrines on the national question, and as it conformed to the Soviet Union's objective of weakening her Rumanian neighbor, it was approved by the Fifth Comintern Congress in the summer of 1924.[118] Though in the spring of the following year it was again endorsed by the Balkan Communist Federation, which was a subsidiary organ of the Comintern dominated by the Bulgarian Party,[119] the Rumanian Communists seem to have accepted it only reluctantly and to have ignored it in practice, for a few years later the Bulgarian Kabakchiev again complained of the failure of the Rumanian Party to support the separationist movements in Bessarabia and the Dobruja.[120]

In the flush of revolutionary optimism in 1919 the Bulgarian Party had called for the establishment of a "Soviet Dobruja." [121] As the revolutionary tide receded, this was modified to "A Free and Independent Dobruja." [122] In the late 1930s, when the popular front policy dictated the adoption by Communist Parties of a patriotic line, the Bulgarian Communists openly called for "the unification of the oppressed Bulgarian districts of South Dobruja and the Western province [i.e., the enclaves ceded to Yugoslavia in 1919] with Bulgaria." [123] As the neighboring Communist Parties now also championed the territorial integrity of their states, considerable confusion resulted which led to some sharp contro-

---

[117] Kolarov, "The National Question in the Balkans," pp. 82-84.

[118] See "Resolution on the National Question in Central Europe and the Balkans," p. 99.

[119] "Die Dobrudscha Frage: Erklärung der K.B.F.," *Inprekorr*, V, No. 35 (March 13, 1925), 530. For the history of this Federation see Chapter XI.

[120] Kabakchiev, "Die Nationale- und die Agrarfrage auf dem Balkan," p. 1957.

[121] *Balgarskata Komunisticheska Partia v Rezolyutsii i Reshenia*, II, 16.

[122] *Inprekorr*, V, No. 35 (March 13, 1925), 531.

[123] "Appeal of the B.C.P.," *Inprecorr* (English edition), XVII, No. 46 (October 30, 1937), 1053.

versies among the Balkan Communist Parties during the Second World War.

If the Communist slogan, "A Free and Independent Dobruja," lacked appeal owing to the inhabitants' preference for outright Bulgarian or Rumanian allegiance, the cry of "A Free and Independent Thrace" was even more unrealistic for the population transfers following the First World War and Greco-Turkish War had virtually eliminated the minority problem in that province.[124] Yet the Communists, driven by their compulsion to universalize the party line of the moment, rigorously applied it to Thrace—the Bulgarian Party again taking the lead.[125] In April and September, 1925, two Bulgarian organizers of an illegal leftist revolutionary organization in Thrace were killed on Bulgarian soil.[126] In the autumn of 1926 an appeal signed by a certain Proikov urged the youth of Thrace to let itself be guided by the Bulgarian Communist Party in the fight for "A Free and Independent Thrace." [127] It was followed in 1927 by the formation of the inevitable front organization, led by the Bulgarian Blagoi Toromanov, which, "following in the footsteps of United-IMRO and the Dobrujan Revolutionary Organization," would fight for the independence of Thrace within a Balkan federation.[128]

It might be argued that all the propaganda for "a free and independent" Macedonia, Dobruja, Thrace, Croatia, Slovenia, even Transylvania, to form an "antiimperialist" Balkan federation could not have been taken seriously even by the Communists and must

[124] See pp. 233-34.
[125] See the Resolutions of the Sixth Conference of the Balkan Communist Federation and of the Fifth Comintern Congress in *The Communist International,* New Series, No. 4 (July-August, 1924), p. 94, and No. 7 (December, 1924–January, 1925), p. 95.
[126] *Inprekorr,* VI, No. 2 (January 5, 1926), 12. Their names were Arnaudov and Majarov.
[127] *La Fédération Balkanique,* III, No. 55 (November 1, 1926), 984.
[128] *Ibid.,* IV, No. 72-73 (August 1, 1927), 1416. The Bulgarian Communists' agitation for the detachment of Thrace from Greece probably enjoyed the sympathy of many Bulgarians for the loss of this area was more deeply resented than any other provision of the Neuilly Treaty. See *Conditions of Peace with Bulgaria: Observations of the Bulgarian Delegation,* p. 26. For the reactions of the Greek government and the Greek Communist Party to this agitation, see the chapter below on Communism and Balkan Federation, pp. 235-41.

have been nothing but the mere mechanical parroting of Stalin's catechism on the national question. Such a view would underestimate both the cynicism and the simultaneous capacity for self-deception of Communists. On the one hand they genuinely believed that this program not only reflected the real wishes of the peasant masses of the Balkan states but was indeed the only solution to the national problem on the Peninsula. On the other hand, the Bulgarian Communists manipulated the policy in order to dominate the other Balkan Communist Parties [129] while their Russian leaders regarded it as a weapon with which to combat French and British influence in the Balkans. Thus when after the Second World War the Soviet Union became the only Great Power in a position to dominate the Peninsula, the local Communist Parties were obliged to bury the federation policy. By the time it was discarded it had, however, given rise to much ill will among the Balkan Communist Parties which probably remains today a political factor in Southeastern Europe. The transformation of the Balkan federation policy from a socialist program for ensuring the peace and prosperity of the peoples of the Peninsula and for excluding Tsarist Russian influence into a political device in the hands of the Bulgarian Communists and their Soviet Russian mentors is a process which must now be examined.

[129] It might be noted that in the patchwork of independent republics which the program foresaw, Bulgaria would be the strongest state.

X

SOCIALISM AND BALKAN FEDERATION

The attitude of Marx and Engels toward the South Slav problem was a function of their revolutionary enthusiasm and of its corollary — hatred of Tsarist Russia, the backbone of European counter-revolution. Their reaction to the first reappearance of the Southern Slavs as active shapers rather than mere objects of European history, the crushing of what they believed was a liberal Magyar revolution in 1848-49 by the Croatian armies of Jelačić acting in cooperation with those of the Russian Tsar, was, consequently, one of vehement hostility, which found expression in bitter editorials in Marx's paper, the *Neue Rheinische Zeitung*, in which the "Pan-Slavistic Southern Slavs" are referred to as "the racial offal (*Völkerabfall*) of a thousand years' confused development" who would soon be "perishing in the storm of world revolution" which, prophesized Engels, would "annihilate the very name of these little pig-headed nations."[1] This political contempt for the Slavs by European radicals at the time was not, of course, confined to Marx and Engels. With the exception of Bakunin, the leading revolutionaries subscribed to it.[2] On closer examination of the problem, however, Marx became

[1] Quoted by Wendel, "Marxism and the Southern Slav Question," p. 292. The attitude of Marx and Engels at this time was similar to that of Hegel, who excluded the Slavs from his historical interests because they had not "hitherto appeared as an independent factor among the forms assumed by Reason in the World."

[2] For Bakunin's position at this time, see Carr, *Michael Bakunin*, pp. 175-77. Marx's attitude should not be confused with the general chauvinism and Slavophobia which gripped the leading German bourgeois revolutionaries of 1848. He was an ardent champion of the Polish national independence movement, expecting its victory not only to contribute to the destruction of both Prussian and Russian absolutism but also to smash the link joining the three subjugators of Poland—Austria, Prussia, and Russia—into a counterrevolutionary bloc. Marx's interests were revolutionary, not chauvinistic.

convinced that the aspirations of the Southern Slavs deserved more sympathetic consideration. Four years after the suppression of the Magyar revolution, a series of articles published over his signature in the New York *Daily Tribune* predicted that should the South Slavic peoples win their independence and establish their own sovereign states, they would cease to be instruments of Russian expansion into the Balkan Peninsula and would become a far more formidable obstruction to it than was the tottering Ottoman Empire.[3] The containment of Tsarist Russia was still Marx's chief concern but his prediction of the future relations between the Balkan Slavs and Russia was now quite the contrary of what he had feared in 1848. He further argued that, though the Balkan Slavs undoubtedly presented a backward economic, political, and social development in comparison to Western Europe, they, together with the Greeks, were still the most progressive elements in the Ottoman Empire, the carriers of commerce and urban civilization on the Balkan Peninsula. The more capitalism developed there, the closer would the Southern Slavs be bound to Western Europe and the more tenuous would become their dependence upon Russia. Marx's belief in the moral superiority of a higher over a less highly developed economy and his conviction of the necessity of opposing Tsarist Russia's influence and restricting her expansion thus combined to induce him to advocate the emancipation of the Southern Slavs from Turkish rule. On the other hand, Engel's suspicions of the South Slav nationalist movements were revived after he had disgustedly observed all the Balkan Slavic nations ally themselves with Russia in the course of the Russo-Turkish War of 1877-78. In a letter written to Eduard Bernstein in 1881, Engels sharply attacks the Southern Slavs. "Tools of Tsardom," he thunders, "they are and remain, and in politics poetic sympathies are out of place." [4] As for other leading socialists of the second half of the nineteenth century, Wilhelm Liebknecht

---

[3] Marx, "What Is to Become of Turkey in Europe?" New York *Daily Tribune*, April 21, 1853, translated in *Die Neue Zeit*, XXVIII, No. 27 (April 1, 1910), 9-12. It is not unlikely that the articles were in fact authored by Engels. There is no doubt, however, that they reflected Marx's thoughts at the time.

[4] Letter from Engels to Bernstein quoted by Wendel, "Marxism and the Southern Slav Question," p. 302. Isaiah Berlin (*Karl Marx*, p. 257) says that "Engels ... had an incurable aversion to everything east of the Elbe." This is a less than just generalization. Engels was interested in the Polish problem and read Polish regularly. In 1852 he studied Russian. In June, 1893, a little more than two years before his death, he corresponded with Bulgarian socialists and happily informed them that he

was opposed to the aspirations of the Balkan Slavs, while Jaurès, though he took a keen interest in the socialist movement among the Balkan peoples, also regretted the expulsion of Turkey from Europe. Bernstein and Rosa Luxemburg on the other hand, were sympathetic toward the Slavs.[5]

By the end of the century the socialists of Europe had not only come to accept the South Slav states but were the most ardent champions of the movement to join them into a federation. After the quarrels of the 1880s and the rupture of friendly relations between Russia and Bulgaria, it was clear that the Balkan Slavs were not simply a stalking horse of Russian expansionism. A federation of Balkan states, transforming the entire Peninsula into one potential market without artificial trade barriers, would, furthermore, stimulate that development of capitalism which socialists advocated and applauded. A federation would have the additional virtue of drawing the fuse from the proverbial Balkan powder keg by limiting the possibility of a Balkan conflict leading to a world war through the clash of interests of the Great Powers seeking to dominate the Peninsula. A Balkan federation would, in fact, establish a large state between Austria and Russia, whose rivalry to fill the vacuum left by the decline of Ottoman power in Europe was then the most explosive element in European diplomacy. The socialists dreaded a war above all other dangers. Engels, in his letter to Bernstein quoted above, had expressed his anxiety that out of Balkan rivalries and uprisings a world war might erupt. To prevent the realization of these fears, it was manifestly more sensible to promote a federation of the Balkan peoples than to demand their continued subservience to crumbling Turkish rule. It was not only immoral but also unrealistic to sacrifice the aspiration for national freedom of seven million Balkan Slavs on the altar of the policy of Russian containment for the benefit of the corrupt government of the Ottoman Empire. A federation would not only free the Slavic peoples from the Ottoman yoke and stimulate technical and economic progress, it would also be its own buffer against Russia.

---

was beginning to understand their language. See "Dva pis'ma Fridrikha Engel'sa k Bolgaram" (Two Letters of Friedrich Engels to Bulgarians), *Letopisi Marksizma* (Annals of Marxism), I (1926), 73-77.

[5] Wendel, "Marxism and the Southern Slav Question," pp. 302-4.

Toward the end of his life even Engels abandoned his earlier hostile attitude toward the Southern Slavs and began to take a keen interest in the Balkans and in particular in the Socialist movements on the Peninsula. In 1893 he began to study the Bulgarian language. Marx, too, had applied himself to Russian and Turkish in the last years of his life in order to be better equipped to study the political and economic developments of Eastern and Southeastern Europe.[6] Balkan federation may be considered to have become the official doctrine of the European Socialists in 1908, the year of the Young Turk revolt, when their supreme theoretical pontiff Karl Kautsky advocated it in the introduction to a Bulgarian translation of his study *Republik und Sozialdemokratie in Frankreich*.[7] Not only, he claimed, would such a federation eliminate the threat of German and Russian imperialist encroachment upon and rivalry in the Balkans, but it would also solve once and for all time the thorny Macedonian issue, which had already led to the bloody uprising of Ilinden in 1903 and which was a bone of contention among the Balkan states.

The idea of a Balkan federation had already been adopted by the Balkan Socialists themselves, long before it won favor among the Western European leaders of the international movement. In the 1870s this solution had been suggested by the Serbian Socialist Vasa Pelagić, and in the 1890s it had been propagated by the Macedonian Socialist Paul Argyriades, who edited a Socialist journal in Paris.[8] In 1885 Dimitar Blagoev, freshly expelled from Russia for illegal Socialist activity, took up the theme, just at the moment when Eastern Rumelia was being annexed to the Principality of Bulgaria, in an article on Balkan Federation and Macedonia written for *Makedonia*, a paper published in Sofia.[9] In 1894 a League for Balkan Confederation was founded which won the immediate support of Socialist leaders. Paul Argyriades, its first president, delivered a policy speech at the opening session in Paris, pointing

[6] Berlin, *Karl Marx*, p. 263.
[7] This introduction was reprinted as an article, "Die Nationalen Aufgaben der Sozialisten unter den Balkanslawen," *Der Kampf*, II, No. 3 (December 1, 1908), 105-10.
[8] M. Popović, "Die Sozialdemokratie in den Balkanländern und die Türkei," p. 156.
[9] Kabakchiev, "Dmitri Blagoev i bolgarskie Tesnyaki," p. 33. Blagoev also propounded the federal solution in *Makedonski Glas*. See Khristov, "Dimitar Blagoev—Osnovatel na Balgarskata nauchna istoriografia," p. 8.

out that the Macedonian question would in the future be the chief obstacle to peace on the Peninsula. The problem could be solved, he insisted, only by the establishment of an autonomous Macedonia within a general confederation of autonomous Balkan states. The confederation would consist, in addition to Macedonia, of Greece (with Crete), Bulgaria, Rumania, Serbia, Bosnia-Herzegovina, Montenegro, Albania, Thrace, the coastal regions of Asia Minor, and even Armenia. Constantinople would be a free city and the confederation's capital. (Inner Anatolia is omitted.) The autonomous states would be self-administered and the general interests of the confederation looked after by delegates in Constantinople who would take all measures necessary to assure the maintenance of the federal pact, to prevent and settle conflicts among member states, and, finally and above all, to place the strength of the confederation at the disposal of any member state threatened from without.[10] Clearly Argyriades, like other Socialists who concerned themselves with Balkan problems, was anxious to erect a barrier to Great Power expansion into the Peninsula. Although this League for Balkan Confederation never exerted any influence over the politics of the Peninsula, its aims were typical of the attitude taken by Balkan Socialists toward the Near Eastern question. The League was not expressly a Socialist one, but Socialists supported and led it.

A stimulus to the development of the idea of a Balkan federation and a spur to Socialist concern with the problem of the nationalities on the Peninsula was the Young Turk revolt of 1908 and its failure to reform the crumbling Ottoman Empire. The specter of Russian or German domination of the Peninsula loomed ever more ominously. The hopes for the reconstitution of the entire Empire on federal lines were dashed by the intransigence of the Young Turk leaders, the annexation of Bosnia-Herzegovina by Austria-Hungary, and the severing of all constitutional suzerain ties between the Ottoman Empire and Bulgaria by the proclamation of Ferdinand, hitherto Prince, as King of independent Bulgaria. Russia, furthermore, regarded any federation which included Turkey as an alliance directed against itself.

In November, 1909, a Congress of Southern Slav Social Democrats within the Austro-Hungarian Empire met at Ljubljana. A delegation

[10] Stavrianos, *Balkan Federation*, p. 151.

of guests from Serbia called for unity of all the Southern Slavs—Slovenes, Croats, Serbs, and Bulgarians.[11] Two months later (January, 1910) the first general Balkan Socialist Conference met in Belgrade. Represented were the Socialists of Serbia, Bulgaria, Rumania, Montenegro, Macedonia, Turkey, and of the Austro-Hungarian provinces of Bosnia and Herzegovina, Croatia and Slavonia, Carinthia, and Carniola.[12] The weak Greek Socialist movement sent no delegates but telegraphed assurances of its solidarity with the aims of the Conference. The Greek working class was at this time Venizelist rather than socialist in orientation.[13] Though both the Narrow and the Broad sections of Bulgarian social democracy were affiliated with the Socialist International, only the former was represented.[14] The Conference demanded the end of both direct and oblique domination of the Balkan peoples by outside powers, the emancipation of these peoples, and their subsequent federation by which the artificial barriers which separate peoples who are interconnected by language, culture, or economic ties were to be removed.[15]

The next Socialist demonstration for a federation directed against Great Power domination of the Balkan Peninsula occurred in the summer of the same year when the Bulgarian Narrow Party invited the Socialist Parties of the other Balkan nations to send delegates to its congress in Sofia so as to offset the effect of the Pan-Slav Congress which had met in the same city a few weeks earlier and to emphasize the distinction between the Socialist conception of a federation of progressive states and the Pan-Slavist one of an agglomeration of Russian vassals.[16] In October, 1911, a conference of delegates from the Socialist Parties of Serbia, Rumania, Croatia, Bosnia, and Turkey and from the Jewish Socialist Federation of Salonika met in Belgrade and recommended that mass meetings be organized in all the Balkan cities to warn against the extension to the Peninsula of the Italo-Turkish War, which had erupted in the

---

[11] Wendel, "Marxism and the Southern Slav Question," p. 307.
[12] Tucović, "Die Erste Sozialdemokratische Balkankonferenz," p. 845.
[13] Stavrianos, *Balkan Federation,* p. 189.
[14] Blagoev would not permit an invitation to be extended to the Broad Party. The Narrow delegation consisted of Blagoev, Kirkov, Kolarov, Dimitrov, and Kabakchiev.
[15] Trotsky, "In den Balkanländern," p. 68.
[16] *Ibid.,* p. 70.

preceding month, and to press for Balkan federation.[17] The demonstrations took place, but their purpose failed.

The Balkan Wars of 1912 and 1913 threatened to make true the nightmare which had haunted the European socialists for over half a century—a world war erupting out of a Balkan clash. In September, 1912, just prior to the opening of hostilities, the Balkan and Turkish Socialist Parties issued a manifesto denouncing the coming war and demanding once again the formation of a federation of democratic Balkan states.[18] As early as September 17/30, 1912, the day of Bulgarian mobilization, *Rabotnicheski Vestnik*, the organ of the Narrow Socialists, had denounced the military alliance of the Balkan states against Turkey, described the coming war as an operation in which the Balkan states would be pulling chestnuts out of the fire for the Great Powers, and demanded in its stead a peaceful federation of Balkan republics.[19] As the war against Turkey was popular in the Balkan states and as mobilization affected the most militant cadres of the young Socialist Parties, their antiwar activities were confined to resolutions, editorials, meetings, and speeches of which one of the most notable was Yanko Sakazov's courageous address to the Sobranie—he was beaten up on leaving the chamber—denouncing the impending war and calling for federation by peaceful means.[20]

With the defeat of Bulgaria in the Second Balkan War in the summer of 1913, public opinion, fickle as always, swung to support the parties which had thundered against the wars and in the

[17] This time neither of the two Bulgarian Socialist Parties was represented. The conference was a preliminary one of the non-Bulgarian parties to consider whether the Broad Party was to be invited to the next plenary conference. It decided affirmatively, but the Balkan and First World Wars intervened before the next conference met in Bucharest in 1915. The Broad Party was then again unrepresented.

[18] "Manifeste des Socialistes de Turquie et des Balkans," reprinted in Grünberg, *Die Internationale und der Weltkrieg*, pp. 14-18. The Extra-Ordinary Congress of the Socialist International, which met in Basel November 24-25 to consider the war danger, approved this policy of the Balkan Parties and urged them to persevere in it. *Ibid.*, p. 22.

[19] Trotsky and Kabakchiev, *Ocherki politicheskoi Bolgarii*, p. 137. For this editorial the government imposed a five months' suspension on the paper. When it reappeared in mid-February, 1913, it was hampered by the censor. During the Second Balkan War its distribution among the troops was prohibited.

[20] See p. 59. Excerpts from Sakazov's speech are quoted by Walling, *The Socialists and the War*, p. 108. It was delivered a few days before the declaration of war. In Serbia the Socialist Skupština deputies, Lapčević and Kaclerović, also voted against war credits. Lapčević made a good speech on this occasion.

elections of December, 1913, 21 Broad and 16 Narrow Socialist deputies were sent to the Sobranie, where but shortly before Sakazov had been alone. They represented a total of 107,146 votes, which may fairly be interpreted as that many ballots for an end to Balkan wars and for the formation of a peaceful federation of states.

In his Sobranie speech against the war, Sakazov made a remark which foreshadowed a major cause of strife among Balkan Socialists and Communists in the coming years. Though deprecating the policy of conquest, he referred to Macedonia as rightfully "ours," that is, Bulgaria's.[21] Though this comment aroused no stir at the time, it marked, in fact, the opening of a quarrel among Bulgarian, Serbian (later Yugoslav), and Greek Socialists and Communists for control of this key territory, a quarrel which plagued their subsequent attempts to formulate a common policy on Balkan questions. Desire for electoral success and the rather unexpected emotion of intense patriotism, which Socialists throughout Europe were somewhat surprised to find burning in their breasts in 1914, moved the Socialist Parties of each of the adjacent states to claim Macedonia for its own country. Sakazov was the first to vent this emotion. In a warmly patriotic article written shortly after the defeat of Bulgaria in the Second Balkan War, he denounced the injustice done to "the taciturn, stubborn, and vigorous race of the Bulgarians," who were being denied their legitimate aspirations.[22] Patriotism also gripped the Socialists of Serbia, and in the course of the First World War the Bulgarian Broad and the Serbian Socialists found themselves each supporting their own country's claim to Macedonia. The Bulgarians simultaneously carried on an identical quarrel with the Greek Socialists. The Balkan Socialist federation thus disintegrated over the issue of Macedonia. The background to this development merits examination.

On July 7/19, 1887, Ferdinand of Coburg was elected Prince of Bulgaria. From that time on, his passion to extend the borders of his new principality to the limits of the Great Bulgaria established by the still-born Treaty of San Stefano of 1878, the clash of policies of the Great Powers on the Balkan Peninsula, and the increased rivalry

---

[21] Trotsky and Kabakchiev, *Ocherki politicheskoi Bolgarii*, p. 136.
[22] Yanko Sakazov, "Bulgarien nach den Balkankriegen," pp. 1667-72.

among the various Balkan states combined to make peace and co-operation in the area distinctly unlikely. The outstanding feature of Balkan politics came to be the rivalry for territorial expansion of each of the Balkan states, especially for the control of Macedonia, which was obviously slipping out of the grasp of the Ottoman government. Macedonia became the main object and cause of Balkan discord.

The Balkan Socialists were disturbed by the heavy migration of refugees, emigrants, and harvest workers out of Macedonia into their own countries where wages were thereby lowered and trade unions weakened. Every spring between 50,000 and 100,000 itinerant Macedonians would invade Greece, Bulgaria, Serbia, and Hungary and depress the labor market, for their living standards were still lower than the already primitive ones of the native workers.[23] This seasonal migration was quite apart from the permanent settlement of Macedonians in Bulgaria, which was also on a considerable scale. The Macedonian laborers had as yet no conception of proletarian solidarity or of workers' organization. Socialist influence among Macedonians had been for long confined to the Jewish proletariat of Salonika. There the Jewish Socialist Federation founded by Abraham Benaroya conducted strikes, published Socialist journals, and in general pioneered in the development of a militant Macedonian working-class movement.[24] Though affiliated

[23] M. Popović. "Die Sozialdemokratie in den Balkanländern und die Türkei," p. 155.

[24] Abraham Benaroya was born in Bulgaria. He had been a member of the Broad Socialist faction before coming to Salonika as a young printer in the summer of 1908, on the eve of the Young Turk revolt. In the same year he founded the Socialist Federation, of which the most militant supporter was the local Jewish tobacco workers' society. In 1918 the Federation, then numbering 60,000 members, joined the Greek Socialist Labor Party. When this party, at its second congress in April, 1920, voted to affiliate with the Communist International, Benaroya strongly opposed the move but remained for a few years in the newly-launched Communist Party, maintaining a vain struggle to bring about its secession from the Comintern. In 1922 the Communists captured control of the Greek Federation of Labor, and the Greek-Turkish population exchange of the following year brought to an end the era of Jewish numerical dominance in Salonika. Thus Benaroya's star was setting even in the city in which he had once been powerful, and his expulsion from the Greek Communist Party in February, 1924, had no serious repercussions within it. His Socialist Federation probably passed away in the following years. Owing to the reluctance of the other nationalities of the city to be associated with it, the Federation had always remained a primarily Jewish organization. Not until 1918 did an appreciable number of Greeks join and their representatives sit on the executive committee. Yet even then the Federation continued to be regarded as a body of Jews. It was always an enthusiastic champion of Balkan federation. On November 4, 1911,

with the Socialist International, it was boycotted by the other nationalities. Not until January, 1911, could representatives of the other ethnic groups of the province be induced to attend a Macedonian Socialist Congress in Salonika and only in the few months immediately preceding the outbreak of the Balkan Wars did genuine cooperation in the form of joint strikes and demonstrations develop within the multinational proletariat of Salonika and Macedonia.[25] The itinerant unskilled farm laborers from the hinterland remained, however, largely unaffected by this process.

Bulgarian, Greek, and Serbian Socialists thus had a direct interest in raising the economic, political, and cultural level of the Macedonians, whose low standards were a threat to the welfare and progress of the weak working class of their own countries. They were convinced that this goal could not be realized as long as Macedonia was ruled by the moribund Ottoman Empire, which governed by terror and plunder. The Socialists of the Christian states bordering on Macedonia thus endorsed the program of Macedonian autonomy not only to forestall an eventual war over the province but also because they were convinced that the advancement of the working class throughout the Balkans depended upon the progress of Macedonia. Socialists were often members of the *komitaji* bands which fought in the name of Macedonian freedom.[26]

From the moment of their first direct championing of the Macedonian cause, the Socialists fought to prevent its subversion by any of the Balkan governments or its degeneration into sheer gangsterism, both perennial dangers. They supported the federalists against the Supremists.[27] Many Narrow and Serbian Social-

---

it sponsored a mass meeting, attended by 8,000 persons, at which Rakovski lectured on this and other current questions. See Starr, "The Socialist Federation of Salonika," pp. 323-36. For Benaroya's own interesting account of the trade union movement in the Ottoman Empire before the First World War, see his article, "Die Türkische Gewerkschaftsbewegung," pp. 1079-81.

In 1897 the population of the city of Salonika was estimated at 120,000, of whom 75,000 (or 62.5 percent) were Sephardic Jews, 14,000 Greeks, 11,000 Slavs, and the remaining 20,000 Turks, Vlakhs, Albanians, and Gypsies. Balugdgitsch, "Saloniki und die Makedonische Frage," p. 368. According to the Greek statistics of 1913, the population of the city then had risen to 153,525 and was composed of 61,439 Jews (39 percent), 45,867 Moslems (Dönmeh, Albanians, and Turks), 39,956 Greeks, 6,263 Slavs. Ancel, *La Macédoine*, p. 291.

[25] Stavrianos, *Balkan Federation*, p. 186.
[26] Wendel, "Marxism and the Southern Slav Question," p. 306.
[27] Yanko Sakazov, "Die Makedonische Frage," p. 8.

ists were even cool toward the Ilinden Rising of 1903, fearing that it might be a machination of Austro-Hungarian diplomacy.[28] The danger of Great Power encroachment on the Peninsula, they felt, was more acute and more immediate than the need to protect the Balkan proletariat by the establishment of an autonomous Macedonia. To this Yanko Sakazov replied on behalf of the Broad Party that, while the entire Macedonian agitation may originally have been stimulated by outside manipulation, it would be both immoral and politically inept for Socialists to sit by and watch a movement for national liberation (which did, after all, correspond to objective conditions in Macedonia) be exterminated by the Turks.[29]

Thus the Broad Socialists of Bulgaria went their way and gradually, perhaps at first unconsciously, their interest in Macedonia ceased to be simply that of a midwife assisting at the birth of an autonomous state. They began to think of Macedonia as their own and Bulgaria's rightful heritage, and their activity on behalf of the Macedonian movement stimulated their Bulgarian patriotism to the point where Sakazov could refer to Macedonia as "ours." The Broad Socialists persisted in their defense of what they believed was Bulgaria's legitimate claim to Macedonia throughout the First World War.

When that war broke out the two Socialists in the Serbian Skupština, Kaclerović and Lapčević, voted against war credits and on July 18/31, 1914, again insisted that only a Balkan federal republic could banish war from the Peninsula, secure it against Great Power domination, and guarantee the political and cultural advancement

---

[28] B., "Die Kommunistische Bewegung in Bulgarien," p. 133; M. Popović, "Die Sozialdemokratie in den Balkanländern und die Türkei," pp. 154-58. The difference in the degree of enthusiasm with which the Broad and Narrow Socialists regarded the Macedonians' armed insurrection was illustrated at joint meetings of Serbian and Bulgarian Socialist student groups held in Sofia in February, 1904. Two sessions had to be held because disciples of the two Bulgarian Socialist Parties refused to meet jointly. The meeting at which the students supporting the Broad faction took part resolved that the youth of Bulgaria and Serbia should cooperate without differentiation of political opinion in support of the struggle for Macedonian autonomy. A resolution was also passed recommending Bulgarian-Serbian political and customs unions to protect the two countries against political and economic pressure from Austria-Hungary and Russia. The meeting at which the Narrow students participated denounced all Socialist collaboration with bourgeois Macedonian agitators and revolutionaries. It insisted, in an unrealistic resolution, that the proletariat of Macedonia—then virtually nonexistent except in Salonika—must independently capture political power and transform Macedonia into a socialist society.

[29] Yanko Sakazov, "Der Ferne Krieg und der Nahe Osten," pp. 521-22.

of its peoples.[30] Their declaration was approved in September and October by the other constituent parties of the Balkan Socialist Federation. For associating themselves with this endorsement, the members of the Bulgarian Narrow Party's Central Committee were summoned before a military tribunal.[31] In November the Party's eleven Sobranie deputies introduced a motion calling on the government to seek, in collaboration with other neutrals, to bring about an early end to the war, but emphasizing their belief that lasting peace on the Peninsula could be assured only by a Balkan federation.[32] The Broad Socialist deputies significantly declined to support this motion. Their Party also rejected the resolution adopted by the Greek, Rumanian, Serbian, and Narrow Socialist Parties at the Second Plenary Balkan Socialist Conference meeting in Bucharest in July, 1915, which denounced the territorial ambitions of the Balkan governments and again issued the inevitable demand for a Balkan republican federation.[33] The Broad Socialists, aware that the two warring camps were vying for Bulgaria's support with competitive offers of territorial aggrandizement, were determined not to embarrass even by implication Bulgaria's demands for Macedonia.

Whereas the Narrow Party met both the Bulgarian mobilization in September and the government's request for war credits in December, 1915, with stirring appeals for peace, labor solidarity, Balkan federation,[34] and even with incitement to defy mobilization orders,[35] the Broad Socialists, though abstaining from the vote for

[30] Lapčević's speech is reprinted in Grünberg, *Die Internationale und der Weltkrieg,* pp. 210-13.

[31] *The American Labor Year Book, 1916,* p. 170.

[32] For the text of this motion, see Walling, *The Socialists and the War,* p. 211. In the elections of February/March, 1914, the Narrow Sobranie representation had been reduced from 16 to 11.

[33] The Resolution of the Second Balkan Socialist Conference is reprinted in Stavrianos, *Balkan Federation,* p. 198. The Conference arranged for a central office to coordinate the antiwar activities of the participating parties, but, as each of the Balkan states was drawn into the war, liaison between the Socialist Parties was interrupted and this central office doomed to ineffectually. It should be noted that each of the Balkan Socialist conferences was evoked by war or the fear of war and discussed little else than problems arising from war or methods of preventing one. The policies of the several parties were evolved independently, not jointly. Cf. Kabakchiev, Boshkovich, and Vatis, *Kommunisticheskie Partii Balkanskikh Stran,* p. 11.

[34] Quoted respectively in Trotsky and Kabakchiev, *Ocherki politicheskoi Bolgarii,* p. 147 and Stavrianos, *Balkan Federation,* p. 200.

[35] Logio, *Bulgaria: Problems and Politics,* p. 146.

war credits in the Sobranie,[36] aided the Bulgarian war effort throughout its duration. The reason why they did so was admitted by Sakazov on his way to Stockholm in 1917. "The Entente," he said, "would never have purchased our neutrality at the price of Macedonia; it would not have promised, much less given, it to us even had we fought for the Entente." [37]

The Broad Party's stand on the Macedonian issue involved it in clashes with both the Greek and the Serbian Socialists. The Jewish Socialist Federation of Salonika, a city occupied by the armies of the Entente after October, 1915, was opposed to Greece's participation in the war, had been represented at the Second Balkan Socialist Conference, and had strongly endorsed its resolution criticizing all the Balkan governments and calling for a federal republic. Once Greece was involved in the war, the Salonika Federation sought to act as a brake on exaggerated nationalism. At the Inter-Allied Labor and Socialist Conference held in London in February, 1918, two of the Federation's leaders, Couriel and Sideris, who were in fact attending with the approval of Venizelos but without the authorization of Benaroya, confined themselves to the modest demands of the evacuation of occupied Greek territory, the restoration of the *status quo ante bellum* as regards Greece's borders, the establishment of a Balkan customs union, and a collective guarantee by all the Balkan states to grant full rights and protection to all the minorities of the Peninsula.[38] This moderation was not, however,

---

[36] Yanko Sakazov, "Die Wahrheit ueber Makedonien," p. 161.

[37] Quoted in Logio, *Bulgaria: Problems and Politics*, p. 155, and in Kabakchiev and Karakolov, "Bolgaria v Pervoi Mirovoi Imperialisticheskoi Voine," p. 65.

[38] Their memorandum is reprinted in A. D. Sideris, A. Couriel, and F. Dimitratos, *La Question d'Orient* (Paris, 1918). In their efforts to maintain Greek neutrality in the First World War, the leaders of the Socialist Federation of Salonika found it expedient to cooperate with the Monarchist Party, which was influenced by the dynastic connection of the Greek royal house with Germany, Queen Sophia being a sister of Kaiser Wilhelm. At this time Benaroya was on the island of Naxos, whither he had been exiled in June, 1914, after a tobacco workers' strike at Salonika, Kavalla, Drama, and other Macedonian centers. He returned to the mainland in January, 1917. Venizelos brought Greece into the war on July 2, 1917, and soon thereafter *Avanti!*, the Ladino organ of the Socialist Federation, was suspended for three months for criticizing the Allies. Though Benaroya throughout the war deprecated Greek chauvinism and excessive claims to territorial aggrandizement, he was equally opposed to Bulgarian or Serbian expansion into areas not ethnically theirs. In July, 1918, he had an interview with Venizelos, who insisted that the Federation urge the Socialist International to oppose the territorial claims which were expected to be submitted to a peace conference by the Bulgarians. See Starr, "The Socialist Federation of Salonika," pp. 331-32.

shared by Greek Socialist leaders, whose demands for Greek control of Macedonia, Thrace, the Aegean Islands, and Constantinople, as well as all Epirus and Smyrna, brought them into conflict with the Bulgarian Broad Socialists, who supported their own government's aspiration toward the first two of these territories. In the course of the war the Broad and Greek Socialists fought their own journalistic battle over the Macedonian question.[39]

The clash between the Broad Party and the Serbian Socialists on the Macedonian question was yet more bitter than those between each of them and the Greek Party, though it came into the open only in 1917. On July 2 of that year Hermann Wendel, the German Social Democrats' expert on Balkan affairs, suggested in the *Vorwärts* that the Macedonian issue might best be settled by a partition along the lines foreseen in the Serb-Bulgarian treaty of March, 1912, which would have left Bulgaria in possession of the fertile Bitolj (Monastir) plain while retaining the territory north and west of the Shar Mountains for Serbia. At the time of the publication of Wendel's article, Serbia had, however, been overrun, and the Bulgarian army stood in occupation of extensive additional territory. The Broad Socialists joined the Bulgarian bourgeois press and parties in rejecting the suggestion that even a fraction of the territory upon which Bulgarian armies were then standing should

---

The Federation likewise opposed Serbian aspirations towards Macedonia. A. D. Sideris, one of its leaders and a deputy in the Greek parliament, rejected a demand by the Serbian Socialist Dušan Popović for the extension of Serbia's frontier to the Vardar River and the internationalization of Salonika as ethnically unjustifiable and requiring too heavy a sacrifice from Greece. He criticized the Serbs for abandoning the traditional socialist program of an autonomous Macedonia within a republican federation and praised both his own Federation and the Bulgarian Narrows for having remained true to it. The Broad Party, which coveted Macedonia for Bulgaria, is dismissed by Sideris as "chauvinist," a group which had placed itself outside the camp of "genuine" Socialism. For this polemic see D. Popović, "The Macedonian Question," pp. 333-39, and Sideris, "The Macedonian Question," pp. 396-401. Sideris, though a leader of Benaroya's Federation, was not a Jew.

[39] The case of the Greek Socialists was presented by Drakoules ("Greece, the Balkans, and the Federal Principle," pp. 113-33). The reply of the Bulgarian Broad Party was by Shopov ("The Balkan States and the Federal Principle," pp. 16-30). In fighting out their feud in an English language publication, both parties were evidently intent on obtaining Western support for their respective claims. In July, 1915, Drakoules was expelled from his party for excessive interventionist agitation. Stavrianos, *Balkan Federation*, p. 200. Yet his policy differed only in degree from that of the Executive Committee of the Greek Socialist Party, which on August 3, 1915, issued a manifesto urging Greece's entry into the war on the Allied side. This manifesto is translated in *The Asiatic Review*, VII (October 1, 1915), 279-82.

be relinquished to Serbia.[40] Wendel perhaps advanced his proposal to entice Serbia into a separate peace with the Central Powers. If so, he no doubt hoped that the antiwar Serbian Socialists could be won over to support it, and the timing of his suggestion was surely influenced by the fact that the proposed Stockholm Socialist Conference, at which ways of bringing the war to an end were to be considered, was being much discussed in the summer of 1917. Unfortunately for Wendel, he had failed to reckon with a change in the outlook of the Serbian Socialists.

The Serbian Socialists had voted against granting war credits to the government in July, 1914, but they were never in doubt that their country had been the victim of aggression. Nor were they likely to view with favor or equanimity the Macedonian claims of Bulgaria, the country which had thrown its armies against the rear of the embattled Serbian forces in October, 1915. Kaclerović and Dušan Popović, the Serbian Socialist delegates at Stockholm, demanded that either Macedonia be declared an autonomous state and the Vardar River internationalized or, in the event of partition, that Serbia be given Western Macedonia up to the right bank of the Vardar River with access to the sea at Salonika. Under no circumstances must Bulgaria be placed astride Serbia's outlet to the Aegean.[41]

The Bulgarian Broad delegation had already left Stockholm by the time the two Serbians arrived in October, but it had made clear its determination that Macedonia be retained by Bulgaria.[42] Unable to confront the Serbians face to face at Stockholm, Sakazov retorted to their demands with a sharp article defending Bulgarian annexation of all of Macedonia. Against the Serbs' geopolitical arguments,

---

[40] Wendel's three articles on this question and the reply to them by the Bulgarian Minister in Berlin, Dmitri Rizov, were published as a pamphlet entitled *Pro Macedonia* (Paris, 1918). Rizov, a Macedonian, had had a long career in the Bulgarian diplomatic service, having served as Minister at Cetinje (1903-5), Belgrade (1905-9), and Rome (1909-15). He played an important part in negotiating the Bulgarian-Serbian agreements of 1904 and 1912.

[41] For the position taken by the two Serbian Socialists at Stockholm, see D. Popović, "Um Makedonien," pp. 334-43. Dušan Popović had been editor of *Radničke Novine* (Workers News), the central organ of the Serbian Socialist Party, since 1910, when he was only twenty-four years old, and was also a founder of *Borba* (Struggle). He died in 1919.

[42] See *The New Europe*, III, No. 32 (May 24, 1917), p. 184.

Sakazov summoned ethnographic ones.[43] By this time the Serbian Socialists had, however, abandoned as impracticable the first of their two suggested solutions of the preceding year, that is, the establishment of an autonomous Macedonian state and the internationalization of the Vardar. They now demanded the partition of Macedonia so as to make the Vardar River Serbia's southeastern frontier. Salonika, they recommended, should be internationalized.[44] Thus was the Balkan Socialist Federation shattered by disputes among the Bulgarian, Greek, and Serbian Socialist Parties over Macedonia.

Toward the close of the war, when the specter of defeat loomed over Bulgaria, the generous territorial demands advanced by her Broad Socialists on their way to Stockholm[45] were of necessity modified. In the spring of 1918, the Party sent a reasonably conciliatory reply to the request of the Third Inter-Allied Labor and Socialist Conference, which had met in London in February, for a precise statement of peace terms which it would find acceptable. The Fourth Inter-Allied Labor and Socialist Conference meeting in September, 1918, in London, expressed its satisfaction with the reply of the Broad Socialists.[46] The Party did not, however, renounce altogether its Macedonian aspirations. The Third Inter-Allied Conference had worked out a War Aims Memorandum on the basis of proposals submitted to it by the British Labour Party which called for a speedy, democratic, and clean peace and advanced a number of specific proposals, one of which was autonomy for Macedonia. The Broad Socialists replied evasively that, while "that part of the program which refers to general principles is quite acceptable," as to the recommendation of an autonomous Macedonia, "the Conference ought to have offered us a mode of settlement which we, the parties most directly concerned in the matter, might have been able to accept without any extraordinary difficulties."[47] This hedging availed little, for the fate of Macedonia was totally dependent on the outcome of the war, which Bulgaria lost.

[43] Yanko Sakazov, "Die Wahrheit ueber Makedonien," pp. 160-75.
[44] D. Popović, "The Macedonian Question," p. 338. For the reply of the Greek Socialists, see p. 218, footnote 38.
[45] See pp. 71-72.
[46] Fainsod, International Socialism and the World War, p. 190.
[47] Quoted by Logio, Bulgaria: Problems and Politics, p. 183.

The Broad Party nevertheless carried its crusade for Bulgarian possession of Macedonia into the postwar period. It had resumed its activities in the Socialist International at the Berne Conference of February, 1919. Though the International, in a special resolution on the Balkan question adopted at its Lucerne Congress in August, 1919, had called upon the Balkan Socialists to act in harmony and concord,[48] the Greek, Yugoslav, and Bulgarian Socialist Parties quarreled ceaselessly at every Congress of the International and between Congresses over the Macedonian issue. At the Marseilles Congress in 1925, the Bulgarian and Greek Socialists clashed over Macedonia and Thrace. The Brussels Congress in 1928 saw a Bulgarian-Yugoslav fight over Macedonia.[49] In that year the German Socialists became involved in the issue when Hermann Wendel once again entered the fray with an article in the *Vorwärts* supporting the Yugoslav case. Sakazov took up his pen in reply, and the two debated the issue in the pages of the *Vorwärts*. Sakazov clashed also with Živko Topalović, then a leader of the Yugoslav Socialist Party, at the Balkan Conference held in Athens in 1930, and in that same year he delivered a lecture to Vardar, an organization of Macedonian students in Bulgaria, then holding a conference, on the theme: How can we regain Macedonia, the Dobruja, Thrace, and the Western Regions? [50] While the leader of the Bulgarian Socialists was thus leading his party along the path of revisionism, the Yugoslav Socialist Party had in 1928 committed itself once more, under the trite slogan of "The Balkans for the Balkan Peoples," to the program of a Balkan federation which would ensure security and progress, both economic and cultural.[51] The resolution had omitted the usual pre-World War insistence that the federation must be a republican one whereupon the Communists gibed that the Socialists contemplated a greater South Slav

---

[48] *Special Resolution Number Six, Concerning the Balkans, Passed by the Congress of the Labor and Socialist International, Lucerne, August 1st-9th, 1919.* Reprinted as Appendix H in Stavrianos, *Balkan Federation,* p. 302. The resolution adopted the Balkan federation scheme as the official policy of the International.

[49] V. Vassileff, "Les Socialistes balkaniques et les questions nationales aux Balkans," *La Fédération Balkanique,* VII, No. 141 (February, 1931), 6.

[50] *Ibid.,* p. 7.

[51] *The Balkans for the Balkan Peoples,* resolution adopted by the Convention of the Social Democratic Party of Yugoslavia, April 15-16, 1928, reprinted in the New York *Times,* May 20, 1928.

federal kingdom under the rule of King Alexander of Yugoslavia.[52] There may indeed have been some truth in this but the Communists had little cause to taunt the Socialists since, as the next chapter will show, their own Balkan policy was as confused, and their own comradely conflicts over Macedonia and Thrace were, if anything, yet more bitter than those of the Socialists.[53]

[52] See Dimitrov, "Die National-Revolutionäre Bewegung auf dem Balkan und die Aufgaben der Kommunistischen Parteien des Balkans," pp. 2625-33.

[53] Both Bulgarian and Yugoslav Socialists participated in the Balkan Conferences in the early 1930s, but as they did so as appointees of their governments rather than as delegates of the Socialist Parties, their activities are beyond the scope of this study. For details, see the article by Yanko Sakazov, president of the Bulgarian National Group for the Balkan Conferences and a leader of the Bulgarian delegation, in *Bulgaria and the Balkan Problems;* also Kerner and Howard, *The Balkan Conferences and the Balkan Entente, 1930-35.* As might be expected, the Communist Parties of all the Balkan states and Turkey denounced these efforts at *rapprochement* as "one of the episodes in the feverish regrouping of imperialist forces . . . which mark the increased preparation for military clashes. . . . The Balkan Pact, in trying to make permanent the Versailles frontiers in the Balkans . . . is a challenge to all these nationalities which are struggling for freedom." "Declaration of the Communist Parties of Rumania, Yugoslavia, Bulgaria, Greece and Turkey on the Balkan Pact," *Inprecorr* (English edition), XIV, No. 27 (May 4, 1934), 692-93.

XI

COMMUNISM AND BALKAN FEDERATION

At a gala congress held in Sofia on May 25-27, 1919, the Bulgarian Narrow Socialist Party changed its name to Communist Party, affiliated with the Third International, and decided that in the face of the "imperialist threat," the independence of the Balkan peoples could be assured only by the establishment of a Balkan Federation of Soviet Socialist Republics.[1] The Communists thereby reaffirmed the prewar program of the Socialist Parties and of the Serres Macedonian federalists. Their resolution was approved by the Russian Comintern leaders in Moscow, then awaiting the world revolution which would transform the globe itself into a federation of soviet socialist republics. The way was thus prepared for the inaugural session of the Balkan Communist Federation, convened in Sofia on January 15, 1920, at the invitation of the Bulgarian Party, at which were also represented the Socialist Labor Party of Greece, the Social Democratic Party of Rumania, and the Socialist Labor Party of Yugoslavia, which were all shortly to be transformed into Communist parties. The Conference released the expected spate of resolutions.[2] It noted that the World War had impoverished the people of the Balkan Peninsula, particularly the proletariat, and that its net effect for the Balkan nations was that Britain, France, and Italy had ousted Austria-Hungary, Germany, and Tsarist Russia in the scramble for the privilege of exploiting them. This condition of semicolonialism could be abolished and the free development of the Balkan countries assured only by a proletarian revolution, which

---

[1] "Resolution des Kongresses der Kommunistischen Partei Bulgariens ueber die Lage in Bulgarien," pp. 729-36.

[2] "Resolutionen der Sozialistenkonferenz des Balkans," pp. 292-96.

would also contribute to the collapse of capitalism in the West by depriving it of one of its colonial areas. The Conference, accordingly, issued a call to the "proletarians and the poor" of the Balkan states to prepare to revolt. The soviet states which would come into being as a consequence of this revolution would then federate. The existing bourgeois governments could not form a federation of Balkan states and even were they able to overcome their mutual jealousies sufficiently to do so, the purpose of such a federation could only be to sharpen the exploitation of the Balkan masses. The Communist Parties of the Balkan states must therefore oppose all federation schemes except their own. The realization of these aims of the Balkan Communist Parties, it was emphasized, depended on mutual cooperation and on coordination with the international Communist movement. The Parties must each affiliate with the Comintern and collectively form a Balkan Communist Federation within it to synchronise methods and aims and thus to hasten the coming of the revolution.

Like other newly formed Communist Parties and organizations, the Balkan Communist Federation from its very beginning put all its influence at the disposal of Soviet Russia. The very first conference called upon the Balkan Communist Parties to give all possible support to the Russian Soviet Republic "and to paralyze thereby the counterrevolutionary forces moved against it from the Balkans or through the Balkans."[3] In May, 1920, the dockworkers of the Bulgarian port of Burgas refused, on Communist urging, to load supplies destined for the White Russian armies in southern Russia,[4] and in the summer of that year, when Wrangel's Crimea-based armies were making extensive gains against the Bolsheviks, the Balkan Communist Federation issued an almost hysterical appeal to all workers of the Peninsula to prevent supplies from reaching the counterrevolutionary armies and in particular to frustrate and avert a Rumanian attack on the embattled Red Army, an attack which was apparently expected in Communist circles at that time.[5]

---

[3] *Ibid.*, p. 294.

[4] Dimitrov, "Die Gewerkschaftliche Bewegung in Bulgarien," p. 331.

[5] "Manifest der Kommunistischen Balkan-Donauföderation: An die werktätigen Klassen der Balkan- und Donauländer," p. 232. In September, 1920, after the Poles had launched their counteroffensive against the Red Army and were again advancing eastwards, another appeal was issued in Sofia in the name of the Balkan Communist Federation calling upon all Balkan Communists to thwart any attempts

The Comintern expected much from this Balkan Communist Federation and supported it enthusiastically, criticizing only its tendency, born of revolutionary ardor and Marxist doctrinairism, to exaggerate the role of the proletariat and to neglect to cultivate the support of the peasantry in the overwhelmingly agricultural Balkan countries.[6]

Toward the end of 1920 it was decided, in view of the great expectations reposed in the Balkan Communist Federation, to supplement it with a Balkan trade union confederation. A congress of trade unions controlled by the Balkan Communist Parties met, accordingly, in Sofia on November 3-4, 1920. Present were Ivan Čolović for the Yugoslav unions, Marcel Pauker for the Rumanian, and a large delegation of Bulgarian functionaries headed by Georgi Dimitrov. The International Trade Union Council in Moscow was represented by N. Glebov.[7] Dimitrov, as Secretary of the Communist-controlled trade union confederation of the host country, presided. The first resolution adopted violently denounced the Social Democratic trade unions and their International in Amsterdam as "yellow" lackeys of the European bourgeoisie and of the League of Nations, which was alleged to be but a cover for aggression against Soviet Russia. All Communist trade union members were warned that they were duty bound to work for the disaffiliation of their unions from the Amsterdam International and their adherence to the new provisional Council in Moscow. Hopes for mediation or compromise between Moscow and Amsterdam were denounced as foolish and illusory.[8] To facilitate coordination with the Moscow

---

by their governments to assist Poland. The possibility of such attempts being made was, however, remote, and the extent to which either the Balkan governments (except the Rumanian) or the Balkan Communist Parties (among which the Rumanian was particularly insignificant) could influence the Russo-Polish War was minimal. This appeal need not, therefore, be taken as a serious political action and may be numbered among the plethora of purely propagandistic Communist verbosities. For its text, see *The Communist,* September 23, 1920, p. 3.

[6] Zinoviev, "An das Proletariat der Balkan- und Donauländer," p. 838.

[7] Dimitrov, "Der Balkan-Donau Gewerkschaftskongress," p. 1682. Among the other Bulgarians were Anton Ivanov, Nikola Penev, Zheko Dimitrov, and Sider Todorov, one of the defectors expelled after the September insurrection who subsequently became a Trotskyist. For the founding of the International Trade Union Council, see Carr, *The Bolshevik Revolution, 1917-1923,* III, 207-8. In July, 1921, it became the Red International of Trade Unions, commonly known as Profintern.

[8] Dimitrov, "Beschlüsse des Ersten Gewerkschaftskongresses der Balkan-Donauländer," p. 356. The Amsterdam International was the continuation of the prewar International Federation of Trade Unions. Though sharing the outlook of the Socialist

organization and to prepare jointly for the coming revolution, it was decided to form a single Balkan Trade Union Secretariat. Sofia was selected as the site for the headquarters whose function was to coordinate the strategic and tactical aims of the Communist trade unions of Bulgaria, Czechoslovakia, Greece, Hungary, Rumania, Turkey, and Yugoslavia.[9]

The secretariat to be established in Sofia was to hold regular plenary sessions every three months and extraordinary ones whenever necessary. It was to cooperate closely in all aspects of its work with the Balkan Communist Federation while the Communist trade union organization of each country was to place itself under the direction of the Communist Party.[10] At the trimonthly meetings of the secretariat, the first 50,000 members of affiliated trade unions of each country were to be represented by two delegates and each additional 50,000 by one. Between these sessions a permanent staff would function in Sofia under the supervision of the Central Committee of the Bulgarian General Trade Union Federation. This arrangement placed considerable potential power in the hands of the Secretary of this Bulgarian trade union federation, Georgi Dimitrov. The November, 1920, congress finally emphasized that one of the main tasks of the proposed secretariat, as well as of each and every Communist trade union member, was to destroy all the "social democratic illusions" to which the workers still clung. In particular the workers must be taught that peaceful transition from capitalism to socialism is a myth, that only a revolutionary class struggle can establish socialism, and that only the Communist Parties can lead this struggle and institute proletarian dictatorship. All this was, of course, standard Communist rhetoric. What is chiefly notable about the resolutions of this congress, which cover eight pages of close print, is that they contain not a single word about

---

International, it was independent of the latter. The Moscow Council, on the other hand, which in 1921 was enlarged and reorganized as the Red International of Trade Unions, or Profintern, was never anything but an adjunct of the Comintern which, in turn, became but an instrument of the foreign policy of the Soviet Union.

[9] Czechoslovakia and Hungary were included as Danubian, not Balkan, states. Austria was excluded presumably because she was considered to lie more properly in the province of German affairs.

[10] This, of course, was essentially a restatement of the ninth of the twenty-one conditions of affiliation to the Comintern, adopted by the Second Comintern Congress on August 6, 1920.

wages, hours, work conditions, or any of the issues of direct and immediate concern to the working man.[11] Nothing could emphasize more forcefully the subordination of the Communists' loudly trumpeted concern with the fortunes of the workers to their main aim, indeed, their sole aim, of achieving political power.

Though this Communist trade union federation from the moment of its birth degenerated into a mere statistics-gathering bureau and never achieved importance, the political Balkan Communist Federation led a more lively existence. It met again in conference in Vienna from February 24 to 28, 1921. The Bulgarian Communists were represented by Vasil Kolarov, secretary of the Party, and by Georgi Dimitrov, secretary of its affiliated trade union federation. Both were members of the Party's Central Committee. Representing the Yugoslav Party were Klemenčić and Cvijić, both members of the Central Committee, and Milkić, the Yugoslav delegate to the ECCI. Credentials for the Rumanian Marcu arrived too late to enable him to vote on resolutions, though he attended most sessions of the conference. Alexander Dobrogeanu-Gherea (son of the Rumanian Socialist leader Constantin Dobrogeanu-Gherea), who by chance happened to be in Vienna at the time, also took part in the discussions on behalf of the Rumanian Communists, though in an unofficial capacity. There were no Greek representatives. The Austrian and Hungarian Communist Parties delegated, respectively, Wertheim and Georg Lukács to attend as nonvoting observers. Two men, identified in the account of the proceedings only as "Comrades A and D" came from Moscow as representatives of the ECCI.[12]

Though Kolarov and Milkić alternated as chairman, the minutes of the Conference leave no doubt that it was dominated by the two men sent from Moscow. After Kolarov had opened with a speech laden with the well-worn jargon about resisting the offensive of the bourgeoisie and frustrating its efforts to sow hatred among the various Balkan peoples, and the necessity of creating a permanent organization to coordinate the policy of the Balkan Communist Parties between congresses of the Balkan Communist Federation, "Comrade A" arose and lectured the Conference on the Comintern's

---

[11] Dimitrov, "Beschlüsse des Ersten Gewerkschaftskongresses der Balkan-Donauländer," pp. 354-62.
[12] "Konferenz der Kommunistischen Balkanföderation," p. 430.

(that is, Moscow's) conception of the tasks of the Balkan Communist Federation. It was to collect information and data for the Comintern and to break the *cordon sanitaire* which Anglo-French diplomacy had erected to contain Soviet Russia and eventually, the Bolshevik government feared, to serve as the springboard for a new war against her. Of course, Comrade A assured the Conference, there need be no fear among the Balkan Communists that it was Moscow's intention to reduce their Federation to a mere "southeastern bureau" of the Comintern organization, a simple institute for gathering statistics, but they must realize that for the time being their main function was to fight Anglo-French influence and imperialism on the Balkan Peninsula, and in this way to defend the interests of Soviet Russia, the workers' state.[13]

The discussion then opened. Neither of the two Bulgarians took exception to the blunt lecture of Comrade A. Kolarov pointed out the necessity of establishing Communist Parties in Albania and Turkey and ventured to oppose associating the Austrian and Hungarian parties directly with the Balkan Communist Federation, though there should, he conceded, be close cooperation with them. In view of the subsequent behavior of Bulgarian Communists within the Balkan Communist Federation, it is not at all unlikely that already at this time the Bulgarians hoped to play the leading role in, even to dominate, the Federation, and that Kolarov's opposition to the affiliation of the Austrian and Hungarian Parties rested on a desire to prevent the devolution of its leadership on either of these two parties, one of which, the Hungarian, had the advantage of having fought for and established, albeit temporarily, a Communist dictatorship in its country, whereas the Bulgarians had remained ingloriously inactive during the one revolutionary situation their country had passed through, the Radomir rebellion. The Hungarians, furthermore, possessed in the persons of Kun, Rákosi, Lukács, and others a leadership of proven political talent and ideological accomplishment far exceeding anything that the Bulgarians had till then demonstrated. Kolarov had every reason to fear that with their revolutionary prestige, the Hungarians might become the group on which Moscow would rely to lead the Balkan Communist Federation. Kolarov did not, of course, explain his opposition to

[13] *Ibid.*, p. 431.

the affiliation of the Austrian and Hungarian Communists with the Balkan Communist Federation in these terms. Rather he sought to justify it by the argument that it was necessary to confine the Federation to the Communist Parties of countries with similar or identical economic and ethnographic structures. This theory, while reasonable, does not fully explain the presence of the Communists of Greece in the Federation, as the economy of that country was not as overwhelmingly agricultural as those of its northern neighbors nor are its people Slavic.[14] Kolarov closed with the traditional prewar Socialist battle cry that only federation could solve the Balkan peoples' problems.

After him Klemenčić rose and, with typical Yugoslav bluntness, told Comrade A that he was not satisfied with the assurance that the Comintern's conception of the tasks of the Federation would not result in its transformation into a mere administrative organ of the Moscow center. He thought that the Federation had intrinsic merit and political functions in addition to, and quite apart from, the struggle against Anglo-French influence on the Balkan Peninsula.[15] This readiness of the Yugoslav Communists to keep an open mind about Comintern policies and suggestions and to persist in their objections even against the highest authorities of international Communism was to result in several purges of the Party's leadership and contributed substantially to the realization of the Bulgarians' hopes to dominate the Federation. Moscow favored the Bulgarian comrades, who accepted orders without back talk, over the Yugoslav Communists, who so often objected to its directives, and who displayed a tendency to accept sincerely or—from Moscow's point of view—naïvely, principles which the latter regarded simply as instrumental devices.

The Conference then proceeded to the main purpose for which it had been called, the creation of a permanent administrative apparatus of the Balkan Communist Federation to maintain the continuity of its activities between conferences. Zinoviev, in a letter of March 5, 1920, had emphasized the necessity for the closest integration of

---

[14] The inclusion of Greek and the exclusion of Hungarian representatives from an organization representing allegedly similar countries could probably be rationalized by reference to a common Byzantine cultural heritage, but it is unlikely that this was in Kolarov's mind.

[15] "Konferenz der Kommunistischen Balkanföderation," p. 433.

the activities of the various Balkan and Danubian Communist Parties, even suggesting that had this existed in 1919, the Hungarian Communist revolution would not have been crushed.[16] His claim was, of course, quite fantastic, for the pitifully weak Communist movement of Rumania, the country whose army, aided by treachery in the Hungarian military command, was the chief instrument of the overthrow of the Bela Kun regime, was powerless to prevent any action decided on by the government, least of all a campaign which had the approval of both the Allies at Versailles and the peasants in Rumania.

The Conference proceeded to establish its permanent organization. It was resolved that each member party was to delegate one comrade to inform all the other parties once a month of the internal state of his own. Copies of these reports were to be forwarded to Moscow. Each party was also to supply the neighbor parties with copies of all its journals and periodicals and abstracts of all its books. The Federation was to establish an Executive Committee of five to seven members which would control the activities of the Federation between conferences as well as those of the individual member parties "insofar as these activities are connected with the aims and tasks of the Balkan Communist Federation"—potentially a rather broad delegation of powers.[17] The Executive Committee was to ensure that all parties developed a unified organizational form and conducted their activities in the spirit of democratic centralism. In all its work the Executive Committee was to act in strictest conformity with the directives of the ECCI and the resolutions of Comintern congresses. It was, in other words, to be a transmission belt between the Comintern and the Balkan Communist Parties. Within a short time, however, the system of direct orders from Moscow made this function redundant. The Executive Committee was further to be in continuous contact with the Communist Trade Union Secretariat of the Balkan countries to ensure the application of all Comintern directives pertaining to trade union matters.

The Executive Committee was authorized to elect one of its members Secretary, responsible to itself. The Secretariat was to be

---

[16] Zinoviev, "An das Proletariat der Balkan- und Donauländer," p. 838.
[17] "Entwurf des Statuts der Kommunistischen Balkanföderation," p. 435.

in permanent session between sessions of the Executive Committee, a quorum for which consisted of representatives of three of the member parties. Conferences of the Federation were to take place every six months, unless emergencies necessitated interim conferences. Delegates to conferences were to be uninstructed by the Central Committee of their respective parties and to vote in accordance with Comintern resolutions. Since the ECCI was to send to such conferences representatives who would be the authoritative interpreters of Comintern resolutions, this clause facilitated the manipulation of conferences for the purpose of purging a member party and, through the device of the uninstructed delegate, to split any recalcitrant Central Committee. The dependence of the Federation on the Comintern was further ensured by a clause to the effect that contacts with Communist Parties not members of the Federation must be maintained only through the ECCI. In addition, a clause stipulating that member parties were to be represented individually at Comintern congresses and ECCI sessions and not by the Federation as a unit was doubtlessly intended to prevent the formation of a Balkan bloc within the Comintern. The final clause underlines these impressions. "This statute," it reads, "must be presented to the ECCI for confirmation." [18]

This imposing organizational structure never became a force in inter-Balkan politics and the Balkan Communist Federation soon crumbled away, owing to quarrels among its constituent parties and their persecution by the Balkan governments. This Vienna conference had styled itself preparatory and had scheduled a more imposing sequel to meet May 4-6, 1921, in Sofia. The May conference, however, turned out to be a dismal failure as governmental intervention prevented any but the Yugoslav and Bulgarian representatives from appearing. These two delegations once again passed the standard Comintern resolutions about the threat of imperialism, of a new war to be unleashed against Soviet Russia, about new inter-Balkan wars, and about the coming revolution. The Little Entente was denounced as a coalition of French lackeys against which the Communist Parties must present their united front of revolutionary solidarity. The Communist Parties were hailed as the

---

[18] *Ibid.*, p. 437.

champions of the national minorities.[19] These vapid and second-hand declarations were symptomatic of the decay into which the Balkan Communist Federation was fast rotting so shortly after its loudly trumpeted birth. The next conference assembled in Moscow December 8-12, 1922, and declared in favor of autonomy for Macedonia, Thrace, and Croatia within the future federation of soviet republics.[20] In December, 1923, the Presidium of the Federation approved the expulsion of Sakarov and his supporters from the Bulgarian Communist Party for having repudiated the September insurrection.[21] In the same month a conference of the Federation took place in Berlin at which the usual orations about oppressed national minorities were declaimed and the expected resolutions in favor of autonomy for Macedonia, Thrace, and Croatia adopted.[22] Though these gestures were well-worn, the situation in which they were made was new, for the Greek-Turkish population exchange had in the meantime fundamentally altered the ethnic composition of Macedonia and Thrace. These traditional resolutions for autonomy therefore caused a grave crisis within the Greek Communist Party which will be discussed presently. The next Federation conference met in Moscow in July, 1924, shortly before Aleksandrov's repudiation of the Vienna Manifesto and at the time of Radić's visit to the USSR. Bulgaria, it predicted, stood on the threshold of a new civil war, and Croatia was about to break away from Yugoslavia.[23] The failure of IMRO and the Croatian Peasant Party to fulfill the expectations of the Communists deprived the Federation of two key levers for affecting Balkan politics.

There were other reasons for the decay of the Federation. It soon became an *émigré* organization, for within a few years of its foundation all member parties except the Greek had been outlawed. A more important and interesting cause of its decline is, however, the process by which the Bulgarians, supported by the Comintern in

[19] "Die Zweite Konferenz der Kommunistischen Balkanföderation," pp. 676-81.

[20] Kabakchiev, "Die Ereignissse in Bulgarien," p. 98. The Greek Party was again not represented.

[21] "Die Kommunistische Balkanföderation zu den Vorfällen in der K.P.B.," *Inprekorr*, IV, No. 3 (January 8, 1924), p. 24.

[22] "Die Balkankonferenz," *Inprekorr*, IV, No. 9 (January 22, 1924), 91.

[23] Dimitrov, "Die Siebte Kommunistische Balkankonferenz," *Inprekorr*, IV, No. 99 (August 1, 1924), pp. 1272-73. This conference is referred to as the seventh of the series, because the Communists appropriated for themselves the prestige of the Socialist conferences of 1910 (Belgrade) and 1915 (Bucharest).

Moscow, turned it into an instrument of their domination over the other member parties. From the very founding of the Federation, Moscow had reposed great confidence in the Communists of Bulgaria and considered the revolutionary situation to be ripest in that country,[24] and from the very beginning of the Federation's life the Bulgarian party had taken advantage of Moscow's favor to dominate the Federation and to impose upon it policies which would suit its own particular electoral and propagandist interests within Bulgaria. Not only did the secretaryship of the Federation revolve exclusively among the three Bulgarians—Kolarov, Kabakchiev, and Dimitrov—but its headquarters and those of its trade-union auxiliary always followed the Bulgarian Communist Party's—from Sofia, to Vienna (after the September insurrection), and finally to Moscow.[25] One of its earliest manifestoes, that of August 10, 1920, not only accused every Balkan state except Bulgaria of persecuting the national minorities on its territory, but even supported Bulgarian revisionist ambitions with an expression of indignation that "the Bulgarian people has been dismembered and split up in the most cruel manner [by the Treaty of Neuilly]. Its compact masses in Macedonia, in the Dobruja, and Thrace, find themselves under foreign yoke." [26] Such support on the Federation's part for Bulgaria's claims to three hotly disputed areas could be to the interest only of its Bulgarian member. It was not long before the other parties revolted against this policy and against the Bulgarian Party's domination of the Federation. The first such explosion took place in the Greek Communist Party in protest against the Comintern's and the Federation's policy on the Macedonian and Thracian questions.

In September, 1922, Mustafa Kemal reoccupied Smyrna, and with this victory the Greek-Turkish War came to an end. Long before the Lausanne Conference culminated on July 24, 1923, in a peace treaty, it had been agreed to exchange the respective minority popu-

[24] See the Zinoviev letter, "An das Proletariat der Balkan- und Donauländer: An die Kommunistischen Parteien Bulgariens, Rumäniens, Serbiens und der Türkei," pp. 835-38.

[25] Kharlakov and Vlakhov, the two editors-in-chief of *La Fédération Balkanique*, which was not officially an organ of the Balkan Communist Federation, were also of the Bulgarian Communist Party.

[26] "Manifest der Kommunistischen Balkan-Donauföderation: An die werktätigen Klassen der Balkan- und Donauländer," p. 234.

lations. Under this repatriation agreement,[27] more than 400,000 Turks living in the Balkan territories that had been acquired by Greece since 1912 were returned to Turkey in exchange for 1,300,000 Greeks from Smyrna and other localities along the littoral of Asia Minor. Of these Greek refugees, 638,000 were resettled in Greek Macedonia and to provide them with living space about 53,000 Bulgarians were expelled to Bulgaria where they joined the approximately 39,000 refugees who had left Greek Macedonia and Greek Thrace for Bulgaria at the end of the World War. Henceforth, 89 percent of the population of Greek Macedonia consisted of Greeks while Greek Thrace was virtually cleared of Bulgarians. There remained in Greece slightly fewer than 100,000 Slavic-speaking people, most of whom lived in the region bordering on Yugoslavia. At the same time (1922-24) about 30,000 Greeks left Bulgaria.[28]

The Fourth Comintern Congress of November, 1922, decided to oppose the coming population transfer and authorized the Balkan Communist Federation to issue a strongly worded hostile manifesto declaring to the refugees that they were all victims of Greek imperialism and that the Federation would champion their right to return some day to their old homes.[29] This policy was an error for which the Communists later paid dearly. History shows that whereas minority treaties and guarantees rarely end disputes, exchanges or expulsions of minority populations, while drastic and painful for

---

[27] The protocol was signed by Ismet and Venizelos on January 30, 1923. The Lausanne Conference had opened on November 20, 1922.

[28] The precise number of Bulgarian refugees is difficult to establish. The figures given above enumerate only those who availed themselves of the services of the League of Nations' Mixed Commission of Emigration and are abstracted from Ladas, *The Exchange of Minorities: Bulgaria, Greece, and Turkey*, pp. 122-23, and from Ancel, *La Macédoine*, p. 114. Figures published by the Bulgarian Statistical Institute in 1926 list the number of people living that year in Bulgaria who had been born in what then was Greek Macedonia as 69,449 and those from Greek Thrace as 38,572. The difference between the total of these two figures (108,000) and the total number of Bulgarian refugees accounted for by the Mixed Commission (92,000) represents roughly those who, prompted by IMRO, boycotted the Mixed Commission. It seems likely that most of these boycotters had fled into Bulgaria before the advancing Allied armies in 1918 and that few of them had emigrated during the population exchange in 1923.

As for the Greek-Turkish population exchange, the 1,300,000 Greek refugee-immigrants formed 22 percent of the population of Greece.

[29] "Manifest der Kommunistischen Balkanföderation," *Inprekorr*, III, No. 8 (January 11, 1923), 61. The Manifesto is dated Sofia, December, 1922, but was probably drafted at the Federation's Fifth Conference held that month in Moscow.

those affected, tend to be permanent settlements. Already in 1922 the Greek Communist Party demurred at this policy adopted by the Comintern and the Federation, a policy not only utopian, not only confusing to the refugees, not only a handicap to the Party's efforts to cultivate support among the other Greek voters, but also liable to present the Greek government with a pretext for taking legal measures against the Party on grounds of sedition. These rumblings of discontent in the Greek Communist Party became so ominous that in March, 1923, on Comintern orders, two leading Bulgarian Communists were sent to Greece where they smashed the incipient revolt.[30]

In March, 1924, the Balkan Communist Federation issued a long statement of its Macedonian program prepared at the Federation's sixth conference held in Berlin in December, 1923.[31] Once more calling for autonomy for Macedonia and Thrace, its entire tone suggests that it was intended to flatter IMRO, to wean it from its alliance with the Tsankov government to an accord with the Communist movement in the Balkans. The effect of the statement on the fortunes of the Greek Communist Party was disastrous. It called on that party to "protest energetically against the attempt to Hellenize [Macedonia and Thrace] by means of the expulsion of Turks and Bulgarians," to "aim at the annulment of the treaty stipulating the exchange of populations," and "to do its utmost, in agreement with the Bulgarian Communist Party, to prevent the conclusion of a similar treaty between the Greek and Bulgarian governments."[32] This last exhortation was as meaningless as the first two were unrealistic for a Greco-Bulgarian Convention Concerning Reciprocal Emigration, under which the respective minorities were being exchanged, had come into effect with the Treaty of Neuilly. These directives and the tone of the declaration savagely attacking the Yugoslav and Greek but not the Bulgarian claims to and policies in Macedonia, suggest that the document was the work of the dominant Bulgarian section of the Federation. The Yugoslav Communists accepted it most unenthusiastically while the Greek Communist

---

[30] Kabakchiev, "Die Ereignisse in Bulgarien," p. 90; Zinoviev, "Die Lehren des Bulgarischen Umsturzes," *Inprekorr*, III, No. 115 (July 9, 1923), 1009.
[31] "Resolution on the Question of Nationalities," pp. 92-98.
[32] *Ibid.*, p. 98.

Party refused to publish it and protested against it to Moscow.[33] In fact, the Greek delegate to the conference which had drawn up the statement, one N. Sargologos, had agreed to sign it only in order to receive the bounty of $15,000 with which Moscow both subsidized and blackmailed the Greek Party.[34]

At an Extraordinary Congress of the Greek Communist Party held in 1924, E. Stavrides, a member of the Central Committee and a Macedonian Greek, pleaded that the Party be permitted to drop the statement in its platform calling for autonomy for Macedonia and Thrace as it was unrealistic and harmful to the Party's electoral chances, but Manuilski, the Comintern's delegate to the Congress, refused to allow any tampering with this clause.[35] Since Moscow held all the trump cards, both organizational and financial, the Congress had to acquiesce, but the seething discontent within the Greek Party was nearing boiling point. When the Fifth Comintern Congress of June-July, 1924, not only once more endorsed the Federation's autonomy slogans but went on to reprove the Yugoslav and Greek Communist Parties for their reluctance to accept them, and thus, by implication, to endorse Bulgarian domination of the Federation, the revolt within the Greek Party bubbled over. Manuilski was the *rapporteur* of the Fifth Comintern Congress on this question and in his speech of June 30 berated the Yugoslav and Greek Parties for their disinclination to accept the policy of national autonomy. The Greek delegate, Maximos, replied tartly on the following day that the policy "fails to take into consideration the conditions of its application to Greece . . . [for] the fact remains that we have in Macedonia 750,000 Greek refugees. The workers and peasants of Greece are therefore not prepared to accept the slogan of the autonomy of Macedonia." [36] This protest, however, availed little and at the seventh conference of the Balkan Communist Federation held in Moscow immediately after the close of the

[33] This was revealed by Manuilski in his report on the National and Colonial Question at the Fifth Comintern Congress. See *Fünfter Kongress der Kommunistischen Internationale: Protokoll*, p. 629.

[34] Christidès, *Le Camouflage macédonien*, p. 121. This incident of the subsidy had an amusing sequel, for once the money was in his pocket, Sargologos, instead of returning to Greece, allegedly absconded with it to America.

[35] *Ibid.*, p. 122.

[36] *Fünfter Kongress der Kommunistischen Internationale: Protokoll*, p. 693. For the resolutions of the Fifth Comintern Congress on the Macedonian and Thracian Questions, see *The Communist International*, New Series, No. 7 (December, 1924–January, 1925), pp. 93-95.

Comintern Congress in July, 1924, the Bulgarian Party, with the aid of the Comintern delegate, reasserted its dominant position. The conference condemned "the right and liquidatory deviation" of many leaders of the Yugoslav and Greek parties who refused to accept the program of autonomy for Macedonia and Thrace.[37]

Maximos's implied defiance of this policy at the Comintern Congress had, however, been no idle threat, for a strong section of the Greek Communist Party was determined to cease compromising itself politically with the electorate and legally with the government in the pursuit of an unrealistic and suicidal policy which only the Bulgarian of all the Balkan Communist Parties supported. Even while the seventh conference of the Federation was in session, Pouliopoulos, who had entered the Greek Party as leader of a group of soldier Communists from the Turkish campaign of 1922 and had been elected Secretary of the Central Committee in the same year, launched a paper in which he definitely broke with the autonomy policy. (The translation of the paper's title is "The New Course.") The Greek government poured oil on the flames by announcing that it would take measures against those advocating autonomy for Greek Macedonia and Thrace. At this time there were ten Communist deputies in the Greek parliament of whom "one section turned out to be opportunists and the others were of the opposition and refused to follow Party instructions," [38]—which, translated into the normal language of politics, means that when threatened by the government with legal consequences, the deputies preferred to jettison the already burdensome autonomy propaganda. A temporary moratorium was imposed on the issue when the Party was declared illegal during the Pangalos dictatorship of June, 1925, to August, 1926. In August, 1925, Maximos, Pouliopoulos, and one Fitsios were tried for publishing the allegedly subversive Communist paper *Rizospastis* (Radical), which was suspended for six months. Maximos was sentenced to one year's imprisonment and the two others to a year and a half.[39] When the Greek Communist Party again emerged into the open in the autumn of 1926, Pouliopoulos and

---

[37] Dimitrov, "Die Siebte Kommunistische Balkankonferenz," *Inprekorr*, IV, No. 99 (August 1, 1924), 1272-73.

[38] *The Communist International Between the Fifth and the Sixth World Congresses, 1924-1928*, p. 261.

[39] Gregorios Dafnis, *E Ellas Metaxy Dyo Polemen, 1923-1940* (Greece between Two Wars, 1923-1940), (Athens, 1955), I, 292.

Maximos continued their heretical agitation. After refusing to heed several warnings and extended criticism made "with the aid of the Comintern"—a phrase suggesting that he enjoyed considerable support within the Greek Party—Pouliopoulos was expelled in October, 1927. He left with two remarks, which rankled because of their truth. "In my opinion," he declared, "our nationality policy has been particularly wrong. The slogan 'Independent and Unified Macedonia and Thrace' has been shown by the facts to be incorrect in principle and has led to catastrophic consequences for the Greek labor movement." [40] How right he was in this charge is indicated by the membership figures, which stood at 860 in March, 1927; even allowing for the fact that the Party had only recently emerged from illegality, there can be no doubt that at least a partial cause of this weakness was the autonomy policy imposed by the Comintern and the Federation. Pouliopoulos's parting shot was to state that "it is inadmissible that any international commando should autocratically decree that other Communist Parties should follow principles incompatible with the objective conditions of their countries." [41] This was, of course, calling into question a basic Comintern principle, but it was the logical consequence of the policies pursued by Pouliopoulos in the months preceding his expulsion when he had constantly demanded greater freedom of discussion and less mechanical discipline within the Party. He had even angled for opposition support from Moscow by entering the polemical lists against Stalin's theory of "socialism in one country." But Trotsky's star had long set by 1927, and Zinoviev in that year suffered his first expulsion from the CPSU (b); Pouliopoulos hitched his wagon to theirs only to go down with them. His expulsion was followed by that of Maximos and several other veteran leaders of the Party, the autonomy slogans were reimposed, and when the Sixth Comintern Congress met in July, 1928, the Bulgarian Dimitrov was able to boast that the Greek Party had been purged and purified.[42]

[40] Šmeral, "Der Kampf gegen das rechte Liquidatorentum in der K.P. Griechenlands," *Inprekorr*, VII, No. 100 (October 14, 1927), 2152.

[41] *Ibid.*, p. 2152. By 1930, after four years of legal existence, the Greek Communist Party still had in Athens but 170 members and in Piraeus, one of the largest proletarian agglomerations in the country, only 70. "The Revolutionary Crisis in Greece and the Tasks of the Communist Movement," *The Communist International*, VII, No. 5 (May 1, 1930), 57.

[42] *Sechster Weltkongress der Kommunistischen Internationale: Protokoll*, I, 241.

The arguments with which the Bulgarian Communists sought to rationalize their refusal to recognize the political implications of the prosaic facts that the population of Greek Macedonia was, after 1923, 89 percent Greek, while in Western (Greek) Thrace there were hardly any Bulgarians, might be amusing were they not so patently fraudulent. When the Presidium, that is, the Bulgarian Secretary, of the Balkan Communist Federation had demanded in January, 1925, that the member parties constantly agitate for the right of the exchanged and expelled populations to return to their original homes, it had given as its reason that the people involved not only had not wanted to be exchanged but still hoped to return to their former homes in Turkey and Greece.[43] By 1925 such pronouncements rested on precariously thin grounds, for there was no evidence that many of the refugees would wish to return to their former homes except some of the Bulgarians who had been ejected or repatriated from Greek Macedonia and Western Thrace. Thus the suspicions of the Greek Communists, that the wishes and interests of 1,300,000 Greeks and 400,000 Turks were being cancelled by those of about 100,000 Bulgarians in determining Communist policy on the question seem to have been not unfounded. By 1928 such arguments were too preposterous even for the Bulgarian Communists, for by then very few even of the Bulgarian refugees still seriously expected to return to their old homes.[44] The Bulgarian

---

Serafim Maximos had followed Pouliopoulos as Secretary of the Central Committee of the Greek Communist Party and held this position from 1925 until his expulsion. In 1926 he had led the Party's parliamentary faction. He and Pouliopoulos founded a "United Opposition" group on the issue of Macedonia and Thrace. After their expulsion they collaborated with the so-called "Archeio-Marxists," a Trotskyite group. In 1933 and 1934 this working coalition split into a number of splinter groups, and by 1936 Maximos was ready to recant. His application for readmission into the Communist Party of Greece was granted after the required self-criticism. See "Eine Erklärung Maximos' an die K.P. Griechenlands," *Basler Rundschau,* V, No. 34 (July 30, 1936), 1406.

[43] "Das Flüchtlingsproblem auf dem Balkan: Stellungnahme des Präsidiums der Kommunistischen Balkanföderation," *Inprekorr,* V, No. 13 (January 20, 1925), 159.

[44] In 1926 Bulgaria received a loan of £2 million from the League of Nations for the purpose of resettling these refugees. One of the conditions of the loan was that each recipient of such aid was required to sign a declaration that he renounced all intentions of returning to his former home across the border. With the aid of this loan, Bulgaria distributed 132,000 hectares of land among the refugees and built 16,000 houses for them. The majority were resettled in the valleys of the Danube and Maritsa rivers and along the Black Sea littoral. See Ancel, *La Macédoine,* pp. 224 ff. It must be born in mind that the total Bulgarian refugee burden, including as it did fugitives from Yugoslav Macedonia and the Rumanian Dobruja,

Communists, however, could not then afford to drop a policy which, if nothing else, still symbolized their domination of the other Balkan Communist Parties. It had become a fetish with them. Accordingly, in 1928 the Bulgarians advanced the thesis that while the refugees who had come out of Anatolia in 1923 may well have been and felt themselves to be Greek, yet after five years of residence in Macedonia and Thrace the spirit and position of these areas had imposed itself on their outlook. "The Greek peasants there," insisted Dimitrov, "are adopting a Macedonian consciousness and are abandoning their self-image as Greeks. They regard as their brothers not the Greeks but the Macedonians across the Bulgarian and Yugoslav borders." [45] There was no evidence for this assertion. Even the Bulgarians must have been aware that it was preposterous to expect Greek Macedonia and Thrace ever to be ceded to an autonomous state by any Greek government. Kolarov himself admitted at the Sixth Comintern Congress in 1928 that since tobacco accounted for 60 percent of the value of Greek exports and since the country's crop was grown almost exclusively in the areas in question, the Greek economy would be hopelessly crippled were the country to lose its portions of Macedonia and Thrace.[46] The fact that this most intelligent of the Bulgarian Communist leaders admitted the utopian character of the autonomy slogans indicates once again that they continued to be imposed as a device in the power struggle among the various Balkan Communist Parties. That the Russian masters of the Comintern were disquieted by the dictatorial conduct of the Bulgarian Communists in these Balkan matters is doubtful, for developments within the Yugoslav Party in the 1920s disappointed Moscow in that party as well as in the

---

was originally a heavy one. For propaganda the Bulgarians usually claimed that it amounted to half a million refugees—a vast exaggeration. The reliable Bulgarian Statistical Institute gave the number of people living in Bulgaria in 1926 who had been born outside her then frontiers as 276,463 (Swire, *Bulgarian Conspiracy*, p. 25). About half of these had by then been integrated into Bulgarian economic life and the Commissioner of the League of Nations found that the number who could still be considered genuine refugees in need of League assistance for settlement did not exceed 31,271 families, or approximately 125,000 individuals. See Ladas, *The Exchange of Minorities: Bulgaria, Greece, and Turkey*, p. 592.

[45] Dimitrov, "Die National-Revolutionäre Bewegung auf dem Balkan und die Aufgaben der Kommunistischen Parteien des Balkans," p. 2632.

[46] Kolarov's speech of August 4, 1928, to the Congress was reprinted in *Inprekorr*, VIII, No. 95 (September 3, 1928), 1756-59.

recalcitrant Greeks, and convinced it that whereas the policies of the Bulgarian Communist Party may not always have been the most intelligently conceived, yet the Bulgarians were the best "bolsheviks" of all the Balkan Communists.

The multinational state of Yugoslavia came into existence as a consequence of the First World War and from its establishment the government of the old Serbian state around which it was built sought to ensure Serbian dominance within the new state. This tendency toward overcentralization had deplorable consequences throughout the country but particularly in Macedonia, which became a Siberia for incompetent Serbian bureaucrats. Government officials who were too corrupt, too inefficient, too brutal, too drunken to be employable in other parts of Yugoslavia were assigned to Macedonia and in consequence administrative standards in that province were lower than elsewhere.[47] Thus discontent with their lot was aroused among the people of Yugoslav Macedonia by the combination of Serbian domination and poor administration. It should be recognized that the second was as important a cause as the first of this dissatisfaction and that the issue was as much one of good government as of local rights. This was always denied by Bulgarian propaganda which claimed that discontent in Yugoslav Macedonia was caused exclusively by a feeling of Bulgarian nationality and by a desire to be united with the rest of the Bulgarian people. In fact, however, the people of Yugoslav Macedonia had lived through as bitter a period under Bulgarian rule during the World War as they were experiencing under Serbian domination after it, and their belief in their capacity to rule themselves was probably as strong as the anxiety of their neighbors to "liberate" them. Neither the Serbians nor the Bulgarians were, however, interested in the actual state of opinion among the population of Macedonia. Domination and corruption from Belgrade and terrorist *komitaji* raids from across the Bulgarian border reacted upon each other in a vicious circle. All this was grist for the Communist mill.

The standard Communist tactic in such a situation required the Communist Parties to come forward as the self-proclaimed defenders of the oppressed and under no circumstances to permit any bourgeois

[47] *The Times*, May 23, 1925.

party or organization to capture the leadership of the struggle of any national minority for freedom.[48] In the case of Macedonia, the Balkan Communist Federation decided, as has been shown, that the proper solution to the problem was the establishment of a united and independent Macedonia rather than the granting of autonomy by each of the three Balkan states involved to its slice of Macedonia.[49] This program, a function of Stalinist doctrine on the national question, of Soviet Russian diplomatic policy, and of the Bulgarian Communist Party's efforts to recruit IMRO as an ally against the Tsankov government, suited the interests of neither the Greek nor the Yugoslav Communist Party. The Yugoslav Communists' revolt against it had stronger repercussions within the Comintern than that of their Greek comrades and merits a short discussion.

From the moment of its birth after the war, the new state of Yugoslavia was anathema to Soviet Russia, for it became the most important outpost of French influence in Southeastern Europe and thus a fulcrum of the *cordon sanitaire* against Russia. Moscow demanded that this state be destroyed. On this question Comintern policy coincided with Bulgarian revisionism and facilitated the propaganda of the Bulgarian Communist Party in addition to strengthening its dominant role in the Balkan Communist Federation. The Bulgarian Communists lost little time in seeking to reinsure themselves with Bulgarian nationalist sentiment by weeping bitter tears for the oppressed Bulgarians of Thrace, the Dobruja and Macedonia and claiming these territories for the fatherland.[50] In their writings for Comintern publications, the Bulgarians reveal a venomous hatred of the Yugoslav state and ceaselessly declaim against its allegedly insufferable oppression of the Bulgarian population of the Tsaribrod salient, of Albanians in Montenegro and the Kossovo region, of Hungarians in the Voivodina, of Croatians, Slovenes, and Macedonians in their respective lands. Kolarov, for example, claimed that in the "prison-house" of the Yugoslav state there were 2,000,000 irredentist Germans, Magyars, Italians, Ru-

---

[48] See Kolarov, "The National Question in the Balkans," pp. 78-85. Also Kabakchiev, "Die Nationale- und die Agrarfrage auf dem Balkan," p. 1625.

[49] "Resolution on the Question of Nationalities," pp. 86-98.

[50] "Weisser Schrecken: Erklärung des Z.K. der K.P. Bulgariens," *Inprekorr,* **IV,** No. 116 (September 5, 1924), 1519.

manians, Albanians, and Bulgarians who wanted to be reunited with their brothers across the borders, in addition to 7,000,000 Croats, Slovenes, Bosnians, Montenegrins, and Macedonians who regarded themselves as separate nations and wished to establish for themselves independent states. Yugoslavia, he concluded, is a monstrosity which must be destroyed.[51] Simultaneously, he severely reprimanded the Yugoslav Communists for not accepting this conclusion and thus allowing bourgeois politicians, such as Radić and Korošec, to win for themselves the leadership of the Croatian and Slovene national movements. In the Balkans, Kolarov insisted, nationalism is as much a peasant as a town ideology, and the Communists could become the dominant political power on the Peninsula by utilizing it in conjunction with an appropriate agrarian program. The Communist Party of Yugoslavia, he charged, "had failed to estimate at its true worth the national factor in the struggle of the toiling masses." [52] The Bulgarian Communists were able to insist on drafting the Balkan Communist Federation's statement of March, 1924, on the national question in this spirit of absolute hostility toward the Yugoslav state as such.[53] The Yugoslav Communist Party, it seems, protested to Moscow, for at the Fifth Comintern Congress held in the summer of that year, the entire question was brought into the open, only to have the Russian Party, in the person of Stalin's chief aide for Comintern matters, Dmitri Manuilski, completely vindicate the Bulgarians' policy against the Yugoslav as well as the Greek malcontents. The Yugoslav Communist leader Sima Marković, who was in prison at the time, and his colleague Miloiković were reproached by Manuilski with holding social democratic, "Bauer-ist" views on the national question. Marković had even dared to claim that the Macedonian issue could be settled only through and after the general European proletarian revolution and that there was nothing which the Balkan Communist Parties could or should do about it in the meantime.[54] The congress resolution on the Macedonian and Thracian questions confirmed the Bulgarian

[51] Kolarov, "The National Question in the Balkans," p. 80.
[52] *Ibid.*, p. 81.
[53] "Resolution on the Question of Nationalities," pp. 86-98. The statement reads as if intended to flatter IMRO, with which the Bulgarian Party at that time hoped to conclude an alliance.
[54] Manuilski's report of June 30, 1924, is in *Fünfter Kongress der Kommunistischen Internationale: Protokoll*, pp. 628 ff.

Party's domination of the Balkan Communist Federation by approving the Bulgarian-inspired decisions of the Federation's sixth conference, which had been held in Berlin in December of the preceding year, and by echoing the Federation's statement of March, 1924.[55] As a result, the Bulgarians were once more enabled to tighten their hold on the Federation at its seventh conference held in Moscow immediately after the close of the Fifth Comintern Congress and to have it condemn the "right and liquidatory deviation" of many leaders and groups of the Yugoslav and Greek Parties.[56]

The Yugoslav Communists did not, however, respond to the rebukes of the Congress with the customary ritual of abject self-criticism. Indeed, they persisted in their "deviationist" views with such stubbornness that the purge of the Yugoslav Party was one of the chief items of business at the Enlarged Plenum of the ECCI, which met in Moscow in March-April, 1925, and witnessed a violent clash between the resentful Yugoslav and the triumphant Bulgarian Communists. A maneuver by the Comintern leaders which exacerbated the feud between the two parties was the appointment as *rapporteur* on the question and thus, in effect, as executioner of the Yugoslav leaders, of the chief complainant, the Bulgarian leader Vasil Kolarov.[57] The Bulgarians had an old score to settle with Marković who had been one of the most acidly contemptuous critics of their neutrality policy at the time of the June coup in 1923.[58] Kolarov paid off this debt with a vengeance, lashing the hapless Marković and other Yugoslavs for having committed a whole series of errors and deviations on the national question. The blindly

[55] "Resolution on the National Question in Central Europe and the Balkans," pp. 93-99.
[56] Dimitrov, "Die Siebte Kommunistische Balkankonferenz," *Inprekorr*, IV, No. 99 (August 1, 1924), 1272-73.
[57] "Bericht des Genossen Kolarow über die Arbeit der Jugoslawischen Kommission: 14. Sitzung vom 6. April 1925 der Tagung des Erweiterten EKKI," *Inprekorr*, V, No. 68 (April 24, 1925), pp. 924-25. In view of the post-1948 statements by Yugoslav Communists that Dimitrov was friendly to their Party in the 1930s when he was Secretary-General of the Comintern and in 1948 even secretly advised them to "be firm" in their struggle with the Russian Politburo (Cf. Dedijer, *Tito Speaks*, pp. 233, 360), it is interesting to note that the chief Bulgarian inquisitor of the Yugoslav heretics in the 1920s was Kolarov while Dimitrov, remaining in the background of this dispute, took a greater interest in that with the Greek Communist Party.
[58] See p. 131.

doctrinaire Yugoslav comrades, complained Kolarov, thought that it was just as essential to oppose Croat and Slovene as Serbian nationalism, all three being equally bourgeois. Did they not realize that they thereby gave aid and comfort to the Serbian ruling clique? They had committed a yet graver sin in refusing to accept the necessity of destroying the Yugoslav state, even having the temerity to assert that the union of several nationalities into one large state had been a progressive act, and that the various national tensions within it could be resolved by a mere federalistic reform of the Vidovdan Constitution of 1921 so as to grant greater autonomy to each of the constituent parts of Yugoslavia within its existing frontiers. Kolarov finished with a self-righteous flourish of smugness and venom, as well he might, for he had been supported in these discussions by none other than the Comintern's oracle on the national question. Stalin had on March 30 rebuked Marković (who was referred to by the pseudonym "Semić") for not recognizing that the national problem in Yugoslavia was essentially a peasant one and for asserting that it was capable of a purely "constitutional" solution.[59] Semić-Marković replied that his statement of views had been incorrectly translated and that Comrade Stalin had thus been given an erroneous impression of these views. The differences between Stalin and himself, he continued, were not wide and could easily be eliminated. Though he replied in a conciliatory manner, Semić-Marković refused to accept the basic contention of the Bulgarians and of the Comintern that it was the duty of the Yugoslav Communists to work for the destruction of the Yugoslav state by supporting all the separatist movements within it. Croatian, Slovene, or Macedonian nationalism, he insisted, was no more progressive than Serbian, while the Serbians had a revolutionary tradition at least as honorable as that of any other Balkan people.[60] Stalin, in effect, rejected the obstinate Yugoslav's explanations and a purge

[59] Stalin, "Zur Nationalen Frage in Jugoslawien: Rede des Genossen Stalin in der Jugoslawischen Kommission des Erweiterten EKKI," *Inprekorr*, V, No. 76 (May 8, 1925), pp. 1013-14; reprinted in his *Sochinenia*, VII, 69-76. The pseudonym was intended to protect Marković, who had been in prison in 1924, from further police persecution. In the Greek Communist Party a similar "deviationist" sect which refused to cooperate with the peasantry and champion its bourgeois national sentiments was led by Kordatos. See Dimitrov, "Die Lage auf dem Balkan und die Aufgaben der Kommunistischen Balkanföderation," p. 747.
[60] Semić, "Zur Nationalen Frage in Jugoslawien," *Inprekorr*, V, No. 120 (August 11, 1925), 1729-30.

of the Party was confirmed.[61] Henceforth no obstacles stood in the way of the supremacy of the Bulgarian among the Balkan Communist Parties.

Why did the Comintern support the claims and ambitions of the Bulgarian Communists against those of the other Balkan Parties? The reasons are several, but each was dictated either by the interests of the Soviet Russian state or by the particular historical-political preferences of the Russian Communist leaders. In the 1920s, Bulgaria and Russia had at least this in common: they were both revisionist states and thus were hostile to three of Bulgaria's neighbors —Greece, Yugoslavia, and Rumania. The first two were anathema to Moscow because it considered them to be pawns of Britain and France respectively in the diplomatic offensive which the two Western powers were conducting against Soviet Russia, while Rumania was loathed because it too was a link in the French alliance system in Eastern Europe and because it had taken advantage of the turmoil of the Russian civil wars to annex Bessarabia. Thus Bulgaria, being the only important Balkan state outside the French or British alliance system and the only one not in some territorial or diplomatic conflict with Soviet Russia, was Moscow's logical choice as a potential protégé. Since the electoral or propaganda success of any of the Balkan Communist Parties could be greatly facilitated by championing the particular national territorial aspirations, it followed, by Moscow's calculations, that the Bulgarian Party's propaganda to this end should be encouraged since Bulgarian revisionism was directed against the same three states which Moscow considered the eastern outposts of her Western enemies. The Bulgarian Communist Party was permitted to make irredentist propaganda with respect to Macedonia, Thrace, the Southern Dobruja, and Tsaribrod.[62]

---

[61] Stalin, "Noch Einmal die Nationale Frage," *Inprekorr*, V, No. 120 (August 11, 1925), 1730-32; reprinted in his *Sochinenia*, VII, 216-26.

[62] "Weisser Schrecken: Erklärung des Z.K. der K.P. Bulgariens," *Inprekorr*, IV, No. 116 (September 5, 1924), 1519. In Vienna the editorial policy of *La Fédération Balkanique* was synchronized with this revisionist campaign. The Sofia government was berated for "betrayal" of the Bulgarian minorities in the three neighboring states to foreign oppression. See, for example, the issues of June 1, August 1, September 1, 1927 (III, No. 69; IV, Nos. 72-73 and 74-75). Neither the Federation's nor the Bulgarian Party's revisionist propaganda was directed against Turkey, with which

The Russian leaders may also have been genuinely convinced of their claims that the Yugoslav state was not viable and had no future because the pent-up pressure of the discontented nationalities would shortly explode. That they were impressed by the Croatian separatist movement is shown by the efforts made to recruit Radić into the International Peasant Council. If they actually believed that the Yugoslav state was destined to collapse sooner or later, there was no point in supporting the Yugoslav Communist Party against that of a homogeneous, permanent state—Bulgaria. Furthermore, it was true, that Serbian administration in Yugoslav Macedonia (or South Serbia as the Belgrade government insisted on calling it until 1929, when it became the Vardarska Banovina) did antagonize the local population. If Moscow supported the Bulgarian Party's slogan of a "united and autonomous Macedonia," there was, it seemed in the early 1920s, the possibility of concluding a "unity of action" agreement between the Bulgarian Communists and IMRO, whereas the adoption of Marković's program of autonomy for Yugoslav Macedonia within the existing Yugoslav state would forfeit this alliance, cement IMRO's ties with the Bulgarian right-wing parties, and gain no new friends for the Communists. In the Yugoslav elections of 1920 the Communist Party had polled an impressive vote, particularly in Macedonia where 17 Communist candidates were elected to the Constituent Assembly.[63] The Comintern leaders probably concluded, however, and rightly so, that this surprising victory did not indicate mass support of Communism so much as mass discontent with the existing state of affairs. They did not allow this success to persuade them that the Yugoslav Communist Party was stronger or enjoyed better prospects of capturing power than did its Bulgarian neighbor, and they declined to transfer their support from the latter to the former.[64]

Moscow hoped to reestablish the *rapprochement* weakened at the Lausanne Conference of 1922-23.

[63] Barker, *Macedonia*, p. 23. The 17 Communists were one third of the deputies elected in Macedonia. Ulam, *Titoism and the Cominform*, p. 8. The total number of Communist votes in the entire country was 198,736. These sent 58 deputies to the Constituent Assembly and made the Communist Party the third strongest in the chamber. The moderate Social Democrats polled only 46,792 votes. Wendel, *Aus der Welt der Südslawen*, p. 54.

[64] Scepticism in regard to the implications of the Yugoslav Communist Party's success was justified. In August, 1921, within a year of the great electoral victory, the government outlawed it and dissolved its legal institutions. In the 1923 elections

When all these probable motives for the Comintern's backing of the Bulgarian Communists have been mentioned, there still remains the most important reason of all—the fact that the Russian leaders had greater confidence in the Bulgarians as "good bolsheviks" than in any other Communist Party. This was owing to several factors—theoretical, historical, and, not least, sentimental. Ever since Klemenčić, at the Balkan Communist Federation conference in February, 1921, had denounced the implication of the Comintern delegate's speech that Moscow looked upon the organization merely as a useful wedge with which to pry open the *cordon sanitaire* and had protested that the Federation had other functions to fulfill within the terms of Marxist theory, the Yugoslav Communists had been in Moscow's bad graces for their tendency to scrutinize critically Comintern directives and for their peculiar idealism, which manifested itself yet again in Semić-Marković's resistance to the tactical opportunism of supporting the demands of the Croatian, Macedonian, and Magyar extremists for the dismemberment of Yugoslavia. Not only did the Bulgarians always dutifully follow Moscow's prescriptions but, with the exception of the swiftly corrected aberration of June, 1923, they had never been contaminated with the disease of ideological naïveté. This, together with their greater ruthlessness, made the Bulgarians the more likely recipients of Moscow's favor. Nor did they entertain any illusions about democracy within the Comintern or autonomy for its various member parties. Dimitrov could justifiably boast:

When the statutes of the Comintern were drawn up, the Bulgarian Communist Party took the position that the Communist International, in contradistinction to the opportunistic Socialist International, must not merely be a free friendly combination of Communist Parties, but a single truly international Communist Party with a compulsory international discipline and the widest rights of control over the activities and policies of its separate national sections.[65]

The Bulgarians had demonstrated their understanding of this basic organizational principle of the Comintern in 1923 when the

---

the Party's cover organization, The Independent Workers' Party of Yugoslavia, polled only 18,000 votes (10 percent of the 1920 figure) which did not suffice to elect even a single deputy to the Skupština. Wendel, *Aus der Welt der Südslawen*, p. 55.

[65] Dimitrov, "The Bulgarian Communist Party and the Communist International," p. 191.

neutrality policy previously endorsed with near unanimity by the Party leadership was promptly reversed on Moscow's orders and the hopeless September insurrection launched.

The Bulgarian Communist leaders, furthermore, had no scruples about giving Moscow an exaggerated impression of their party's strength. Their delegates to the early Comintern Congresses had boasted "we shall seize power when we so desire." [66] They had told Wilhelm Pieck, Comintern representative to their Fourth Party Congress in 1922, that they were sufficiently strong to seize power but preferred to wait for it to drop into their hands, as it inevitably must with the "sharpening" of the "contradictions" of the Stamboliski regime.[67] It is quite probable that the ever-optimistic Zinoviev, who headed the Comintern in these early years, took these boasts at their face value, for they only confirmed the exaggerated notions which he held of the ability of the Bulgarian Communists and of the degree of revolutionary ripeness in their country at the time he penned his open letter to the Balkan proletariat in the summer of 1920.[68]

The fundamental, though never openly admitted, reason why not only Zinoviev but almost all the other Russian Communist leaders were already prepared in 1920 to regard the Bulgarian as the Balkan Communist Party with the greatest potentialities was the fact that it was a party thoroughly in the Russian tradition, whereas the old Serbian and Greek Socialist Parties had been more influenced by the German and French Socialist movements. Blagoev's founding of the first Marxist circle in Russia in 1883-84 at St. Petersburg, Kirkov's participation in Narodnaya Volya activities at Nikolaev, Bakalov's, Kabakchiev's, and Kolarov's association with Plekhanov at Geneva—these were considerations carrying weight with the Russian masters of the Comintern. Blagoev's struggle against the non-political Social Democratic Union in the 1890s—equated by Bulgarian Communist propagandists with Lenin's campaign against the Economists—and the Narrow-Broad split, consummated at the same time as the Bolshevik-Menshevik one, enabled the Bulgarian

---

[66] Serge, *From Lenin to Stalin*, p. 58.
[67] Pieck, "Der Vierte Bulgarische Parteikongress," p. 597.
[68] Zinoviev, "An das Proletariat der Balkan- und Donauländer," pp. 835-38. Because his expectations in the Bulgarian Party had been so high, Zinoviev's disappointment at the time of the June, 1923, neutrality fiasco was all the more bitter.

Party to boast of a long record of struggles for orthodoxy even before the Comintern was founded. The Narrow Socialists had also earned Lenin's affection by assisting the Bolshevik underground movement in Russia before the First World War. Bakalov organized and another Bulgarian named Ivan Zagubanski operated the smuggling of *Iskra* into Russia via the Varna-Odessa shipping route.[69] The Narrow Socialists also supplied Lenin's agents with false Bulgarian passports to facilitate their travels across and behind the Russian borders.[70] Blagoev endeared himself to Lenin and particularly to Stalin by facilitating the escape of the latter's friend, the *boyevik* Kamo (Ter-Petrossian) from a Bulgarian prison cell in 1912.[71] Unlike Western socialists, these Bulgarians neither flinched at Lenin's "expropriations" nor blushed at handling his "dirty monies." They were the ideal raw material from which good bolsheviks could be moulded. Such considerations weighed at least as heavily as those of international diplomacy or of Marxist theory in determining Moscow's decision to support the Bulgarian against the other Balkan Communist Parties. They carried especially great weight with a man like Stalin to whom cadres were the most precious assets in the world.[72]

It remains now to sketch in brief outline the disintegration of the Balkan Communist Federation. The ECCI Plenum of March-April, 1925, before closing its sessions, had called upon the Balkan Communist Parties to integrate their policies and to coordinate their activities so as to strengthen the Federation.[73] In view of the sharp criticism which had been leveled against the leaders of the Yugoslav Party at that very session and of the crisis which was convulsing the Greek Party at the time, this resolution amounted to an order to these two parties to submit to Bulgarian domination. As the Bulgarian Party was, however, itself illegal and weak in the following

---

[69] See p. 1, footnote 4.

[70] Bakalov, "Staraya 'Iskra' sredi Bolgar," pp. 81-83.

[71] Souvarine, *Stalin*, p. 102.

[72] Souvarine (*Stalin*, p. 605) quotes Stalin as saying at the height of the purge terror of the 1930s: "You must reach the understanding that of all the precious assets existing in the world, the most precious and decisive are the cadres."

[73] "Thesen und Resolutionen angenommen auf der Tagung des Erweiterten EKKI: Thesen über die Bolschewisierung der Parteien der Kommunistischen Internationale," *Inprekorr*, V, No. 80 (May 11, 1925), 1076.

years, and as the various Balkan governments were slowly feeling their way toward improved relations, the Balkan Communist Federation, which had never been a real force, became a phantom. It remained important only to the Bulgarian Communist leaders as a symbol of their party's supremacy. Once again it was Kolarov, with whom this supremacy was an obsession, who raised the question at the Sixth Comintern Congress in the summer of 1928. Before proceeding to demand fresh sanctions against the recalcitrant parties, Kolarov sought to convince the assembled delegates that the Bulgarians were still the best of the Balkan Communists and therefore deserving of continued support. Whereas the Yugoslavs and Rumanians had still not managed to purge themselves completely of all opportunist elements and the Greeks had only just managed to liquidate their deviationist wing, the Bulgarian Communist Party, he proudly assured the Congress, had overcome its internal crisis "most quickly and most radically." [74]

Having thus successfully prepared the way, Kolarov took the opportunity of his next speech to berate violently the other Balkan Communist Parties for each going its own unsynchronized way, and once again to deliver a bitter diatribe against Sima Marković. [75] The latter had in the meantime been brought on charges of sedition before a Yugoslav court where he had said in his defense that the Communist Party of Yugoslavia would oppose bands invading Macedonia from Bulgaria. These, he had claimed, only sought, as agents of Italian imperialism, to destroy the Yugoslav state by their raids, not to liberate the Macedonian peasants. This assurance by Marković to the Yugoslav authorities whipped Kolarov into a frenzy, for it amounted to another rejection of the Bulgarian-imposed Macedonian autonomy plank of the Federation's platform and thus to a renewed revolt against Bulgarian domination of the Federation. Though Marković had been removed from leadership, Kolarov feared that on this issue the stubborn Yugoslav was expressing the sentiments of his entire party. Kolarov's insistence that a long overdue conference of the Federation be summoned for the correction of such deviations was approved by the Sixth Comintern

[74] "Rede des Genossen Kolarow: 7. Sitzung," *Inprekorr*, VIII, No. 77 (August 2, 1928), 1385.
[75] "Rede des Genossen Kolarow: 21. Sitzung," *Inprekorr*, VIII, No. 95 (September 3, 1928), 1756-59.

Congress, which admonished the Balkan Communist Parties to co-ordinate their policies "far better than they have done hitherto." The general slogan of "A Workers' and Peasants' Balkan Feder-ation" was to be sustained.[76]

Thus it came about that early in 1929 delegates from the Commu-nist Parties of Bulgaria, Greece, Rumania and Yugoslavia, and an Albanian Communist (though formally no Albanian Communist Party as yet existed) assembled for the eighth conference of the Balkan Communist Federation and demonstrated once again, if proof were needed, that collectively as well as individually they and their Federation were but pawns of Soviet policy. Before proceeding to redefine its position on the national question in the Balkans, the conference commented on the European diplomatic outlook.[77] In the early 1920s France had been considered the foe most dangerous to Soviet Russia. Then, after the severing of Anglo-Soviet diplomatic relations in May, 1927, the Kremlin for a time professed to fear that Great Britain was the chief plotter of an imperialistic war against the USSR, and accordingly the conference, not anticipating the resumption of Anglo-Soviet relations in the autumn of 1929, promptly launched an Anglophobic tirade in its first resolution, on The Political Situation and the Tasks of the Balkan Communist Federation. It also insisted that the oppressed peasants of Bes-sarabia and Bukovina should be allowed to realize their allegedly fondest hopes of being incorporated into the Soviet Union, and went on to abuse the Little Entente, denounce Serbian chauvinism in Macedonia, decry plans allegedly being considered to unite Yugo-slavia and Bulgaria under the Karageorgević dynasty, and flatter IMRO. As was to be expected, the conference declared all the ills of the Balkan states to be a consequence of Western imperialism and concluded that all national movements deserved Communist support as they were potential revolutionary forces which could be utilized to slash the imperialist net by severing its local strands, the Balkan bureaucratic state structures. Accordingly, the old hobby-horses of "free and independent" Macedonia, Thrace, Dobruja, Croatia, Montenegro, Slovenia, were once again paraded. One

[76] *Communism and the International Situation. Theses Adopted at the Sixth World Congress of the Communist International,* p. 39.
[77] "Resolutionen der 8. Konferenz der KBF," *Inprekorr,* IX, No. 35 (April 23, 1929), 842, and No. 36 (April 26, 1929), 867-68.

wonders if the delegates were aware of the incongruity of withholding only Bessarabia and Bukovina from this procession.

After these declarations of policy and propaganda, the conference proceeded to a lusty bout of self-criticism for the failure of the Federation to develop into a politically significant force on the Balkan Peninsula.[78] The reasons for this sterility, it was decided, were the "temporary" defeat of the various member parties in their respective countries, the inner crises which had wracked each of them, and organizational laxity both within the parties severally and the Federation. To correct this last error, it was resolved to hold conferences with greater frequency and absolute regularity—at least once every two years and extraordinary sessions in an emergency. No delegate at this eighth conference was so tactless as to recall that the original regulations of 1921 required semiannual conferences. An interesting discussion on the functions of the Executive Committee of the Balkan Communist Federation and its powers to enforce coordination within and among the various affiliated parties then ensued. It was resolved that the Executive Committee had no competence to interfere in the strictly internal affairs of any party since this would be encroaching upon the competence of the ECCI. On the other hand, it was emphasized, no affiliated Communist Party might undertake any political or economic action which would have repercussions beyond the borders of its country without prior consultation with the Executive Committee. That party, in turn, could appeal against the Committee's decision to the ECCI. The conference closed with the reminder that among the Federation's principal tasks were the exchange of information among the member parties and, particularly, the transmission of political and economic information to Moscow.

But neither this conference nor subsequent efforts could revive the Balkan Communist Federation. It was in the year 1929 that its death blow was dealt by a *rapprochement* among the Balkan governments. Venizelos's return to power in July of the preceding year,

---

[78] "Die Tätigkeit der Kommunistischen Balkanföderation: Resolution der 8. Konferenz der KBF," *Inprekorr*, IX, No. 37 (April 30, 1929), 885-86. The Bulgarian Kabakchiev significantly ascribed the cause of the Federation's ineffectiveness to the "incorrect approach" of "some" Communist Parties toward the national question. Past statements by Bulgarian Communist leaders leave little doubt that Kabakchiev had in mind the Greek, Rumanian, and Yugoslav Parties. Kabakchiev, Boshkovich, and Vatis, *Kommunisticheskie Partii Balkanskikh Stran*, p. 239.

though initially unwelcome to the Bulgarian government, as the veteran republican leader had been a champion of a Greater Greece, nevertheless led to a *détente* in relations as he showed a readiness to discuss outstanding problems. Also, in Rumania, Maniu had formed a cabinet in November, 1928, and proceeded to relax the persecution of the Bulgarian minority in the Southern Dobrudja. After the royal coup in Yugoslavia in January, 1929, King Alexander had reopened the Bulgarian frontier, closed since the murder of General Kovačević at Štip by IMRO terrorists in October, 1927. This conciliatory action was followed by the establishment of the Pirot Mixed Commission to discuss and relieve Bulgarian-Yugoslav border tension. Though the Commission did not achieve any startling results, the new spirit of negotiation was helpful. It was at this time, also, that internecine war broke out within IMRO between the two wings led by Alexander Protogerov and Ivan Mikhailov. This facilitated the final suppression of the organization by the Velchev-Georgiev government in 1934. With that event and with the temporary increase in cooperation among the various states initiated by the Balkan conferences in the early 1930s[79] the opportunities for Communist maneuvering on the national question were reduced and the Federation's propaganda prospects attenuated.

The growing concern of Moscow and the Comintern with the threat of National Socialist Germany in the mid-1930s also contributed to the demise of the Federation. In December, 1935, the Sixth Congress of the Communist Party of Greece—then the only legal Communist party on the Balkan Peninsula—took advantage of Moscow's preoccupation with Germany to drop the Federation-imposed slogans of autonomy for Macedonia and Thrace which the Party had until then honored at the price of several hundred imprisoned members and of political impotence.[80] The Greek Communist Party henceforth combined its defense of the country's territorial integrity with invitations to agrarian and liberal groups to form a united front against fascism—the tactic prescribed at the Seventh

---

[79] See Kerner and Howard, *The Balkan Conferences and the Balkan Entente, 1930-35.*

[80] Christidès, *Le Camouflage macédonien,* p. 124. Despite this reversal of its propaganda on the question of the territorial integrity of Greek Macedonia and Thrace, the Greek Communist Party was seriously handicapped in the civil war (1946-49) by the widespread fear that its victory would result in the cession of these territories to the northern neighbors.

Comintern Congress in the summer of 1935. During the brief period of free parliamentary activity which followed the restoration of King George II in November, 1935, the fifteen Communists elected to the legislature in 1936 held a pivotal position between the rather evenly matched royalist and republican wings. The establishment, with the King's consent, of the Metaxas dictatorship in August, 1936, drove the Greek Communist Party underground.

In 1937 Tito became head of the Communist Party of Yugoslavia. If he had ever accepted the Federation's Macedonian policy, he certainly abandoned it in the surge of Yugoslav patriotism which gripped him and on which he rode to power in the course of the Second World War. Since the profession of patriotic sentiments was the general Communist line between the Seventh Comintern Congress of July-August, 1935, and the signing of the Molotov-Ribbentrop Pact four years later, the autonomy slogans had become obsolete. Even the Bulgarian Communist Party reverted to open revisionist propaganda at least in regard to "the oppressed Bulgarian districts of South Dobruja and the Western Province" (the enclaves ceded to Yugoslavia in 1919).[81]

Thus each of the Balkan Communist Parties went its own way, and the Axis invasion of the Peninsula in the spring of 1941 found Communist policy on the national question in confusion. While the Greek and Yugoslav Communists rejected the traditional formula of an independent Macedonia, their Bulgarian comrades not only failed to protest against Bulgarian military occupation of the area but sought to exploit this occupation in order to bring the area under their own organizational jurisdiction. This involved them in a conflict with the Yugoslav Communist Party which, under Tito's leadership, was determined to retain Yugoslav Macedonia within its own sphere of activity even though the local Communist organization in the territory was weak in 1941.[82] Thus in the summer of 1941 for the first and only time resort was had to that provision of the dormant Balkan Communist Federation's regulations providing for the settlement of disputes by the ECCI. Tito simply

---

[81] "Appeal of the Communist Party of Bulgaria," *Inprecorr* (English edition), XVII, No. 46 (October 30, 1937), 1053.

[82] In April, 1941, after the destruction of the Yugoslav state by the Axis armies and the occupation of Yugoslav Macedonia by Bulgarian troops, Metodi Shatarov-Sharlo, the representative of the Yugoslav Communist Party in Macedonia, on a visit

asserted that the Yugoslav Macedonians now preferred to remain within a federalized Yugoslav state and no longer cared to exercise their right of secession. Stalin had left open this loophole in 1925 when he had ended his speech reprimanding Semić-Marković with the words, "To avoid misunderstanding, I must say that the right to separation ought not to be understood as an obligation, as a duty, to secede. A nation may utilize this right and secede, but it may also forego it." [83] In accordance with its empirical doctrine that nationality questions must be decided by tactical-political, not theoretical-ideological considerations, Moscow, through the ECCI, decided in August, 1941, in favor of the Yugoslav Communist Party's claims, as its contribution to the anti-Hitler war effort was heavier than that of the Bulgarian.[84] The Soviet leaders thus demonstrated once again that far from having had a definite Macedonian policy based on principle, they simply considered the area as a prize to be awarded to their most promising and obedient pupil among the Balkan Communist Parties. As such, Macedonia served the additional purpose of being a source of rivalry among the Balkan Communist Parties, rivalry which could only be of benefit to Moscow in making it the perpetual arbiter and in preventing the formation of a close bloc within the international Communist movement.

That the slogan of an "independent and united Macedonia" had never represented a firm Communist principle is further suggested by the fact that no attempt had ever been made to organize a specifically Macedonian Communist Party. This patent contradiction between propaganda and organization resulted in crises within the Greek and Yugoslav Communist Parties while the Bulgarian one took advantage of it to persuade Moscow that the

---

to Sofia transferred the Communist organization in Macedonia to the jurisdiction of the Bulgarian Communist leaders who, in a letter to Tito, defended this procedure on grounds of administrative expediency. Tito's response was prompt, forceful, and negative. At the end of May he sent Lazar Koliševski to the area to replace Sharlo and to reorganize Communist cells under the control of the Yugoslav Communist Party. In July Tito demanded that the Bulgarians disown Sharlo and recognize the Yugoslav Communist Party's jurisdiction in the area. The Bulgarian Communists refused, and the dispute was referred to the Comintern for a decision. See Barker, *Macedonia*, pp. 84-88. Koliševski became postwar President of the Macedonian People's Republic within Yugoslavia. After the Tito-Soviet split, Sharlo's memory was honored by the Bulgarian Communist Party as that of one of its heroes. See *Novo Vreme*, XXVII, No. 8 (August, 1951), 13.

[83] Stalin, *Sochinenia*, VII, 75-76.

[84] Barker, *Macedonia*, p. 88.

"independent Macedonia" slogan had the greatest revolutionary possibilities as it would be received most enthusiastically by the local population. Events showed, however, that the Bulgarian Communist Party was too weak to pursue a Macedonian policy independently of IMRO and the attempt to recruit that organization as an ally was a fiasco.

Just as its jurisdictional decision of August, 1941, showed that Moscow pursued a thoroughly pragmatic policy on the Macedonian issue, so too its actions after the war proved that two decades of agitation for a "Balkan federation" had been merely a manipulative device, to be exploited when France, Great Britain, or Germany threatened to draw the Balkan states into their sphere of influence but to be suppressed when Soviet Russia had replaced them as the Great Power dominating the Peninsula. With the elimination of any but Soviet Russian power in East Central Europe as a consequence of the Second World War, the federation policy was dropped, as Moscow preferred to dictate directives to half a dozen isolated satellite states rather than to negotiate with a single, powerful, albeit Communist, neighbor on its southwestern border. When Georgi Dimitrov once again raised the federation issue early in 1948, *Pravda* tartly advised him and the other leaders of the satellite states that instead of concerning themselves with such "questionable and artificial" projects they would do better to devote their attention to the internal consolidation of their regimes.[85] Even discussion of

[85] *Pravda*, January 28, 1948. The background to this incident is as follows: On January 16, 1948, Dimitrov went to Bucharest to sign the Bulgaro-Rumanian Treaty of Friendship. During his return journey the following day, he gave a press conference on the train at which he was asked, "There is talk about a forthcoming creation of a Balkan federation, a federation of Balkan nations and of whole parts of Eastern and Southeastern Europe to embrace also Hungary, Czechoslovakia, and Poland. In case such an organization is created, will other countries also be able to join it?" To this Dimitrov replied, "The question of federation or confederation is a premature question to us. It is not on the agenda now, and that is why this question was not examined at our conference. When the question is ripe—and it will ripen at all costs—then our peoples of the People's Democracy of Rumania, Bulgaria, Yugoslavia, Albania, Czechoslovakia, Poland, Hungary, and Greece—remember, Greece also—will decide it. They it is who will decide whether there should be a federation or confederation; and when and how it is to be formed. I can say that what our nations are doing now facilitates to a great extent the solution of this question in the future. I can also stress that when such a federation or confederation is created our peoples will not ask the imperialists and will not consider their objections, but will solve the question alone in accordance with their interests and the interests of international cooperation." Quoted by Sharp, "Federation in Eastern Europe," p. 616.

the issue apparently became taboo, as is indicated by the fact that whereas in the first edition of the *Bolshaya Sovetskaya Entsiklopedia* there appeared a long and presumably authoritative (though inaccurate) article by Georgi Dimitrov on Balkan Federation, in the new post-Second World War edition all references to the subject have been omitted. The men in the Kremlin have not forgotten that the idea of Balkan federation was introduced into socialist policy in the nineteenth century as a device for preventing the extension of Russian power into the Peninsula.

XII

UNDERGROUND DECADE

On April 14, 1925, General Kosta Georgiev, a Sobranie deputy and a leading member of the Democratic Entente, was assassinated. Two days later Sofia's Sveta Nedelya Cathedral, where many ministers, officers, and deputies were gathered for the funeral ceremonies, was torn by an explosion which killed 128 mourners, including three deputies, fourteen generals, the Chief of Police, and the Mayor of Sofia, and wounded 323. Two weeks previously the government had announced the interception of a message from the ECCI to the underground Bulgarian Communist Party ordering mobilization in preparation for another insurrection by April 15,[1] and it now immediately declared the outrage to be the work of the Communists. In Moscow prompt denials of complicity were issued on behalf of the Comintern by the ECCI Plenum then in session,[2] on behalf of the Soviet government by Chicherin,[3] and on that of the Bulgarian Communist Party by Kolarov and Dimitrov who declared the alleged message from Moscow ordering an insurrection to be a forgery by the *agent provocateur* Druzhilovski, a Russian working for the Polish intelligence service in Berlin.[4] For more than two decades

---

[1] *Deutsche Allgemeine Zeitung*, April 5, 1925. A photostat of this alleged message, dated March 12, and signed "A. Dorot," is reproduced in the government's white paper *La Conspiration bolchéviste contre la Bulgarie*, pp. 85-89.

[2] "Erklärung des EKKI zu den Bulgarischen Ereignissen," *Inprekorr*, V, No. 66 (April 24, 1925), 891.

[3] *Le Temps*, April 25, 1925. Chicherin's statement was issued on April 21 in response to a press inquiry on the alleged Soviet complicity in the cathedral outrage. *Izvestia* printed it on April 23.

[4] "Wortlaut der Deklaration der Auslanddelegation der K.P.B.," *Inprekorr*, V, No. 84 (May 19, 1925), 1148. This Druzhilovski was briefly arrested by the German police in June *(Manchester Guardian*, June 27, 1925). In 1927 he was brought to trial in Moscow, having allegedly crossed the Soviet frontier illegally, and reportedly confessed to having been involved in the forgery of the document produced by the Tsankov government in the spring of 1925 as well as of the notorious "Zinoviev Letter" which was a factor in the British General Election of October, 1924. Kolarov was a witness at the trial which resulted in Druzhilovski's execution.

the Communists persisted in their denial of responsibility for the cathedral calamity, asserting that it had been instigated by the Tsankov government as a pretext to launch a White Terror and thus to strengthen its dictatorship. In support of this claim they cited the fact that the cabinet ministers in the cathedral at the time of the explosion all escaped injury. At the Reichstag fire trial in 1933 Dimitrov protested that "the outrage in the Sofia Cathedral . . . was not organized by the Bulgarian Communist Party . . . . That provocation . . . was actually organized by the Bulgarian police." [5] Fifteen years later, in the course of his political report to the Fifth Congress of the Bulgarian Communist Party, Dimitrov finally confessed that the disaster had been "an ultra-left deviation . . . an act of desperation perpetrated by the leadership of the military organization of the Party." [6]

The Tsankov government seems to have been aware of this. Immediately after the explosion the police were ordered to take into custody Lieutenant-Colonel Kosta Yankov, a Narrow and Communist Party member of twenty years' standing, who had been assigned at the Vitosha Conference in May, 1924, to take charge of the military aspects of Communist underground work.[7] He was killed resisting arrest, as was his assistant, Captain Ivan Minkov, who had joined the Communist Party after the First World War.[8] A state of siege was declared and, with the permission of the Inter-Allied Control Commission, 10,000 volunteers were recruited into the army for temporary duty. By April 22 the government reported 1,500 arrests.[9] Within the next four months 124 death sentences were imposed,[10] and, though a number of these were subsequently commuted, many

---

See *Inprekorr*, VII, No. 71 (July 15, 1927), 1515-17 and *Die Epoche Liaptscheff*, p. 4. Other versions of the trial state that Druzhilovski declared the "Zinoviev Letter" to have been forged by other Russian *émigrés* also working for Paciorkowski, the Polish press attaché in Berlin and alleged member of the Polish intelligence service. See *Inprekorr*, VIII, No. 10 (January 31, 1928), 189, and No. 32 (March 27, 1928), 597-98, as well as L. Fischer, *The Soviets in World Affairs*, p. 496.

[5] *The Reichstag Fire Trial*, p. 227.

[6] Dimitrov, *Politicheski otchet na Ts.K. na BRP(k)*, p. 28.

[7] See p. 159.

[8] "Unsere Märtyrer: Jankow und Minkow," *Inprekorr*, V, No. 76 (May 8, 1925), 1015. A list of the Internal Bureau of the Central Committee of the Communist Party had fallen into the government's hands a few days before the explosion. *Le Temps*, April 10, 1925.

[9] Maus, *What Is Happening in Bulgaria?*, p. 16.

[10] *Inprekorr*, V, No. 124 (August 25, 1925), 1790.

other victims were murdered without trial. Among the latter were Dimitar Grancharov and Nikola Petrini, Peasant Union leaders who supported the united front with the Communists,[11] the socialist pioneer Nikola Gabrovski,[12] the ex-Communist defector Ivan Ganchev,[13] Ivan Nedelkov (Schablin), who had represented the Bulgarian Communist Party at the early Comintern Congresses,[14] and, in August, Zheko Dimitrov, who had succeeded Georgi Dimitrov as leader of the Communist-controlled General Trade Union Federation after the September insurrection.[15] Georgi Dimitrov's brother Todor, a Communist courier who had been arrested before the explosion, was afterwards killed by the police.[16] It was at this time that Traicho Kostov's name first achieved prominence in the press. Then a twenty-eight year old law student at Sofia, he was arrested after the explosion and, to escape continued torture, sought death by throwing himself out of a window at police headquarters. He lived but was left a cripple.[17]

Of the many trials, the most spectacular was that of Marko Fridman, a young Communist lawyer thought by the government to be a member of the Central Committee, Lieutenant-Colonel Georgi K. Koev, charged with briefly sheltering Minkov on April 16 and alleged by the government to be the contact man between Moscow and the Bulgarian and Rumanian Communist military undergrounds, the cathedral sacristan Petar Zadgorski, charged as an accessory to the planting of the explosive charge, and two lesser defendants. At the trial, which opened on May 1, Zadgorski played

[11] Inprekorr, V, No. 87 (May 26, 1925), 1197. Petrini was an associate of Kosta Todorov and of Petko Petkov. See p. 148. For Grancharov's career see p. 135, footnote 12.

[12] Inprekorr, V, No. 111 (July 21, 1925), 1543.

[13] La Fédération Balkanique, IV, No. 94 (June 15, 1928), 1916.

[14] Inprekorr, V, No. 90 (June 5, 1925), 1233.

[15] Ibid., V, No. 126 (August 28, 1925), 1827.

[16] Le Temps, April 8, 1925; also "Vydayushchisya deyatel' mezhdunarodnogo rabochego dvizhenia," p. 8.

[17] Inprekorr, V, No. 98 (June 23, 1925), 1322. Another leader of contemporary Communist Bulgaria whose name first appears in connection with the White Terror of 1925 is Tsola Dragoicheva. While awaiting execution in Plovdiv jail, she became pregnant—whether with or against her consent has been disputed—and had her sentence commuted to life imprisonment. (Inprekorr, VI, No. 62 [April 23, 1926], 904). Released in 1932, she went to the USSR. Active in the work of the Communist Party-in-exile, she became a member of its Central Committee and Politburo in 1940. During the Second World War, she was parachuted into Bulgaria for sabotage work and after the war became a deputy to the Sobranie and Minister of Post, Telegraph, Telephone, and Radio.

a role similar to that which Van der Lubbe was to fill eight years later at Leipzig. A dull-witted wretch, only partly aware of the proceedings, he admitted having received 12,000 leva and a promise of safety abroad for his participation in the plot.[18] Fridman initially adopted the posture which Dimitrov was to imitate at Leipzig. Conducting his own defense, he turned the dock into a platform for Communist propaganda, boasting of his bolshevik convictions but insisting that as these deprecated individual terrorism, he could not have been an accomplice in the dynamite plot.[19] Soon, however, he was giving evidence on the organization of the Communist Party, his own activities in its military section, and the funds which were passed to him from Yankov, who allegedly received them from the Communist center in Vienna.[20] The post-September defector Nikola Sakarov testified concerning the organizational and financial control of the Communist Party by Moscow.[21] The two minor defendants received prison terms for having hidden Zadgorski, who was sentenced to death as were Fridman and Koev. Their public execution by gypsy hangmen on May 27 was witnessed by 50,000 onlookers.[22] The same court pronounced posthumous death sentences on the murdered Peasant Union radicals Grancharov, Petrini, and Kosovski, as well as on the exiled Communists Georgi Dimitrov and Abajiev. The latter was reported to have personally planted the explosive.[23]

Later in May were tried a French couple, M. and Mme. Eugène Léger, Adèle Nikolova, a Frenchwoman married to a Bulgarian, and a Peasant Union member, Ivan Perchemliev, on the charge of having hidden the principals of the plot. All except Marie Léger were sentenced to death and she to life imprisonment.[24] Perchemliev was hanged on June 11,[25] but, at the intercession of the French ambassador, the sentence on the others was commuted to life imprisonment.[26] Shortly thereafter Léger was released under mysterious

[18] *Manchester Guardian*, May 4, 1925.
[19] *Le Temps*, May 3, 1925.
[20] *Le Temps*, May 14, 1925; *La Conspiration bolchéviste*, p. 93.
[21] *Le Temps*, August 10, 1925; *La Conspiration bolchéviste*, p. 94.
[22] *Manchester Guardian*, May 28, 1925.
[23] *The Times*, May 12, 1925. Nothing was heard again of this mysterious Abajiev until his death was reported in Berlin in 1930. See *The Times*, December 30, 1930.
[24] *Le Temps*, May 28, 1925.
[25] *Deutsche Allgemeine Zeitung*, June 13, 1925.
[26] *Le Temps*, June 8, 1925.

circumstances, went to the Soviet Union where, according to Victor Serge, he was clapped into solitary confinement at Yaroslavl, went mad, and disappeared into a mental asylum.[27]

Other ex-Communists who allege GPU complicity in the cathedral plot are Ruth Fischer[28] and Grigori Besedovski.[29] As the remarks of the former are conjectural while the latter is a man of exceedingly active imagination, proof is lacking. Besedovski asserts that the explosive was supplied through the Communist center in Vienna. Balkan conditions being what they were, it would seem unnecessary to import such substances from Austria, especially as the principals of the plot were high officers in the Bulgarian army, presumably with access to its munition supplies. In any event, early in June the director of the Sofia arsenal was arrested on the charge of having supplied the Communists with war material.[30] The outrage had probably been planned for a considerable time, as it seems unlikely that a sufficient supply of explosives could have been smuggled into the cathedral between the assassination of General Georgiev on April 14 and the funeral two days later, especially as the building was presumably being made ready for the ceremony. It is possible that the general had in fact been killed for the express purpose of providing an occasion at which the entire political and military elite of the country would be gathered together in the cathedral where they might be eliminated at one stroke.[31] In 1948 Georgi Dimitrov asserted that in March, 1925, the External Representation, or Foreign Bureau, of the Communist Party (i.e., he and Kolarov), having become aware of the "imminent danger of an ultraleft deviation disastrous for the Party and the revolutionary movement,"

---

[27] Serge, *Mémoires d'un révolutionnaire*, pp. 196-97.

[28] R. Fischer, *Stalin and German Communism*, p. 468.

[29] Besedovski, *Im Dienste der Sowjets*, p. 99. Kosta Todorov (*Balkan Firebrand*, p. 223) asserts that Gavril Genov bought the explosive (ecrasite) in Yugoslavia and sent it to Yankov in Sofia.

[30] *Deutsche Allgemeine Zeitung*, June 5, 1925.

[31] This conjecture, if true, might help to explain an unsuccessful attack on King Boris, also perpetrated on April 14, 1925, by unknown assailants at Arabo-Konak Pass while he was motoring to Sofia. His chauffeur and guard were killed. The government claimed that this assault was the work of the same Communist–Peasant Union group which blew up the cathedral (*Manchester Guardian*, May 1, 1925) but it was generally assumed to have been mere brigandage by men unaware that their intended victim was the King (*The Times*, April 15, 1925). In 1949 the Fédération Anarchiste-Communiste Bulgare claimed credit for the affair (*Les Bulgares parlent au monde*, p. 6), but as so many of the allegations in this organization's publication are questionable, this one cannot be considered proven.

sought to forestall it by demanding the replacement of the policy of preparing another insurrection by one of mass organizational work. Too late.[32] Ironically, it had been the henchmen of Dimitrov and Kolarov who at the Vitosha Conference in May, 1924, had committed the Communist Party to the continuation of the insurrectionary policy over the objections of the moderates.

In Bulgaria the cathedral outrage resulted in the decimation of the Party cadres.[33] In the Soviet Russian Communist Party and in the Comintern it shook Zinoviev's prestige at the critical time of the preparations for the pivotal Fourteenth Congress of the CPSU (b), which, after being twice deferred, met in December, 1925, and at which Stalin emerged as the effective ruler of the Soviet Union. Though Zinoviev was probably not directly involved in the plot, he now unwittingly paid the penalty for his perennial assurances that new revolutionary upsurges were imminent. Whereas the German Communists, after the collapse of their attempted seizure of power in 1923, confined their demonstrations of "revolutionary temper" to the blowing of whistles in the Reichstag, Yankov and Minkov took Zinoviev at his word and decided to blow up the government. Once again the Bulgarian Communists demonstrated their "hard" heritage.

In 1923 the insurrection by the Communists had been suppressed. In 1924 their efforts to recruit the *émigré* Peasant Union and IMRO as allies had aborted. In 1925 the terrorist interlude was ruinous. In 1926 they reverted to the policy of trade-union unity with the Socialists, hitherto maligned as vicious enemies of the working class.

At the time of its dissolution under the terms of the Law for the Defense of the Realm in April, 1924, the Communist-controlled General Trade Union Federation had about 35,000 members.[34] This expansion from the prewar years[35] had been supervised by Georgi Dimitrov. In September-October, 1920, at the time of the defection of a section of the Socialist Party to the Communists, the trade-union federations controlled by the two parties had been amalga-

---

[32] Dimitrov, *Politicheski otchet na Ts.K. na BRP(k)*, p. 28. This claim is probably true. *Inprekorr*, V. No. 30 (February 27, 1925), 442, had carried a warning by Dimitrov to refrain from terrorism.

[33] Dimitrov, *Politicheski otchet na Ts.K. na BRP(k)*, p. 28.

[34] *Inprekorr*, V, No. 92 (June 9, 1925), 1249.

[35] See p. 55.

mated [36] and this united organization affiliated to the International Trade Union Council [37] which had been founded in Moscow in the summer of 1920 during the Second Comintern Congress and enlarged in July, 1921, in synchronization with the Third Comintern Congress, to form the Red International of Trade Unions. In July, 1922, however, a number of the old Socialist leaders split away and refounded the Free Trade Union Federation as a nominally nonparty political body for which in that year they claimed 14,803 members—a figure disputed by the Communists.[38] There is some confusion over the Free Federation's strength in the critical year of 1925. Addressing its congress in October, 1925, Dimo Kazasov boasted of a total membership of 27,118, a figure apparently accepted by the Communist economist Varga.[39] In the report which the Socialist Party submitted to the Congress of the Socialist International meeting in Marseilles in August, 1925, however, it was stated that the total membership of trade unions under the Socialist Party's influence was a more modest 15,000.[40] The pillars of the Free Federation were the railwaymen and transport workers, teachers and civil servants. The hard core of the industrial workers, on the other hand, joined the Independent Trade Union Federation founded in the summer of 1925 as a Communist "front" organization. Its journal was *Edinstvo* (Unity), and its member unions were organized on the principle of "democratic centralism." [41]

Late in 1925 the Independent Federation proposed amalgamation to the Free Federation.[42] This was an attempt by the Communists to break out of their isolation. The Socialist leaders of the Free Federation initially returned a negative response, citing the Independent Federation's domination by Communists—an allegation which *Inprekorr* professed to find "preposterous." [43] They were, however, shortly obliged to modify their position as a strong current

---

[36] Dimitrov, "Die Revolutionäre Gewerkschaftsbewegung in den Balkanländern," *Inprekorr*, III, No. 11 (January 15, 1923), 79.
[37] Dimitrov, "Die Gewerkschaftsbewegung Bulgariens," *Inprekorr*, III, No. 24 (February 5, 1923), 183.
[38] *Ibid.*, p. 183.
[39] Varga, *Sotsial-demokraticheskie partii*, p. 240.
[40] *II. Kongress der Sozialistischen Arbeiter-Internationale: Tätigkeitsbericht*, p. 150.
[41] *Die Internationale Gewerkschaftsbewegung in den Jahren 1924-1927*, p. 156. Circulation of *Edinstvo* was 6,000.
[42] "Der Kampf um die Gewerkschaftseinheit in Bulgarien," *Inprekorr*, VI, No. 9 (January 12, 1926), 119-21.
[43] *Ibid.*, pp. 119-21.

favoring cooperation with the Communist trade-union movement was then running in the Socialist "Amsterdam" International Federation of Trade Unions. Its most enthusiastic proponent was the Dutchman Edo Fimmen and its most spectacular manifestation the formation of the Anglo-Russian Trade Union Committee in 1925.

The Soviet leaders sought to take advantage of this mood as offering both an opportunity to infiltrate the non-Communist labor movement and a possible escape from their isolation and the ideological dilemma of "socialism in one country." The Fifth Plenum of the ECCI, meeting in Moscow March 21-April 6, 1925, recommended trade-union unity to its parties.[44] It was probably in response to these instructions that the Bulgarian Independent Federation had proposed an amalgamation to its rivals.

In the spring of 1926, the "Amsterdam" International Federation of Trade Unions sent Fimmen, Mertens, and Johann Sassenbach to the Balkans. They persuaded a conference of Balkan Socialist trade unions, meeting in Sofia April 9-10, to pass a resolution urging the Bulgarian Free Federation to reopen unity negotiations with the Independent Federation.[45] On the invitation of the Free Federation, accordingly, joint May Day demonstrations were held, and in June and July the negotiations took place. The Free Federation agreed to suspend temporarily its membership in the "Amsterdam" International while the Independent Federation consented to the establishment of interim "informational connections" with "Amsterdam" until a joint congress to be held within six months could decide the issue of full affiliation. In the meantime every support would be given to the efforts to achieve international trade-union unity through the Anglo-Russian Committee. The united federation would be independent of all Bulgarian political parties. These protocols were initialled on July 21, 1926. Separate conferences of the two federations to ratify the agreement were scheduled for August 8. The conference of the Free Federation, however, resolved by a vote of 38 to 23 to require of the leaders of the Independent Federation preliminary assurances that the industrial unions of the united organization would affiliate with the "Amster-

[44] Lozovski, *Za yedinstvo*, pp. 31-33.
[45] "Die Balkan-Gewerkschaftskonferenz in Sofia," *Inprekorr*, VI, No. 62 (April 23, 1926), 905-6.

dam" International. These assurances were refused, the Communists angrily charging that the Socialist Party had packed the conference with enemies of workers' solidarity and that Grigor Danov, the leader of the Free Federation who had returned from consultations with Western trade-union leaders just before the conference at which he insisted on these unacceptable conditions, was acting on the instructions of Sassenbach, now frightened at the consequences of his advice to open unity negotiations.

The Communists appealed to the rank and file of the Free Federation to transfer to the Independent one. The Socialists were vulnerable, for to the workers "Amsterdam" was a remote issue while the weakness of a divided trade-union movement in their backward country was manifest. On October 3-4, 1926, the Typographers' Union removed Grigor Danov from its secretaryship[46] and quit the Free Federation, though it remained within the "Amsterdam-affiliated" Printers' International. On the other hand the Waiters' Union, which had been a branch of the Independent Federation, seceded from it in protest against its leaders' refusal to promise affiliation with the "Amsterdam" International and against its excessive centralization. The waiters had perhaps not previously been aware of the Independent Federation's domination by the Communists. On October 7 the leaders of the Independent Federation warned those of the rival organization that unless the agreement of July 21 was honored, the Independent Federation would "raid" local groups of the Free Federation. The leaders of the latter organization, probably in an attempt to dispel the impression that they had negotiated in bad faith and deliberately sabotaged trade-union unity, once more proposed fusion on December 2, but as affiliation with "Amsterdam" was again their condition, the offer was rejected by the Independent Federation on December 15, 1926.[47]

---

[46] He was dismissed as Secretary of the Free Federation on December 1, 1929.

[47] Detailed accounts of this episode appeared throughout the year 1926 in *Inprekorr*, VI. See in particular Lippert, "Die Balkan-Gewerkschaftskonferenz in Sofia," No. 62 (April 23), 905-6; Kolarov, "Auf dem Wege zur Gewerkschaftseinheit in Bulgarien," No. 108 (August 24), 1803-4; "Vor dem Gericht des Internationalen Proletariats," No. 126 (October 19), 2172-73; Szántó, "Die Einheit in Bulgarien auf dem Vormarsch," No. 134 (November 5), 2330-31; and Chronik, Nos. 125 and 151 (October 13 and December 8). See also Dimitrov, "Der Kampf um die Gewerkschaftseinheit in Bulgarien," pp. 86-91.

Competition for membership ensued. In April, 1926, on the eve of the negotiations, the Communist-controlled Independent Federation numbered 5,082 members. In December, after the defection of the waiters and the adhesion of a few other groups, it counted 5,018, which rose to 6,926 by the time of its first congress of November 6-8, 1927.[48] Six months later it claimed 8,000 [49] and in 1934, on the eve of the suppression of the trade-union movement, 11,000 members.[50] It is clear that the Independent Federation never attained the numerical strength of 35,000 members claimed for the openly Communistic General Federation at the time of the dissolution of the latter in April, 1924. Yet, despite severe government persecution, frequent arrests of its leaders, repeated confiscations of its journal, recurrent raids on its various headquarters,[51] it retained the loyalty of the core of the industrial workers. To a considerable extent this is a tribute to the organizational work of Georgi Dimitrov during his secretaryship of the General Federation from 1909 to 1923 and a testimonial to the Independent Federation's defense of the workers' interests. By 1928 only 2,500 workers remained in unions affiliated with "Amsterdam." [52] The Socialists still controlled the officially nonpolitical unions of teachers, civil servants, and railway men which totaled about 30,000 members in 1929.[53] An attempt by Sassenbach in 1930 to persuade the neutral unions of railway men, teachers, and postal workers (claiming respectively 4,326, 11,000, and 2,500 members), to affiliate with the "Amsterdam" International failed as these state employees were legally prohibited from joining "political" unions. Their representatives later agreed, however, "voluntarily" to cooperate with the political party representing their interests—by which was meant the Socialist Party.[54]

[48] "Der Erste Kongress der Unabhängigen Gewerkschaften Bulgariens," *Inprekorr*, VII, No. 123 (December 16, 1927), 2850.

[49] *The Communist International Between the Fifth and Sixth World Congresses, 1924-1928*, p. 255.

[50] *Kommunistischeski Internatsional pered VII Vsemirnom Kongressom*, p. 331.

[51] These incidents are thoroughly documented in *Frankfurter Zeitung* and *Inprekorr* for the 1927-34 period.

[52] *III. Kongress der Sozialistischen Arbeiter-Internationale*, I, Sect. 4, p. 20. In 1931 the figure still hovered around 2,500. See *IV. Kongress der Sozialistischen Arbeiter-Internationale*, p. 19.

[53] Tchitchovsky, "Political and Social Aspects of Modern Bulgaria," p. 281.

[54] *The American Labor Year Book, 1930*, p. 267.

Insurrection had failed in 1923; alliances had snapped in 1924; terrorism had led to catastrophe in 1925; trade-union unity negotiations had aborted in 1926. On February 24, 1927, Communist policy turned full circle: with the permission of Prime Minister Lyapchev, who had replaced Tsankov in January, 1926, with a promise to end the White Terror, a Labor Party was founded.[55] It was secretly controlled by the illegal Communist Party. Its leader was Yordan Milev. On March 5, 1927, it began issuing the journal *Rabotnichesko Delo* (Workers' Action).[56] Another mouthpiece of Communist policy was the ostensibly independent paper *Novini* (News), beginning in January, 1926, and boasting a circulation of 8,000-10,000. *Edinstvo* (Unity), the organ of the Communist-controlled Independent Trade Union Federation, was sold in issues of about 6,000 copies.[57] *Komunistichesko Zname* (Communist Banner), a monthly paper of four or five sheets, had been distributed clandestinely since January, 1926.[58]

The Communists' decision to found a legal cover party was probably influenced by the fact that the life of the Sobranie elected in November, 1923, would expire and new elections be held in 1927. Their hopes in the overthrow of the Democratic Entente government, which was still anathema to them despite the fact that it was now led by the milder Lyapchev, had been fanned by the results of the municipal elections of November 7 and the departmental elections of November 14, 1926. In the former, the government received 13,600 votes to the opposition parties' 22,500,[59] while in the latter the figures were 539,944 for the government and 558,991 for the opposition, of which the Socialist Party's share was 39,560, that of the independent Peasant Union 66,000, of the Artisan Party (a satellite of the Peasant Union) 4,000, while various workers' groups polled 6,000 votes.[60] Altogether 16,000 invalid

[55] *Inprekorr*, VII, No. 25 (March 2, 1927), Chronik.

[56] *Novo Vreme*, XXVIII, No. 3 (March, 1952), 69.

[57] Kabakchiev, Boshkovich, and Vatis, *Kommunisticheskie Partii Balkanskikh Stran*, p. 125. *Nakovalnya* (Anvil), a literary journal, and *Mladezhka Duma* (Word of Youth) were other Communist propaganda journals.

[58] Bad, "Illegale Kommunistische Zeitschriften auf dem Balkan," p. 278.

[59] *La Fédération Balkanique*, III, No. 57 (December 1, 1926), 1027.

[60] *Inprekorr*, VI, No. 145 (November 24, 1926), Chronik. Though the government received only 49 percent of the votes in these departmental elections, it took, through gerrymandering and sheer force, 60 percent of the seats on the councils. See *III. Kongress der Sozialistischen Arbeiter-Internationale*, I, Sect. 4, p. 21.

ballots had been cast, and the Communists believed that many of these were tokens of protest by their sympathizers. The Communists probably hoped that a large share of the ballots cast for the left opposition parties in these elections could be won to their cause, albeit camouflaged, and in February, 1927, they founded the Labor Party on the basis of the scattered workers' groups of the November, 1926, polls.

As usual when engaging in "front" tactics, the Communists over-played their hand. The proposal by the Labor Party to the Socialist, Peasant, and Artisan Parties to fight the coming Sobranie election as a four-party coalition on a program of exterminating the "fascist regime" was rejected, and the Peasant Union center group together with the Socialist and Artisan Parties formed an Iron Bloc from which the Labor Party was excluded, to the great chagrin of the Communists.[61] Behind the decision of the Socialists to join the left opposition lies a story of bitter internal party strife.

The participation of the Socialist Dimo Kazasov in the June, 1923, coup and the subsequent endorsement by the Socialist Party's Central Committee of his acceptance of the Ministry of Transport in the Democratic Entente government had for a time enabled Tsankov to pose to the West as an efficient, liberal administrator around whom were gathered the "healthiest" elements of Bulgarian political life. After the September insurrection and the ensuing White Terror, qualms about the policy of Socialist participation in the Tsankov government began to agitate the leaders of the Socialist International. The Bureau of the International met in Brussels in October, 1923, to discuss this issue. A questionnaire was sent to the Bulgarian Socialist Party requesting explanation of its conduct.[62] On December 12, 1923, the Sofia *Epokha* (Epoch), a journal with a circulation of 4,000 which, though not the official organ of the Socialists, expressed the view of their more radical wing led by Pastukhov, confessed that Socialist participation in the government was a mistake. At its next session in Luxembourg in February, 1924, the Bureau of the Socialist International decided to convene a

---

[61] Dimitrov, "Die Parlamentswahlen in Bulgarien," *Inprekorr*, VII, No. 54 (May 24, 1927), 1058-60.

[62] *II. Kongress der Sozialistischen Arbeiter-Internationale: Tätigkeitsbericht*, p. 48.

Conference of Balkan Socialist Parties (the first since before the war) in March to examine this issue as well as the general war danger on the Peninsula.[63]

In Bulgaria, in the meantime, the Socialist Party had resolved at its congress of February 3-6, 1924, to demand the reconstruction of the cabinet. This was taken to mean the replacement of Minister of Justice Smilov, a National Liberal, by a Socialist.[64] Premier Tsankov was prepared to part with Smilov but not to award his portfolio to a Socialist. Kazasov was thereupon withdrawn from the cabinet, which resigned in mid-February and was reconstructed without Socialists. When the Balkan Socialist Conference, attended for the Socialist International by Friedrich Adler and I. G. Tsereteli, for the Yugoslav Socialist Party by Živko Topalović and Divac, for the Rumanian by Ion Flueraş, Ilie Moscovici, and Dr. Pistiner, and for the Bulgarian by Yanko Sakazov, Dimitar Neikov, and Assen Tsankov (brother of the Premier) assembled on March 11, 1924, in Bucharest,[65] the Bulgarians could claim that they had complied with the implied wishes of the International in withdrawing from the government, though their motives for having done so were mixed. The Bulgarian delegation assured the conference that the worst excesses of the White Terror had been perpetrated against the will of the government, which had not always been able to control its paramilitary allies in the hectic days of the June coup and the September insurrection. They explained that Kazasov's participation in the cabinet had been approved in an attempt to mitigate the severity of the terror and to prevent anarchy. Both these assertions are at best doubtful. The three Bulgarians then gave a distorted version of the reasons for their party's withdrawal from the Tsankov government, claiming that they had taken this action, as they had always intended, when the danger of anarchy had manifestly passed. In conclusion, they promised henceforth to remain in opposition and to fight for fully constitutional government, for freedom of the press and assembly, and for proportional representation.[66] A second Balkan Socialist Conference meeting in Prague on June 12, 1925, declared itself satisfied with the efforts

---

[63] *Ibid.*, p. 48.
[64] Assen Tsankov, "Bulgarien nach dem Umsturz," p. 117.
[65] *II. Kongress der Sozialistischen Arbeiter-Internationale: Tätigkeitsbericht*, p. 109.
[66] *Ibid.*, pp. 50-52.

of the Bulgarian Socialist Party to honor these promises.[67] In the meantime, the policy of opposition had borne fruit in the departmental elections of May 4, 1924, in which the Socialist Party claimed to have received 54,287 votes.[68] In that year it counted 28,761 members of whom about 5,000 were urban workers, about 19,000 peasants, and the remainder drawn from the petite bourgeoisie and the free professions.[69]

At the time of the cathedral outrage the Socialist deputies, while regretting that their principles prevented their voting for the declaration of martial law, assured the government that they considered its campaign to root out the united front of Communists and radical Peasants to be a "patriotic war" against the agents of a foreign power—the USSR.[70] The Party remained, nevertheless, in opposition. Later in 1925, however, when the Tsankov government found itself in difficulties because of the White Terror in its attempts to float a loan in Western Europe (where Tsankov had an unsavory name) the Socialist leaders Kazasov, Djidrov, and Assen Tsankov demanded that the Party support the Premier or at least not collaborate with the opposition. They were defeated at the Party's congress of October 5, 1925,[71] by Pastukhov's wing and expelled at a special Socialist Party Congress in January, 1926.[72] They thereupon formed a fractional Socialist Federation supporting the government. Though Socialist groups in Sofia, Varna, Plovdiv, and Khaskovo ultimately affiliated with it,[73] and though it was at one time reported that 13 of the 29 Socialist Sobranie deputies adhered to it,[74] this Socialist Federation remained weak. With the

[67] *Ibid.*, p. 49. This Conference was attended by Adler, de Brouckère, and Shaw for the International, and Topalović and Korun for the Yugoslav, Yannios for the Greek, and Sakazov, Neikov, and Pastukhov for the Bulgarian Socialist Parties.

[68] *Ibid.*, p. 151. Varga (*Sotsial-demokraticheskie partii*, p. 241) asserts it received only 46,916 votes.

[69] *Balgarskata Rabotnicheska Sotsialdemokraticheska Partia*, p. 9; Varga, *Sotsialdemokraticheskie partii*, p. 239.

[70] *La Bulgarie*, II, No. 540 (April 22, 1925); Cf. *Die Judasrolle der Bulgarischen Sozialdemokratie*, p. 6, for the speech of April 23 by the Socialist spokesman Chernoukov, who in March, 1927, went over to the Democratic Entente.

[71] Varga, *Sotsial-demokraticheskie partii*, p. 242. In 1925 Kazasov published his reminiscences of the conspiracy which culminated in the June coup. The participants, especially Tsankov, are lauded. See Kazasov, *V tamnite na zagovora.*

[72] *III. Kongress der Sozialistischen Arbeiter-Internationale*, I, Sect. 4, p. 22.

[73] *Inprekorr*, VI, No. 129 (October 27, 1926), Chronik; Kazasov, *Burni godini: 1918-1944*, p. 295.

[74] *Inprekorr*, VI, No. 134 (November 3, 1926), Chronik.

exception of Kazasov and Assen Tsankov, most of its leaders were readmitted into the Socialist Party at the congress of October, 1926,[75] and in the departmental elections of the following month it won only 728 votes to the Socialist Party's 39,560.[76] It was at its congress of October, 1926, that the Socialist Party had resolved to fight the Sobranie elections of May, 1927, in alliance with the Peasant and Artisan Parties. Thus was born the Iron Bloc.

The electoral campaign for the Sobranie waged by the Iron Bloc of Socialist, Peasant, and Artisan Parties in the spring of 1927 was based on demands for the restoration of political freedom, an amnesty for political prisoners, suppression of paramilitary bands (IMRO), legislation against speculation, reduction of indirect taxes, and the widening of social legislation for the benefit of workers. In the areas of Kazanlak, Stara Zagora, and Pernik, the Communist-controlled Labor Party managed to conclude agreements with the more radical Peasant Union groups. A third section of the Peasant Union, led by Tomov, allied itself with Malinov's Democrats and Kyorchev's Liberals while still a fourth, led by old Dragiev, a founder of the Union, fought the election in combination with Kosturkov's Radicals.[77] The party which under Stamboliski had dominated Bulgaria was thus splintered. The Labor Party reserved its most vitriolic abuse for the Iron Bloc, to the subsequent regret of the Communist leaders who feared that the Socialists had been thereby benefited.[78]

The demand of the entire opposition, proposed on February 8, 1927, that proportional representation be reintroduced had been rejected by the government. The subsequent campaign, in view of the participation of eighteen parties and groups, was confused, with 4,000 candidates standing for 273 Sobranie seats.[79] In the provinces it was characterized by the customary terror and police chicanery.[80]

[75] Ibid., VI, No. 127 (October 20, 1926), Chronik.
[76] Ibid., VI, No. 145 (November 24, 1926), Chronik.
[77] Ibid., VII, No. 48 (May 4, 1927), Chronik.
[78] Kabakchiev, Boshkovich, and Vatis, Kommunisticheskie Partii Balkanskikh Stran, p. 126.
[79] The Times, May 28 and 30, 1927.
[80] During the reading of the Speech from the Throne to the newly elected So-branie on June 19, 1927, Boris asserted that the elections had been free. At this point the Socialist Yanko Sakazov, still resentful over the refusal of the government to reintroduce proportional representation, over which issue Socialist and Democratic

Election day was May 29, 1927. The Democratic Entente received 504,703 votes, or 39 percent of the total, but the inequitable electoral law awarded it 167 of the 273 seats in the Sobranie. The Iron Bloc's 285,758 votes won 56 seats of which 42 went to the Peasant Union, 10 to the Socialists, and 4 to the Artisan Party. The Communist-controlled Labor Party received 29,210 votes. Two of its candidates won direct election, and two more were sent to the Sobranie with the support of Peasant groups. The Socialist Federation won no seats. The remaining 450,000-odd ballots and 46 seats were divided among the bourgeois opposition parties.[81] In the cities, where terror could not so conveniently be applied, the government did poorly. Of the 11 seats for Sofia, it won only 4 and the Labor Party 2. The Labor Party's 2 other seats were won in Plovdiv and Sliven.[82]

On June 8, 1927, the Labor Party offered to join the Iron Bloc which it had maligned throughout the preceding campaign.[83] The Socialists, resentful over their loss of seats from 29 to 10 and angry with the government, whose terror they believed largely responsible for this reduction, responded at their congress on October 23, 1927, with a resolution advocating a coalition of all leftist opposition parties.[84] Before the matter could be pursued, however, the Communist leaders in Moscow disallowed it. At the ECCI Plenum on February 9, 1928, Kolarov explained:

Under the influence of the White Terror, there has arisen in certain Communist parties, particularly in the Bulgarian Communist Party, the illusion that it is possible to win over Social Democracy to the fight against Fascism. This is a myth.... Social Democracy cannot participate in the struggle against Fascism. It serves, on the contrary, as a tool of Fascism in the fight against the proletariat.[85]

Entente deputies had come to blows on the floor of the Sobranie in April, and still smarting over police persecution, dramatically shouted, "That is not true, Your Majesty. The elections were held under terror and violence." *La Fédération Balkanique*, III, No. 70-71 (July 1, 1927), 1372.

[81] These statistics were compiled from Bell, *The Near East Year Book, 1931-1932*, p. 135; Kazasov, *Burni godini: 1918-1944*, p. 312; *III. Kongress der Sozialistischen Arbeiter-Internationale*, I, Sect. 4, p. 22; Yotsov, "Upravlenieto na 'Demokraticheski Sgovor,'" p. 468.

[82] The names of three of the Labor Party deputies were Avram Stoyanov, Kh. Kalaijiev, and D. Dimitrov. *La Fédération Balkanique*, IV, No. 88 (March 15, 1928), 1834.

[83] *Inprekorr*, VII, No. 63 (June 15, 1927), Chronik.

[84] *Inprekorr*, VII, No. 108 (November 2, 1927), Chronik.

[85] "Rede des Genossen Kolarow zur Diskussion zum Referat des Genossen Bucharin ueber die Opposition: Tagung des EKKI Plenums," *Inprekorr*, VIII, No. 18 (February 23, 1928), 387.

The Comintern was entering the era of the "social-fascist" line. The Bulgarian Socialist Party, against which the government conducted a mild campaign of persecution in 1927 and 1928, once more announced its readiness to form temporary alliances with other "labor groups"—meaning the Labor Party and the Socialist Federation—at its congress in October, 1928, but again this offer was without result.[86] The Socialist Party henceforth oscillated in regard to both votes and membership around the 30,000 mark. It had become one of the static institutions of Bulgarian political life.[87]

From the moment of its founding in 1927 the Labor Party had been persistently harassed by the government which was aware of its control by the Communist Party. The Labor Party's leaders were frequently imprisoned, its Sobranie deputies suspended, its journals confiscated, its offices raided, and its functionaries arrested.[88] Yet it thrived. At each local, municipal, and departmental election its vote increased. Though the Iron Bloc was formally augmented by the adhesion of the Radical Party, many workers and peasants deserted it for the Labor Party in elections. In the departmental elections held on November 9, 1930, in half the country's districts, the Labor Party polled 80,000 votes, 11 percent of the total and second only to the Democratic Entente.[89] In the municipal elections of February, 1931, it emerged as the largest party in Russe, where it doubled its vote, and made striking gains in Nova Zagora.[90] Between November 1, 1931, and February 14, 1932, another series of municipal elections was held in all cities except Sofia. This time the Labor Party won absolute majorities on the town councils of Sliven and Troyan and pluralities in Russe, Varna, Burgas, Plovdiv, Khaskovo, Yambol, Stara Zagora, Shumen, Gabrovo, and Teteven. It polled 50,087 votes and won 294 seats on the councils. The Democratic Entente received 25,389 votes and 136 seats, the Socialists 7,778 and 15, and all the oppositional bourgeois parties combined 105,085 votes and 740 seats.[91] The Labor Party's membership

---

[86] *IV. Kongress der Sozialistischen Arbeiter-Internationale,* p. 22.

[87] *Balgarskata Rabotnicheska Sotsialdemokraticheska Partia,* p. 9. In 1930 its membership totaled 28,146 consisting of 6,875 employees, 17,391 peasants, 2,242 artisans, and 1,638 from the free professions. In the early 1930s both its membership and its votes declined slightly, probably in consequence of the depression which drove people to the more radical parties.

[88] Avram Stoyanov was deprived of his Sobranie seat in December, 1928.

[89] *Inprekorr,* XI, No. 74 (July 31, 1931), 1668.

[90] *Inprecorr* (English edition), XI, No. 11 (March 5, 1931), 212.

[91] *Ibid.,* XII, No. 8 (February 25, 1932), 145.

rose from 6,000 at the end of 1930 to 12,000 in July, 1931, to 25,000 at the end of that year, to 30,000 in June and 35,000 in October, 1932. About three fourths of this membership was drawn from the villages, in 1,600 of which Labor Party cells were established.[92] In 1931, despite frequent police confiscations, 42 legal labor papers with a weekly circulation of 250,000 were published in addition to illegal Communist leaflets, of which 100,000 were distributed in 1933.[93]

On June 21, 1931, Sobranie elections were held under a new and complicated system of proportional representation. To its intense surprise and dismay, the Democratic Entente was defeated. Together with its allies, Smilov's Liberals, it received 417,000 votes and 78 seats, of which the Liberal share was 15. A newly formed National Bloc, consisting of Malinov's Democrats, the Peasant Union wing controlled by Dimitar Gichev, Kyorchev's Liberals, and Kosturkov's Radicals won 590,000 votes, 152 mandates, and the right to form a government. Its seats were apportioned among 69 Peasants, 43 Democrats, 32 Liberals, and 8 Radicals. A group calling itself the Left Bloc, which consisted of Dragiev's Peasant followers, the Artisan Party and a splinter group from the Radical Party, received 14,800 votes and no seats. The Socialists, this time standing without allies, won 5 seats on 26,000 ballots. The 11 deputies from Petrich were, as usual, virtually IMRO appointees. The Labor Party, supported in various localities by radical peasant groups, stood under the label of Toilers' Bloc and received 166,000 votes entitling it to 31 seats in the Sobranie[94]—a striking recovery of Communist influence.

The crest of the Labor Party tide was, however, still to be reached. A critical municipal election was held in Sofia on September 25, 1932. In the Sobranie elections of the previous year, the National Bloc (now the government) had polled 22,382 votes in the capital. This was now reduced to 10,738 while the Labor Party's vote rose

[92] *Inprekorr*, XI, No. 74 (July 31, 1931), 1668; No. 107 (November 10, 1931), 240; XII, No. 49 (June 14, 1932), 1551; No. 51 (June 21, 1932), 1637; No. 87 (October 21, 1932), 2784.

[93] *Kommunisticheski Internatsional pered VII Vsemirnom Kongressom*, pp. 331-32. In 1933 seven illegal numbers of *Rabotnicheski Vestnik*, the official organ of the Bulgarian Communist Party, appeared and in 1934, fifteen.

[94] Statistics from Bell, *The Near East Year Book, 1931-32*, p. 134; *Inprecorr* (English edition), XI, No. 35 (July 2, 1931), 645.

from 9,658 to 16,104, which qualified it for a majority of 19 out of the 35 seats on the Sofia Municipal Council, leaving 12 for the National Bloc and 4 for the Democratic Entente.[95] The government, alarmed, petitioned the Sofia District Court to set aside the election results (under Article 28 of the Law for the Defense of the Realm) on the ground that the Labor Party was a cover for the illegal Communist Party. Initially the Court ruled in December that the government had not proved its allegations but, on appeal, it invalidated 15 of the 19 Labor Party seats in February, 1933.[96] Two months later the Sobranie expelled 29 of its Labor Party deputies on the same grounds. The other two were exempted on declaring that they had left the Communist Party.[97] The expelled deputies, who during their tenure in the Sobranie had several times provoked uproars and fights,[98] now walked out of the chamber singing the *Internationale* while in the streets the police arrested 100 demonstrators protesting against the expulsion.[99]

A campaign of terror against the Labor Party and the illegal Communist Party had been in progress for some time. On October 30, 1931, the Secretary of the illegal Communist Party, Nikola "Sasho" Kofarjiev, had been shot in a Sofia street shortly after his clandestine return to Bulgaria from Moscow where he had been instructed to make certain changes in tactics and personnel. The police claimed that, having been wounded, he killed himself to avoid interrogation.[100] A few days later, on November 5 and 6, 1931, the tobacco worker Khristo Kochev and the student Tsacho Nenov, respectively treasurer and head of the technical department of the underground Communist Party, committed suicide at the Sofia police headquarters.[101] In October and November, 1931, the police arrested ten suspects on the charge of being members of the underground central committees of either the Communist Party or the Communist Youth League. They were tried in June, 1932,

[95] *Inprekorr*, XII, No. 81 (September 30, 1932), 2578. The vote of the Democratic Entente and Smilov's Liberals in Sofia fell slightly from 13,031 to 12,270 and that of the Socialists from 1,900 to 1,596. A Nazi-like group received 147 votes.
[96] *Basler Rundschau*, II, No. 1 (January 1, 1933), 6; No. 3 (March 1, 1933), 47.
[97] *The Times*, April 13, 1933.
[98] *Neue Freie Presse*, October 29, 1931; *Manchester Guardian*, October 29, 1932.
[99] *Pester Lloyd*, April 13, 1933; *Le Temps*, April 14, 1933.
[100] *Inprekorr*, XII, No. 50 (June 17, 1932), 1602.
[101] *Ibid*.

together with two others *in absentia*, one of whom was Blagoi Popov, shortly to be a codefendant with Dimitrov at the Reichstag fire trial. Six of the accused, including these latter two, were sentenced to twelve and one-half years imprisonment, three to seven and one-half years, and three to four and one-half years. They were further deprived of political rights for 15, 10 and 8 years and fined 270,000, 125,000, and 90,000 leva respectively.[102]

The government next turned its attention to the still legal Labor Party. In December, 1932, its leading functionaries were arrested on the charge of being Communist agents.[103] A few weeks later, on January 24, 1933, the Labor Party deputy Khristo Traikov was murdered by Mikhailov's IMRO gunmen after he had ignored several warnings to cease his political activities. A thirty-six year old shoemaker, he had edited, together with the Labor Party deputies Martulkov and Naumov, the *Makedonsko Zname* (Macedonian Banner) and had been a coeditor of the *Rabotnichesko Delo* (Workers' Action).[104] On June 26, 1933, Assen Boyajiev, for many years secretary of the Independent Trade Union Federation, editor of its paper *Edinstvo*, and a Labor Party deputy, was killed by the police in the course of a general roundup of political suspects.[105] Ironically, he had shortly before been expelled from the Communist Party for his warnings that its social-fascist line and semi-insurrectionary tactics were suicidal.[106] A few days before his murder, Petko Napetov, Secretary of the Labor Party, had also been killed.[107]

Was the government really so frightened by the Labor Party and the menace of Communism? In the autumn of 1931 Prime Minister Mushanov told the Reuters correspondent that he believed there were 12,000 confirmed Communists then in the country.[108] The

[102] *Ibid.*

[103] *Inprekorr*, XII, No. 107 (December 23, 1932), 3432. One of those arrested was Zhak Natan, who was to become the "dean" of Communist historians in post-Second World War Bulgaria and editor-in-chief of *Istoricheski Pregled* (Historical Review).

[104] *Inprekorr*, XIII, No. 14 (January 31, 1933), 509. It has been claimed that Traikov's murderer was Vlado Chernozemski, the assassin of D. H. Dimov in 1924 and of King Alexander and Barthou in 1934. See Plantagenet, *Les Crimes de l'ORIM*, p. 36.

[105] *Basler Rundschau*, II, No. 24 (July 14, 1933), 850.

[106] This was later revealed in *Basler Rundschau*, II, No. 43 (November 17, 1933), 1684.

[107] *Inprecorr* (English edition), XIII, No. 26 (June 16, 1933), 568.

[108] Swire, *Bulgarian Conspiracy*, p. 38.

chief concern of the government was not the absolute number of Communists but their activities within the armed forces, the main target of Communist infiltration in the early 1930s. Shortly before the Seventh Comintern Congress in 1935, the Bulgarian Communists boasted that their Youth League had established cells in almost every garrison in Bulgaria.[109] In 1932, 7 soldiers were convicted of conspiracy at Kazanlak and executed in 1934.[110] In August, 1933, 6 "revolutionary" soldiers were tried in Plovdiv and publicly hanged a year later on December 8, 1934.[111] In September, 1933, 16 soldiers of the Shumen garrison were condemned to death for Communist activities, and in December the same sentence was pronounced on 7 soldiers at another trial in the same town, 18 others being condemned to prison terms of five to fifteen years.[112] Early in 1934 2 naval officers and 10 enlisted men were condemned to death for attempted mutiny at Varna. Fifteen others received prison sentences.[113] In the summer of 1934 a Communist ring was uncovered in the Plovdiv garrison. Altogether 122 defendants were indicted before a court martial of whom 9 were sentenced to death, 71 to hard labor for three to five years, and 42 were acquitted.[114] In June, 1935, the soldier Alexander Voikov, a member of the Communist Youth League, was executed for revolutionary propaganda among the troops.[115] Cumulatively, the Communist infiltration into the army was a causative factor in the *coup d'état* of May, 1934.

Another, and more important factor leading to the accelerated disintegration of Bulgarian political life and the growing strength of the Labor Party was the economic collapse of the early 1930s. The economies of the Danubian states had been precarious at the best of times but the "scissors," the disparity between agricultural and industrial prices which was an aspect of the world depression, brought catastrophe. Though the nadir of the agricultural de-

[109] *Kommunisticheski International pered VII Vsemirnom Kongressom,* p. 331.
[110] *The Times,* December 19, 1934.
[111] "Helft dem heroischen Proletariat Bulgariens," p. 516.
[112] *Pester Lloyd,* September 10 and December 27, 1933.
[113] *The Times,* February 13, 1934.
[114] *Manchester Guardian,* October 3, 1934. Three of those sentenced to death were reprieved as minors.
[115] *Basler Rundschau,* IV, No. 30 (July 11, 1935), 1515.

pression was not reached in Southeastern Europe until after the collapse of the Vienna Kreditanstalt in May, 1931, as a result of which wheat prices fell by half in the next two years, Bulgaria's economy had been wracked by crisis since the depression in the late 1920s of the market for her chief money crop, tobacco.

With the acquisition of the Rhodope Mountain area and the loss of the Southern Dobruja during the Balkan Wars of 1912 and 1913, wheat had yielded to tobacco as Bulgaria's primary export crop. Indeed, in 1925 the government imported 50-million leva worth of grain into a country 80 percent of whose population depended on agriculture for its livelihood.[116] In the 1920s about 200,000 peasant holdings, or one third of the total, were devoted to tobacco culture; the crop, 90 percent of which was exported, accounted in 1926 for 41 percent of the total value of Bulgarian exports.[117] The country's economy as well as the solvency of her government, most of whose revenue came from the tobacco tax, were thus vulnerable to fluctuations in the world price of this crop. In 1926 a sharp decline in the value of the tobacco exports began. Whereas it had stood at 3-billion leva in 1925 it had fallen by 1927 to 1.9-billion leva and was to sink yet lower in the depression of the early 1930s.[118] Then came the collapse of the grain market, as can be seen from the following tables:

Price of Bulgarian Grain Exports in Leva per Kilogram[119]

Crop	Spring 1930	Spring 1931	Spring 1932
Wheat	5.62	3.06	2.20
Oats	4.30	2.71	—
Corn	3.12	2.27	1.20

[116] Ordon, "Bemerkungen ueber die Bauernbewegung in Europa," p. 272.

[117] *Ibid.*, p. 272; *La Fédération Balkanique,* IV, No. 94 (June 15, 1928), 2007. Cf. Basch, *The Danube Basin and the German Economic Sphere,* p. 38.

[118] Kazasov, *Burni godini: 1918-1944,* p. 326.

[119] These figures are abstracted from *Inprekorr,* XI, No. 64 (June 30, 1931), 1443; XII, No. 87 (October 21, 1932), 2792-93. It should be noted that the leva had been stabilized in 1928 at .03745 gold francs. The official exchange rate of the leva was applied in foreign trade until June, 1933, when the National Bank authorized private compensations in foreign trade transactions. By paying a higher price for foreign exchange, it was hoped to bridge the gap between domestic and foreign prices and thus to encourage the export of Bulgarian products.

Bulgarian Foreign Trade during the World Depression[120]

YEAR	EXPORTS		IMPORTS	
	Volume	*Value*	*Volume*	*Value*
	(in 1000 kg.)	*(in 1000 leva)*	*(in 1000 kg.)*	*(in 1000 leva)*
1928	382,067	6,231,247	357,162	7,040,935
1929	313,167	6,397,061	508,123	8,324,633
1930	543,148	6,191,140	316,880	4,589,725
1931	769,185	5,934,174	294,734	4,660,063
1932	584,941	3,382,845	261,164	3,471,233
1933	430,528	2,846,349	230,859	2,202,256
1934	396,145	2,534,630	246,203	2,247,232
1935	327,067	3,253,284	276,403	3,008,954

A comparison of the years 1929 and 1934, for example, indicates that whereas the *volume* of Bulgarian exports—overwhelmingly agricultural products—actually rose by 26.5 percent, the *value* of these increased exports in 1934 was only 39.6 percent of what it had been in 1929.

The operation of the price scissors between Bulgarian exports and imports may be illustrated graphically by the reduction of the value of these two categories of foreign trade for each year of the crisis to a leva-per-kilogram ratio. Then taking the average of the years 1928 and 1929 as an index of 100, the following scale emerges, manifestly demonstrating that the decline in value of Bulgaria's exports proceeded more precipitously and to a deeper trough than the value of her imports:

Cost per Kilogram

YEAR	EXPORTS		IMPORTS	
	Leva	*Percent*	*Leva*	*Percent*
1928	16.3 } 18.35 = 100		19.7 } 18.05 = 100	
1929	20.4 }		16.4 }	
1930	11.4	62.1	14.5	80.3
1931	7.7	42.0	15.8	87.5
1932	5.8	31.6	13.3	73.7
1933	6.6	36.0	9.5	52.6
1934	6.4	34.9	9.1	50.4
1935	9.9	54.0	10.9	60.4

Despite the disastrous decline in the value of agricultural products, the Bulgarian peasant, caught in an inelastic productive system, failed to reduce either total production or cultivated area.

---

[120] Piperow, *Bulgariens Agrarkrise und Agrarverschuldung,* p. 29. These are the official figures of the Bulgarian Statistical Institute.

The National Bloc government of 1931-34 was unable to cope with the catastrophe which by 1934 had reduced the estimated national income to 61.4 percent of its 1929 level.[121] As the Peasant Union leader Gichev held alternately the two vulnerable portfolios of Agriculture and, after December 1932, Commerce (he was succeeded in the former ministry by his party colleague Muraviev, a nephew of Stamboliski), it is not surprising that many peasants turned in despair to the Labor Party which glibly promised panaceas for a world depression that any Bulgarian government, no matter how able or well-intentioned, would have been powerless to solve.

The crisis rapidly enveloped commerce and industry. In May, 1929, a strike of employees in tobacco-processing factories (mainly women and children) spread from Khaskovo until it affected 26,000 workers.[122] The Labor Party initially had not been involved, and the strike leaders, not wishing to be embarrassed by its interference, emphasized that their demands were purely economic, not political, and that they would welcome governmental mediation.[123] An attempt by the Labor Party and the Independent Trade Union Federation to extend the strike and give it a political character failed, though 2,000 textile workers in Sliven also walked out and the country's shoemakers staged a twenty-four hour sympathy strike.[124] The government advised the employers to be accommodating toward the strictly economic demands of the strikers and simultaneously attacked those seeking to introduce political issues. The entire Committee of the Independent Tobacco Workers Union in the most important center of Plovdiv was arrested.[125] By July 2 all but 10,000 tobacco workers in the lesser tobacco towns had returned to work.[126] As the crisis deepened and unemployment spread during the following years, the Communists, through the Labor Party, did manage to control and manipulate the workers. As prolonged strikes in a period of unemployment often failed, the Communists developed the technique of the short work-stoppage and demonstration, which

---

[121] Basch, *The Danube Basin and the German Economic Sphere*, p. 91n.
[122] *The Times*, June 19, 1929.
[123] Kolarov's report of July 6, 1929, to the Tenth ECCI Plenum in *Zehntes Plenum des Exekutivkomitees der Kommunistischen Internationale: Protokoll*, p. 313.
[124] *Inprecorr* (English edition), IX, No. 32 (July 5, 1929), 694.
[125] *Inprecorr* (English edition), IX, No. 65 (November 22, 1929), 1386.
[126] *Inprecorr* (English edition), IX, No. 34 (July 19, 1929), 736.

often resulted, as they had hoped, in violence.[127] In order to facilitate the manipulation of this industrial discontent, the illegal Communist Party reorganized itself on the "production-unit cell" principle.[128] The wages-and-hours type of strike was also called on the slightest pretext. In December, 1933, it was reported to the Thirteenth ECCI Plenum that between 1929 and 1932 there had been 570 strikes involving 135,000 men, one fourth of the country's urban working class.[129] These figures, together with the increasing discontent engendered by the lowering of wages and the growing dissatisfaction in the impoverished villages,[130] whither many of the unemployed semiproletarians drifted to swell the already inflated ranks of the underemployed and undernourished, encouraged the Communists. "All this raises before our party the serious task of preparing the proletariat and the toiling masses for the impending decisive battles for the dictatorship of the proletariat, for a Soviet Bulgaria," the Thirteenth ECCI Plenum was assured by the Bulgarian Dybov-Planinski, who went on to analyze the political strategy required by the situation as follows:

Directing its main blow against the Peasant Union, the Communist Party of Bulgaria must systematically expose the "left" groups. . . . In the present circumstances, when the fascist dictatorship is crumbling to pieces, when the majority of the working class follows our party, the major task confronting the party is the preparation of the working class and all the toiling masses for the decisive battles for the dictatorship of the proletariat.[131]

In Bulgaria, as in Germany, however, the Communists, blinded by this preposterous tactic of social fascism, misread utterly the political omens of the depression crisis. The dictatorship to which it gave birth was one, not of the proletariat, but initially of the Army and subsequently of the Crown.

[127] Report of Dybov-Planinski to the Thirteenth ECCI Plenum of December, 1933, in *Trinadtsati plenum IKKI: Stenograficheski otchet*, p. 266. Cf. *Pester Lloyd*, July 10, 1931; *Neue Freie Presse*, July 23, 1931.
[128] Kabakchiev, Boshkovich, and Vatis, *Kommunisticheskie Partii Balkanskikh Stran*, p. 128.
[129] Report of Iskrov in *Trinadtsati plenum IKKI: Stenograficheski otchet*, p. 545.
[130] At times the peasants chased tax collectors out of their villages, and clashes with the police occurred. See *Kommunisticheski International pered VII Vsemirnom Kongressom*, p. 330.
[131] Report of Dybov-Planinski in *Trinadtsati plenum IKKI: Stenograficheski otchet*, pp. 267-68.

On May 19, 1934, a military coup led by Colonel Damyan Velchev, organizer of the Military League,[132] seized power and installed a government headed by Kimon Georgiev, a lieutenant-colonel of the reserve. Though only a colonel, Velchev enjoyed great influence among the junior officers by virtue of his having been for many years commandant of the Cadet School. The new government was supported by a small group of about 300 intellectuals known as Zveno (Link) who published a journal of the same name read by about 2,500 other intellectuals. Zveno had been founded in June, 1927, by Dimo Kazasov, then an expellee from the Socialist Party, and other "idealists." Encouraged by army officers, it worked for "national regeneration" through a supraparty authoritarian government.

The coup of May 19, 1934, was evoked by the political and economic collapse of the country. Its immediate causes were the threat of another putsch by Alexander Tsankov, who had by then founded a Bulgarian Nazi-like party and had summoned his followers to stage "an action" on May 20, and the demands of the Peasant Union to be invested with complete power.[133] The Sobranie was prorogued, the parties liquidated,[134] and the Tirnovo Constitution of 1879 replaced by one based on the Portuguese model. Henceforth the Sobranie was to consist of 160 members elected, without party labels, from "approved" lists of candidates. Local government was centralized. IMRO was suppressed, incipient Nazi-type clubs disbanded, a *rapprochement* with Yugoslavia effected, Italy replaced by France as the country's principal Great Power patron, and diplomatic relations with the USSR established. A moratorium on debts was decreed. The trade unions were dissolved into a government-organized Workers' League which was to inculcate the principles of devotion to the state and social solidarity instead of revolution and class struggle. There was, however, some

[132] Velchev had organized the Military League in 1922. Its members were mainly junior officers and it was therefore dubbed "The Captains' League" by its detractors. It participated in the coup against Stamboliski. Dissolved in 1927, it was secretly revived by Velchev in 1929.

[133] *Inprecorr* (English edition), XIV, No. 32 (June 1, 1934), 836; *South-Eastern Europe: A Political and Economic Survey*, p. 101.

[134] Until 1937 the Labor and Communist Parties remained separate underground organizations, the latter at a deeper level than the former. In 1937 they fused into one illegal Labor Party, which was renamed Communist Party at the Fifth Congress in December, 1948.

effective resistance among the workers. In Sofia they rejected the government-nominated candidate for the secretaryship of the capital's key branch of the Workers' League and elected a former leader of the Communist-guided Independent Federation, Milev.[135] The new government's experiment with a propaganda ministry, the Directorate of Social Renovation, which attacked the old bourgeois parties and politicians, was also brought to grief by their resistance. Indeed, the Velchev-Georgiev government was too radical for the taste of the vested interests of the old order, among which was the Crown, and these were strong enough to bring about its downfall in January, 1935, and its replacement by a regime headed by General Zlatev, who retained the authoritarian constitutional innovations but emasculated the political and social radicalism which had characterized the Velchev-Georgiev program. Several more changes of regime in the following years led to the concentration of power in the hands of King Boris. In October, 1935, Velchev was arrested, together with several other military and civilian colleagues, on a charge of plotting to overthrow the monarchy. His death sentence was commuted to life imprisonment in 1936, and he was released in 1940, to become a leading figure in the Communist-dominated Fatherland Front during the Second World War.[136] Velchev then served as War Minister from September, 1944, until September, 1946, when he fell victim to the Communists' decision to assume complete control openly.[137] Appointed Minister to Switzerland, he died there in 1954. Georgiev became the first Prime Minister of Communist-dominated Bulgaria in September, 1944, being replaced in that office by Georgi Dimitrov in November, 1946, at which time he became a Vice-Premier and Foreign Minister. Ten years later he was serving as Minister of Electrification.

In 1935, however, even after their fall from power, Velchev and Georgiev were regarded by the Communists as fascist beasts and the

---

[135] Kabakchiev, "Glavnie etapi i osobennosti razvitia fashizma v Bolgarii," p. 59. The government reserved the right to veto the election of unacceptable officers.

[136] Velchev's codefendant at the trial of 1935-36, General Vladimir Zaimov, was executed early in June, 1942, on charges of having committed espionage on behalf of the USSR.

[137] Velchev was obliged to resign as War Minister after the Communists had purged the officer corps and reproached him with having been implicated in the overthrow of Stamboliski as well as for his known correspondence with the Serbian General Draža Mihajlović.

"real" enemies.[138] That the Communists persisted in this evaluation even after Velchev's imprisonment is but one more example of their incapacity to adjust the line of the moment to circumstances except in mechanical obedience to orders from Moscow. The year before, hypnotized by their doctrine of social fascism, the Communists had been caught completely unawares by the Velchev coup. Until Moscow signalled the new policy of the "Popular Front," however, they continued to bleat that the main threat came from the moribund Socialists and "left" Peasant Union.[139] Early in 1935 the *émigré* Central Committee in Moscow received new instructions and promptly and without embarrassment appealed to the social fascists of yesterday to join the Communists in an "anti-fascist people's front." [140] In November, 1935, after the Seventh World Congress had officially proclaimed the new line, Willi Muenzenberg in Paris invited Kosta Todorov, who had been denounced by the Communists as a Yugoslav jackal since the collapse of his negotiations with Dimitrov in 1924, to go to Moscow to cement a new alliance.[141] Even the discredited bourgeois parties were flattered. The Tirnovo Constitution of 1879, scrapped by Velchev, which until 1935 had been to the Communists but a screen for bourgeois exploitation, suddenly became an almost mystical guarantor of the People's rights.[142] As usual in the interwar history of the European Communist Parties, the delay between external political events and the creaking adjustment to them of the party line was sufficient to reduce the latter to virtual ineffectuality. That the paralysis of the Bulgarian Communist Party in May, 1934, had been a consequence of the Moscow-imposed doctrine of social fascism could not, of course, be admitted. An inquest had to be held and "wreckers" found. The cycle of chiliastic optimism, vainglorious boasts, paralysis, and purge had again to be turned.

---

[138] "An Appeal by the C.C. of the C.P. of Bulgaria," *Inprecorr* (English edition), XV, No. 61 (November 16, 1935), 1515-16.

[139] Kolarov, *Protiv lyavoto sektantstvo i Trotskizma v Balgaria*, p. 145.

[140] "Enlarged Plenum of the C.C. of the C.P. of Bulgaria," *Inprecorr* (English edition), XV, No. 13 (March 23, 1935), 367.

[141] K. Todorov, *Balkan Firebrand*, p. 268.

[142] "The Sixth Plenum of the C.C. of the C.P. of Bulgaria," *Inprecorr* (English edition), XVI, No. 25 (May 30, 1936), 684. In subsequent elections during the 1930s, the Communists had their sympathizers write across the ballot the words, "Restore the Tirnovo Constitution." *Inprecorr* (English edition), XVII, No. 23 (May 29, 1937), 533-34.

XIII

PURGE

That tension should develop between the Foreign Bureau of the Communist Party, comfortably installed at Moscow's Hotel Lux, and the persecuted cadres being hounded and tortured by the police in Bulgaria was well-nigh inevitable. In the later 1920s this antagonism between the hunted and the secure became, in effect, a revolt of the underground Communist Youth League, the nucleus of the most radical and militant elements of the illegal Communist movement in Bulgaria, against the veterans of the parent party led from abroad by Kolarov and Dimitrov. Like the senior Party, the Youth League operated through a legal cover organization, The Union of Working Youth (RMS) which was founded in 1926, and held its constituent conference in February, 1927. In 1928 the illegal core numbered 500, which by December, 1932, was expanded to 2,254. The legal RMS counted 1,100 members at the end of 1930 and 20,000 two years later.[1] At the second Party Conference in exile,[2] held in Berlin, December 8, 1927-January 15, 1928, the delegates of the Youth League, "Rossen" (pseudonym of Georgi Lambrev), "Boikov" (Ilya Vasilev) and Petar Iskrov, vigorously attacked the "June [1923] leadership." Though only Todor Lukanov and Georgi Popov, who had continued to question the wisdom of the September insurrection, were expelled,[3] Kolarov and Dimitrov uneasily felt that this merciless criticism of "the entire previous Party activity"[4] was directed against themselves as well, and they subsequently accused the representatives of the Youth League at the Berlin Conference of

---

[1] *Kommunisticheski International pered VII Vsemirnom Kongressom*, p. 546.

[2] The first Conference in exile had been an uneventful inquest in Moscow on the cathedral outrage of April, 1925.

[3] See Dimitrov's report to the Sixth Comintern Congress of 1928 in *Sechster Weltkongress der Kommunistischen Internationale: Protokoll*, I, p. 241.

[4] *The Communist International between the Fifth and Sixth World Congresses, 1924-1928*, p. 258.

"factional activities," especially among the delegates from the underground movement and of "underhand agitation in order to . . . usurp the leadership of the Party." [5]

Developments within the Comintern, which was about to embark on the ultraleft era of the social-fascist line, favored the militants of the Youth League. At the Sixth Comintern Congress, meeting in Moscow in the summer of 1928, Schüller, the leader of the Communist Youth International, reproached the leaders of the Bulgarian Party with not permitting adequate scope to its Youth League and brushed aside Kolarov's protest against this accusation.[6] Schüller also referred here to clashes between the senior leaders and the Youth League delegates at the Berlin Party Conference. The Congress elected Iskrov of the Bulgarian Youth League to the International Control Commission.[7] When the Fifth Congress of the Communist Youth International met later in the same year, August 20-September 18, Rossen and Boikov of the Bulgarian Youth League repeated Schüller's charges in yet more bitter tones.[8] Boikov was promoted to the Executive Committee of the Communist Youth International, to the vexation of Kolarov, who later complained that this had been engineered without the prior knowledge of the senior Party leadership.[9] In May, 1929, at the second Plenum of the Central Committee of the Bulgarian Communist Party held in Berlin, the radical rebels against the veteran leadership captured control.[10] A year later Boikov took charge of the underground apparatus in Bulgaria where he was assisted by Ivan Pavlov, called "Encho," who had attended the 1929 Plenum of the Central Com-

[5] Kolarov, *Protiv lyavoto sektantstvo i Trotskizma v Balgaria,* p. 172; Dimitrov, *Politicheski otchet na Ts.K. na BRP(k),* p. 31.

[6] "VI. Weltkongress der K.I., 16. Sitzung vom 30. Juli 1928," *Inprekorr,* VIII, No. 85 (August 16, 1928), 1593-96.

[7] *Inprekorr,* VIII, No. 135 (December 4, 1928), 2695.

[8] "V. Weltkongress der K.J.I.," *Inprekorr,* VIII, No. 98 (September 7, 1928), 1869; No. 101 (September 11, 1928), 1918. Kolarov later accused Iskrov, Rossen, and Boikov of having inspired Schüller's attack. See Kolarov, *Protiv lyavoto sektantstvo i Trotskizma v Balgaria,* p. 172.

[9] Kolarov, *Protiv lyavoto sektantstvo i Trotskizma v Balgaria,* p. 172.

[10] Karakolov, "Kharakterni momenti ot borbata na Balgarskata Rabotnicheska Partia—Komunisti," p. 151. Here it is charged that the rebels were supported by Bela Kun, Lenski, and Knorin. Dimitrov, in his report to the Fifth Party Congress in 1948 (p. 33) said they were aided by "secret elements in the apparatus of the ECCI and of other Communist Parties." In 1935 Kolarov (*Protiv lyavoto sektantstvo i Trotskizma v Balgaria,* p. 124) had charged Heinz Neumann and V. Lominadze with being the culprits.

mittee as chairman of the Youth League and within two months of his return to Bulgaria was coopted to the underground section of the Central Committee.[11] In December, 1930, the new leadership consolidated its position at another Central Committee Plenum held illegally in Bulgaria. This time Nikola "Sasho" Kofarjiev, who was to die within a year,[12] emerged as another leader of the opposition to Dimitrov and Kolarov.[13] The latter charged that this Plenum had been held without the knowledge of the rank-and-file and lamented that such maneuvers by his and Dimitrov's rivals were rendered possible only by the illegal conditions in which the Party had to operate.[14]

The Russian leaders of the Comintern were, of course, aware of the struggle within the Bulgarian Communist Party. For the time being they gave free rein to the young militants who had captured control and who, in pursuance of the current Comintern doctrine that the period of capitalist stabilization had come to an end, proceeded to intensify underground preparations for the great day of civil war, concentrating particularly on the infiltration of the army.[15] Simultaneously, however, Dimitrov and Kolarov, who had long since proven their subservience to Moscow, were kept in reserve by the Russian leaders, possibly on Manuilski's initiative, against the day when the line would be reversed. Articles by Kolarov and Dimitrov in *Inprekorr* between 1928 and 1932 became rare, usually dealt with non-Bulgarian matters, and were often indexed in the lists of contributions by members of the CPSU (b) rather than in those of the Bulgarian Communist Party. The two also retained their positions on the ECCI, of which Kolarov was then a full member and Dimitrov a candidate member. At the Thirteenth Plenum of the ECCI held in Moscow in December, 1933, Dybov-Planinski and Iskrov (rivals of Kolarov and Dimitrov) represented the Bulgarian Communist Party; Kolarov participated as an official of the Comintern apparatus, together with Kun, Kuusinen, Manuilski, and Marty.[16] Dimitrov was then in the prisoner's dock at

---

[11] Kolarov, *Protiv lyavoto sektantstvo i Trotskizma v Balgaria*, pp. 125, 173.
[12] See p. 277.
[13] Kolarov, *Protiv lyavoto sektantstvo i Trotskizma v Balgaria*, p. 126.
[14] *Ibid.*, p. 126.
[15] See p. 279.
[16] *Inprekorr*, January-March, 1934, *passim*.

the Reichstag fire trial, laying the basis of his future leadership. He had spent the previous years on a series of Comintern errands in Western Europe while Kolarov had been appointed a director of the Soviet Agrarian Institute and editor of *Agrarnie Voprosy* (Agrarian Problems).[17] Their colleague from the old Narrow Party Kabakchiev, who had been removed from the Central Committee in 1928, was also given membership in the CPSU (b) and became a contributor to *Istorik Marksist* (Marxist Historian) and *Die Kommunistische Internationale*. Gavril Genov, one of the triumvirate which had commanded the September insurrection, went to the USSR in 1926, was given membership in the CPSU (b) and a post in the International Peasant Council.[18] The Russian leaders were marking time during the Bulgarian dissensions.

In Bulgaria the new young leaders, under the stimulus of the chiliastic Comintern line of the moment, pursued an aggressive semi-insurrectionary policy: they hoped to gain a foothold in the army; workers were urged to "dominate the streets" and the peasants "to occupy the land"—a rather inept parroting of Russian revolutionary phraseology in a land where the peasants already owned their plots. "A general, open, universal offensive" for "Soviet power" and "proletarian dictatorship" was demanded. The legal parliamentary activities of the Labor Party were despised and the Labor Party as such regarded with hostile suspicion as "a nursery of opportunism" even though it had been founded as a Communist-directed cover party. A united front with the Peasant and Socialist Parties was disdained.[19] Were these not obscurantist reactionaries and social fascists? Was not the rapid "radicalization" of the masses, both urban and rural, rendering such tactics unnecessary? Was not the bourgeois order about to collapse? Not a united front but a tight Communist cadre to direct the revolutionary masses was declared to be the need of the moment. After their recapture of Party control, Kolarov and Dimitrov correctly criticized

---

[17] For Dimitrov's travels in Western Europe before his arrest after the Reichstag fire on March 9, 1933, see *Il Processo di Lipsia.*

[18] Genov died in the Soviet Union in January, 1934, and Kabakchiev on October 6, 1940. See the obituaries in *Basler Rundschau,* III, No. 12 (February 1, 1934), and *Istorik Marksist,* XI, No. 87 (1940), 158-59.

[19] Sakun, "Organisationsfragen der Kommunistischen Parteien des Balkans," pp. 1294-1305; Kolarov, *Protiv lyavoto sektantstvo i Trotskizma v Balgaria,* pp. 32-34; Dimitrov, *Politicheski otchet na Ts.K. na BRP(k),* p. 35.

this policy as unrealistic and sectarian[20] but neglected to recall that these preposterous illusions had been nourished and these extravagent slogans fostered by the Comintern line and that their own vituperation against the social fascists had been as shrill as anyone's at the turn of the decade.[21]

Against this infiltration of the army and the semirevolutionary tactics of "domination of the streets" and short, violent strikes, the government retorted with terror.[22] Many young Communists faced firing squads with vain heroism. Some committed suicide on capture.[23] Others, when arrested, betrayed the secrets of the organization to the police, were released, and resumed Party work.[24]

What frightened and enraged Kolarov and Dimitrov in particular was the attack of the young militants on the entire Narrow heritage of the Party. It is easier for a camel to pass through the eye of a needle, judged Boikov, than for an old *Tesnyak* (Narrow Socialist) to become a true bolshevik.[25] Had the Narrow Party been purged at the time of its admission into the Comintern in 1919, he argued, Bulgaria would have been a Soviet state by the 1930s. Boikov insisted that the surviving leaders of the Narrow period must be removed so

[20] Kolarov, *Protiv lyavoto sektantstvo i Trotskizma v Balgaria, passim;* Dimitrov, *Politicheski otchet na Ts.K. na BRP(k),* pp. 33-38.

[21] See the speeches of Kolarov and Dimitrov reprinted in *Sechster Weltkongress der Kommunistischen Internationale: Protokoll* and Kolarov's lengthy introduction to Kabakchiev, Boshkovich, and Vatis, *Kommunisticheskie Partii Balkanskikh Stran.* The tone for the line of "social fascism" was set at ECCI meetings in the late 1920s and early 1930s by Manuilski and Kuusinen. Trotsky denounced the irresponsibility of such slogans as "dominate the streets" long before Dimitrov and Kolarov dared to criticize them from hindsight. See Trotsky, *La "Troisième période" d'erreurs de l'Internationale Communiste.*

[22] After an abortive attempt to blow up the Burgas-Sofia express near Nova Zagora in February, 1931, the police uncovered the Communist cells in Burgas, Yambol, Sliven, Kharmanli, and Khaskovo.

[23] See p. 277.

[24] For bitter complaints about this "shameful phenomenon," see Sakun, "Organisationsfragen der Kommunistischen Parteien des Balkans," pp. 1294-1305; "Die Wappung der Parteikader in der Bekämpfung des 'Auffliegens' in den Ländern des Faschismus," *Inprekorr,* XII, No. 60 (July 22, 1932), 1944-46; "Der K.J.V. Bulgariens auf der Spitze des Kampfes der Arbeiterjugend," *Basler Rundschau,* II, No. 24 (July 14, 1933), 864; *Kommunisticheski International pered VII Vsemirnom Kongressom,* p. 587. The same charge of having turned police agent on capture was made against Traicho Kostov in 1949.

[25] In August, 1930, the Political Secretariat of the ECCI drafted a statement on the Bulgarian question which both praised the Narrow Party for its struggle against reformism and simultaneously chided it for not having been truly Leninist. The two rival factions in the Bulgarian Communist Party each claimed that the statement supported its respective position, but the statement was probably intentionally inconclusive on this issue. See Kabakchiev, "Lenin i bolgarskie Tesnyaki," p. 187.

that a party "of a new type" might be formed.[26] Kolarov and
Dimitrov were denounced as defeatists because in their "Open Letter
to the Workers and Peasants in Bulgaria" of October, 1923,[27] they
had charged that the September insurrection had been provoked by
the government instead of proudly hailing it as the deliberate policy
of the Communist Party, and because they claimed that the aim of
the insurrection had been a Worker-Peasant rather than a Soviet
government.[28] In the issue of the clandestine *Rabotnicheski Vestnik*,
1933, No. 4, celebrating the tenth anniversary of the September
insurrection, Kolarov, Dimitrov, Genov, and Kabakchiev were condemned together with the critics of the September, 1923, policy as
opportunists—presumably because they had offered an alliance to
the Peasant Union and "social fascists" while preparing the insurrection. At this very moment, on September 23, 1933, Dimitrov was
eulogizing the insurrection at the Reichstag fire trial as a heroic
deed.[29] It was later charged that Boikov and his colleagues had
deprecated any demonstrations of support for Dimitrov within Bulgaria at this time when protest rallies and counter-trials were being
staged in London, Paris, and New York.[30]

[26] Boikov's article on Communist Party policy in the clandestine *Komunistichesko
Zname*, 1932, No. 6, as quoted and discussed by Kolarov in his *Protiv lyavoto
sektantstvo i Trotskizma v Balgaria*, pp. 77, 132. As early as the Berlin Party
Conference of December, 1927–January, 1928, the entire Narrow period had been
stigmatized as "Menshevik," to the anger of Dimitrov, who rebutted this charge.
See *Balgarskata Komunisticheska Partia v Rezolyutsii i Reshenia*, II, 343-44. The
"Narrow heritage" was again denounced as a hindrance to the "bolshevization" of the
Party by Z. Serebryansky in *The Communist International*, IX, No. 7 (April 15,
1932), 238-46. The young critics seized every opportunity to advertise the fact that
Blagoev had sided with Plekhanov against Lenin before the First World War. See,
for example, Bazhenov, "Sentyabr'skoe vosstanie v Bolgarii," p. 255. Dimitrov, in
turn, asserted that Blagoev had stood for a policy of "Class against Class"—the
Comintern slogan of the period of "social fascism" in the early 1930s. See Dimitrov,
"Zum zehnten Todestag von Blagoew," *Basler Rundschau*, III, No. 36 (June 14,
1934), 440-41.

[27] See p. 146, footnote 49.

[28] Boikov in *Komunistichesko Zname*, 1932, No. 9, cited by Kolarov (*Protiv
lyavoto sektantstvo i Trotskizma v Balgaria*, p. 140).

[29] Reed, *The Burning of the Reichstag*, p. 52.

[30] See the apology of the Bulgarian Krumov at the Seventh Comintern Congress
on July 30, 1935 in *Inprecorr* (English edition), XV, No. 52 (October 10, 1935),
1300-301.

A word about the Reichstag fire trial: Ruth Fischer (*Stalin and German Communism*, p. 308*n*.) has claimed that there was nothing courageous about Dimitrov's
defiance at the trial as he was aware that it had been arranged between the Gestapo
and the GPU that he and his two Bulgarian codefendants, Blagoi Popov and Vasil
Tanev, would be freed and permitted to go to the USSR, while the German Communist leader Ernst Torgler would be retained in a German concentration camp. This

In the course of 1933 the "left sectarians" (as they were dubbed by Kolarov and Dimitrov) in the leadership of the underground

account presents certain problems. It is, of course, obvious that neither the Gestapo nor the GPU would have scrupled about concluding such a deal had they found it expedient. These questions must be asked, however: Should Ruth Fischer's allegations be correct, why was a trial held and why was Dimitrov permitted to make a fool of Goering before the entire world? The Gestapo was at that time still subordinated to Goering, and Dimitrov's baiting involved the possibility that Goering might be provoked into canceling a "deal" had one been made. Goering's apoplectic threat to "get" Dimitrov after the trial does not seem to have been play-acting (*The Reichstag Fire Trial*, p. 190). It seems probable, therefore, that even if an arrangement such as the one alleged by Ruth Fischer existed between the Gestapo and the GPU, Dimitrov was not aware of it and that his conduct at the trial was genuinely courageous. His ignorance of any such deal is further suggested by the fact that on March 4, 1934, five days after his arrival in Moscow, he wrote that to work for the release of Torgler and Thaelmann was "a question of honor for the international antifascist movement." See Dimitrov, "The Victory of Proletarian Solidarity," *Inprecorr* (English edition), XIV, No. 16 (March 9, 1934), 405. On March 23, however, *Inprecorr* (XIV, No. 19, 501) carried another article by Dimitrov in which he repeated the identical phrase but omitted Torgler's name. He had no doubt been advised to do so in the interval. Torgler, incidentally, survived a Nazi concentration camp and after the Second World War became a functionary of the Social Democratic Party in a provincial German town.

These circumstances lead the writer of the present study to conclude that a deal, if any, was arranged only toward the end of the trial or after the acquittal of the three Bulgarians and Torgler on December 23, 1933, and that in any event Dimitrov's conduct at the trial was based on the conviction that he was fighting for his life. Throughout the summer of 1933 the articles in *Inprecorr* had referred to "four revolutionaries" arrested after the Reichstag fire and heroized Torgler as much as the others. Only after March, 1934, was his name dropped. In October, 1935, a German Communist Party conference allegedly meeting in Brussels expelled Torgler for his "unbolshevik" conduct at the trial. See "Ausschluss Torglers aus der K.P.D.," *Basler Rundschau*, IV, No. 73 (December 12, 1935), 2825. (David J. Dallin [*Soviet Espionage* (New Haven, 1955), p. 122] asserts that this co-called "Brussels" meeting actually convened in Kuntsevo, near Moscow.) Popov and Tanev were also severely rebuked for having failed to follow Dimitrov's example of turning the dock into a tribune. This criticism was unfair, as neither spoke German. Tanev had attempted suicide before the opening of the trial. Although they both groveled to the Communist Party for forgiveness, they disappeared. When Kolarov wrote a biographical sketch on Dimitrov in the *Bolshaya Sovyetkaya Entsiklopedia* (1st edition) in 1935, he instructed the reader to see also the articles on Popov and Tanev, but when the "P" and "T" volumes appeared in 1940 and 1946, their names were omitted. Their reserve toward Dimitrov during the trial may be an indication that they adhered to Boikov's wing of the underground leadership. Both were high functionaries of the Communist Party—Popov was even a member of the Central Committee—at a time when it was in the control of rivals of Kolarov and Dimitrov. In 1929, when Boikov had assumed direction of the Communist Party, Popov had returned from the USSR to Bulgaria to take up the secretaryship of the illegal Communist Youth League.

The entire episode may be followed in *Die Kommunistische Internationale*, XVI, No. 21 (December 30, 1935), 1883-88: Kolarov, "Ueber die Haltung der Genossen Taneff und Popoff im Leipziger Prozess"; "Erklärung der Genossen Popoff und Taneff ueber ihre Haltung vor dem Leipziger Gericht"; "Beschluss des Z.K. der K.P. Bulgariens zur Erklärung der Genossen Popoff und Taneff." See also the separate declarations of Popov and Tanev, "An Genossen Dimitrov und das Z.K. der K.P. Bulgariens," pp. 538-43.

Communist Party, exasperated by the fact that Kolarov and Dimitrov, though having lost control of the Party, continued to enjoy at least the passive protection of the Russian Comintern leaders, proposed the liquidation of the Foreign Bureau, then consisting of Kolarov, Dimitrov, and Iskrov, and suggested the return of Iskrov, their partisan, to Bulgaria. It was simultaneously decided to oppose the reelection of Kolarov to the ECCI at the next Comintern Congress and in the meantime to despatch from Bulgaria a delegate to the ECCI who would be a more accurate interpreter of the views of the underground cadres. A Communist Party Congress would be convened within Bulgaria, thus rendering impossible the attendance of Kolarov and Dimitrov as death sentences awaited both of them there.[31] At the same time a campaign was conducted among the underground cadres against leaders who "stand between the Central Committee and the Comintern."[32]

In the aftermath of the Reichstag fire trial, which resulted in the elevation of Dimitrov to the Secretary-Generalship of the Comintern, these plans came to nought and their authors to grief. "In May, 1934 . . . Vasil Kolarov and Georgi Dimitrov obtained through the ECCI a change in the Party leadership."[33] The rejection in 1929 of control by Kolarov and Dimitrov was denounced as an underhand machination while the coup which this pair now engineered with the support of the Russian leaders was hailed as a healthy reconstitution of the Communist Party along bolshevik lines.[34]

In the course of their feud, prosecuted with all the shameless vituperation which characterises "domestic" quarrels within the Communist movement, each Bulgarian faction sought to pin the damning label of Trotskyist on the other.[35] The charge was in both cases unwarranted. There did, however, exist a small but genuine Trotskyist movement in Bulgaria led by Stefan Manov and Sider Todorov, who had each belonged to both the Broad Socialist and the Communist Parties, and had been expelled from the latter on

[31] Kolarov, *Protiv lyavoto sektantstvo i Trotskizma v Balgaria*, p. 127.
[32] *Ibid.*, p. 137.
[33] Savova, *Vasil Kolarov: Bio-Bibliografia*, p. 54.
[34] Kolarov, *Protiv lyavoto sektantstvo i Trotskizma v Balgaria*, p. 184.
[35] *Ibid.*, p. 146, and on p. 138, the citation from Boikov's article in *Komunistichesko Zname*, 1932, No. 9.

denouncing the September insurrection.[36] Other prominent Trotskyists were Samnaliev, D. Gachev, Edorov (three more expellees from
the Communist Party), and one Spas Zadgorski, a veteran of the
ultraleft Communist Workers' Party (founded in 1920 in protest
against the Communist Party's decision to retreat from the great
railway strike of the winter of 1919-20) [37] who had subsequently
been readmitted into the orthodox Communist Party. On February
16, 1927, as the Communists were about to launch their cover Labor
Party, Manov had cofounded an Independent Socialist Party, the
journal of which was *Nov Pat* (New Road). It disbanded a few
weeks later on April 8, after having vigorously attacked the Communist Party and vainly flattered the Socialist Party, which many of
its members then joined.[38] The next year Samnaliev formed a small
Trotskyist cell in Sliven.[39] Early in 1931 he, Manov, Todorov, and
their colleagues began publishing *Osvobozhdenie* (Liberation), a
political journal for which they claimed a circulation of 1,000.[40]
Trotsky advised his Bulgarian disciples to infiltrate into the Labor
and Communist Parties.[41] Instead of founding a separate party, they
termed themselves the Left Marxist Opposition and agitated for
severing the Labor Party's alliance with the Peasant Union and
pursuing a "pure" proletarian policy.[42] The Communist Workers'
Party of 1920 [43] was now held up as a model. This position coincided
in general with the views of Boikov's "left sectarians." On the
other hand, the Trotskyists condemned as futile, irresponsible, and
dangerous the tactics—so beloved by the left sectarians—of street
riots and strike violence. The slogan of "dominate the streets" was

---

[36] See pp. 152-56. Manov was a contributor to Ivan Ganchev's *Lach*. Todorov had
attended the first congress of Balkan Communist-controlled trade unions in November,
1920. See p. 225.

[37] See pp. 99-100.

[38] *Inprekorr*, VII, No. 23 (February 23, 1927); No. 37 (April 6, 1927); No. 43
(April 20, 1927); Kolarov, "Die Umgruppierung der Kräfte des Klassenkampfes im
Faschistischen Bulgarien," p. 704.

[39] Letter from Samnaliev published in *Osvobozhdenie* (Liberation), I, No. 5 (December 10, 1931).

[40] Vol. I, Nos. 2-5, of *Osvobozhdenie* are filed at the Internationaal Instituut voor
Sociale Geschiedenis in Amsterdam. They are dated March 15, April 25, September
10, and December 10, 1931. The irregularity of their appearance suggests that the
Trotskyist group was small and poor.

[41] Trotsky letter of October 17, 1931, in *Osvobozhdenie*, I, No. 5 (December 10,
1931), 6.

[42] *Osvobozhdenie*, I, No. 3 (April 25, 1931), 31.

[43] See pp. 99-100.

denounced as an imbecility[44] and the policy of political strikes as an invitation to the police to destroy the trade unions.[45] Here the Trotskyists' evaluation was less unrealistic than that of the Communist leadership at that time, but their belief that a "pure" proletarian policy would be more fruitful was utopian or meaningless.

Being a small minority within the Labor Party, the Trotskyists naturally demanded greater freedom to criticize the leadership of both the Labor Party and the Independent Trade Union Federation.[46] They proclaimed their faith in the soundness of the political intelligence of the ordinary Party activist were he only freed from the oppressive control of "political illiterates," "bureaucratic mandarins," and Stalinist "cretins." [47] The inevitable quotation from Lenin demanding criticism and self-criticism was cited.[48] Had the Trotskyists been in a majority, they would as easily have found a contrary, yet equally authoritative, passage in Lenin's writings.

The Bulgarian police made no distinction between the Trotskyists and Stalinists. *Osvobozhdenie* was permitted to be published, as was *Novini* (News), but activists of both persuasions were herded indiscriminately into the same prison compounds, with the result that fights and riots broke out in the jails. The Trotskyists, being fewer, got the worst of these clashes.[49] While the Trotskyists charged that Assen Boyajiev, chief of the Independent Trade Union Federation, was a traitor and a *provocateur*, the orthodox Communists accused Samnaliev of being a police spy.[50]

It was a foregone conclusion that the Trotskyists would lose out against the Communist leadership. They were few and poor. Trotsky's encouragement was no substitute for the Comintern's organizational and financial resources. The policies advocated by the Trotskyists were not sufficiently daring, original, or realistic to galvanize the workers to rally to them. The Left Marxist Opposition was soon wracked by the dissensions which appear to be inevitable in Trotskyist sects. Manov and Todorov quarreled, each took to publishing his

[44] *Osvobozhdenie*, I, No. 3 (April 25, 1931), 3.
[45] *Osvobozhdenie*, I, No. 4 (September 10, 1931), 5.
[46] *Osvobozhdenie*, I, No. 2 (March 15, 1931), 24-25.
[47] *Osvobozhdenie*, I, No. 3 (April 25, 1931), 3-4; No. 4, (September 10, 1931), 6.
[48] *Osvobozhdenie*, I, No. 4 (September 10, 1931), 14.
[49] *Osvobozhdenie*, I, No. 5 (December 10, 1931), 2.
[50] *Ibid.*, pp. 3, 22. Boyajiev was killed by the police on June 26, 1933.

own *Osvobozhdenie*, and the Bulgarian Trotskyist movement eroded away into insignificance.[51]

Having been reinstated to the leadership of the Bulgarian Communist Party by the Comintern in May, 1934, in consequence of Dimitrov's tour de force at the Reichstag fire trial in 1933 and the utter paralysis of the left sectarians in the face of Velchev's *coup d'état* of May 19, 1934,[52] Dimitrov and Kolarov proceeded to consolidate their control. The *émigrés* in the Soviet Union were first purged. In January, 1935, the Fifth Enlarged Plenum of the Central Committee of the Bulgarian Communist Party "exposed with ruthless bolshevik self-criticism the political and tactical mistakes committed by the Party leadership since 1933" and resolved to coopt new members to the Central Committee. It also replaced "social fascism" with "united frontism" as the Party policy.[53] A general meeting of Bulgarian political *émigrés* in Moscow sat from March 28 to April 3, 1935. Harangued on its opening day by Kolarov, who demanded a thorough overhaul of the apparatus,[54] it resolved to demote Rossen and Omirov-Bratanski, both left sectarians. Iskrov was still permitted to appear at the Seventh Comintern Congress in the summer of 1935. He made no mention of internal problems within the Bulgarian Communist Party and confined his remarks largely to general warnings against German imperialism. Unlike Kolarov and Krumov, he indulged in no breast beating for past sins.[55] He was purged at

[51] After the Second World War, Manov reappeared, surprisingly, as a functionary on the staff of the People's Courts of Communist Bulgaria. In March, 1950, he was sentenced to life imprisonment as a Trotskyist.

[52] After issuing a bombastic appeal for a general strike to overthrow Velchev, these left leaders subsided into inactivity. They then rationalized that the coup had liberated the masses from the illusion that the Peasant and Socialist Parties were significant political forces, that it had served to define more sharply the tasks of the Communist Party, and that it was simply a further instance of the bourgeoisie digging its own grave. See Kolarov, *Protiv lyavoto sektantstvo i Trotskizma v Balgaria*, p. 24. This evaluation was but a continuation of the social-fascist line which the Comintern was now preparing to jettison.

[53] "Enlarged Plenum of the C.C. of the C.P. of Bulgaria," *Inprecorr* (English edition), XV, No. 13 (March 23, 1935), 367.

[54] Kolarov's speech, "For a Decisive Turnabout in the Bulgarian Communist Party," is reprinted in his *Protiv lyavoto sektantstvo i Trotskizma v Balgaria*, pp. 11-78.

[55] Compare Iskrov's speech to the Seventh Comintern Congress with those of Krumov and Kolarov in *Inprecorr* (English edition), XVI, No. 3 (January 11, 1936), 80-81; XV, No. 52 (October 10, 1935), 1300-301; XV, No. 62 (November 21, 1935), 1537-40. At the Thirteenth ECCI Plenum of December, 1933, Iskrov had still denounced as a "right-wing opportunist" the trade-union leader Assen Boyajiev,

the Sixth Plenum of the Party Central Committee meeting in Moscow, February-March, 1936.[56] Boikov, who had returned to the USSR, probably in 1933, had suffered the same fate earlier.[57]

Now came the turn of the underground cadres in Bulgaria to be purged. Here a scramble to return to the right side of the fence had followed Dimitrov's triumph. Encho-Pavlov,[58] who had succeeded Boikov as leader of the underground Party, accepted the criticism of his policy of May 19, 1934, in the hope of surviving in a position of leadership.[59] This and other stratagems, such as sycophancy toward Dimitrov, were unavailing. In October, 1935, an "open letter" from the Central Committee in Moscow to all Communist Party cells had insisted on the complete liquidation of the left sectarian leadership[60] and in 1936, after the Sixth Plenum of the Central Committee in Moscow, a three-man punitive commission led by Traicho Kostov with Stanke Dimitrov (Marek) and Georgi Damyanov as assistants was authorized to purge the underground cadres in Bulgaria—a task which it executed with great thoroughness.[61]

---

who had warned that reaction was consolidating itself and had been killed by the police on June 26, 1933, after his expulsion from the Communist Party. See *Trinadtsati plenum IKKI: Stenograficheski otchet*, p. 543.

[56] "The Sixth Plenum of the C.C. of the C.P. of Bulgaria," *Inprecorr* (English edition), XVI, No. 25 (May 30, 1936), 684.

[57] The last appearance of Boikov's name is as a cosignatory of the obituary notice for Dimitrov's wife Lyuba, who died in Moscow on May 27, 1933.

[58] See pp. 288-89.

[59] Kolarov, *Protiv lyavoto sektantstvo i Trotskizma v Balgaria*, p. 128.

[60] "An Historical Letter from the C.P. of Bulgaria," *Inprecorr* (English edition), XV, No. 61 (November 16, 1935), 1516-17.

[61] Zhak Natan, "Vasil Kolarov i osnovite problemi na nashata istoria," p. 57. Kostov, one of the few underground leaders to side with Kolarov and Dimitrov in the intraparty quarrel, had escaped to the USSR in 1933. He was himself purged and executed in 1949. Marek had managed the Vitosha Conference of May, 1924, on behalf of Kolarov and Dimitrov. He died in April, 1944. Georgi Damyanov, having completed his underground work in Bulgaria, operated after 1937 as a functionary of the Foreign Bureau of the Central Committee of the Bulgarian Communist Party as well as of the ECCI. He helped to organize the International Brigade during the Spanish Civil War. In the Second World War, Damyanov served as an officer in the Soviet Army, having received his military training at the Frunze Academy in Moscow after his flight to the Soviet Union in 1925. He returned to Bulgaria after its conquest by the Soviet Army. A deputy to the Grand Sobranie in 1946, he served first on the commission that prepared the new draft constitution adopted by the Grand Sobranie on December 4, 1947, and later—November, 1946 - May, 1950—as Minister of Defense, becoming Chairman of the Presidium of the Sobranie in 1950. Elected to the Politburo of the Central Committee in 1954, he is not to be confused with Raiko Damyanov, his colleague on these two bodies. Georgi Damyanov died November 27, 1958.

Having won their political feud with left sectarianism, Kolarov and Dimitrov set about rewriting its history. The embarrassing question of how it was possible for a gang of alleged Trotskyist hyenas to retain the control of the Communist Party, the support of the rank-and-file, and the acquiescence of the Comintern for seven years had to be met. The answer was to claim that these wretches had deceived the Comintern by sending it false reports of Communist political fortunes within Bulgaria and had cheated the rank-and-file by passing to them distorted versions of Comintern directives.[62] In fact, of course, Iskrov, Boikov, Encho, Rossen, and their colleagues had fallen victim to the occupational hazards which every Communist leader faces—personal vendetta and an abrupt reversal of the political line. The latter they were not sufficiently nimble to anticipate. In the Stalinist doctrine every misjudgment was a sin; thus every change of policy required its scapegoat.

[62] Kolarov, "Some Lessons from the Struggle Against the Trotskyist Agents of Fascism," a speech delivered to a meeting of Bulgarian refugees in Moscow, June, 1937, and reprinted in *Protiv lyavoto sektantstvo i Trotskizma v Balgaria,* pp. 161-90.

CONCLUSION

The traditional attachment of the Bulgarian peasant to Russia accounted to a considerable degree for the toleration, if not support, which the Bulgarian masses extended to the Communists. Within the Communist Party, however, until the Second World War, this sentimental Panslavism was derided. Its main cultivators were, indeed, the conservative parties. The Bulgarian Communists were convinced adherents of Leninist doctrine, and they played a role out of all proportion to their numbers in the international Communist movement.

Of the three socialist mass parties which joined the Bolsheviks in the Comintern in 1919-20—the Italian, Norwegian, and Bulgarian Narrow ones—only the latter proved itself thoroughly "Leninist," an undeviating observer of the twenty-one conditions.[1] Indeed, when Moscow felt it necessary to purge the first two parties, it chose Bulgarian "executioners" for this task, despatching Kabakchiev with the Hungarian Rákosi to the Leghorn Congress in January, 1921,[2] and Kolarov together with Radek to Oslo in February, 1923.[3] Kabakchiev had learned the technique of splitting a socialist party when he had accompanied Zinoviev to the Congress of the Unabhängige Sozialdemokratische Partei Deutschlands (USPD) at Halle in October, 1920,[4] while Kolarov was in 1922 and 1923 the Comintern's roving envoy in Western Europe, participating also at congresses and conferences in Rome, Paris, Frankfurt, Leipzig, and Prague.[5] He was Secretary of the ECCI between the Fourth and Fifth Comintern Congresses, November, 1922—June,

---

[1] The Bulgarian General Trade Union Federation was also the only mass organization to affiliate with the International Trade Union Council at the time of its inception. See pp. 264-65.

[2] Kabakchiev, *Die Gründung der Kommunistischen Partei Italiens.*

[3] Kolarov, "Le Congrès du Parti Ouvrier Norvégien," *Le Bulletin communiste,* IV, No. 12 (March 22, 1923), 196-97.

[4] Karakolov, "Revolyutsionniat i tvorcheski pat na Khristo Kabakchiev," p. 209.

[5] *Vasil Kolarov: Important Dates of His Life and Work,* pp. 37-38; R. Fischer. *Stalin and German Communism,* p. 229.

1924, head of its Balkan Secretariat 1928-29, and a member of the Presidium until its dissolution on May 15, 1943. His colleague Georgi Dimitrov was elected a candidate-member of the ECCI at the Fifth Comintern Congress of June-July, 1924, and served as Secretary-General during the Comintern's last decade. Many other Bulgarians exercized important functions in the international Communist apparatus. Blagoev's daughter Stella, who is said to have been at one time the wife of the Sofia Cathedral dynamiter Kosta Yankov,[6] was in the 1930s the head of the Latin States Department of the Comintern's Cadres Section.[7] Many Bulgarian Communists served in Spain during the Civil War. Among them were Ferdinand Kozovski, who was to become Deputy War Minister and head of the Political Education Administration of the Bulgarian Army after the Communist seizure of power. A postwar president of the Fatherland Front, he was elected president of the Sobranie on January 17, 1950. Another Bulgarian active in Spain was a mysterious Lebedev-Stepanov ("Vanini") who apparently operated as a GPU spy and *agent provocateur* among anti-Stalinist opposition groups.[8] The Chief of Staff of the International Brigade, Colonel Belov, was a Bulgarian. He became a Soviet Army Cavalry Commander in the Second World War.[9] Apart from Comintern activities, 600 Bulgarians were at one time, according to *Pravda*, occupying important positions in the Soviet state administration.[10] The best known of these was Christian Rakovski, nephew of the Bulgarian revolutionary patriot Georgi Rakovski and a leading Soviet politician and diplomat, ultimately purged for Trotskyism. Stomonyakov, sometime Soviet Assistant Commissar for Foreign Affairs, was also a Bulgarian, as was Telalov, an adviser to the Soviet Mission to China in the 1920s.[11] Language, sentiment, irredentism, and the tradition, established by Blagoev and his colleagues, of peculiarly close relations between the Bulgarian and Russian Marxist movements, explain this unique trust reposed in the Bulgarian Commu-

---

[6] *La Fédération Balkanique*, III, No. 70-71 (July 1, 1927), 1376.

[7] Castro-Delgado, *J'ai perdu la foi à Moscou*, p. 23. After World War II she was Bulgarian ambassador to Moscow, where she died on February 16, 1954.

[8] Castro-Delgado, *J'ai perdu la foi à Moscou*, p. 27; Serge, *Mémoires d'un révolutionnaire*.

[9] K. Todorov, *Balkan Firebrand*, p. 283.

[10] Cited by Logio, *Bulgaria: Past and Present*, p. 363.

[11] *Ibid.*, p. 363.

nists by the Russian leaders. Among the most backward of European countries, Bulgaria produced international Communism's best bolsheviks.

Within Bulgaria, the ability of the Communists to survive persecution was a consequence of the moral erosion of the superficially imposing state machine. The top-heavy educational system produced more university graduates than the backward structure of the peasant society warranted. This intelligentsia despised the peasantry from which it sprang and scorned any occupation other than state service or politics, which became one of Bulgaria's leading industries.

The bureaucratic legacy of the country was inherited from the Turks, by whom the Bulgarians were the first of the Balkan Christian peoples to be conquered and from whom they were the last to be liberated. Corruption was a tradition. As the number of university-trained aspirants for state employment far exceeded the number of positions rationally available, the consequence was an inordinate swelling of a redundant bureaucratic apparatus. In 1931 there were seventeen government officials per thousand citizens in this peasant society.[12] The civil servant, poorly paid and convinced that his academic degree transformed him into a being infinitely superior to the lowly peasant, who in fact supported this rotten edifice, quickly taught the latter that the cumbersome bureaucratic machine must be lubricated with bribes. In addition, there was considerable diversion of public funds into the pockets of politicians and officials. Politics rivaled industry and commerce as sources of personal wealth. Idealistically-inclined young people turned in desperation to Communism.

Yet more disastrous, perhaps, than financial corruption was the contempt of these politicians and officials for the peasant masses whom they claimed to serve but in fact treated most callously. The venality and debasement of public life evoked cynicism on the part of the governed. The peasant came to regard the state as something separate from and hostile to himself and his interests. He knew that the inordinate proliferation of political parties, each attaching to itself a moralistic label like Liberal or Democratic, had no social substance and was based on no fundamentally diverging principles, that the parties were but syndicates to capture and exploit power.

[12] *Ibid.*, p. 43.

The Communists beat the drum of social justice and social revolution. The peasant, stagnating in underemployment and undernourishment in his overpopulated village, would have preferred a radical agrarian government like Stamboliski's, but he was not prepared, especially after many Peasant Union leaders had pushed their way to the political trough in 1931, to resist the capture of power by the Communists even if, or, perhaps, especially when, they were installed, as happened in 1944, by the relentless Grandfather Ivan—Russia.

APPENDIX

LABOR LEGISLATION AND LABOR ORGANIZATION
IN BULGARIA BEFORE THE FIRST WORLD WAR

Committed to a policy of rapid modernization, Bulgarian governments initiated a policy of encouraging and fostering the development of the country's industries. In 1889 the War Ministry decreed that all military uniforms were to be cut from domestic textiles, and in 1897 a largely abortive attempt was made to extend this policy to the dress of civil servants.[1] In 1894, under the National Party government of Stoilov, the Law for the Encouragement of Industry was enacted, under which industrial raw materials could be imported tariff-free and transported within Bulgaria to the factories at a 35 percent reduction in railway charges. New factories converting these materials into manufactured products were exempt from taxation during their first years. Foreign capitalists were thus encouraged to take advantage of Bulgaria's cheap labor to invest in the country. The growth of industries benefiting from this law justified the expectations of its drafters:[2]

Year	Factories Benefiting from the Law	Workers Employed	H. P. of Machines	Fixed Capital (in leva)	Annual Production (in leva)
1894	72	3,027	—	10,916,000	—
1900	103	4,716	—	19,823,000	—
1904	166	6,149	8,976	36,145,000	32,777,975
1907	206	7,646	—	53,961,900	41,552,000
1909	266	12,943	17,677	66,032,440	78,317,396
1911	345	15,886	27,885	91,098,000	122,512,000

Thus, in a little more than a decade and a half the number of factories and workers quintupled and the value of investment and production multi-

[1] Sakarov, *Die Industrielle Entwicklung Bulgariens*, p. 78.

[2] Ivan Sakazov, *Bulgarische Wirtschaftsgeschichte*, pp. 278-79. The benefits of this law of 1894, which came into force in January, 1905, could be claimed only by owners of factories employing more than 20 workers or with a fixed capital of more than 25,000 leva and in either case using mechanical power. Since Staneff, *Das Gewerbewesen und die Gewerbepolitik in Bulgarien,* p. 94, records on the basis of official statistics the existence of 501 nonartisanal industrial units employing 5,732 workers in 1894, it is obvious that there were more which did not meet these minimum standards than did. The above statistics do not, moreover, cover the state-owned railways. In 1909, about 22 percent of the capital invested in factories benefiting from the law was foreign.

Before the First World War the Bulgarian lev was equivalent at par to the French franc.

plied prodigiously. In fact, since the industrialists, to avoid higher tax assessments, tended to undervalue their investments, it is probable that they rose in value more rapidly than these figures suggest. The chief beneficiaries were the light consumer industries. Of the 15,886 workers employed in the encouraged industries in 1911, only 1,862, or 12 percent, were miners.[3] In the absence of heavy industry, most of the coal mined was used for heating, a fraction of it to drive locomotives, and none to fire steel furnaces.

Complementing the bounties on raw materials and subsidies for the mines were the tariffs on essential finished consumer products. These, together with the state monopolies for salt, matches, and cigarette paper, were responsible for the fact that already at the turn of the century the state's revenue from indirect taxation exceeded that from direct taxes.

The intent of the 1894 Law for the Encouragement of Industry with its premium on the larger enterprise, was to promote industrial development. The law, therefore, was incompatible with the attempts to protect the artisans. That the legislation of 1898 and 1901, allegedly designed to aid the artisans, became in effect a device to facilitate the exploitation of apprentice labor is not surprising. In 1908, when the Young Turks raised the Ottoman tariff on imported textiles from 7 to 11 percent ad valorem, the small textile manufacturers and the remaining artisan weavers were hit hard.[4] The modern mills easily hurdled this raised bar and in the following year exported 92 percent of their output, mostly to the Ottoman Empire.[5]

To meet the financial difficulties created by tax exemptions to successful manufacturers combined with the impoverishment of the peasants, the chief taxpayers, the government attempted in 1899 to impose a land tithe, an attempt which almost led to a revolution and did in fact provoke the founding of the Peasant Union.[6] Thenceforth the government resorted to Western European, especially French, loans which were used partly to finance railway development and partly to maintain the swollen bureaucracy. Some of the money sank into the political swamp. In these chaotic conditions the labor movement developed.

In the years 1902 and 1903 there occurred the first strikes involving hundreds rather than dozens of workers. Five hundred workers at a sugar refinery in Sofia and 600 girls in a Varna cotton mill who, a decade after the founding of the Socialist Party, had still not been organized by its quarreling ideologists into a trade union, struck for better conditions and higher wages, as did 600 textile workers in Sliven, 600 tobacco processors

[3] Ivan Sakazov, *Bulgarische Wirtschaftsgeschichte*, p. 279. It is also significant that in 1910 over 52 percent of the workers in the encouraged industries had been born of peasant parents (many of the others were sons of ruined artisans) and of these 38.7 percent had themselves actually been peasant cultivators before drifting into the towns to seek a livelihood in industry.

[4] Sidarov, "Die Revolutionäre Bewegung in Bulgarien," p. 523.

[5] Ivan Sakazov, *Bulgarische Wirtschaftsgeschichte,* p. 278.

[6] Logio, *Bulgaria: Past and Present,* p. 357.

of Khaskovo and the 150 streetcar drivers in the capital.[7] The government replied with decrees outlawing strikes by government employees, among whom were included the railway men and streetcar drivers, and with a law providing up to three years' imprisonment for the "ringleaders" of strikes.[8] The trade unions had in 1903 only 1,300 members,[9] many of them from the still semiartisan trades such as tailoring, smithing, printing, shoemaking.[10] Although these unions had been promoted by the Socialist Party, it is not unlikely that their members were more Luddite than Marxist in outlook.

The growth of the trade unions in the subsequent years followed a pattern similar to that of the Socialist Parties, as can be seen from the following membership figures:[11]

Year	Free Federation (Broad)	General Federation (Narrow)	"Proletarian" Federation (Liberal Socialist)	Total
1904	1,190	1,500	—	2,690
1905	1,670	1,460	—	3,130
1906	1,890	1,390	970	4,250
1907	1,880	1,690	1,180	4,750
1908	—	2,080	*	—

* Merged with Free Federation in June, 1908.

These figures, taken in conjunction with those on the growth of the government-encouraged industries, indicate that the total trade-union membership fluctuated roughly between 45 and 65 percent of the number of workers employed in those factories. Since, however, many of the trade-union members were employed in nonencouraged industries, such as printing and the surviving artisan trades, the unionized workers evidently formed only a fraction of all those employed in Bulgaria's few modern plants. The trade-union figures for 1906 and 1907 seem to suggest that in the first of these years the Proletarian unions of the Liberal Socialists drew their members mainly from the General Federation of the Narrow Party, from which their leaders had split away in protest against Blagoev's dictatorship over the workers,[12] while in 1907 their growth was at the expense of the Free Federation, with which they merged a year later. It is to be noted that the Proletarian Federation had in one year won the adherence of 25 percent of

[7] Tchitchovsky, The Socialist Movement in Bulgaria, p. 17.
[8] Bakalov, "Die Sozialdemokratische Bewegung in Bulgarien," p. 602.
[9] Assen Tsankov, "Der Sozialismus in Bulgarien," p. 627.
[10] Kabakchiev, Boshkovich, and Vatis, Kommunisticheskie Partii Balkanskikh Stran, p. 53.
[11] The table is extrapolated from Blagoev, "Die Sozialistische Arbeiterbewegung in Bulgarien," p. 566; Rainoff, Die Arbeiterbewegung in Bulgarien, p. 94, and the periodic "Rundschau" of the Sozialistische Monatshefte. The above statistics enumerate only paid-up members. For propaganda purposes the federations would pad their membership estimates with hundreds of sympathizers and lapsed members. Since the trade unions were weak and poor, it is quite likely that every strike and lockout resulted in the defection of members who could not pay their dues and that the turnover in membership was considerable.
[12] See pp. 38-39.

the unionized workers and when it fused with the Free Federation had about two thirds as many members as that body. The accelerated growth of both groups was a reflection of the increasing vehemence of industrial strife at this time.

In 1905 and 1906 a series of strikes erupted. Whether this was a repercussion of the Russian Revolution, as the Communists have claimed,[13] is difficult to demonstrate or to disprove conclusively, but it appears more likely that this convulsion, which undoubtedly had political overtones, was evoked more by the harsh, semidictatorial policies of the Liberal Petrov-Petkov government than by events in Russia. The movement began in mid-January, 1905, with a strike of printers in Sofia which dragged on for fifty-two days, ended in victory for the workers as their union was recognized and the workday reduced to eight and one-half hours, and was a feather in the Free Federation's cap.[14] This was the signal for strikes by tobacco, leather, shoe, textile, mine, arsenal, and railway depot workers, some of which were successful, like the two months' strike of the Sofia shoemakers whose working day was lowered from fourteen to twelve hours and wages raised 8-30 percent,[15] while others, like that of the Gabrovo leatherworkers, collapsed. The movement continued into 1906, and industrial strife became even more bitter when employers resorted to lockouts which often broke the strikes. The sheer enthusiasm of the workers could not compensate for their objective weakness.

The statistics are as follows:[16]

YEAR	STRIKES LED BY FREE FEDERATION (BROAD)			STRIKES LED BY GENERAL FEDERATION (NARROW)			STRIKES LED BY "PROLETARIAN" FEDERATION (LIBERAL SOCIALIST)			TOTAL STRIKES		
	Won	Lost	Total	Won	Lost	Total	Won	Lost	Total	Won	Lost	Total
1904	—	—	—	7	23	30	—	—	—	7	23	30
1905	11	8	19	12	35	47	—	—	—	23	43	66
1906	21	6	27	19	39	58	2	0	2	42	45	87
1907	22	8	30	29	54	83	2	0	2	53	62	115

The Narrow Socialist account[17] reports that between 1905 and 1909 their General Federation led 282 strikes of which 139 were "defensive" and 143 "offensive"—categories which distinguish strikes fought in protest against

[13] See, for example, Bazhenov, "Sentyabr'skoe vosstanie v Bolgarii," p. 254. Also Blagoeva, *Dimitrov: A Biography,* p. 22, and *Georgi Dimitrov: Short Biographical Notes,* p. 6.

[14] Rainoff, *Die Arbeiterbewegung in Bulgarien,* p. 96.

[15] Kazasov, *Burni godini: 1918-1944,* p. 549.

[16] From Rainoff, *Die Arbeiterbewegung in Bulgarien,* p. 94, and "Rundschau: Gewerkschaftsbewegung: Bulgarien," p. 1068. Only 676 strikers were involved in the 19 strikes led by the Free Federation in 1905—an indication of the weakness of the trade-union movement at the time. The most important strike was that of 264 Sofia printers.

[17] Blagoev, "Die Sozialistische Arbeiterbewegung in Bulgarien," p. 567.

proposed lowering of wages from those launched to support demands for higher pay. This official Narrow Socialist account then evaluates the results as successful in 63 cases and partially successful in 71, while 159 failed altogether. (This, however, adds up to 293 strikes and not 282.)

Certain conclusions can be drawn from these two sets of figures. Whereas the Broad-affiliated Free Federation usually won between two thirds and three quarters of its strikes, those organized by the Narrow-controlled General Federation were successful only in one quarter to one third of the cases. Blagoev sought to explain the poor performance of his organization by claiming the existence of a "lockout cartel" among the employers.[18] This argument does not account for the relative success of the rival Federation which was active in the same industries and among the same trades. The real reasons for the failure of the General Federation's strikes were probably poor preparation and excessive resort to the strike weapon, often without any hope of success. This is suggested by the figures showing that between 1905 and 1907 the General Federation called 188 strikes to the Free Federation's 76. Blagoev, Kirkov, and Dimitrov, the Narrow Socialist leaders in charge of trade-union questions, seem to have operated on the theory, which was adopted by the Communists in the 1920s, that the essential function of the strike weapon is not so much to achieve wage-and-hour benefits as to create an industrial *climat de combat* which can be utilized for political purposes; therefore the probability of success is not a consideration which must be weighed with great care before calling a strike. The purpose of creating this atmosphere of struggle was probably to smash the rival Free Federation. If the workers could be aroused to a high pitch of belligerence by frequent, sharp, industrial struggles they would, Blagoev reasoned, then desert the cautious Free Federation for the militant General Federation. If this was indeed his aim—and it is difficult to detect an alternative explanation for the storm of semipolitical strikes unleashed in the years immediately following the socialist schism—he failed to take into account the psychological effect upon the workers of the long series of lost strikes which he imposed upon them. In any event, the Free Federation was not shattered. That its destruction was Blagoev's primary aim—his obsession, one might say—is indicated by the questionable tactics of the Narrow leaders in the railway men's and printers' strikes of 1907.

From May, 1903, to January, 1908, the Liberal Party was in power. It sought to entrench itself permanently through control of the state machinery. Permanency of tenure of civil servants was abolished, the opposition parties were harried, corruption stimulated, and all government employees forbidden to strike. Included in this last category were the railway men, closely associated with the Broad Socialist leaders. In protest against this strike-prohibiting decree and in support of demands for better working conditions, an eight-hour day, and an end to corruption, all railway workers and staff

[18] *Ibid.*, p. 568. In 1909 there were ten lockouts, the most important of which were those of 800 Sliven textile workers and of an equal number of Pernik miners. In neither case was the trade union smashed.

employees—about 3,400 men—struck on December 20, 1906/January 2, 1907. The railway men's organizations affiliated with the Free and Proletarian Federations as well as the nonpolitical union of staff employees formed a joint committee to direct the strike. The government decided upon ruthless countermeasures. Though it was midwinter, about 25 percent of the workers' families were evicted from their state-owned houses and the entire railway labor force of military age was called to the colors to run the trains under army control. The men resorted to "working to rule," [19] and in this way dragged out the paralysis of the transport system for forty-two days, at the end of which the government was forced to accept a compromise.[20] In the course of the strike the three railway men's organizations merged into one, under Broad Socialist influence, and began publishing a single strike paper.[21]

The Narrow Party was caught by this strike in a dilemma. To join the rival "traitor" groups under a united leadership was unthinkable for Blagoev but to break the strike was equally out of the question. The Narrow Socialists announced that their General Federation would support the strike out of a sense of duty to proletarian solidarity but that they suspected the political motives of the strike leaders, who were allegedly tools of the bourgeois opposition, and reserved the right to criticize tactics and results. This equivocation, which resembled the later Communist tactic in the European Popular Front era of the mid-1930s, earned Blagoev a special vote of condemnation by the strikers.[22] He then asserted that the railway men were only being used as tools by Sakazov and Malinov in the campaign to overthrow the Liberal government, a campaign which reached its culmination early in 1907 with the jeering by the students of Prince Ferdinand, the subsequent closing of the Sofia University, and the assassination of Prime Minister Petkov.[23] Blagoev's affectation of outrage at the alleged manipulation of the labor movement for political purposes was not without irony. When it made no impression on the workers, he tried to explain away both the strike and his evasive conduct toward it with the flimsy assertion that the entire affair had been but a provocation on the part of the Director of Railways and his chief assistants to blackmail the government into raising their own salaries.[24] Such feeble excuses availed little. Instead of smashing the Broad Socialists' trade-union federation, Blagoev's party lost the confidence of the railway men, never to regain it.

[19] Bakalov, "Die Sozialdemokratische Bewegung in Bulgarien," p. 602.
[20] Rainoff, *Die Arbeiterbewegung in Bulgarien,* p. 98.
[21] Such cooperation culminated in June, 1908, in the merger of the Proletarian with the Free Federation, followed shortly thereafter by the fusion of the Broad Socialist, Liberal Socialist, and Progressive Socialist Parties.
[22] Manoff, "Ce qui se passe en Bulgarie," p. 258.
[23] See p. 37.
[24] Blagoev, "Die Sozialistische Arbeiterbewegung in Bulgarien," p. 570. In later Communist interpretations Blagoev is severely reproached for his inept handling of this strike. See, for example, Tsonev and Vladimirov, *Sentyabr'skoe vosstanie v Bolgarii 1923 goda,* p. 17.

The Narrow Socialists again resorted to similar shabby tactics in a printers' strike shortly afterwards. Here their resentment against the rival organizations and their determination to destroy them were revealed even more sharply. In November, 1906, the Free (Broad) and Proletarian (Liberal Socialist) trade unions had agreed to wage a joint campaign for the extension of social legislation and the abolition of the reactionary and abused law to protect artisan industry. An invitation to the General (Narrow) unions to join in this united effort was declined, though Narrow Socialist propaganda was constantly making the same demands. Some weeks later a strike broke out among the printers and typographers, the majority of whom were affiliated with the Free Federation. The Narrow Socialists, in what they thought was a subtle maneuver, suggested the formation of a united strike front, but this time the Broad leaders, still resenting the previous spiteful tactics of their rivals, refused to dignify the small group of printers adhering to the Narrow Party with coresponsibility for and coleadership of the strike. The latter, led by Georgi Dimitrov, thereupon turned strikebreakers and returned to work.[25] Earlier, in 1906, Dimitrov had been active as a labor organizer and agitator during the strike of Pernik miners but had been forced to accept defeat when, after thirty-five days, the strike collapsed.[26]

With the fall of the Liberal government in January, 1908, the political overtones of the strike wave faded. The Sliven textile workers' strike of 1908, that of the Kostenets match workers in 1909, both of which lasted three months, as well as those of the Plakalnitsa ore and Plovdiv tobacco workers in 1910, were strictly economic in cause and aim. It was in the organization of such "wage-and-hour" struggles that Dimitrov's competence as an organizer and agitator revealed itself.

[25] Bakalov, "Die Sozialdemokratische Bewegung in Bulgarien," p. 602.
[26] Rainoff, *Die Arbeiterbewegung in Bulgarien*, p. 97.

BIBLIOGRAPHY

Aleksandri, L. N. God uzhasov belogo terrora v Bolgarii (A Year of the Horrors of White Terror in Bulgaria). Moscow, 1924.

American Labor Year Book, The. New York, 1916-32.

Ancel, Jacques. La Macédoine: Etude de colonisation contemporaine. Paris, 1930.

––––– "La Politique bulgare: Union Paysanne et Entente Démocratique," Le Monde slave, May, 1926, pp. 294-306.

"Après le révolte communiste," Selections de la presse bulgare, 5. Sofia, 1923.

Army of Resistance in Bulgaria, The. Sofia, 1946.

Arnaudov, M. "Bulgariens nationale Wiedergeburt," Osteuropa, XII (July 12, 1937), 613-26.

Avramov, R. "Der Zehnte Kongress der Sozialdemokratischen Arbeiterpartei Bulgariens," Die Neue Zeit, XXII, No. 7 (November 14, 1903), 205-10.

B. "Die Kommunistische Bewegung in Bulgarien," Die Kommunistische Internationale, No. 11 (1920), 126-45.

B., G. "Shiroki Sotsialisti ili Obshtodeltsi" (Broad Socialists or Common Cause-Makers), Rabotnichesko delo (Workers' Action), II, No. 10 (October, 1904), 581-87.

Bad, A. "Illegale kommunistische Zeitschriften auf dem Balkan," Die Kommunistische Internationale, VII, No. 15 (October 25, 1926), 278-79.

Bading, H. "Das Agrarproblem des Donaugebiets," Sozialistische Monatshefte, XXXVIII (July 1, 1932), 593-97.

Bakalov, Georgi. "G. V. Plekhanov v Bolgarii" (G. V. Plekhanov in Bulgaria), Letopisi Marksizma (Annals of Marxism), V (1928), 45-55.

––––– "Die Sozialdemokratische Bewegung in Bulgarien," Die Neue Zeit, XXV, No. 18 (January 30, 1907), 596-603.

––––– "Staraya 'Iskra' sredi Bolgar" (The Old Iskra Among the Bulgarians), Proletarskaya revolyutsia (Proletarian Revolution), No. 91-92 (1929), pp. 67-95.

Balabanoff, Angelica. Erinnerungen und Erlebnisse. Berlin, 1927.

––––– "Die Zimmerwalder Bewegung," in Archiv für die Geschichte des Sozialismus und der Arbeiterbewegung, XII, 310-413; XIII, 232-84.

Balgarskata Komunisticheska Partia v Rezolyutsii i Reshenia. II. 1919-23 (The Bulgarian Communist Party in Resolutions and Decisions. Vol. II. 1919-23). Sofia, 1951.

Balgarskata Rabotnicheska Sotsialdemokraticheska Partia, XXXIII Redoven Kongres. Otchet na Tsentralnia Komitet (The Bulgarian Social Democratic Labor Party, XXXIII Regular Congress. Report of the Central Committee). Sofia, 1930.

Balkanicus. The Aspirations of Bulgaria. London, 1915.

Balkanski, P. Revolyutsia v selo (Revolution in the Village). Plevna, 1932.

Balugdgitsch, Zivoin. "Die Oekonomischen Ursachen der Gährung in Makedonien," Die Neue Zeit, XIX, No. 10 (December 8, 1900), 292-301.

—— "Saloniki und die Makedonische Frage," Die Neue Zeit, XVI, No. 38 (June 18, 1898), 368-72.

Barker, Elisabeth. Macedonia: Its Place in Balkan Power Politics. Royal Institute of International Affairs Publication. London, 1950.

Basch, Antonin. The Danube Basin and the German Economic Sphere. New York, 1943.

Bashmakov [B——off], A. Mémoire sur le mouvement communiste en Bulgarie durant les années 1921 et 1922. Belgrade [1923?].

Basler Rundschau. Basel, 1932-39.

Bazhenov, L. "Sentyabr'skoe vosstanie v Bolgarii" (The September Insurrection in Bulgaria), Istorik Marksist (Marxist Historian), No. 26-27 (1932), pp. 253-92.

Bell, H. T. Montague, ed. The Near East Year Book. London, 1927; 1931-32.

Benaroya, Abraham. "Die Türkische Gewerkschaftsbewegung," Sozialistische Monatshefte, XIV, No. 16-18 (August 11, 1910), 1079-81.

Berdyaev, N. The Origin of Russian Communism. London, 1937.

"Bericht der K.P. Bulgariens," Die Kommunistische Internationale, No. 15 (1921), pp. 466-74.

"Berichte des Z.K. der K.P. Bulgariens; Berichte des Z.K. des Kommunistischen Jugendverbandes Bulgariens," Die Kommunistische Internationale, XIII, No. 5 (March 10, 1932), 411-13.

Berlin, Isaiah. Karl Marx: His Life and Environment. 2d ed. London, 1948.

"Beschluss des Z.K. der K.P. Bulgariens zur Erklärung der Genossen Popoff und Taneff," Die Kommunistische Internationale, XVI, No. 21 (December 30, 1935), 1886-88.

Besedovski, G. Im Dienste der Sowjets. Leipzig, 1930.

Birman, M. A. "Narastanie revolyutsionnoi situatsii v Bolgarii v 1917-1918gg. i Vladaiskoe Vosstanie" (The Growth of the Revolutionary Situation in Bulgaria in 1917-1918 and the Vladaya Insurrection), Uchenie Zapiski Instituta Slavyanovedenia (Scientific Papers of the Institute of Slavistics), V (1952), 5-77.

Black, C. E. The Establishment of Constitutional Government in Bulgaria. Princeton, 1943.

—— "The Influence of Western Political Thought in Bulgaria," American Historical Review, XLVIII (April, 1943), pp. 507-20.

Blagoev, Dimitar. Kratki belezhki iz moya zhivot (Short Notes from My Life). Sofia, 1945.

—— "Po vaprosa za organizatsiata na Partia" (To the Question of the Organization of a Party), *Novo vreme* (New Time), No. 2 (1906).

—— Prinos kam istoriata na sotsializma v Balgaria (Contribution to the History of Socialism in Bulgaria). Sofia, 1949 (first published in Sofia in 1906).

—— [Bratanov, D.] Shto e sotsializam i ima li toi pochva u nas? (What Is Socialism and Do We Have a Basis for It [i.e., in Bulgaria]?). Tirnovo, 1891.

—— "Die Sozialistische Arbeiterbewegung in Bulgarien," *Die Neue Zeit,* XXVIII, No. 16 (January 14, 1910), 563-71.

—— "Yambolskia partien kongres i negovit reshenia" (Yambol Party Congress and Its Decisions), *Novo vreme* (New Time), XI, No. 9 (September, 1908).

Blagoeva, Stella. Dimitrov: A Biography. London, 1935.

Bogart, Ernest L. Direct and Indirect Costs of the Great World War. No. 24 of Preliminary Economic Studies of the War, published for the Carnegie Endowment for International Peace. New York, 1919.

Borkenau, Franz. The Communist International. London, 1938.

—— Der Europäische Kommunismus. Bern, 1952.

Boshkovich, B., *see* Kabakchiev, Khristo, B. Boshkovich, and C. Vatis.

Bourchier, J. D. "Alexander Stambolisky," *The Contemporary Review,* No. 660 (December, 1920), 784-89.

Brailsford, H. N. Macedonia: Its Races and their Future. London, 1906.

Bratanov, D., *see* Blagoev, Dimitar.

Buchan, John, ed. The Nations of Today: Bulgaria and Romania. London, 1924.

Bulatsei', A. Ocherki sotsial'no politicheskoi zhizni sovremennoi Bolgarii (Sketches of the Social-Political Life of Contemporary Bulgaria). Moscow, 1925.

Bulgare, Ein. "Die Gewitterwolken in Bulgarien," *Die Neue Zeit,* XXVI, No. 17 (January 25, 1908), 586-91.

Bulgares parlent au monde, Les. Paris, 1949.

Bulgaria and the Balkan Problems. Sofia, 1934.

Bulgaria: Basic Handbook. London, 1943.

Bulgarie: Nouvelle Espagne, La. Paris, 1948.

Bulgarie sous le régime de l'assassinat, La. Représentation de l'Union Paysanne Bulgare à l'Etranger. Paris, 1925.

Bulletin communiste, Le. Paris, 1920-24.

Carr, Edward Hallett. The Bolshevik Revolution, 1917-1923. 3 vols. London, 1951-53.

—— The Interregnum, 1923-1924. New York, 1954.

—— Michael Bakunin. London, 1937.

Castro Delgado, E. J'ai perdu la foi à Moscou. Paris, 1950.

Chilingirov, Stilian. Balgarski chitalishta predi osvobozhdenieto: Prinos kam istoriata na Balgarskoto vazrazhdane (Bulgarian Reading Rooms before the

Liberation: A Contribution to the History of the Bulgarian Renaissance). Sofia, 1930.

Christidès, C. Le Camouflage macédonien. Athens, 1949.

Christowe, Stoyan. Heroes and Assassins. London, 1935.

Collins, J. W. "Bulgaria," *The Slavonic Review*, III, No. 9 (March, 1925), 704-12.

Communism and the International Situation. Theses Adopted at the Sixth World Congress of the Communist International. London, 1928.

Communist International Between the Fifth and Sixth World Congresses, 1924-1928, The. London, 1928.

Conditions of Peace with Bulgaria: Observations of the Bulgarian Delegation. Paris, 1919.

Conspiration bolchéviste contre la Bulgarie, La. Sofia, 1925.

Danilov, J. "Les Tentatives de constitution d'un bloc balkanique en 1914-15," *Le Monde slave*, May, 1928, pp. 201-29; June, 1928, pp. 352-78.

Dedijer, Vladimir. Tito Speaks. London, 1953.

Dellin, L. A. D. Bulgaria. New York, 1957.

Denkoff, R. "Le Huitième Congrès National du Parti Ouvrier Social Démocrate Bulgare," *Le Mouvement socialiste*, No. 69 (November 1, 1901), pp. 567-72.

—— "La Lutte de la social démocratie bulgare contre l'opportunisme," *Le Mouvement socialiste*, No. 124 (July 15, 1903), 435-46.

Dilovska, Elena. "Borbata sreshtu voenno-fashistkia prevrat na 9 Yuni 1923 v Plevenski Okrag" (The Struggle Against the Military-Fascist *Coup d'Etat* on June 9, 1923, in the Plevna District), *Izvestia na Instituta za Balgarska Istoria* (News of the Institute for Bulgarian History), Vol. 3-4 (1951), 63-84.

Dimitrov, Georgi. "Der Balkan-Donau Gewerkschaftskongress," *Kommunismus*, I, No. 46 (December 14, 1920), 1682-86.

—— "Beschlüsse des Ersten Gewerkschaftskongresses der Balkan-Donauländer," *Die Kommunistische Internationale*, No. 16 (1921), pp. 354-62.

—— "The Bulgarian Communist Party and the Communist International," *The Communist International*, New Series, No. 1 (April, 1924), pp. 191-92.

—— "The European War and the Labour Movement in the Balkans," *The Communist International*, New Series, No. 5 (September-October, 1924), pp. 93-103.

—— "Die Gewerkschaftliche Bewegung in Bulgarien," *Die Kommunistische Internationale*, No. 15 (1921), pp. 324-31.

—— Der Kampf um Arbeiterschutz in Bulgarien. Sofia, 1912.

—— "Der Kampf um die Gewerkschaftseinheit in Bulgarien," *Die Kommunistische Internationale*, VII, No. 11 (September 24, 1926), 86-91.

—— "Die Kommunistische Internationale und die K.P. Bulgariens," *Die Kommunistische Internationale*, No. 30-31 (1924), pp. 135-36.

—— "Die Lage auf dem Balkan und die Aufgaben der Kommunistischen

Balkanföderation," *Die Kommunistische Internationale*, VI, No. 7 (July, 1925), 741-60.

—— "Die National-Revolutionäre Bewegung auf dem Balkan und die Aufgaben der Kommunistischen Parteien des Balkans," *Die Kommunistische Internationale*, IX, No. 43 (October 24, 1928), 2625-33.

—— Oeuvres choisies. Paris, 1952.

—— Politicheski otchet na Ts.K. na BRP(k) pred 5. Kongres na BRP(k) (Political Report of the Central Committee of the Bulgarian Labor Party [Communist] before the Fifth Congress of the Bulgarian Labor Party [Communist]). Sofia, 1948.

—— The United Front. London, 1938.

—— *see also* Georgi Dimitrov; G. M. Dimitrov; *and* Vydayushchisya.

Dimitrova, E. and V. Filipova. "Iz deinostta na Komunistite v Parlamenta sled Septemvriiskoto Vastanie" (From the Activity of the Communists in Parliament after the September Insurrection), *Istoricheski pregled* (Historical Review), XII, No. 1 (1956), 59-74.

Dimker. "La Crise socialiste en Bulgarie," *Le Mouvement socialiste*, No. 136 (May 15, 1904), pp. 65-76.

Drakoules, Platon E. "Greece, the Balkans, and the Federal Principle," *The Asiatic Review*, VI (February 15, 1915), 113-33.

Dritter Kongress der Sozialistischen Arbeiter-Internationale. Brussels, 5. - 11. August 1928. Zürich, 1928.

Dvadeset i peta godishninata na Septemvriiskoto vastanie (The 25th Anniversary of the September Insurrection). Sofia, 1948.

Ein Bulgare, *see* Bulgare, Ein.

Eleventh Plenum of the E.C.C.I., The. April, 1931. Theses, Resolutions and Decisions. London [1931?].

"Entrée en guerre de la Bulgarie, L'," *Le Monde slave*, April, 1929, pp. 115-44; May, 1929, pp. 275-301; July, 1929, pp. 109-34; August, 1929, pp. 269-302.

"Entwurf des Statuts der Kommunistischen Balkanföderation," *Die Kommunistische Internationale*, No. 17 (1921), pp. 434-37.

Epoche Liaptscheff, Die: Die Entwicklung des Bulgarischen Faschismus. Berlin, 1927.

"Ereignisse auf dem Balkan und die Aussichten der Arbeiter- und Bauernrevolution, Die," *Die Kommunistische Internationale*, VI, No. 2 (February, 1925), 180-94.

"Erklärung der Genossen Popoff und Taneff über ihre Haltung vor dem Leipziger Gericht, Die," *Die Kommunistische Internationale*, XVI, No. 21 (December 30, 1935), 1885-86.

Erste Kongress der Kommunistischen Internationale, Der. Protokoll der Verhandlungen in Moskau vom 2. bis zum 19. März 1919. Hamburg, 1921.

"Exekutive der Kommunistischen Internationale an den Kongress der Kommunistischen Partei Bulgariens, Die," *Die Kommunistische Internationale*, No. 17 (1921), pp. 421-23.

Fainsod, Merle. International Socialism and the World War. Cambridge, Mass., 1935.

Fédération balkanique, La. Vienna, 1924-31.

Fischer, Louis. The Soviets in World Affairs. 2 vols. London, 1930.

Fischer, Ruth. Stalin and German Communism. Cambridge, Mass., 1948.

Fisher, H. H., see Gankin, Olga Hess and H. H. Fisher.

Fournol, E. "L'Europe centrale et l'Hitlerisme," *Le Monde slave*, June, 1934, pp. 321-46.

From the Fourth to the Fifth World Congress: Report of the Executive Committee of the Communist International. London, 1924.

Fünfter Kongress der Kommunistischen Internationale: Protokoll. Hamburg, 1924.

Gankin, Olga Hess and H. H. Fisher. The Bolsheviks and the World War: The Origin of the Third International. Stanford, 1940.

G. B., see B., G.

Genadiev, N. "Rapport sur la position à prendre par la Bulgarie," *Le Monde slave*, September, 1936, pp. 407-34.

Genov, Gavril, see Tsonev, G.

Gentizon, Paul. Le Drame bulgare: De Ferdinand de Bulgarie à Stamboulisky. Paris, 1924.

—— "Stamboulisky et le peuple bulgare," *La Revue de France*, III, No. 19 (October 1, 1923), 593-608.

"Georg Kirkov" [obituary], *Die Kommunistische Internationale*, No. 14 (1920), 330-33.

Georgi Dimitrov: Short Biographical Notes. Sofia, 1946.

Georgi Dimitrov: A Short Biographical Sketch. Sofia, 1948.

Georgiev, Petar. "Rolyata i znachenieto na vestnik *Rabotnik* v istoriata na partiata i na rabotnicheskoto dvizhenie u nas" (The Role and the Significance of the Newspaper *Worker* in the History of Our Party and Labor Movement), *Istoricheski pregled* (Historical Review), IX, No. 1 (1953), 78-88.

G. M. Dimitrov. Moscow, 1949.

Gibb, H. A. R. and H. Bowen. Islamic Society and the West. Royal Institute of International Affairs Publication. London, (Vol. I, Pt. I) 1950; (Vol. I, Pt. II) 1957.

Gopčević, Spiridon. Bulgarien und Ostrumelien: Mit besonderer Berücksichtigung des Zeitraumes von 1878-1886 nebst militärischer Würdigung des Serbo-Bulgarischen Krieges. Leipzig, 1886.

Grogan, Lady Ellinor F. B. "Bulgaria under Prince Alexander," *The Slavonic Review*, I, No. 3 (March, 1923), 561-71.

—— "The Bulgarian Aspect of the Near East Question," *Journal of the British Institute of International Affairs*, II, No. 1 (January, 1923), 35-37.

Grünberg, Carl. Die Internationale und der Weltkrieg. Leipzig, 1916.

Handelsman, Marcel. "La Guerre de Crimée, la question polonaise, et les origines du problème bulgare," *Revue historique,* CLXIX (March-April, 1932), 271-315.

"Helft dem heroischen Proletariat Bulgariens," *Die Kommunistische Internationale,* XVI, No. 6 (March 20, 1935), 513-16.

Herb, M. Südosteuropa: Form und Forderung. Paris, 1938.

Hodža, Milan. Federation in Central Europe: Reflections and Reminiscences. London, 1942.

Howard, H. N., *see* Kerner, R. J. and H. N. Howard.

Inprecorr, see International Press Correspondence.

Inprekorr, see Internationale Presse-Korrespondenz.

Internationale Gewerkschaftsbewegung in den Jahren 1924-1927, Die: Bericht des Vollzugsbüros der Roten Gewerkschafts-Internationale an den Vierten Kongress in Moskau am 15. März 1928. Moscow, 1928.

International Press Correspondence [Inprecorr]. Vienna, London, 1923, 1930-38.

Internationale Presse-Korrespondenz [Inprekorr]. Berlin, Vienna, 1921-1936?

Iskrov, P. "Eine Neue Welle des weissen Terrors in Bulgarien," *Die Kommunistische Internationale,* XII, No. 40 (November 25, 1931), 1838-44.

—— "Sowjetfeindlicher Block unter der Flagge einer 'Balkanföderation'," *Die Kommunistische Internationale,* XI, No. 36 (September 24, 1930), 1964-72.

Istoria Bolgarii (History of Bulgaria). Vol. II. Publication of the Academy of Sciences of the USSR. Moscow, 1955.

Judasrolle der bulgarischen Sozialdemokratie, Die. Vienna, 1925.

Kabakchiev, Khristo. "Balgaria v Pervata Imperialisticheska Voina" (Bulgaria in the First Imperialist War), *Istoricheski pregled* (Historical Review), IV, No. 1 (1947), 40-56.

—— "Der Balkan am Vorabend der Revolution," *Die Kommunistische Internationale,* No. 16 (1921), pp. 96-103.

—— "Die Balkanpolitik der Entente," *Die Kommunistische Internationale,* No. 21 (1922), pp. 112-17.

—— "Dmitri Blagoev i bolgarskie Tesnyaki" (Dimitar Blagoev and the Bulgarian Narrows), *Istorik Marksist* (Marxist Historian), No. 44 (1935), pp. 31-57.

—— "Dmitri Nikolaevich Blagoev, 1855-1924," *Letopisi Marksizma* (Annals of Marxism), XI (1930), 54-66.

—— "Bulgarien nach dem Imperialistischen Kriege," *Die Kommunistische Internationale,* No. 14 (1921), pp. 155-64.

—— "Die Ereignisse in Bulgarien," *Die Kommunistische Internationale,* No. 28-30 (1923), pp. 74-103.

—— "Für die Arbeiter- und Bauernregierung in Bulgarien," *Die Internationale,* VI, No. 11 (June 1, 1923), 345-52.

—— "Fürstenbund oder Balkanrepublik?," *Die Neue Zeit,* XXXI, No. 9 (November 29, 1912), 311-20.

—— "Glavnie etapi i osobennosti razvitia fashizma v Bolgarii" (The Principal Stages and Peculiarities of the Development of Fascism in Bulgaria), *Istorik Marksist* (Marxist Historian), No. 58 (1936), pp. 44-67.

—— Die Gründung der Kommunistischen Partei Italiens. Hamburg, 1921.

—— "Lenin i bolgarskie Tesnyaki" (Lenin and the Bulgarian Narrows), *Istorik Marksist* (Marxist Historian), No. 35 (1934), pp. 173-88.

—— "Die Nationale- und die Agrarfrage auf dem Balkan," *Die Kommunistische Internationale,* IX, No. 27-28 (July 11, 1928), 1618-35; No. 29-30 (July 25, 1928), 1775-88; No. 31-32 (August 1, 1928), 1946-61.

—— "Die Neuen Ereignisse auf dem Balkan," *Die Internationale,* III, No. 1 (1921), 5-10.

—— "Der Septemberaufstand in Bulgarien," *Die Kommunistische Internationale,* VIII, No. 40 (October 5, 1927), 1965-73; No. 43 (October 26, 1927), 2118-26.

—— "Der Weg zur Kommunistischen Internationale," *Die Kommunistische Internationale,* X, No. 9-11 (March 13, 1929), 616-27.

Kabakchiev, Khristo, B. Boshkovich, and C. Vatis. Kommunisticheskie Partii Bakanskikh Stran (The Communist Parties of the Balkan Countries). Moscow, 1930.

Kabakchiev, Khristo and R. K. Karakolov. "Bolgaria v Pervoi Mirovoi Imperialisticheskoi Voine" (Bulgaria in the First World Imperialistic War), *Istorik Marksist* (Marxist Historian), No. 89 (1941), pp. 58-72.

—— *see also* Trotsky, Leon D. and Khristo Kabakchiev.

Kaltscheff, Kaltscho. Die Bulgarische Zollpolitik seit 1878. Nürnberg, 1912.

Karakolov, R. K. "Kharakterni momenti ot borbata na Balgarskata Rabotnicheska Partia—Komunisti" (Characteristic Moments from the Struggle of the Bulgarian Labor Party—Communists), *Istoricheski pregled* (Historical Review), V, No. 2 (1948), 129-56.

—— "Revolyutsionniat i tvorcheski pat na Khristo Kabakchiev" (The Revolutionary and Creative Path of Khristo Kabakchiev), *Istoricheski pregled* (Historical Review), IV, No. 2 (1947), 194-213.

—— *see also* Kabakchiev, Khristo and R. K. Karakolov.

Kautsky, Karl. "Der Baseler Kongress und die Kriegshetze in Oesterreich," *Die Neue Zeit,* XXXI, No. 10 (December 6, 1912), 337-46.

—— "Der Krieg und die Internationale," *Die Neue Zeit,* XXXI, No. 6 (November 8, 1912), 185-93.

—— "Die Nationalen Aufgaben der Sozialisten unter den Balkanslawen," *Der Kampf,* II, No. 3 (December 1, 1908), 105-10.

Kazasov, Dimo. Burni godini: 1918-1944 (Stormy Years: 1918-44). Sofia, 1949.

—— Political Bulgaria between 1913 and 1944. Sofia, 1945.

—— V tamnite na zagovora (In the Gloom of Conspiracy). Sofia, 1925.

Kennedy, A. L. "A Peasant Statesman: Alexander Stambulisky," *The Fort-*

nightly Review, New Series, DCLXXX (August 1, 1923), 177-86.

Kerner, R. J. and H. N. Howard. The Balkan Conferences and the Balkan Entente, 1930-35. Berkeley, Calif., 1936.

Kheimo, M., *see* Tivel', A. and M. Kheimo.

Khristov, Khristo. "Dimitar Blagoev—Osnovatel na Balgarskata nauchna istoriografia" (Dimitar Blagoev—Founder of the Bulgarian Scientific Historiography), *Izvestia na Instituta za Balgarska Istoria* (News of the Institute for Bulgarian History), I-II (1951), 8-36.

—— "Laiptsigskiat protsess i otzvukat mu v Balgaria" (The Leipzig Trial and Its Echo in Bulgaria), *Istoricheski pregled* (Historical Review), IX, No. 2 (1953), 156-79.

Kibalchich, Viktor Lvovich, *see* Serge, Victor.

Kirshevskaya, A. N. "Padenie pravitel'stva Zemledel'cheskogo Soyuza v Bolgarii" (The Downfall of the Government of the Peasant Union in Bulgaria), *Uchenie Zapiski Instituta Slavyanovedenia* (Scientific Papers of the Institute of Slavistics), XI (1955), 63-118.

—— "Reformi pravitel'stva Zemledel'cheskogo Soyuza v Bolgarii i ikh krakh" (The Reforms of the Government of the Peasant Union in Bulgaria and their Failure), *Uchenie Zapiski Instituta Slavyanovedenia* (Scientific Papers of the Institute of Slavistics), X (1954), 5-71.

Klincharov, Ivan. Dimitr Blagoev. Sofia, 1926.

Kolarov, Vasil. "Der 'Agrarismus' als Theorie des 'Sozialen Friedens'," *Die Kommunistische Internationale,* IX, No. 22 (May 30, 1928), 1231-40.

—— "Bauernparteien und Verbände," *Die Kommunistische Internationale,* VI, No. 3 (March, 1925), 257-71.

—— "Ein Beitrag Zur Geschichte der Agrarthesen des Zweiten Weltkongresses," *Die Kommunistische Internationale,* IX, No. 47-48 (November 28, 1928), 2918-21.

—— "Der Brandherd des Balkans," *Die Kommunistische Internationale,* VII, No. 18 (November 16, 1926), 387-97.

—— "Dimitry Blagojew — der Gründer und Führer der Bulgarischen K.P.," *Die Kommunistische Internationale,* No. 34-35 (1924), pp. 197-204.

—— "Die Komintern und das Revolutionäre Bündniss der Arbeiter und Bauern," *Die Kommunistische Internationale,* X, No. 9-11 (March 13, 1929), 555-74.

—— "Die K.P. und die politische Lage Bulgariens," *Die Kommunistische Internationale,* No. 17 (1921), pp. 437-48.

—— "The National Question in the Balkans," *The Communist International,* New Series, No. 4 (July-August, 1924), pp. 78-85.

—— "Die Perspektiven des Klassenkampfes in Bulgarien," *Die Kommunistische Internationale,* IX, No. 18 (May 2, 1928), 986-97; No. 19 (May 9, 1928), 1039-50.

—— Protiv lyavoto sektantstvo i Trotskizma v Balgaria (Against Left Sectarianism and Trotskyism in Bulgaria). Sofia, 1949.

—— "Der 'Rote Tag' auf dem Balkan," *Die Kommunistische Internationale*, X, No. 28 (July 10, 1929), 1583-98.

—— "Der Sinn der Ereignisse in Bulgarien," *Die Kommunistische Internationale*, VI, No. 5 (May, 1925), 559-77.

—— "Die Sozialen Grundlagen des Zankowregimes," *Die Kommunistische Internationale*, VI, No. 8 (August, 1925), 883-96.

—— "Die Taktik der K.P. Bulgariens im Lichte der Ereignisse," *Die Kommunistische Internationale*, No. 31-32 (1924), pp. 253-71.

—— "Ueber die Haltung der Genossen Taneff und Popoff im Leipziger Prozess," *Die Kommunistische Internationale*, XVI, No. 21 (December 30, 1935), 1883-85.

—— "Die Umgruppierung der Kräfte des Klassenkampfes im Faschistischen Bulgarien," *Die Kommunistische Internationale*, VIII, No. 14 (April 5, 1927), 697-705.

—— "Die Weltagrarkrise und die Bauernbewegung," *Die Kommunistische Internationale*, XII, No. 40 (November 25, 1931), 1838-44.

—— "Wie die Faschisten den Klassenkampf in Bulgarien 'begruben'," *Die Kommunistische Internationale*, XVII, No. 7 (July, 1936), 613-22.

—— Za Oktomvriskata Revolyutsia, Sovyetskia Sayuz, i Balgaro-Sovyetskata druzhba: Studii, statii, rechi, 1919-1948 (For the October Revolution, Soviet Union, and Bulgarian-Soviet Friendship. Studies, Articles, Speeches, 1919-48). Sofia, 1949.

—— *see also* Vasil Kolarov.

Kommunisticheski International pered VII Vsemirnom Kongressom (The Communist International Before the Seventh World Congress). Moscow, 1935.

"Konferenz der Kommunistischen Balkanföderation," *Die Kommunistische Internationale*, No. 17 (1921), pp. 430-34.

Koren'kov, A. M. "Internatsionalistskaya pozitsia Bolgarskikh Tesnykh Sotsialistov v period Pervoi Mirovoi Voiny, 1914-1918gg." (The Internationalist Position of the Bulgarian Narrow Socialists in the Period of the First World War, 1914-1918), *Uchenie Zapiski Instituta Slavyanovedenia* (Scientific Papers of the Institute of Slavistics), X (1954), 351-88.

Kostov, P. "Borbata na Balgarskata Komunisticheska Partia protiv likvidatorstvoto sled Septemvriiskoto vastanie v 1923 godina" (The Struggle of the Bulgarian Communist Party against Liquidationism after the September Insurrection in the Year 1923), *Novo vreme* (New Time), XXVII, No. 12 (December, 1951), 134-43.

Kuhne, Victor. Bulgaria Self-Revealed. London, 1919.

Kun, Bela. "Der Anti-Sowjetblock der Donau-Balkanstaaten," *Die Kommunistische Internationale*, VIII, No. 18 (May 3, 1927), 871-78; No. 19 (May 10, 1927), 902-20.

—— (editor). Kommunisticheski Internatsional v dokumentakh: 1919-1932 (The Communist International in Documents: 1919-32). Moscow, 1933.

Kunsi, S. "Der Bauer in der Revolution," *Der Kampf*, XVI, No. 8 (August, 1923), 353-57.

Kuusinen, Otto V. Fascism, the Danger of War and the Tasks of the Communist Parties. Report to the XIII Plenum of the E.C.C.I. London, 1934.

—— The International Situation and the Tasks of the Sections of the Comintern. Report to the XII Plenum of the E.C.C.I. London, n.d.

Ladas, S. P. The Exchange of Minorities: Bulgaria, Greece, and Turkey. New York, 1932.

Lamouche, Léon. "La Bulgarie et l'Entente Démocratique," *Le Monde slave*, February, 1926, pp. 231-49.

—— "La Population de la Bulgarie d'après les recensements de 1920 et 1926," *Le Monde slave*, July, 1927, pp. 132-44.

Lazard, Max. Compulsory Labour Service in Bulgaria. International Labour Office. Studies and Reports. Series B (Economic Conditions), No. 12. Geneva, 1922.

Lazitch, Branko. Lénine et la IIIᵉ Internationale. Neuchatel, 1951.

Lebedev, V. "Bolgarski perevorot" (The Bulgarian *Coup d'Etat*), *Volya Rossi* (Freedom of Russia), II, No. 12 (July 1, 1923), 49-56; No. 14 (September 1, 1923), 71-89.

—— Novym putem (By a New Way). Berlin, 1923.

Logio, G. C. Bulgaria: Past and Present. Manchester, 1936.

—— Bulgaria: Problems and Politics. London, 1919.

Londres, Albert. Terror in the Balkans. London, 1935.

Lozovski, A. Za yedinstvo (For Unity). Moscow, 1925.

Macedonicus, see Mikhailov, Ivan.

Mackinder, W., see Wedgwood, J. C., W. Mackinder, and C. L. Malone.

Madol, Hans Roger [pseudonym of Gerhard Salomon]. Ferdinand of Bulgaria. London, 1933.

Malone, Cecil l'Estrange. "Bulgaria, the Bulgarian Social Democratic Party and the Labour and Socialist International," *The Plebs*, XVII, No. 6 (June, 1925), 223-30.

—— see also Wedgwood, J. C., W. Mackinder, and C. L. Malone.

"Manifest der Kommunistischen Balkanföderation: An die werktätigen Klassen der Balkan- und Donauländer," *Die Kommunistische Internationale*, No. 14 (1920), pp. 231-41.

"Manifesto of the Greek Socialist Party: Greece in Danger," *The Asiatic Review*, VII (October 1, 1915), 279-82.

Manoff, S. "Ce qui se passe en Bulgarie," *La Revue socialiste*, XLV, No. 267 (March, 1907), 254-63.

Manuilski, D. Z. The Communist Parties and the Crisis of Capitalism: Speech Delivered at the XI Plenum of the E.C.C.I. Held in March-April 1931. London, 1931.

Marin, T. "Die Erwerbslosigkeit auf dem Balkan," *Die Kommunistische Internationale*, XII, No. 40 (November 25, 1931), 1844-56.

Markham, Reuben H. Meet Bulgaria. Sofia, 1931.

Markham, Sydney F. A History of Socialism. London, 1930.

Marx, Karl. The Eastern Question: A Reprint of Letters Written 1853-56 Dealing with the Events of the Crimean War. Edited by E. M. and E. Aveling. London, 1897.

—— "What Is to Become of Turkey in Europe?," New York *Daily Tribune,* April 21, 1853.

Maus, Karl. What is Happening in Bulgaria? Vienna, 1925.

Mikhailov, Ivan. Macedonia: A Switzerland of the Balkans. St. Louis, 1950.

—— [Macedonicus]. Stalin and the Macedonian Question. St. Louis, 1948.

Mitrany, David. The Effects of the War in Southeastern Europe. New Haven, 1936.

—— Marx Against the Peasant: A Study in Social Dogmatism. Chapel Hill, N.C., 1951.

Moissov, L. Bugarska Radnichka Partia (Komunista) i makedonsko natsionalno pitanje (The Bulgarian Labor Party (Communist) and the Macedonian National Question). Belgrade, 1948.

Mosely, Philip E. "The Distribution of the *Zadruga* within Southeastern Europe," *in* The Joshua Starr Memorial Volume: Studies in History and Philology. Jewish Social Studies Publication No. 5; New York, 1953, pp. 219-30.

Natan, Zhak. "Vasil Kolarov i osnovite problemi na nashata istoria" (Vasil Kolarov and the Basic Problems of Our History), *Izvestia na Instituta za Balgarska Istoria* (News of the Institute for Bulgarian History), III-IV (1951), 17-61.

—— "Vasil Kolarov protiv lyavoto sektantstvo i Trotskizma v Balgaria" (Vasil Kolarov against Left Sectarianism and Trotskyism in Bulgaria), *Istoricheski pregled* (Historical Review), VI, No. 3 (1950), 276-94.

Nenoff, D. The Bulgarian Communist Party. New York, 1951.

Nevski, V. I., ed. Deyateli revolyutsionnogo dvizhenie v Rossii: Bio-Bibliograficheski slovar'. Tom 5: Sotsial-Demokraty 1880-1904 (Workers of the Revolutionary Movement in Russia: A Biographical-Bibliographical Dictionary. Vol. 5: Social Democrats 1880-1904). Moscow, 1931.

—— Materiali dlya biograficheskogo slovar' Sotsial-Demokratov (Materials for a Biographical Dictionary of Social Democrats). Moscow, 1923.

New Europe, The. London, 1916-20.

Nicolson, Harold. Curzon: The Last Phase. London, 1934.

Nokov, Stoyan. "Studentski spomeni ot Zheneva (1889-1894g.)" (Student Memories of Geneva (1889-94)), *Istoricheski pregled* (Historical Review), XII, No. 4 (1956), 81-103.

Obbov, Alexander and Kosta Todorov. La Bulgarie sous la terreur du bourreau Liaptchev. Prague, 1927.

Ordon. "Bemerkungen ueber die Bauernbewegung in Europa," *Die Kommunistische Internationale,* VIII, No. 6 (February 8, 1927), 267-76.

Osvobozhdenie (Liberation). [N. p.], 1931.

Padev, Michael. Dimitrov Wastes No Bullets; Nikola Petkov: The Test Case. London, 1948.
—— "The Petkov Tradition," *Eastern Quarterly*, VI, No. 3-4 (October-December, 1953), 59.
Panaiotov, L. "Borbata na Balgarskata Komunisticheska Partia (T.S.) protiv likvidatorite sled Septemvriiskoto vastanie (1923-1925)" (The Struggle of the Bulgarian Communist Party (Narrow Socialists) Against the Liquidators After the September Insurrection (1923-25)), *Istoricheski pregled* (Historical Review), VIII, No. 4-5 (1952), 380-409.
Pandov, D. M. Grazhdanskata Voina (The Civil War). Sofia, 1926.
Pantsuktilova, O. V. "Rabochee dvizhenie v Bolgarii v 1905-1907 godakh" (The Labor Movement in Bulgaria in the Years 1905-7), *Voprosy istorii* (Problems of History), No. 6 (June, 1953), pp. 113-22.
Pastukhov, K. "Le Rapport de M. Wedgwood," *La Bulgarie*, II, No. 556 (May 13, 1925).
Patek, V. [pseudonym of B. Slavich]. Bolsheviki v Bolgarii (Bolsheviks in Bulgaria). Sofia, 1924.
Petkoff, Georg. Die Sozialen und wirtschaftlichen Verhältnisse in Bulgarien vor der Befreiung. Erlangen, 1906.
Petkov, G. "Die Bulgarische Sozialdemokratie und die Bauern," *Der Kampf*, XXII, No. 3 (March, 1928), 113-17.
Pieck, Wilhelm. "Der Vierte bulgarische Parteikongress," *Die Internationale*, IV, No. 26 (June 27, 1922), 597-601.
Piperow, Andreas. Bulgariens Agrarkrise und Agrarverschuldung. Berlin, 1938.
Plantagenet, E. E. Les Crimes de l'ORIM. Paris [1935?].
Plekhanov, G. V. O voine (About the War). 5th ed. Petrograd [1917?].
—— Sochinenia (Works). 2d ed. Moscow, 1923-27.
Popov, Blagoi and Vasil Tanev. "An Genossen Dimitroff und des Z.K. der K.P. Bulgariens," *Die Kommunistische Internationale*, XVII, No. 6 (June, 1936), 538-43.
"D. S. Popov" (obituary), *Die Kommunistische Internationale*, No. 34-35 (1924), pp. 204-8.
Popović, Dušan. "The Macedonian Question," *The New Europe*, VI, No. 76 (March 28, 1918), 333-39.
—— "Um Makedonien," *Der Kampf*, X, No. 11-12 (November-December, 1917), 334-43.
Popović, Milorad. "Die Makedonischen Komitees und die internationale Sozialdemokratie," *Die Neue Zeit*, XXII, No. 49 (September 3, 1904), 734-35.
—— "Ein Nationaler Kampf in der Türkei," *Die Neue Zeit*, XX, No. 44 (August 2, 1902), 566-68.
—— "Die Nationalitäten Kämpfe und die Reformen in der Türkei," *Die Neue Zeit*, XXII, No. 46 (August 13, 1904), 617-21; No. 47 (August 20, 1904), 659-63.

—— "Die Sozialdemokratie in den Balkanländern und die Türkei," *Die Neue Zeit*, XXII, No. 31 (April 30, 1904), 153-58.

—— "Die Sozialpolitische Lage in der Türkei," *Die Neue Zeit*, XX, No. 52 (September 27, 1902), 821-25.

Pravdin. "Revolutionäre Taktik und revolutionäre Phraseologie," *Kommunismus*, I, No. 21 (May 29, 1920), 690-92; No. 22 (June 12, 1920), 733-37.

Processo di Lipsia, Il. Documenti, litteri e noti di G. Dimitrov. Moscow, 1944.

"Programatische Erklärung der Bulgarischen Kommunistischen Partei (Engherzige Sozialisten) angenommen vom Ersten Kongress der BKP am 25-27. Mai 1919 in Sofia," *Die Kommunistische Internationale*, No. 4-5 (1919), pp. 161-68.

Proletarii (Proletarian). [N. p.], 1924-25.

Rabotnicheska iskra (Labor Spark). Varna, 1920-23.

Radek, Karl. "Der Umsturz in Bulgarien: Bericht in der Sitzung des Erweiterten Exekutiv-Komitees vom 23. Juni 1923," *Die Kommunistische Internationale*, No. 27 (1923), pp. 115-20.

Radoslavov, Vasil. Bulgarien und die Weltkrise. Berlin, 1923.

Rainoff, Witscho. Die Arbeiterbewegung in Bulgarien. Grüningen, 1909.

Rakovski, Christian. "Aus Bulgarien," *Die Neue Zeit*, XXIX, No. 46 (August 18, 1911), 685-89.

—— "Die Kommunistische Bewegung in Rumänien," *Die Kommunistische Internationale*, No. 13 (1920), pp. 245-48.

—— "Der Sozialistische 'Allgemeine Gewerkschaftsbund' in Bulgarien," *Die Neue Zeit*, XXIX, No. 34 (May 26, 1911), 277-78.

—— "Transylvania and Macedonia," *The New Europe*, VI, No. 73 (March 7, 1918), 254-56.

"Rapport du Parti Ouvrier Social Democrate Bulgare (Unifié) au Bureau Socialiste International" *in* Rapports sur le mouvement ouvrier et socialiste soumis au Congrès Socialiste International de Copenhagen, No. 21, 1910.

Rasshirennyi Plenum Ispolnitel'nogo Komiteta Kommunisticheskogo Internatsionala (12-23 Iyunya 1923 goda) (The Enlarged Plenum of the Executive Committee of the Communist International [June 12-23, 1923]). Moscow, 1923.

Reed, Douglas. The Burning of the Reichstag. London, 1934.

Reichenbach, B. "Zur Geschichte der KAPD," *Archiv für die Geschichte des Sozialismus und der Arbeiterbewegung*, XIII, 117-40.

Reichstag Fire Trial, The: The Second Brown Book of the Hitler Terror. London, 1934.

Report of the Seventh World Congress of the Communist International. London, 1936.

"Resolution des Kongresses der Kommunistischen Partei Bulgariens ueber die Lage in Bulgarien," *Die Kommunistische Internationale*, No. 5 (1919), pp. 729-36.

"Resolution des Zweiten Kongresses der K.P. Bulgariens ueber die innere und die internationale Lage des Landes und der K.P.," *Die Kommunistische Internationale*, No. 15 (1921), pp. 369-76.

"Resolution on the National Question in Central Europe and the Balkans," *The Communist International*, New Series, No. 7 (December, 1924-January, 1925), pp. 93-99.

"Resolution on the Question of Nationalities," *The Communist International*, New Series, No. 4 (July-August, 1924), pp. 86-98.

"Resolutionen der Sozialistenkonferenz des Balkans," *Die Kommunistische Internationale*, No. 12 (1920), pp. 292-96.

"Richtlinien der Parlamentsgruppe der K.P. Bulgariens," *Die Kommunistische Internationale*, No. 17 (1921), pp. 449-51.

Rizov, D., *see* Wendel, Hermann and D. Rizoff.

Roberts, Henry L. Rumania. New Haven, 1951.

Roucek, Joseph S. Balkan Politics. London, 1948.

"Rundschau: Gewerkschaftsbewegung: Bulgarien," *Sozialistische Monatshefte*, VIII, No. 10 (October, 1904), 853; IX, No. 12 (December, 1905), 1067-68.

"Rundschau: Sozialistische Bewegung: Bulgarien," *Sozialistische Monatshefte*, VIII, No. 10 (October, 1904), 848-49.

Sakarov, Nikola. Die Industrielle Entwicklung Bulgariens. Berlin, 1904.

Sakazov, Ivan. Bulgarische Wirtschaftsgeschichte. Berlin, 1929.

Sakazov, Yanko. "Die Balkanwirren," *Die Neue Zeit*, XXV, No. 3 (October 17, 1906), 84-87.

—— "Bulgarien an der Schwelle des neuen Jahrhunderts," *Die Neue Zeit*, XVIII, No. 30 (April 21, 1900), 81-86.

—— "Bulgarien nach den Balkankriegen," *Sozialistische Monatshefte*, XIX, No. 26 (December 23, 1913), 1667-72.

—— "Der Ferne Krieg und der Nahe Osten," *Die Neue Zeit*, XXII, No. 43 (July 23, 1904), 518-22.

—— "Die Makedonische Frage," *Die Neue Zeit*, XXI, No. 27 (April 4, 1903), 5-12.

—— "Die Nächsten Aufgaben der bulgarischen Sozialdemokratie," *Sozialistische Monatshefte*, XIV, No. 16-18 (August 11, 1910), 1075-79.

—— "Neoslawismus, Balkanföderalismus, und Sozialdemokratie," *Der Kampf*, IV, No. 5 (February 1, 1911), 209-14.

—— "Les Socialistes bulgares et la situation actuelle de notre pays," *La Bulgarie*, II, No. 563 (May 21, 1925).

—— "Die Spaltung in der Bulgarischen Sozialdemokratischen Arbeiterpartei," *Die Neue Zeit*, XXII, No. 15 (January 9, 1904), 472-75.

—— "Das Unabhängige Bulgarien," *Sozialistische Monatshefte*, XII, No. 22 (November 5, 1908), 1379-83.

—— "Die Wahrheit ueber Makedonien," *Der Kampf*, XI, No. 3 (March, 1918), 160-75.

—— "Was geschieht in Bulgarien?," *Die Neue Zeit*, XXI, No. 47 (August 22, 1903), 645-52.

—— "Ziele und Wege der Bulgarischen Sozialdemokratie," *Sozialistische Monatshefte*, XI, No. 8 (August, 1907), 649-54.

—— *see also* Yanko Sakazov.

Sakun, W. "Organisationsfragen der kommunistischen Parteien des Balkans," *Die Kommunistische Internationale*, XI, No. 22-23 (June 18, 1930), 1294-1305.

Salomon, Gerhard, *see* Madol, Hans Roger.

Savadjian, Léon. La Bulgarie en guerre. Geneva, 1917.

Savinski, A. A. "La Declaration de guerre de la Bulgarie aux Alliés," *Le Monde slave*, December, 1929, pp. 389-413; January, 1930, pp. 31-60.

Savova, E. Georgi Dimitrov: Letopis na zhivota i revolyutsionnata mu deinost (Georgi Dimitrov: Chronicle of his Life and Revolutionary Activity). Sofia, 1952.

—— Vasil Kolarov: Bio-Bibliografia (Vasil Kolarov: Biographical Bibliography). Sofia, 1947.

Sechster Weltkongress der Kommunistischen Internationale. Moskau. 17. Juli-1. September 1928. Protokoll. 3 vols., Hamburg [1928?].

Second and Third Internationals and the Vienna Union, The: Official Report of the Conference Between the Executives Held at the Reichstag, Berlin, on 2nd April, 1922 and Following Days. London, 1922.

Serebryansky, Z. "Comrade Stalin's Letter and the Purging of the Communist Parties of Social Democratic Relics," *The Communist International*, IX, No. 7 (April 15, 1932), 238-46.

Serge, Victor [pseudonym of Viktor Lvovich Kibalchich]. From Lenin to Stalin. London, 1937.

—— Mémoires d'un révolutionnaire. Paris, 1951.

Sergievski, N. L. Partia Russkikh Sotsial-Demokratov: Gruppa Blagoeva (The Party of Russian Social Democrats: The Group of Blagoev). Moscow, 1929.

—— "Plekhanov i gruppa Blagoeva" (Plekhanov and the Group of Blagoev), *Proletarskaya revolyutsia* (Proletarian Revolution), No. 79 (1928), pp. 133-51.

Service obligatoire du travail en Bulgarie, 1922-1925, Le. Sofia, 1926.

Seton-Watson, Hugh. The East European Revolution. London, 1950.

—— Eastern Europe between the Wars: 1918-1941. Cambridge (England), 1946.

Sharova, Krumka. "Raztseplenieto na BRSDP prez 1903g. i sindikalnoto dvizhenie" (The Split of the Bulgarian Social Democratic Labor Party in 1903 and the Trade Union Movement), *Istoricheski pregled* (Historical Review), IX, No. 2 (1953), 180-210.

Sharp, S. L. "Federation in Eastern Europe," *American Perspective*, March, 1948, pp. 612-27.

Shnitman, A. "K voprosu o vlianii russkogo revolyutsionnogo dvizhenia 1885-1903 godov na revolyutsionnoe dvizhenie v Bolgarii" (To the Question of the Influence of the Russian Revolutionary Movement of the Years 1885-1903 on the Revolutionary Movement in Bulgaria), *Voprosy istorii* (Problems of History), No. 1 (1949), pp. 39-55.

Shopov, A. "The Balkan States and the Federal Principle," *The Asiatic Review*, VII (July, 1915), 16-30.

Sidarov. "Die Revolutionäre Bewegung in Bulgarien," *Kommunismus*, I, No. 16-17 (May 1, 1920), 522-25; No. 18 (May 8, 1920), 561-66.

Sideris, A. D. "The Macedonian Question," *The New Europe*, VI, No. 78 (April 11, 1918), 396-401.

Slavich, B., *see* Patek, V.

Smoljanski, G. "Die Tagesaufgaben der kommunistischen Parteien innerhalb der Gewerkschaftsbewegung," *Die Kommunistische Internationale*, VII, No. 24 (December 28, 1926), 680-87.

South-Eastern Europe: A Political and Economic Survey. Royal Institute of International Affairs Publication. London, 1939.

"Southern Slav Socialist Manifesto, A," *The New Europe*, V, No. 61 (December 13, 1917), 281-84.

Souvarine, Boris. Stalin: A Critical Survey of Bolshevism. New York, 1939.

Spassow, Athanas D. Der Verfall des alten Handwerks und die Entstehung des modernen Gewerbes in Bulgarien während des 19. Jahrhunderts. Greifswald, 1900.

Spiridonoff, F. "Der Kampf gegen das Vordringen des Hitler-faschismus auf dem Balkan," *Die Kommunistische Internationale*, XVIII, No. 2 (February 28, 1937), 138-47.

Stalin, J. V. Sochinenia (Works). Vol. VII. Moscow, 1947.

Stamboliski, Alexander. Politicheski partii ili saslovni organizatsii? (Political Parties or Estatist Organizations?). 2d ed. Sofia, 1920 (first published, 1909; 3d ed., 1945).

Staneff, Stoil. Das Gewerbewesen und die Gewerbepolitik in Bulgarien. Russe, 1901.

Starr, Joshua. "The Socialist Federation of Saloniki," *Jewish Social Studies*, VII, No. 4 (October, 1945), 323-36.

Stavrianos, L. S. Balkan Federation: A History of the Movement Toward Balkan Unity in Modern Times (Smith College Studies in History, Vol. 27). Northampton, Mass., 1944.

—— "The Balkan Federation Movement—A Neglected Aspect," *American Historical Review*, XLVIII, No. 1 (October, 1942), 30-51.

Struggle of the Bulgarian People Against Fascism, The. Sofia, 1946.

Sumner, B. H. Russia and the Balkans: 1870-1880. Oxford, 1937.

Svobodin, P. "El Movimiento anarquista en Bulgaria," *Timon*, November, 1938, pp. 148-61.

Swire, Joseph. Bulgarian Conspiracy. London, 1939.

Tanev, Vasil, *see* Popov, Blagoi and Vasil Tanev.

"Tätigkeit der Sozialdemokratie (der 'Tesnjaki') in Bulgarien, Die," *Die Kommunistische Internationale*, No. 5 (September, 1919), pp. 785-89.

Tchitchovsky, T. The Socialist Movement in Bulgaria. London, 1931.

—— "Political and Social Aspects of Modern Bulgaria," *The Slavonic Review*, VII, No. 20 (January, 1929), 272-87; No. 21 (March, 1929), 595-603; VIII, No. 22 (June, 1929), 176-87.

Theses and Decisions. XIII Plenum of the E.C.C.I. Held in Moscow 1933. London, 1934.

Third Congress of the Communist International, The. London, 1921.

Tivel', A. and M. Kheimo. 10 Let Kominterna v resheniakh i tsifrakh (10 Years of the Comintern in Pronouncements and Statistics). Moscow, 1929.

Todorov, Kosta. Balkan Firebrand: The Autobiography of a Rebel, Soldier and Statesman. Chicago, 1943.

—— "The Macedonian Organization Yesterday and Today," *Foreign Affairs*, VI, No. 3 (April, 1928), 473-82.

—— La Vérité sur l'ORIM. Paris, 1927.

—— *see also* Obbov, Alexander and Kosta Todorov.

Todorov, N. "Leninskata 'Iskra' i balgarskite revolyutsionni Marksisti" (The Leninist *Iskra* and the Bulgarian Revolutionary Marxists), *Istoricheski pregled* (Historical Review), VII, No. 3 (1951), 283-90.

Topalović, Živko. "Im Neuen Orient," *Der Kampf*, XVIII, No. 12 (December, 1925), 445-60.

—— "Kolonisierung oder Befreiung des Balkans?," *Die Gesellschaft*, IV (1927), 385-96.

—— "Zehn Jahre Kommunismus auf dem Balkan," *Der Kampf*, XX, No. 11 (November, 1927), 512-18.

Toynbee, Arnold J. "Communism in South-East Europe," *in* Survey of International Affairs, 1924. London, 1926.

"Traité secret agraro-communiste signé en mars 1924 à Moscou," *La Bulgarie*, II, No. 563 (May 21, 1925).

Traitres à la cause macédonienne, Les. Paris, 1929.

Trial of Nikola D. Petkov, The: Record of the Judicial Proceedings 5th-15th August 1947. Sofia, 1947.

Trinadtsati plenum IKKI: Stenograficheski otchet (Thirteenth Plenum of the E.C.C.I.: Stenographic Report). Moscow, 1934.

Trotsky, Leon D. "In den Balkanländern," *Der Kampf*, IV, No. 2 (November 1, 1910), 68-74.

—— The Lessons of October, 1917. London, 1925.

—— My Life. London, 1930.

—— La "Troisième période" d'erreurs de l'Internationale Communiste. Paris, 1930.

Trotsky, Leon D. and Khristo Kabakchiev. Ocherki politicheskoi Bolgarii (Sketches of Political Bulgaria). Moscow, 1923.

Tsankov, Alexander Ts. "Die Wirtschaftlichen Ursachen der revolutionären Gährung in der Türkei," *Die Neue Zeit*, XXIV, No. 48 (August 25, 1906), 739-44.

Tsankov, Assen. "Die Balkankrise und die innere Zersetzung der Türkei," *Die Neue Zeit*, XXXI, No. 6 (November 8, 1912), 193-202.

—— "Bulgarien nach dem Umsturz," *Sozialistische Monatshefte*, XXX, No. 2 (February 18, 1924), 114-19.

—— "Der Sozialismus in Bulgarien," *Sozialistische Monatshefte*, VIII, No. 8 (August, 1904), 624-31.

Tsonev, G. and A. Vladimirov. Sentyabr'skoe vosstanie v Bolgarii 1923 goda (The September Insurrection in Bulgaria of the Year 1923). Moscow, 1934.

Tucović, D. "Die Erste Sozialdemokratische Balkankonferenz," *Die Neue Zeit*, XXVIII, No. 24 (March 11, 1910), 845-50.

Ulam, Adam B. Titoism and the Cominform. Cambridge, Mass., 1952.

Valev, L. B. "Zhizn' i deyatel'nost' D. N. Blagoeva" (Life and Activity of D. N. Blagoev), *Uchenie Zapiski Instituta Slavyanovedenia* (Scientific Papers of the Institute of Slavistics), II (1950), 69-77.

Valko Chervenkov: Bio-Bibliografia (Valko Chervenkov: Biographical Bibliography). Sofia, 1950.

Vandervelde, Émile. Les Balkans et la paix. Brussels, 1925.

Varga, Eugen. Sotsial-demokraticheskie partii (Social-Democratic Parties). Moscow, 1927.

—— "War Losses," *The Communist International*, New Series, No. 5 (September-October, 1924), pp. 30-33.

Vasil Kolarov: Important Dates of his Life and Work. Sofia, 1948.

Vasilev, Orlin. Vaorazhenata saprotivata sreshtu fashizma v Balgaria (The Armed Resistance Against Fascism in Bulgaria). Sofia, 1946.

Vatis, C., see Kabakchiev, Khristo, B. Boshkovich, and C. Vatis.

Vierter Kongress der Sozialistischen Arbeiter-Internationale in Wien 25. Juli-1. August 1931: Berichte der Angeschlossenen Parteien. Zürich, 1931.

Vladimirov, A. "Nekrolog: Kh. S. Kabakchiev" (Obituary: Kh. S. Kabakchiev), *Istorik Marksist* (Marxist Historian), No. 87 (1940), pp. 158-59.

—— "Zum 15. Jahrestag des Septemberaufstandes in Bulgarien," *Die Kommunistische Internationale*, XIX, No. 10 (October 24, 1938), 1034-49.

—— see also Tsonev, G. and A. Vladimirov.

Vlakhov, Dimitar. Iz istorije makedonskog naroda (From the History of the Macedonian People). Belgrade, 1950.

"Vydayushchisya deyatel' mezhdunarodnogo rabochego dvizhenia: Pamyati Georgia Mikhailovicha Dimitrova" (An Outstanding Worker of the

International Labor Movement: In Memory of Georgi Mikhailovich Dimitrov), *Bol'shevik*, XXVI, No. 13 (July 15, 1949), 8-15.

Walling, William E. The Socialists and the War. New York, 1915.

Wedgwood, J. C., W. Mackinder and C. L. Malone. Report of a Visit to Bulgaria. London, 1925.

Wendel, Hermann. Aus der Welt der Südslawen. Berlin, 1926.

—— Der Kampf der Südslawen um Freiheit und Einheit. Frankfurt, 1925.

—— "Marxism and the Southern Slav Question," *The Slavonic Review*, II, No. 5 (December, 1923), 289-307.

Wendel, Hermann and D. Rizov. Pro Macedonia. Paris, 1918.

Willard, M. Was ich in Bulgarien gesehen habe. Vienna, 1925.

Winter, E. K. "Problèmes de la confederation danubienne," *Le Monde slave*, April, 1936, pp. 137-55.

Wolfe, Bertram D. Three Who Made a Revolution. New York, 1948.

Woods, H. C. "The Bulgarian Revolution," *Fortnightly Review*, New Series, DCLXXX (August 1, 1923), 294-304.

World News and Views. London, 1938-43.

X.Y.Z. "Le Peuple bulgare et l'Union Paysanne," *Le Monde slave*, November, 1925, pp. 236-56.

Yanko Sakazov yubileyen sbornik (Yanko Sakazov Jubilee Symposium). Sofia, 1930.

Yotsov, Yaroslav. "Upravlenieto na 'Demokraticheski Sgovor' " (The Government of the "Democratic Entente"), *Istoricheski pregled* (Historical Review), V, No. 1 (1948-49), 13-58; No. 3-4 (1948-49), 451-88.

—— "Upravlenieto na Zemledelskia Sayuz" (The Government of the Peasant Union), *Istoricheski pregled* (Historical Review), VI, No. 3 (1950), 305-27; VII, No. 3 (1951), 249-82.

Zehntes Plenum des Exekutivkomitees der Kommunistischen Internationale: Protokoll. Berlin, 1929.

Zinoviev, Grigori E. "An das Proletariat der Balkan- und Donauländer: An die Kommunistischen Parteien Bulgariens, Rumäniens, Serbiens und der Türkei," *Kommunismus*, I, No. 24 (June 26, 1920), 835-38.

—— "Die Lage in der Kommunistischen Internationale: Bericht auf dem Zehnten Kongress der K.P. Russlands," *Die Kommunistische Internationale*, No. 16 (1921), pp. 550-76.

—— "Die Lehren des bulgarischen Umsturzes: Den Sektionen der Kommunistischen Internationale zur Beachtung," *Die Kommunistische Internationale*, No. 27 (1923), pp. 41-47.

—— "Die Partielle 'Stabilisierung' des Kapitalismus und die Aufgaben der Komintern und der K.P. Russlands: Bericht auf der XIV. Parteikonferenz der Sowjetunion April 1925 ueber die Ergebnisse der Tagung der Erweiterten Exekutive ergänzt durch Auszüge aus den Berichten des Genossen Sinowjew in den Versammlungen der aktiven Parteiarbeiter Leningrads und Moskaus ueber das selbe Thema," *Die Kommunistische Internationale*, VI, No. 4 (May, 1925), 481-518.

—— Twelve Days in Germany. Glasgow, 1921.

Zur Frage der Internationale. Charlottenburg [1922?].

"Zweite Konferenz der Kommunistischen Balkanföderation, Die," *Kommunismus*, II, No. 19-20 (July 1, 1921), 676-81.

Zweiter Kongress der Sozialistischen Arbeiter-Internationale in Marseille 22.-27. August 1925: Tätigkeitsbericht Ueber die Zeit vom 23. Mai 1923 bis 30. Juni 1925, vorgelegt vom Sekretariat der SAI. Zürich, 1925.

Z., X. Y., *see* X.Y.Z.

INDEX